PERGAMON INTERNATIONAL LIBRARY
of Science, Technology, Engineering and Social Studies
The 1000-volume original paperback library in aid of education,
industrial training and the enjoyment of leisure
Publisher: Robert Maxwell, M.C.

Readings in
Managerial Economics

THE PERGAMON TEXTBOOK
INSPECTION COPY SERVICE

An inspection copy of any book published in the Pergamon International
Library will gladly be sent to academic staff without obligation for their
consideration for course adoption or recommendation. Copies may be retained
for a period of 60 days from receipt and returned if not suitable. When a
particular title is adopted or recommended for adoption for class use and the
recommendation results in a sale of 12 or more copies, the inspection copy may
be retained with our compliments. If after examination the lecturer decides that
the book is not suitable for adoption but would like to retain it for his personal
library, then a discount of 10% is allowed on the invoiced price. The Publishers
will be pleased to receive suggestions for revised editions and new titles to be
published in this important International Library.

Other Titles of Interest

DUBRIN, A. J.
The Practice of Managerial Psychology

DUBRIN, A. J.
Fundamentals of Organizational Behavior

EILON S. *et al.*
Applied Productivity for Industry

FREDERIKSEN, N. *et al.*
Prediction of Organizational Behavior

GOLD, B.
Technological Change: Economics, Management and Environment

HUSSEY, D. E.
Introducing Corporate Planning

HUSSEY, D. E.
Corporate Planning: Theory and Practice

KING, J. R.
Production Planning and Control: An Introduction to Quantitative Methods

LETHBRIDGE, D. G.
Government and Industry Relationships

MELNYK, M.
Principles of Applied Statistics

MAXWELL TOWERS J.
Role-playing for Managers

TOWNSEND, H.
Scale, Innovation, Merger and Monopoly

The terms of our inspection copy service apply to all the above books. Full details of all books listed will gladly be sent upon request.

Readings in
Managerial Economics

Edited by

I. B. IBRAHIM, K. K. SEO, and P. G. VLACHOS

*College of Business Administration,
University of Hawaii*

PERGAMON PRESS

OXFORD · NEW YORK · TORONTO
SYDNEY · PARIS · FRANKFURT

U.K.	Pergamon Press Ltd., Headington Hill Hall, Oxford OX3 0BW, England
U.S.A.	Pergamon Press Inc., Maxwell House, Fairview Park, Elmsford, New York 10523, U.S.A.
CANADA	Pergamon of Canada Ltd., P.O. Box 9600, Don Mills M3C 2T9, Ontario, Canada
AUSTRALIA	Pergamon Press (Aust.) Pty. Ltd., 19a Boundary Street, Rushcutters Bay, N.S.W. 2011, Australia
FRANCE	Pergamon Press SARL, 24 rue des Ecoles, 75240 Paris, Cedex 05, France
WEST GERMANY	Pergamon Press GmbH, 6242 Kronberg/Taunus, Pferdstrasse 1, Frankfurt-am-Main, West Germany

Copyright © 1976 Pergamon Press Ltd.

First edition 1976

Library of Congress Cataloging in Publication Data
Ibrahim, Ibrahim B   comp.
Readings in managerial economics.

1.   Managerial economics--Addresses, essays, lectures.
I.   Seo, K. K., joint comp. II. Vlachos, P. G., joint comp. III. Title.
HD58.5.I27   1975   658.1'5'08   75-4618
ISBN 0-08-019605-5
ISBN 0-08-019604-7 pbk.

Printed in Great Britain by A. Wheaton & Co., Exeter

Contents

*A = Applications (mostly). T = Theory (mostly). A, T = A mixture favoring application. T, A = A mixture favoring theory.

PART IV: PRICING AND MARKET STRUCTURE

PART V: CAPITAL BUDGETING AND PROFIT

Preface

THE past decade has been marked by the establishment of higher-level university courses in quantitative methods of business analysis, in the information sciences, and in systems approaches to management theory. In the same period we have also witnessed increased sophistication of business management, increased application of scientific methods to business planning, and impressive growth in the complexity of business organizations and activities.

Managerial economics is a field of study that has been developed to bridge the gap between economic theory as taught in universities and economic practice as applied in the day-to-day activities of the business world. Managerial economics employs a multidisciplinary approach, utilizing analytical and decision-making tools derived from accounting, finance, marketing, and administrative theory, as well as from economic theory and quantitative analysis.

This book of readings in managerial economics combines a number of diverse articles, selected from recent issues of over fifty leading professional publications, that show to both students and executives the application of theoretical concepts to business decision making. The articles are grouped into five parts dealing with the major subject areas of decision making; forecasting and demand analysis; production and cost; pricing and market structure; and capital budgeting and profit.

Some of the articles deal principally with theory, some with applications, some with both; and each article has been labeled accordingly in the contents pages. We have also included a cross-reference table (p. xv) which relates articles in this book to chapters in suggested reading in leading textbooks on managerial economics.

The articles in this book have been selected for excellence of their content rather than for ease of reading. Consequently, some of the material presented may be difficult, particularly for undergraduate students. In order to alleviate this problem, each selection is preceded by an introduction which summarizes and explains the main points of the article, and in some instances cites additional reference material which may be helpful. We believe that this feature will help all students, and particularly those whose background in economics or quantitative techniques is relatively weak.

The sequence of the subject matter is the same as that in most standard textbooks on managerial economics. Indeed, the collection can be used as a managerial economics text. However, each article is self-contained, and the student may concentrate on any article that interests him.

Our deep appreciation goes to the authors and publishers who have kindly permitted us to edit and to print their material. The editors are much indebted to our colleagues William Long and Rosalind Ibrahim, University of Hawaii, whose remarkable ability to spot errors and to smooth rough drafts has made it a much improved product. Also we would like to thank Ms. Yuri Shimahara, a graduate assistant, for her library research. We extend our thanks also to Ms. Masayo Matsukawa and Ms. Gail Masaki, without whose secretarial support and patience the work never would have been completed. If any errors have crept in during our editing and transcription, the blame is wholly our own.

I. IBRAHIM
K. K. SEO
P. G. VLACHOS

The Editors

I. B. IBRAHIM (Ph.D. New York University) is Associate Professor of Business Economics and Quantitative Methods at the University of Hawaii. He has published a number of articles and monographs, including recent articles in such journals as *Risk and Insurance* and *Marketing Research*.

K. K. SEO (Ph.D. University of Cincinnati) is Professor of Business Economics and Quantitative Methods and Director of Research and Development at the College of Business Administration, University of Hawaii. He served as Department Chairman during 1968–72 and had an appointment as Senior Fellow, at East–West Center (1972–3). He is the author of numerous articles and monographs in economics and business-related fields which have appeared in such journals as *Simulation, Economic Development and Cultural Change, Policy Sciences, Engineering Economist, Annals of Regional Science*, etc. He is co-author of the book *Managerial Economics, Texts, Problems and Short Cases*, fourth edition, by Richard D. Irwin, Inc.

P. G. VLACHOS (Ph.D. University of Cincinnati) is Economics Affairs Officer, Water Resources Branch, Natural Resources Division, Economic and Social Commission for Asia and the Pacific (ESCAP), Bangkok, on leave from the University of Hawaii, where he is Associate Professor of Business Economics and Quantitative Methods. Dr. Vlachos has taught at the collegiate level at eight institutions, here and abroad; and has conducted research whose spectrum includes articles, professional papers, monographs, case studies, and transliterations.

List of Contributors

PETER ASCH, *Professor of Economics*, Rutgers University, State University of New Jersey.

R. J. BALL, *Deputy Principal and Professor of Economics*, London Graduate School of Business Studies.

WILLIAM J. BAUMOL, *Professor of Economics*, Princeton University.

JOHN R. CANADA, *Professor of Industrial Engineering*, North Carolina State University.

D. T. CARROLL, *Vice President*, Booz, Allen & Hamilton, Inc.

JOSEPH G. COWLEY, *Managing Editor*, The Research Institute of America, Inc.

DWIGHT B. CRANE, *Officer*, Mellon National Bank of Trust Co.

JAMES R. CROTTY, *Professor of Economics*, Bucknell University.

J. M. CUMMINGS, *Consultant*, Woods, Gordon & Co.

WARD S. CURRAN, *Professor of Economics*, Trinity College.

B. R. DARDEN, *Professor of Marketing*, University of Georgia.

JOEL DEAN, *Professor Emeritus of Economics*, Columbia University.

MICHAEL D. GEURTS, *Assistant Professor*, University of Hawaii.

R. G. GOLLEDGE, *Professor of Geography*, Ohio State University.

CLIFFORD F. GRAY, *Professor*, Oregon State University.

PAUL E. GREEN, *Professor of Marketing*, Wharton School, University of Pennsylvania.

RICHARD T. HISE. *Professor and Chairman*, Shippensburg State College.

BARRY G. KING, *Dean of Business Administration*, North Texas State University.

PETER J. LLOYD, *Senior Fellow*, Australian National University.

BURTON G. MALKIEL, *Professor of Economics*, Princeton University.

MATITYAHU MARCOS, *Professor and Chairman*, Rutgers University, State University.

J. B. MASON, *Professor of Marketing*, University of Alabama.

M. L. MAYER, *Professor and Head*, University of Alabama.

J. P. MCINERNEY, *Professor of Agricultural Economics*, University of Manchester.

M. C. MURPHY, *Professor*, University of Cambridge.

J. NIEDEREICHHOLZ, *Professor*, University of Karlsruhe, Federal Republic of Germany.

E. A. ORBECK, *Officer*, The US Air Force.

JOHN W. PRATT, *Professor of Business Administration*, Harvard University.

HOWARD RAIFFA, *Professor of Business Administration*, Harvard University.

ROBERT E. REIMAN, *President and General Manager*, Foamat Foods Corporation, Corvallis, Oregon.

JAMES E. REINMUTH, *Associate Professor*, University of Oregon.

JOHN F. ROCKART, *Professor*, MIT.

GARY M. ROODMAN, *Associate Professor*, The Amos Tuck School of Business Adm., Dartmouth University.

JOHN W. ROWE, JR., *Professor of Economics and Chairman*, University of Houston.

STUART A. SAMUELS, *Group Product Manager*, Warner/Chilcott, Morris Plains, N.J.

ROBERT SCHLAIFER, *Professor of Business Administration*, Harvard University.

A. ROSS SHEPHERD, *Professor of Economics*, University of Missouri, Kansas City.

EDWARD A. SILVER, *Professor of Management Science*, University of Waterloo, Canada.

EZRA SOLOMON, *Dean Witter Professor of Finance*, Stanford University.

ROBERT H. STRAWSER, *Associate Professor of Accounting*, The Pennsylvania State University.

L. G. TELSER, *Professor of Economics*, University of Chicago.

ROBERT C. WEISSELBERG, *Manager-Systems*, Citizens Utilities Co., Stanford, CT.

BRUCE YANDLE, JR., *Head and Professor of Economics*, Clemson University.

Text Cross-reference Table

	Part I Decision making	Part II Forecasting and demand analysis	Part III Production and cost	Part IV Pricing and market structure	Part V Capital budgeting and profit
Brigham and Pappas	1, 3*	4, 5, App. B	6, 7, 8	10, 11	13, App. A
Colberg, Forbush, and Whitaker	1	2, 3, 4	5	9, 12, 14	6, 7
Hague	1, 7	3	5	4, 13, 14	6, 15
Christenson, Vancil, and Marshall	4, 5	6	1, 2, 3	3, 7	9, 11
Haynes and Henry	1	3, 4, 10	2, 6, 7	8, 9	5, 11
Mantell and Sing	16	2, 3, 4, 5, 6	7, 8	9, 10	11, 12, 13, 14
Riggs	1, 8, 10		2		5, 6, 7, 9
Spencer, Seo, and Simkin	1, 2, 3	4, 5, 6	7, 8, 11	12, 13	9, 10, 14, 15
Stokes	2	3, 10	4	5, 13	11

*The figures refer to the chapters of the works of the authors quoted in column 1.
Complete references follow:

BRIGHAM, EUGENE F., and JAMES L. PAPPAS, *Managerial Economics*. Hinsdale, Illinois: The Dryden Press Inc., 1972. 493 pp.

CHRISTENSON, CHARLES J., RICHARD F. VANCIL, and PAUL W. MARSHALL, *Managerial Economics: Text and Cases*. Homewood, Illinois: Richard D. Irwin, Inc., 1973. 581 pp.

COLBERG, MARSHALL R., DASCOMB R. FORBUSH, and GILBERT R. WHITAKER, JR., *Business Economics: Principles and Cases*, 5th ed. Homewood, Illinois: Richard D. Irwin, Inc., 1975. 613 pp.

HAGUE, D. C., *Managerial Economics: Analysis for Business Decisions*. New York: John Wiley & Sons, Inc., 1969. 350 pp.

HAYNES, W. WARREN, and WILLIAM R. HENRY, *Managerial Economics: Analysis and Cases*. Dallas, Texas: Business Publications, Inc., 1974. 646 pp.

MANTELL, LEROY H., and FRANCIS P. SING, *Economics for Business Decisions*. New York: McGraw-Hill Book Company, 1972. 460 pp.

RIGGS, JAMES L., *Economic Decision Models for Engineers and Managers*. New York: McGraw-Hill Book Company, 1968. 401 pp.

SPENCER, MILTON H., K. K. SEO, and MARK G. SIMKIN, *Managerial Economics: Text, Problems, and Short Cases*. Homewood, Illinois: Richard D. Irwin, Inc., 1975. 562 pp.

STOKES, CHARLES J., *Managerial Economics: A Textbook on the Economics of Management*. New York: Random House, 1969. 414 pp.

PART I

Decision Making

Introduction

Since decision making is so much a human activity it is not surprising that it is largely subjective, depending upon the personality, temperament, and experience of the decision maker. Yet within the framework of subjective decision making there are analytical tools which can be combined with disciplined, logical thinking to introduce at least a modicum of objectivity into the decision-making process.

There is no doubt that modern decision theory has resulted largely from the work of the eminent scientist Abraham Wald (1902–50), who is chiefly responsible for conceiving statistics in a decision-making context. Much of recent developments in decision theory stems from the concept of probability, despite some conflicting ideas among mathematicians and philosophers.

When probability considerations are introduced, the theory of choice can be extended to the theories of decision making under risk and uncertainty. This leads to a discussion of the choice of strategies and to the role of "subjective" probability theories developed mainly in the early fifties by Professor L. H. Savage. Savage's theories were later extended to a more operational form by Professors Raiffa and Schlaifer, one of whose works is included in this part.

1

The objective of this part of the book is to bring the student to a fuller appreciation of quantitative methods as "formal" aids to managerial decision making by illuminating just a few of the many ways in which quantitative methods can be applied to practical problems.

SUMMARIES OF ARTICLES IN PART I AND COMMENTS

Article 1

In "The foundations of decision under uncertainty: an elementary exposition" John W. Pratt, Howard Raiffa, and Robert Schlaifer show how the decision maker, who is operating in an uncertain world, can arrive at a rational decision. The decision problem can be greatly simplified if it is reduced to a payoff table. In this table all the relevant states (E_j)'s and all the possible sources of actions (a_i)'s are specified. In addition, the conditional consequences (c_{ij})'s are estimated. A conditional consequence c_{ij} is a numerical value of cost, profit, or loss that results when state E_j occurs and action a_i is chosen.

The second step in arriving at a rational decision is to ask the decision maker to express his judgment concerning the chance of E_j occurring and to scale his preference regarding the outcome c_{ij}† using the following definitions:

1. A canonical experiment: an experiment with equally likely outcomes.
2. A canonical lottery: a lottery that is based on a canonical experiment.
3. C^*: an outcome that is at least as desirable as any of the (c_{ij})'s in the problem.
4. C_*: an outcome that is at least as undesirable as any of the possible (c_{ij})'s.

The decision maker expresses his judgment concerning the occurrence of E_j by specifying a number $P(E)$ such that he is indifferent between two lotteries: (1) if E_j occurs he gets C^* and if E_j does not occur he receives C_*; (2) a lottery with a chance $P(E)$ that he gets C^* and a chance $(1 - P[E])$ of receiving C_*. In addition, the decision maker is supposed to

---

†Scaling the preference of the decision maker is not needed if this preference is a linear function of money.

scale his preference by specifying a number $\pi(c)$ such that he is indifferent between getting c for certain and a canonical lottery with a chance $\pi(c)$ of receiving C^* and a chance of $(1 - \pi[c])$ of receiving C.

The decision maker is assumed to abide by the rules of consistent behavior but he is not assumed to be consistent when faced with complex alternatives. The analysis is geared to simplifying the alternatives available so that he is able to choose between them in a consistent manner. This is achieved by reducing each alternative into a simple contract with only two possible outcomes: best (C^*) with a π chance and worst (C_*) with a $(1 - \pi)$ chance, where

$$\pi = \sum_i P(E_i)\pi(c_i).$$

Obviously the contract with the highest π is supposed to be preferred. The following example illustrates the above analysis:

TABLE 1

	1a Contract A			1b Contract B		
	c_i	$P(E_i)$	$\pi(c_i)$	c_i	$P(E_i)$	$\pi(c_i)$
E_1	9000	0.40	0.99	3000	0.40	0.6
E_2	5000	0.25	0.70	3000	0.25	0.6
E_3	− 5000	0.35	0	3000	0.35	0.6

Let $C^* = 10,000$ and $C_* = -5000$.

Columns 1 in Table 1a and 1b are the conditional consequences. Columns 2 represent the decision maker's judgment concerning the occurrence of E_i; column 3 his preference concerning c_i. For instance, 0.99 in column 3, Table 1a, means that the decision maker is indifferent between getting 9000 for certain and a canonical lottery with 0.99 chance of getting 10,000 and 0.01 chance of getting − 5000. The act to be selected is found as follows:

$$\pi_A = (0.99 \times 0.4) + (0.7 \times 0.25) + (0 \times 0.35) = 0.571,$$
$$\pi_B = (0.6 \times 0.4) + (0.6 \times 0.25) + (0.6 \times 0.35) = 0.60.$$

The best act would be to choose contract B. Notice that if the expected monetary value was the criterion, then A should have been selected.

If the decision maker wants to consider some piece of information that may have bearing on the act, such as E^* occurring, then the probability that should be considered is the conditional probability. This would be found from the Bayesian formula:

$$P(E/E^*) = \frac{P(E^* \cap E)}{P(E^*)}.$$

Two explanations may be given to justify the use of $P(E/E^*)$ instead of $P(E)$. The first and the most common is that before knowing whether E^* occurs or not the decision maker decides on what to do given every piece of information. The second interpretation is that the decision maker's posterior behavior is governed by the same four assumptions mentioned in the paper but reworded so it deals with posterior behavior. This is a philosophical question, and regardless of the interpretation $P(E/E^*)$ is the relevant probability.

This paper is an excellent one in showing the steps and demonstrating the logic of decision making under uncertainty.

Students are advised to acquaint themselves with the following concepts:

Payoff table	Preference (utility)
Events	Transitive preference
Acts (alternatives)	Conditional probability vs.
Conditional consequences	posterior probability
Canonical experiment	Joint probability
Canonical lottery	

Article 2

In "Bayesian statistics and product decisions" Paul E. Green nicely complements the preceding article by giving an example of the use of Bayesian analysis in product development. One can clearly identify all the steps discussed in the preceding article with the exception of stating the utility function of the decision maker, since it is implicitly assumed to be linear with respect to money.

The alternatives available to the decision maker are:

(a) Make a decision now⟨terminate the project.
⟨go ahead with the project.

(b) Delay the decision for one year or more to gather additional information.

In addition there are four states of nature (F_i), and associated with each is a certain sales outcome. The decision maker expresses judgment concerning the occurrences of the states. These are given in Table 1.

A terminal decision involves making a decision before gathering enough information and thus entails the high cost of uncertainty. On the other hand, delaying the decision affects the outcomes as follows: (a) decreases the present values of the profit, (b) increases the risk of competition, (c) increases the cost of gathering information.

The best act would be the one with payoffs having the highest expected value. The four available alternatives are:

1. The alternative, "terminate," has an expected value of 0 since the cost incurred so far in developing the project is a sunk cost and has no bearing on the choice of any of the various alternatives.
2. The expected value of "go" is 1.15. This is found by multiplying each outcome by the prior probability distribution. (Table 1.)
3. Computing the expected value of the payoffs by delaying the project one year is more complicated. The conditional outcome would change because the payoff will be received in the future instead of now, and because the firm loses 25% of its market as a result of the delay. For example, outcome 4 which was 10 million dollars becomes:

$$10 \times \left(\frac{1}{1+0.1}\right)0.75 = 6.82.$$

In addition, the probabilities of the four outcomes have to be reassessed as a result of gathering new information. This information is assumed to make predicting the outcome 70% accurate. Thus if F_j is the outcome and f_j is the predictor of F_j, then $P(f_j|F_j)$ is 0.7 while $P(f_j|F_k) = 0.1$, where $k \neq j$. If outcome 1 is predicted, then $p(f_1|F_1) = 0.7$, $P(f_1|F_2) = 0.1$, $P(f_1|F_3) = 0.1$ and $P(f_1|F_4) = 0.1$.

This assumption is made in the article in order to simplify the analysis. To evaluate this alternative, the conditional probabilities of F_j's given various predictors must be found according to the Bayesian formula discussed in the preceding article. These probabilities are given in Table 3 and are derived from Table 2. The derivation is explained very clearly in the text; however, since the information may lead to either of the four predictors f_j, the expected value of the alternative "delay one year" must be based on the probabilities of these predictors. This is found to be, after deducting the cost of gathering information, 1.24 million.

In a similar way alternative 4 "delay for two years" is evaluated and the expected value of its payoff is found to be 0.88 million. Thus alternative 3, "delay one year," is the best course of action.

The student should study the following concepts:

Prior probability	Joint probability
Posterior probability	Payoff table (matrix)
Marginal probability	Decision tree
Conditional probability	

Article 3

In "Maximin programming: an approach to farm planning under uncertainty" J. P. McInerney expands the conventional linear programming models applied to farm planning. The conventional approach takes little or no formal account of imperfect knowledge in the production environment. Because such an omission makes the models unrealistic, McInerney's paper attempts to make uncertainty at least partially manageable within the framework of the linear programming model, using some of the notions embodied in the theory of games.

Although game theory was highly praised at the outset it is now considered to be not as important an operational concept. However, McInerney attempts a resurrection of the theory to elaborate his model on farm planning.

The theory of games is employed in analyzing situations of conflict between two or more participants. It is best developed in relation to two-person games; and the most common examples relate to zero-sum (or constant-sum) games, where the gains by one player completely represent the losses by the other. The elements of the game are the set of alternative possible courses of action, or strategies, available to each player, and a corresponding set of potential outcomes resulting from the implementation of any pair of opposing strategies.

As a basis for rational action in an environment of complete uncertainty the criterion of *maximin* is selected as a particular alternative applicable to such situations. This approach assumes that the decision maker is interested in that strategy which secures for him the maximum minimum gain, that is, his minimum gain from a player of the game will be as large as possible.

For agricultural purposes the problem becomes one of a "game against Nature," where Nature represents the spectrum of uncertainties in the biological and institutional complex. A major assumption of the theory applied to agriculture relates to absolute uncertainty on the part of the decision maker regarding the occurrence of any particular state of Nature.

The farmer has two strategies from which to choose:

1. The "pure" maximin strategy involves "saddle-point" payoff matrices in which one element is both the minimum of its row and the maximum of its column.
2. The "mixed" maximin strategy involves a combination of two or more courses of action. Here, a fundamental and amazing theorem of game theory states that, in such unstable situations, there exists some combination of strategies for each player such that a stable solution is reached.

For farm planning, the derived mixed strategy when interpreted in terms of proportions of resource allocated to each activity indicates the best combination of farm activities to derive some guaranteed minimum level of income in the uncertainty situation specified. McInerney calls this an "optimal scheme of diversified production in the face of uncertainty."

The reader should be aware of the following concepts:

Game theory   Minimax programming
Linear programming models   Mixed maximin strategy
Maximin programming   Pure maximin strategy

Article 4

The object of J. P. McInerney's "Linear programming and game theory models: some extensions" is to present a complete account of the application of game theoretic criteria in linear programming models by extending the initial work in this field.

For farm planning, several criteria for selecting among alternatives which are applicable to game situations are:

1. The maximin (Wald) criterion.
2. The minimax regret (Savage) criterion.
3. The Laplace criterion.
4. The Hurwicz decision rules.

There are at least two different ways of applying these decision rules in determining an "optimal" farm plan under conditions of uncertainty.

First, any decision rule can be incorporated into an LP model and generate a single programmed solution which satisfies the requirements of both the programming and the decision rule constraints. The second way is to generate a series of farm plans using the LP model alone, and then selecting among the plans by applying the decision criteria.

Because the maximin model was adequately discussed in his "Maximin programming: an approach to farm planning under uncertainty," McInerney merely repeats some of his major observations in this part.

The minimax regret model, when adopted, implies that the farmer feels a dissatisfaction equal in magnitude to the difference between the return he actually achieved and the (maximum) return he could have achieved had he correctly predicted the state of Nature which would occur. It might be, therefore, that the farmer wishes to minimize the maximum possible value of this *ex post* regret.

The Laplace decision rule states that, for lack of any better information, equal probabilities are assigned to each state of Nature; and selections are made to maximize the expected value of the return.

The Hurwicz decision rule is a simple model for forming expectations of uncertain outcomes based on the general pessimistic or optimistic attitudes of the decision maker. The practical application of the Hurwicz model flounders on the difficulty of altering the value of any individual's general pessimistic attitude.

McInerney has demonstrated how all the classical decision rules of game theory can be applied in a constrained choice context as opposed to the usual unconstrained selection procedure of game theory models. There are still problems to consider—nothing is yet known of how these models work in general over a wide variety of planning situations.

The following concepts should be noted by the reader:

Game theory	Linear programming
Hurwicz decision rule	Maximin model
Laplace model	Minimax regret model

Article 5

In "Risk evaluation in farm planning: a statistical approach" M. C. Murphy incorporates risk into the planning of farm production. The following five steps are followed to achieve this end.

(1) The gross margin made on a certain area of land is maximized by finding the optimal mix of crops such as wheat, barley, beets, etc. (The gross margin is defined to mean net income plus fixed cost.)

(2) In addition to the mean gross margin arrived at in the first step, the variance of this gross margin is computed. The variance of the gross margin is equal to the sum of the variances of the crop multiplied by the amount of acreage of each crop squared (A_i^2) plus twice the sum of the covariances multiplied by A_iA_j. This can best be understood by using the formula for the variance of the sum of two random variables:

$$V(c_1x_1 + c_2x_2) = c_1^2 V(x_1) + c_2^2 v(x_2) + 2c_1c_2 \operatorname{cov}(x_1x_2).$$

To arrive at the variance of the gross margin, the variance–covariance matrix is computed in Table 2c. The diagonal elements in this matrix are brought from column 3, Table 2a. It should be noted that these variances can be estimated from time series or cross-section data on each crop. The other elements in Table 2c are computed from column 2 of Table 2a and Table 2b as follows: the correlation coefficient between the two crops is multiplied by the multiple of their standard deviations. For example, the covariance between the gross margins of barley and wheat (6.51) is equal to the correlation between barley and wheat (0.160) in Table 2b multiplied by 7.12 × 5.71 from column 2, Table 2a. The computation follows directly from the formulas for the covariance and the correlation coefficient:

$$\operatorname{cov}(xy) = \frac{\Sigma(x - \bar{x})(y - \bar{y})}{n - 1},$$

$$r(xy) = \frac{\Sigma(x - \bar{x})(y - \bar{y})}{(n - 1)s_xs_y},$$

where s_x, s_y are the standard deviations of x, y estimated from the samples.

(3) By allowing for fixed cost, net income is found. From the mean of net income and its standard deviation the cumulative probability distribution is derived.

(4) This distribution can be used to determine whether the risk involved is acceptable. One method would be to determine a cutoff value for net income, such that any year producing lower income is considered a failure and a higher income year is considered a success. The value chosen in the article is 15. Given a mean of 21.98 and a standard deviation of 9.6, the probability of 15 or less is equal to

$$P\left(Z < \frac{15 - 21.98}{9.6}\right) = 0.23.$$

The probability of the number of years that will be considered as failures during a certain future period, say 5 years, is found by using the binomial distribution with $P = 0.23$ and $n = 5$.

(5) If the probability distribution of the number of years that are considered failures is not satisfactory, it can be improved by reducing the variance of the gross margin. To do this the crop mix has to be changed. However, the reduction in the variance can be achieved only at the expense of the gross margin, since in step (1) the optimal mix was chosen.

This article is especially interesting because it ties linear programming to a risk evaluation model. The model is easy to apply and appears to be a very useful tool to farm planning.

Understanding the following concepts would be very helpful in reading the article:

The expected value of a random variable.
The expected value of the sum of random variables.
The variance of a random variable.
The variance of the sum of random variables.
Cumulative probability distribution.
The normal distribution.
The binomial distribution.
The covariance of two random variables.
The correlation coefficient between two random variables.

The following formulas are useful in this respect:

$E(x) = \Sigma\, xP(x)$, if x is a discrete random variable.
$V(x) = \Sigma\, (x - E(x))^2 P(x)$ if x is a discrete random variable.
$E(x_1 + x_2) = E(x_1) + E(x_2)$.
$V(x_1 + x_2) = V(x_1) + V(x_2) + 2\,\mathrm{cov}(x_1, x_2)$.
$\mathrm{cov}(x_1, x_2) = \dfrac{\Sigma\, (x_1 - \bar{x}_1)(x_2 - \bar{x}_2)}{n - 1}$.
$r(x_1 x_2) = \dfrac{\Sigma\, (x_1 - \bar{x}_1)(x_2 - \bar{x}_2)}{(n - 1)S_{x_1} S_{x_2}}$.
$V(cx) = c^2 V(x)$, where c is a constant.

Article 6

In "Business simulation and management decisions" J. Niedereichholz discusses the application of simulation in business and economics. There are still many practical limitations on the construction of large scale dynamic models of the firm or of a whole economy, but the author finds it interesting to look at some aspects of these compact simulation methods, especially at those of Industrial Dynamics with DYNAMO and the General Purpose Simulation System (GPSS).

There are two fundamental possibilities in constructing a simulation model and in building a simulation language:

1. The time-oriented approach (fixed time increment simulation).
2. The event-oriented approach.

Time-oriented simulation can be compared with sampled data systems used in cybernetics and systems engineering. Of the many models possible, only Industrial Dynamics can be viewed as a conception to deal with total dynamic models. This model was developed to analyze particularly the effects of managerial decision processes on highly interdependent organizations, with dynamic conditions and information feedbacks of many orders. The focus of this philosophy is the proposal that management should recognize the character of industrial organizations as a highly interconnected network of information and material feedback processes.

The basic components used by Industrial Dynamics are the two fundamental variables—rates and levels. The rates of flow represent the activities and decisions in the organization and include such activities as payments, movements of goods, etc. The varying rates of flow result in changes of levels of variables in the system. The levels represent accumulations of resources such as inventories, cash balances, etc.

Industrial Dynamics uses a special flow chart technique preceding the construction of the model as a system of equations.

The fixed time-increment model just discussed requires the user to specify the size of the time increment DT (Delta Time, the time interval used). However, a variable time-increment model processes the event occurrences by the next-event mode. After the processing of an event, simulation time is advanced to the time of the nearest future occurrence of a coming event. The correct choice of the next processing time-point is done by a sequencing set.

Because of its simplicity, the writer selects the GPSS over other next-event simulation languages. This involves a block diagram where blocks represent the subroutines of the activities and the lines linking the blocks indicate the logical sequence for the execution of the activities.

The application field for both models is very large including airport systems, operating systems of time-sharing computers, etc.

Noteworthy to the reader are the following concepts:

Blocks	Industrial Dynamics
DYNAMO	Levels
Event-oriented approach	Rates
General Purpose Simulation System	Simulation
(GPSS)	Time-oriented approach

Article 7

In "PERT simulation: a dynamic approach to the PERT technique" Clifford F. Gray and Robert E. Reiman explain the method and provide two applications: highway design and product and process development.

The basic PERT model is a closed system network of activities and events that represent a project from its inception to its completion. It depicts events and activities in their chronological sequences and in their explicit interrelationships as conceived and scheduled within the project by its designers and managers. The authors feel that standard PERT and Critical Path Method (CPM) analyses are deterministic in their solution and static in their scope.

Thus Gray and Reiman present a relatively new technique, PERT Simulation (PS). The PS approach allows management to cope with the uncertainty and instability of time estimates used in the early planning stages of project management. By simulating the PERT network, the PS model reveals the likelihood of shifting critical paths while the project is still in the planning or bidding stages. This model injects a vital dimension, *dynamics*, into the PERT model and makes it a more powerful and flexible management tool.

The article explores in detail the PERT problem and the desirability and need for the dynamic approach. This discussion is followed by a nontechnical description of the method used to transform the standard PERT model to PS. In turn, some of the key points of network analysis under the PS system are noted.

The conversion of the static PERT model into a dynamic one is done by applying the Monte Carlo (simulated sampling) method. The method uses random numbers to generate simulated activity times for each activity in the network.

PS offers the following advantages:

1. PS uses essentially the same input data as does standard PERT, but

also provides a means to incorporate subjective or intuitive factors into the data.

2. It tests the network to identify what paths are sensitive to delays or early completion of activities.
3. It copes with the uncertainty associated with activity duration times and the dynamic interaction between the activities of the closed network.
4. The criticality indices for the activities reveal the likelihood of activities becoming critical *before* the project begins. The indices also serve as an indication of the degree of management attention an activity should receive.
5. Accuracy and flexibility are increased since any probability distribution or mix of distributions may be used by the estimator.
6. It identifies those activities that will rarely or never occur on any of the possible critical paths.

In conclusion, the criticality concept is more useful for management by exception than the single critical path concept used in network analysis. The PS model is valuable to management whether or not the network is sensitive or insensitive to changes in activity duration times. Since PS fully utilizes the manager's experience and subjective feelings, more accurate results occur.

The reader should know the following terms:

Critical path method	PERT cost
Monte Carlo method	PERT/LOB
Network analysis	PERT simulation (PS)

Article 8

Robert C. Weisselberg and Joseph G. Cowley, in "Quicken the queue," deals with methods of handling the waiting customer faster and better by concentrating on the application of scientific decision tools to management problems rather than in the techniques themselves.

The typical waiting line exists because it is usually cheaper to have such a line than not to have it. And the length of the line that is most economical can be determined by operations research techniques. The trick is to balance demand against service, thus minimizing total cost (the cost of having a line versus the cost of idle time).

The stages of queue include the following:

1. The most elementary is the *single-channel, single-phase* operation, that is, the first-come, first-served discipline.
2. *Multichannel* service.
3. *Three-phase, sequential* operation.

Some questions to ask with reference to strategies for service facilities are:

1. Can you reduce the service time?
2. Can you reduce the variation in service time?
3. Can you increase the number of service channels?
4. Can you reduce the number of phases?

Some questions to ask with reference to customers are:

1. Can you reduce the arrival rate?
2. Can you vary the arrival times?
3. Can you vary the batch sizes?
4. Can you predict and therefore prepare for the arrival rate?

The ratio between the arrival rate and the service rate is an essential consideration in solving queuing problems. This ratio is often called the *traffic intensity* or *load factor*. The formulas for these are:

1. *Average waiting-line length:*

$$\frac{(\text{average arrival rate})^2}{\text{service rate} \times (\text{service rate} - \text{arrival rate})}.$$

2. *Average waiting time:*

$$\frac{\text{average arrival rate}}{\text{service rate} \times (\text{service rate} - \text{arrival rate})}.$$

The examples provided by the authors are on a simple level. Other complications which are not discussed include the last-come, first-served discipline, impatient customers, batching problems, and unstable queues. Whatever formulas are used, the results have to be interpreted in the light of the measure of effectiveness (lowest overall cost, minimal customer wait, etc.).

The following concepts are of interest to the reader:

Arrival rate	Service rate
Load factor	Sequential operation
Multichannel service	Single-channel, single-phase
Operations research	Traffic intensity
Queuing	

1

The Foundations of Decision Under Uncertainty: An Elementary Exposition*

JOHN W. PRATT, HOWARD RAIFFA, and ROBERT SCHLAIFER

Bayesian rules for decision under uncertainty are derived constructively from two principles of consistent behavior and two principles asserting that the decision maker can scale his preferences for consequences and judgments concerning unpredictable events by reference to simple lotteries involving only two consequences and based on an imaginary experiment with subjectively equally likely outcomes. It is shown that the two principles of consistent behavior require the decision maker's scaled judgments to obey the axioms of probability, and by use of one further principle of consistent behavior it is shown that they should also agree with the usual definition of conditional probability and hence with Bayes' rule.

1. GENERAL APPROACH

In this paper we consider the problem faced by a person who on most occasions makes decisions intuitively and more or less inconsistently, like all other mortals, but who on some one, particular occasion wishes to make some one, particular decision in a reasoned, deliberate manner. To do so he must, of course, start by defining his problem; and we therefore assume that he has already specified the set of *acts* that he believes it worth his while to consider and has reflected on the *consequence* that each act will have given each of a set of mutually exclusive *events* some one of which he feels sure must occur (or must already have occurred but is still unknown to him). The data of his problem can then be described by a payoff table of the kind shown schematically in Table 1, where a_i is the i'th act, E_j is the j'th event, and c_{ij} is the consequence that a_i will have if E_j occurs.

*From *Journal of the American Statistical Association*, Vol. 59, No. 306, 1964, pp. 353–375. Reproduced by permission.

TABLE 1

Act	Event				
	E_1	$\cdots$	E_j	$\cdots$	E_n
a_1	c_{11}	$\cdots$	c_{1j}	$\cdots$	c_{1n}
$\cdots$	$\cdots$	$\cdots$	$\cdots$	$\cdots$	$\cdots$
a_i	c_{i1}	$\cdots$	c_{ij}	$\cdots$	c_{in}
$\cdots$	$\cdots$	$\cdots$	$\cdots$	$\cdots$	$\cdots$
a_m	c_{m1}	$\cdots$	c_{mj}	$\cdots$	c_{mn}

We first show that if the decision maker is willing (1) to scale his *preferences* for the possible consequences and his *judgments* concerning the possible events in a manner to be described in a moment, and (2) to accept two simple principles of *consistent* behavior, then it is possible by straightforward calculation to determine which of the acts he *should* choose in order to be consistent, in the sense of these principles, with his own preferences and judgments.

We then consider the special case where the decision maker wishes to evaluate separately the import of some particular piece of information (possibly but not necessarily the outcome of a sample or experiment), and we show that if he accepts one additional principle of consistent behavior, then it is possible by straightforward calculation to determine what effect this information *should* have on his judgments as assessed in its absence. The calculations required are shown to agree with the usual definition of conditional probability and hence under appropriate conditions to involve the formula commonly known as Bayes' rule.

In one sense this paper merely adds one more axiomatization of decision under uncertainty to the many logically equivalent systems that already exist, and the sophisticated reader will find nothing here that he does not already know.[1] We hope, however, that the paper will help some readers to a better understanding of the foundations of the so-called

[1] The best known system is of course the one developed and very fully discussed by L. J. Savage in his book *The Foundations of Statistics* (New York: John Wiley and Sons, 1954). For references to earlier systems, see Savage's very complete bibliography. In several respects our approach to the problem is very close to that of F. J. Anscombe and R. J. Aumann in "A definition of subjective probability," *Annals of Mathematical Statistics*, **34** (1963), 199–205, although these authors take utility for granted and derive only subjective probability whereas we derive both from first principles. They and we both obtain simplification mainly by assuming directly the existence of a random variable whose distribution is subjectively (or objectively) uniform. Their discussion of the relation of their assumptions to Savage's is relevant here also.

"Bayesian" position. To this end, we have first of all avoided any reference to the behavior of idealized decision makers all of whose acts are perfectly self-consistent; instead, we have taken a strictly "constructive" approach to the problem of analyzing a single problem of decision under uncertainty, hoping thereby to dispel such apparently common misconceptions as that a utility function and a system of judgmental probabilities necessarily exist without conscious effort, or that they can be discovered only by learning how the decision maker would make a very large number of decisions. Second, we have tried to choose axioms that will make it as easy as possible for the reader to understand and internalize, not only the behavioral implications of each axiom taken individually, but also the way in which the axioms combine to produce the principal results of the system as a whole.

We should mention that sometimes the axioms seem unreasonable when the acts, events, and consequences are defined casually but become acceptable under more careful definitions. In particular, each consequence must be defined in sufficient detail that the decision maker has the same attitude toward it whatever act and event give rise to it. This is further discussed by Savage (*op. cit.*, p. 25).

2. INFORMAL STATEMENT OF ASSUMPTIONS AND PRINCIPAL CONCLUSIONS

To orient the reader among the technicalities which will have to follow, we shall start by giving a brief, informal statement of our basic assumptions and our principal results. We trust that any ambiguities in this introduction will be cleared up as the reader continues with the main part of the paper.

2.1. The Canonical Basis

As a basis for scaling of preferences and judgments and as a standard for comparison of acts, we shall ask the decision maker to consider some very simple hypothetical lotteries in which the consequence depends on an experiment that he, the decision maker, is to imagine. Concerning this experiment and the lotteries based on it we shall make two assumptions the psychological essence of which is as follows:

1a. The decision maker *can imagine* an experiment all of whose outcomes are "equally likely" in the sense that *he* would be *indifferent* between any two lotteries one of which entitles him to a certain valuable prize if some one, particular outcome occurs while the other entitles him to that *same* prize if some other one, particular outcome occurs.

1b. As regards any two lotteries one of which entitles him to a valuable prize if *any one* of n_1 particular outcomes occurs while the other entitles him to that same prize if any one of n_2 particular outcomes occurs, he will prefer the former lottery to the latter if and only if n_1 is greater than n_2.

Any experiment having the "equally likely" property defined by the first assumption will be called a *canonical experiment,* and any lottery in which the payout depends upon a canonical experiment will be called a *canonical lottery.* If a canonical experiment has N possible outcomes, we shall say that the *canonical chance* that any particular one of these outcomes will occur is $1/N$; and similarly we shall say that the canonical chance that *some* one of any n particular outcomes will occur is n/N. We call the reader's particular attention to the fact that canonical chances need have nothing to do with "objective probability," whatever that expression may mean. We have not assumed and do not need to assume that anyone can design an experiment all of whose outcomes are equally likely in some frequency sense; all we need is an experiment, which may be imaginary, towards whose possible outcomes the *decision maker* holds the attitudes of indifference and preference called for by the assumption. If he happens to believe that some real experiment has "objectively" equally likely outcomes, it will serve for him, of course.

In the sequel, we shall assume the existence of a continuous version of the experiment described above. Thus canonical chances need not be rational numbers, but include all real numbers between 0 and 1.

2.2. Scaling of Preferences and Judgments

Concerning the scaling of preferences and judgments we shall make the following assumptions.

2. The decision maker can select reference consequences c^* and c_* such that c^* is *at least* as attractive as any possible consequence of any of the available acts and c_* is *at least* as unattractive as any possible consequence of any of the available acts; and he can then:

a. Scale his *preference* for any possible *consequence c* by specifying a number $\pi(c)$ such that *he* would be *indifferent* between (1) c

for certain, and (2) a lottery giving a canonical chance $\pi(c)$ at c^* and a complementary chance at c_*;

     b. Scale his *judgment* concerning any possible *event E_0* by specifying a number $P(E_0)$ such that *he* would be *indifferent* between (1) a lottery with consequence c^* if E_0 occurs, c_* if it does not, and (2) a lottery giving a canonical chance $P(E_0)$ at c^* and a complementary chance at c_*.

The event E_0 in part (b) *may* be one of the events $E_1, \ldots, E_n$ some one of which will determine the consequence of the decision maker's chosen act, but the assumption is to be understood as asserting that the decision maker can if necessary scale his judgment concerning any event whatever.

Although we assume that the decision maker *can* scale his preference for any c and his judgment concerning any E_0 by direct, intuitive evaluation, this by no means implies that he *must* do this for every conceivable c and E_0 in the world, or even for every c and E_0 involved in his immediate decision problem. If the set of possible consequences has structure—if, e.g., all consequences are sums of money or numbers of hours of effort—the decision maker may if he likes make a preliminary assessment of $\pi(c)$ for only a few c's and then fair a curve or select a formula giving $\pi(c)$ for all c's; and in so doing he *may* wish to revise those $\pi(c)$ which he originally assessed directly in order to make π a "smoother" function of c. Similarly, if the set of possible events has structure—if, e.g., each event corresponds to a particular value of some unknown quantity—the decision maker may if he likes evaluate $P(E_0)$ directly for only a few of the possible E_0's and then fair a curve or select a formula which gives $P(E_0)$ for all E_0, again possibly revising his original assessments in the process.

2.3. Principles of Consistent Behavior

We next come to two principles of *consistent* behavior which we submit for the decision maker's approval. In stating them we shall use the word "lottery" to mean *either* a hypothetical lottery in which the payout depends upon the outcome of an imaginary canonical experiment *or* a real-world act whose consequence depends upon which of a number of real-world events occurs (or has occurred but is still unknown to the decision maker).

     3. As regards any set of lotteries among which the decision maker

has evaluated his feelings of preference or indifference, these relations should be *transitive*. If, for example, he prefers lottery A to lottery B and is indifferent between lottery B and lottery C, then he should prefer lottery A to lottery C.

4. If some of the prizes in a lottery are replaced by other prizes such that the decision maker is indifferent between each new prize and the corresponding original prize, then the decision maker should be indifferent between the original and the modified lotteries.

The word "prize" in this latter principle is to be interpreted as meaning *either* a consequence *or* the right to participate in another lottery whose payout *will* be a consequence; under the other assumptions, the principle implies, among other things, that replacing one of the prizes in a lottery by a *less* desirable prize cannot make the lottery as a whole *more* desirable.

We call the reader's particular attention to two points. First, we do not assume that the decision maker has established his preferences between *all conceivable* pairs of lotteries by direct, intuitive evaluation; and second, we do not assume even as regards those lotteries which he *has* evaluated intuitively that his intuitive evaluations will agree with our two principles of consistent behavior. On the contrary, we ask the decision maker whether he would *like* his decisions in complex problems to be consistent in the sense of these two principles with his preferences and judgments as expressed after careful consideration of very simple problems. All that we have to offer the decision maker is a method of calculation that will insure this kind of consistency; ideal decision makers whose intuitive behavior is perfectly consistent have no use for our services.

2.4. Choice Among Acts

The essence of the method by which the two principles of consistency discussed in the last section permit the decision maker to infer a choice among acts from his scaled preferences for consequences and judgments concerning events is contained in the following theorem.

Let a be any one of the acts which the decision maker wishes to compare, let $\{E_1, \ldots, E_i, \ldots, E_n\}$ be a set of mutually exclusive and collectively exhaustive events, let c_i be the consequence that a will have if the event E_i occurs, let $\pi(c_i)$ be his scaled preference for c_i, let $P(E_i)$ be his scaled judgment concerning E_i, and compute the *index*

$$\Pi \equiv \sum_i P(E_i)\pi(c_i).$$

Then it follows from the two basic principles of consistency that the *decision maker* should be *indifferent* between the real act a and a canonical lottery giving a chance Π at c^* and a chance $(1 - \Pi)$ at c_*.

In other words, to *every* available act there corresponds an equivalent canonical lottery between the *same* two consequences c^* and c_*, the lotteries differing only as regards the *chances* Π and $(1 - \Pi)$ of obtaining the two respective consequences. The most desirable of these "reference lotteries" is obviously the one giving the *greatest* chance Π at the superior consequence c^* (and hence automatically the smallest chance at the inferior consequence c_*); and from this observation we can immediately derive the following *rule for choice among acts*.

Let a' and a'' be any two of the acts which the decision maker wishes to compare, and let Π' and Π'' be their respective indices as defined in the previous theorem. Then it follows from the two basic principles of consistency that the decision maker should prefer a' to a'' if and only if Π' is greater than Π''.

2.5. Probability and Utility

As a preliminary lemma to these principal results we prove that the scaled judgments $P(E_i)$ which the decision maker attaches to the events E_i *should* obey the usual axioms of the mathematical theory of probability, viz.: for any event E_0,

$$P(E_0) \geq 0;$$

if E is an event certain to occur,

$$P(E) = 1;$$

and if $E_1, E_2, \ldots, E_n$ are mutually exclusive events,

$$P(E_1 \text{ or } E_2 \text{ or } \cdots \text{ or } E_n) = P(E_1) + P(E_2) + \cdots + P(E_n).$$

It follows that the reader can, if he likes, give the name *probabilities* to the scaled judgments $P(E_i)$. He can also, if he likes, give the name *utilities* to the scaled preferences which the decision maker attaches to the various consequences c; and he can then call the index Π that is computed for any act the *expected utility* of that act and say that our principal result shows that the decision maker should choose so as to "maximize his expected utility."

Whether or not anyone *does* prefer to give the name utility to π or probability to P is a question of linguistic taste; and although we ourselves like this use of the word probability and dislike this use of the word utility, we do not propose to argue over questions of taste. The *essential* point is simply that the decision maker who accepts the two consistency principles *can* solve any decision problem, no matter how complex, by merely expressing his basic preferences and judgments with regard to very simple problems and then performing straightforward computations. Whether he will feel that he can express his preferences and judgments *more effectively* by intuitive analysis of simple problems than by intuitive analysis of complex problems is another matter; but even though there is a good deal of empirical evidence to show that many practical decision makers instinctively want to avoid the rather awful clarity that surrounds a really simple decision, we nevertheless believe that most responsible decision makers who take the trouble to train themselves to support this clarity will end by preferring to make decisions in such a way that they can see what they are doing.

2.6. Conditional Preference and Conditional Probability

In some situations the decision maker will wish to pay particular attention to the import of some one particular piece of information for his choice of an act. The information can be thought of as knowledge that some event $E^\dagger$ has occurred, where $E^\dagger$ *may* be the outcome of some sample or experiment but more generally represents *any* piece of information that bears on the choice of an act. We shall conclude our analysis by showing how such information "should" be processed by the decision maker, i.e., how he "should" choose one of the available acts after learning that $E^\dagger$ has occurred; but since our results will require the direct or indirect use of probabilities of joint events such as the occurrence of E_i and $E^\dagger$, we first digress to consider ways in which such probabilities can be conveniently assessed.

2.6.1. *Joint and Conditional Probability*

Let E' and E'' be any two events such that $P(E')$ is greater than zero, and suppose that for some purpose the decision maker wishes to assign a probability to the "joint event" (E' *and* E''). The probability of such an event can of course be assessed directly, like that of any other event, but the decision maker will often find it more convenient to assess joint probabilities indirectly, by a method the validity of which rests on the following theorem.

Let $l_E^\dagger$ and $l_Y^\dagger$ be lotteries neither of which pays anything unless E'

occurs. *Provided that E' does occur, $l_E^\dagger$ will pay c^* if E'' occurs,
otherwise c_*, while $l_Y^\dagger$ will give a canonical chance p at c^* and a
complementary chance at c_*. Then the decision maker should be
indifferent between $l_E^\dagger$ and $l_Y^\dagger$ if and only if

$$p = \frac{P(E' \text{ and } E'')}{P(E')}.$$

In the abstract theory of probability, the right-hand side of this equation
is usually taken as the *definition* of the *conditional probability of E'' given
E'*,

$$P(E''|E') \equiv \frac{P(E' \text{ and } E'')}{P(E')} \quad \text{if} \quad P(E') > 0,$$

and from this is obtained the "multiplication rule"

$$P(E' \text{ and } E'') = P(E')P(E''|E').$$

What the *theorem* says is that, because $P(E''|E')$ has a behavioral
interpretation in terms of "conditional lotteries" that are called off unless
E' occurs, this conditional probability can be assessed by direct application of judgment; and this being true, the decision maker can if he likes
compute the probability of the event (E' *and* E'') from the multiplication
rule; he does not *have* to assess it directly.

2.6.2. *Optimal Acts Given $E^\dagger$*

We now return to the problem of selecting an act that is optimal given
that $E^\dagger$ occurs. We continue to assume that the consequence of any
available act will depend on which of a set $\{E_1, \ldots, E_n\}$ of mutually
exclusive and collectively exhaustive events occurs; what we shall show
is that, if we compute for each available act the *conditional* index

$$\Pi^\dagger = \sum_i P(E_i|E^\dagger)\pi(c_i),$$

then the act which maximizes $\Pi^\dagger$ is *optimal given $E^\dagger$* in two senses that we
shall now define.

2.6.3. *Optimal Decision Rules*

The most common approach to the problem of selecting an act given
the information that $E^\dagger$ has occurred is to say that, *before* it is known
whether or not $E^\dagger$ will occur, the decision maker should select a *decision
rule* telling him what to do given *every possible* piece of new information

(e.g., every possible outcome of a sample or experiment). Considering the problem in this way, we show that the four basic assumptions stated in Sections 2.1 through 2.3 above imply that the act which maximizes the index $\Pi^\dagger$ is optimal given $E^\dagger$ in the following sense:

> Let d' and d'' be two decision rules that *agree* concerning the act to be chosen if $E^\dagger$ does *not* occur but *disagree* concerning the act to be chosen if $E^\dagger$ *does* occur; let a' and a'' be the acts called for by d' and d'' respectively in the case that $E^\dagger$ occurs; and let $\Pi^{\dagger\prime}$ and $\Pi^{\dagger\prime\prime}$ be the conditional indices of a' and a'' given $E^\dagger$. Then the decision maker should prefer d' to d'' if and only if $\Pi^{\dagger\prime}$ is greater than $\Pi^{\dagger\prime\prime}$.

2.6.4. *Action After $E^\dagger$ Is Known to Have Occurred*

The conditional probabilities $P(E_i|E^\dagger)$ that are used in computing the conditional indices $\Pi^\dagger$ are often called "posterior" probabilities, i.e., probabilities assigned to the E_i posterior to learning that $E^\dagger$ has occurred; and it may therefore seem that the result just stated is equivalent to an assertion that after learning that $E^\dagger$ has occurred the decision maker "should" proceed to reassess the probabilities of the E_i in accordance with the usual definition of conditional probability given $E^\dagger$ and then select the act whose "posterior expected utility" $\Pi^\dagger$ is greatest. This interpretation is illegitimate, however, since our four original basic assumptions deal only with relations among preferences in a situation which is static as regards knowledge about events, and therefore all that those assumptions entitle us to say is that if the decision maker *binds* himself to a decision rule *before* knowing what the new information will be, then he should bind himself according to the stated result. It is a new behavioral assumption, albeit an obvious one, that the decision maker should actually follow his chosen decision rule *after* he has actually learned that $E^\dagger$ has in fact occurred; and we formalize the essence of this principle in the following new basic assumption.

> 5. Lottery l' should be preferred to lottery l'' given knowledge that $E^\dagger$ has occurred if and only if l' would be preferred to l'' without this knowledge but with an agreement that both lotteries would be called off if $E^\dagger$ did not occur.

From our four original assumptions concerning preferences held *prior* to learning that $E^\dagger$ has occurred and our fifth assumption relating prior to *posterior* preferences, it can be proved as a *theorem* that the decision maker's posterior behavior "should" be governed by the four original assumptions reworded to deal with posterior rather than prior preferences; and it can also be proved that the *scaled judgment* that the decision maker forms concerning any event E_0 posterior to learning that $E^\dagger$ has occurred "should" agree with the usual definition of $P(E_0|E^\dagger)$. From these results it then follows, by exactly the same reasoning that led to our original theorem on comparison of acts, that *after* learning that $E^\dagger$ has occurred the decision maker "should" choose the act which maximizes the index $\Pi^\dagger$. Or in other words: even though the decision maker is *free* to deviate from the act called for by the decision rule which was optimal when chosen before it was known whether or not $E^\dagger$ would occur, our fifth basic assumption implies that he should not do so.

3. INTRODUCTION TO THE FORMAL SYSTEM

To help the reader over the step from the very informal statement of principles and results that we have just given to the formal language and formal proofs that will follow, we shall in the present section introduce the basic concepts of the formal system in as suggestive a manner as possible.

3.1. Real-world Events

As we have already seen in Section 2.6, it is often necessary to group two or more events into a single event or to subdivide an event into two or more subevents. We therefore introduce the idea of an "elementary event" which is so finely described that we shall never need to subdivide it further; and we let e denote a typical one of these elementary events, let E denote the collection or set of all possible e's, and consider the generic event E_0 to be a subset of E. The expression $e \in E_0$ will mean that the "true" elementary event e belongs to the subset E_0; the symbol $\bar{E}_0$ will denote the complementary subset to E_0 (the event that E_0 does not occur); and any collection $\{E_1, \ldots, E_n\}$ of mutually exclusive and collectively exhaustive events will be called a partition of E.

3.2. The Canonical Basis

In our informal discussion of a canonical basis, we introduced the idea of an imaginary *canonical experiment* with a finite number of possible outcomes all of which were equally likely in the behavioral sense defined by assumption (1a) in Section 2.1. We shall now be more specific about the way in which the outcome of this experiment is to be described, and at the same time we shall make some slight technical changes in our assumptions about the experiment itself, although without in any way altering the psychological essence of these assumptions.

Specifically, we shall think of an *outcome* of the canonical experiment as being described by *two numbers* both between 0 and 1 inclusive. Denoting these two numbers by x and y, we can also think of the experiment as one which selects a *point* (x, y) in a *unit square* with one side extending along an x axis from 0 to 1 while an adjacent side extends from 0 to 1 along an orthogonal y axis. If the numbers x and y were to be decimal fractions with a fixed number of places, we would have an experiment with a finite number of possible outcomes, exactly as in our original assumption; but it will be much more convenient to get rid of the discreteness inherent in this assumption, and we shall therefore ask the decision maker to imagine an experiment such that the point (x, y) can lie *anywhere* in the unit square. All that is needed for this purpose is to imagine a process capable of generating an infinite sequence of random digits that are assigned alternately to the decimal representations of x and y.

The "equally likely" property was originally defined in terms of indifference between lotteries each of which paid off for a *single one* of the possible outcomes of the experiment. Since the point (x, y) now has an infinity of possible locations, this definition of equally likely is no longer adequate, and we shall therefore modify it as follows. Using the expression "generalized interval" to denote any rectangle or finite union of rectangles with sides parallel to the x and y axes, we shall consider lotteries which will yield a valuable prize if the point (x, y) falls within some specified generalized interval such as I or J in Figure 1; and as a

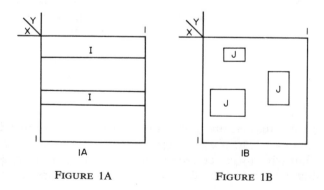

FIGURE 1A   FIGURE 1B

first approximation we shall say that the experiment is canonical if the decision maker is indifferent between any two such lotteries in which the *areas* of the intervals yielding the prize are equal. Adding in our original assumption (1b), which says that if two lotteries offer unequal chances at the same prize, then the decision maker will prefer the one offering the greater chance, we arrive at the following revision of our original assumptions (1a) and (1b).

> The decision maker can *imagine* an experiment which will determine a point (x, y) in such a way that, if I and J are any two generalized intervals in the unit square, if l_I is a lottery that will yield a valuable prize if $(x, y) \in I$, and if l_J is a lottery that will yield this same prize if $(x, y) \in J$, then *he* will prefer l_I to l_J if and only if the area of I is greater than the area of J.

This definition of a canonical experiment is only a first approximation because it neglects one point of considerable importance. If the canonical experiment is to serve as a kind of "standard" for scaling of preferences and judgments and for comparison of acts, then clearly it must be of such a nature that its outcome in no way depends on the real-world events involved in the decision maker's real decision problem. In our original, informal discussion we took this independence for granted, but in the formal system we shall make the following additional assumption which requires it specifically.

> Let E_0 denote any real-world event, and let I and J denote any two generalized intervals whose areas are equal. The decision maker can imagine that (x, y) will be determined in such a way that he will be indifferent between any two lotteries one of which yields a valuable prize if *both $e \in E_0$ and $(x, y) \in I$* while the other yields that same prize if *both $e \in E_0$ and $(x, y) \in J$*.

That this additional assumption does in fact require the decision maker to think of x and y as independent of e is easily seen. Suppose, for example, that the decision maker feels that if e belongs to some particular E_0, then high values of x and y are "more likely" than low values. He would then prefer a prize contingent on E_0 and an interval I in the upper right-hand corner of the unit square to the same prize contingent on E_0 and an interval J of the same area as I but located in the lower left-hand corner of the unit square, in contradiction to the assumption just stated. Notice, on the other hand, that we cannot *combine* this additional assumption with the previous one by saying that he will *prefer* the prize contingent on E_0 and I to the prize contingent on E_0 and J if I is *larger* than J. The event E_0 may be such that the decision maker would attach no value to the chance whatever the areas of I and J might be.

3.3. Lotteries and Prizes

3.3.1. *Diagrammatic Representation of Lotteries*

Most of the real-world acts and hypothetical lotteries that we shall have to consider can be represented by diagrams of the kind shown in Fig. 2.

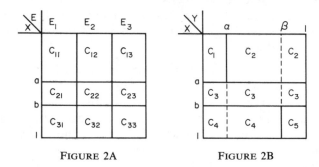

FIGURE 2A   FIGURE 2B

Figure 2A is to be interpreted as defining a lottery that pays, for example,

$$c_{11} \quad \text{if} \quad 0 \le x \le a \quad \text{and} \quad e \in E_1,$$
$$c_{23} \quad \text{if} \quad a < x \le b \quad \text{and} \quad e \in E_3,$$

and so forth. Figure 2B is to be interpreted as defining a lottery that pays

$$c_1 \quad \text{if} \quad 0 \le x \le a \quad \text{and} \quad 0 \le y \le \alpha,$$
$$c_3 \quad \text{if} \quad a < x \le b \quad \text{regardless of } y,$$

and so forth.

3.3.2. *Lotteries with Lotteries as Prizes*

In evaluating *hypothetical* lotteries whose payoffs depend in whole or in part on x and/or y, we shall ask the decision maker to imagine that he will *never actually learn* the true values of these quantities—what he will learn is simply the consequence that the lottery pays out; but we shall nevertheless sometimes ask him to look at and compare such lotteries *conditionally* upon some given e, x, or y.

Suppose then, for example, that we consider the lottery defined by

Figure 2A *given* that $e \in E_2$; what we have is a lottery in which the payoff depends only on x, being

$$c_{12} \quad \text{if} \quad 0 \le x \le a, \qquad c_{22} \quad \text{if} \quad a < x \le b, \qquad c_{32} \quad \text{if} \quad b < x \le 1.$$

If we consider the lottery defined by Fig. 2B *given* that $0 \le x \le a$, we have a lottery that pays

$$c_1 \quad \text{if} \quad 0 \le y \le \alpha, \qquad c_2 \quad \text{if} \quad \alpha < y \le 1;$$

if we consider the lottery defined by Fig. 2B *given* that $a < x \le b$, we have a "constant lottery" that pays c_3 regardless of the value of y; and so forth. In short, every row in a diagram like those in Fig. 2 defines a *row lottery*, and every column defines a *column lottery*.

This way of looking at the rows and columns of diagrams like those in Fig. 2 means that there are three possible ways of looking at the figures as a whole; we illustrate with Fig. 2A as an example.

1. Figure 2A may be regarded as a lottery in which e and x jointly determine a particular cell in the table and thus a particular consequence. Regarded in this way we shall call Fig. 2A a *lottery on $E \times X$* with *consequences as prizes*.

2. Figure 2A may be regarded as a lottery in which e determines a column and x determines a cell within the column. Regarded in this way we shall call Fig. 2A a *lottery on E* with *lotteries on X as prizes*.

3. Figure 2A may be regarded as a lottery in which x determines a row and e determines a cell within the row. Regarded in this way we call Fig. 2A a *lottery on X* with *lotteries on E as prizes*.

The reader must remember, however, that the second and third "aspects" which we have just defined do *not* imply that the value of one of the two "variables" is revealed to the decision maker *after* the other.

3.3.3. *Notation for Lotteries*

The diagrams in Fig. 3 represent notational devices which are virtually self-explanatory. As shown in Fig. 3A, we shall sometimes find it convenient to regard a lottery as a lottery *on $X \times Y$* (say) even though the prize *actually depends* only on y, and similarly for lotteries depending only on x or e. As shown in Fig. 3B, we shall sometimes find it convenient to consider even a particular consequence as a "lottery" which is sure to pay out that particular consequence; we have already referred to the second row of Fig. 2B as defining a row lottery even though that row lottery is sure to pay c_3.

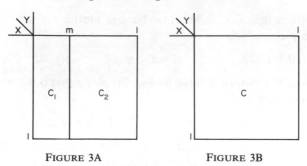

FIGURE 3A   FIGURE 3B

The formal notation for lotteries which we shall introduce in Section 4 will be based on a complete systematization of this point of view. In order to avoid having to deal with preference relations between different *kinds* of entities, *all* lotteries (including row lotteries and column lotteries) will be formally treated as *functions* with *all three* of e, x, and y as arguments, even though the *value* of such a function will almost never *actually depend* on more than two of its three arguments and may depend on only one or even none. Thus a consequence c will sometimes be treated as a "function" of e, x, and y *whose value is c for all e, x, y*; a lottery on E with consequences as prizes will be treated as a function of e, x, and y *whose value depends only on e*; and so forth.*

ACKNOWLEDGMENTS

We are very grateful to L. J. Savage and the referees for their many comments.

*Editors' footnote: At the request of the authors, note is here made that the original article of 23 pages has been abridged. It appears intact, except for the final 11 pages of more technical material based on the exposition presented above.

2

Bayesian Statistics and Product Decisions*

Paul E. Green

The purpose of this article is to show the relevance of the Bayesian approach to product development decision making. More specifically, we shall illustrate how these techniques can be used to help answer two persistent questions related to each stage in the development of a new product:

1. Should we make a decision *now* (with respect to passing a product along to the next development stage vs terminating the project), or should we *delay* this decision until some future date, pending the receipt of additional information regarding the new product's chances for commercial success?

2. Given a decision on *when* to make the decision, *what* action ("go" vs "stop") should we take?

The power of the Bayesian approach as applied to these basic questions is described in two parts. First, we shall review the nature of the costs associated with moving too slowly vs too quickly through the product development process. Second, an illustrative case will show how these groups of costs can be introduced within a Bayesian framework to guide both the "when to" and "what to do" classes of decisions.

TIME-RELATED COSTS

The ultracautious decision maker tends to incur sizable costs when he delays each development decision until he has assembled enough information to make the choice patently clear. These costs are partly as-

*From *Business Horizons*, Vol. 5, No. 3, Fall 1962, pp. 101–109. Reproduced by permission.

sociated with time and partly associated with the cost of the information gathering activity itself (which also takes time to accomplish).

An illustration should make clear the nature of these time-related costs. Assume that a new chemical product has reached the development stage where the company must either (1) decide now whether to construct a semiworks unit or to terminate the project, or (2) delay, pending the receipt of additional information regarding the anticipated outcomes associated with the alternative to proceed. Apart from sunk costs (that is, historical costs, not relevant from an economic standpoint), termination at this point would result in a payoff of zero. The decision to proceed, however, is related to a series of future decisions up to and including commercialization before a positive payoff could be forthcoming. The decision maker should be concerned with at least three groups of costs that can be associated with delay. First, as a function of delay time, the present value of all future revenues attendant with commercialization would be reduced as a consequence of delaying the start of the receipt of these revenues until a more distant time. This type of delay cost merely gives recognition to the time value of money.

Second, also as a function of delay time, the present value of all future revenues attendant with commercialization could be lowered as a consequence of the increased risk of competitive imitation or supersedure of the product (at the hands of competitors or conceivably of a future product of the decision maker's own research organization).

Finally, gathering the information obviously costs money and incurs time for its development. If one assumes some linear relationship of money spent for information with the period required to obtain the information, then this cost also can be associated with the time variable.

On the other side of the coin, an impatient decision maker who eliminates or gives short shrift to vital steps of information gathering runs the risk of incurring sizable costs associated with acting under a high degree of uncertainty (and perhaps costs associated with "crashing" the program, that is, telescoping development steps, as well). The behavior of these groups of costs can be viewed as a function of time, which, in turn, is a function of the amount of information collected. Thus, the decision maker must view the change in payoff associated with the go vs no-go decision now vs the payoff associated with delay of this decision, pending receipt of additional data. Why collect additional data at all? Additional data would be collected for the purpose of reducing the variance associated with the estimated distribution of payoffs related to acting now. Other things equal, it is clear that when the costs of uncertainty are large the decision maker could suffer by moving too rapidly to the next stage of the development process. On the other hand, if the costs of wrong decisions are low, he should move rapidly.

APPLYING BAYESIAN THEORY

While the preceding remarks have focused on the nature of the costs associated with moving too quickly vs too slowly at any stage in the development process, we must still illustrate how Bayesian decision theory utilizes these costs to provide a rationale for answering both the "when to" and "what to do" questions. The following illustration is deliberately simplified to deal with the simplest of cases, a one-stage choice.

Assume that a point has been reached in the development of a new product regarding whether or not a semiworks should be constructed now vs delaying this decision (pending receipt of further market information). To be more explicit, three options will be considered:

1. Build a semiworks vs terminate project now.
2. Delay this decision until one period (year) into the future.
3. Delay this decision until two periods (years) into the future.

Options 2 and 3 imply, of course, that better marketing information than now exists could be secured over the next year or two and that the more extensive this inquiry, the better the quality of the information. However, the development of the additional marketing data will cost something itself and will delay subsequent steps toward commercialization.

Some present marketing information, which is rather imprecise, indicates that four alternative forecasts of potential sales, given commercialization, bracket the possible levels of future sales. Subjective probabilities have been stated for the occurrence of each forecast and, given each forecast, it has been possible to calculate the payoff, given commercialization. These data are noted in Table 1 where F_i stands for each sales forecast deemed admissible and $P(F_i)$ stands for the likelihood that the decision maker assigns to the occurrence of each forecast.

TABLE 1. *Conditional payoffs and expected values (in millions of dollars)*

Acts	F_1	$P(F_1)$	F_2	$P(F_2)$	F_3	$P(F_3)$	F_4	$P(F_4)$	EP
Go	−$12	.15	−$1	.30	$5	.45	$10	.10	$1.15
No-go	$ 0	.15	$0	.30	$0	.45	$ 0	.10	$0

Under the go alternative, Table 1 indicates that if forecasts F_1 or F_2 actually occurred, negative payoffs (in present value terms) would result, while under the more optimistic forecasts, F_3 or F_4, payoffs would be positive. According to the Bayesian approach the expected payoff (EP) of the go option is found by summing over the product of each payoff times its probability. The present value of future returns of the no-go alternative (termination) is, of course, zero.[1] In this oversimplified problem situation, the decision maker—in the absence of the opportunity to collect additional market information—would go with the project, that is, construct the semiworks. The expected payoff associated with this alternative is $1.15 million.

More realistically, however, the decision maker frequently has the option of delaying his decision pending the receipt of additional data regarding the occurrence of the alternative sales forecasts. These additional data will cost something to collect, delay construction time, and rarely, if ever, be perfectly reliable.

One-year Delay Option

We shall first consider the one-year delay option. For purposes of illustration we will assume that a delay of one year in construction would have the following results: (1) the cost of delayed revenues amounts to payoffs that are only 91 per cent of the former payoff (interest rate equal to 10 per cent annually); (2) the firm's market share would drop from 100 per cent, under the no-delay case, to 75 per cent because of the resulting greater lead time for competitive imitation; and (3) the cost of collecting additional information concerning future sales would be $150,000. However, information obtained at this early stage of development is assumed to be only 70 per cent reliable. That is, if the market survey results indicate f_1 (namely, that forecast F_1 will occur), there is a 30 per cent chance that this information could have been assembled if the true underlying sales potential were not F_1 but really F_2, F_3, or F_4.

To evaluate the cost of this alternative, several sets of new probabilities have to be derived by application of Bayes's theorem, a central tenet of this approach. We shall need to compute marginal, joint, and posterior

---

[1]A project payoff of zero, on a present value basis, would imply that the project's cash flow back (over its anticipated life) would just be sufficient to pay back all cash outlays and to earn some net rate of return, say 10 per cent, on the present value of those outlays. Adoption of the no-go alternative thus assumes that other projects exist that could just earn this return; an opportunity cost concept is involved here.

probabilities. Their meaning will be made clear in the computations to follow.

First we consider the calculation of the *marginal* probabilities, .190, .280, .370, and .160 of the market survey results f_1, f_2, f_3, and f_4, respectively. These calculations are shown in Table 2. The cell entries represent

TABLE 2. *Marginal and joint probabilities under the one-period delay option*

Survey results	Joint probabilities				Marginal probabilities
	F_1	F_2	F_3	F_4	
f_1	.105	.030	.045	.010	.190
f_2	.015	.210	.045	.010	.280
f_3	.015	.030	.315	.010	.370
f_4	.015	.030	.045	.070	.160
	.150	.300	.450	.100	1.000

joint probabilities (the probability assigned to the joint occurrence of each survey result f_i and each underlying event F_i). For example, the joint probability of survey result f_1 and event F_1 occurring is found, under the oversimplified assumptions of our problem, by multiplying the conditional probability, $P(f_1|F_1)$, by the prior probability, $P(F_1)$, which the decision maker assigned to F_1; $.70 \times .15 = .105$. The conditional probability of observing survey result f_1, given the fact that the true underlying forecast is F_2, is assumed equal to .10. (Similarly, for the sake of simplicity, the probability of obtaining the survey result f_1 if the true forecast is F_3 or F_4 is also assumed to be .10.) Hence the joint probability of survey result f_1 and event F_2 occurring is, by way of illustration, $P(f_1|F_2) \cdot P(F_2) = .10 \times .30 = .030$ as shown in the second column of row f_1. The other cell entries are computed analogously.

The *marginal probabilities* f_1, f_2, f_3, and f_4 are then found by merely summing over the column entries for each row—$P(f_1) = P(f_1$ and $F_1) + P(f_1$ and $F_2) + P(f_1$ and $F_3) + P(f_1$ and $F_4)$ or $.190 = .105 + .030 + .045 + .010$. Also note that the marginal probabilities, found by summing over rows for each column F_i, are simply the prior probabilities that the decision maker had originally assigned to the occurrence of these four events.

We can next proceed to the calculation of the *posterior probabilities*, $P(F_i|f_i)$, and to a brief description of how Bayes's theorem can be used to derive them. These calculations are shown in Table 3.

TABLE 3. *Posterior probabilities under the one-period delay option*

Survey results	Posterior probabilities				
	F_1	F_2	F_3	F_4	Total
f_1	.553	.158	.237	.052	1.000
f_2	.054	.750	.161	.035	1.000
f_3	.041	.081	.851	.027	1.000
f_4	.094	.188	.281	.437	1.000

Each cell is computed by utilizing Bayes's formula:

$$P(F_i|f) = \frac{P(f|F_i) \cdot P(F_i)}{\sum_{j=1}^{n} P(f|F_j) \cdot P(F_j)}.$$

Hence the first row of Table 3 is derived by merely dividing each entry in Table 2 (.105, .030, .045, and .010) by the marginal probability (.190) associated with f_1. *Before* observing f_1 we would have assigned the prior probabilities .15, .30, .45, and .10 to events F_1, F_2, F_3, and F_4, respectively. *After* having observed f_1 we would then revise these probabilities to .553, .158, .237, and .052, respectively, so as to reflect the fact that the observance of f_1 was deemed more likely under F_1 than under F_2, F_3, or F_4. Analogous considerations apply to the calculation of posterior probabilities shown in the remaining rows of Table 3.

All of the assumptions and calculations of our simple expository case can be summarized in Fig. 1, which should be examined by working from right to left. To illustrate, the upper branch (do not delay) summarizes the results of Table 1. The conditional payoffs under each forecast, given go, are −$12 million, −$1 million, $5 million, and $10 million. Multiplying these payoffs by their respective probabilities and summing the results yields, of course, the expected payoff of $1.15 million. Since this is clearly higher than the $0 associated with no-go, this latter alternative is blocked off, and the best alternative, *given no delay*, is go.

However, the second main branch of the tree is still to be evaluated. The conditional payoffs, −$10.91 million, −$0.91 million, $3.41 million, and $6.82 million at the extreme right of the lower branch, reflect the

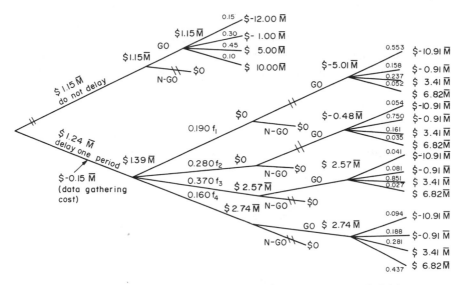

FIGURE 1. Build semiworks—terminate project now vs one-period delay.

penalties associated with (1) the discount penalty for delay and (2) the effect on the firm's market share, due to delay if the product were successful.

If f_1 is observed, however, the best action to be taken after the survey is no-go—terminate the project. Hence, the go alternative branching from f_1 is blocked off. Similar results pertain to survey results f_2. Under survey results f_3 and f_4, however, the resulting best action is to build the semiworks. On an expected payoff basis, collecting the additional information produces a gross payoff of $1.39 million. From this gross figure must be subtracted the $0.15 million cost of collecting the information, yielding an expected payoff of $1.24 million associated with the one-year delay option.

The power of this technique is found in the recursive nature of solution. That is, the two payoffs, $1.24 million and $1.15 million, *summarize completely the whole series of moves along the decision tree.* Moves have been optimally planned from this point forward by, in effect, solving the problem backward.

Two-year Delay Option

We now consider the third option: delaying the decision pending a two-year inquiry into the sales potential of the product.[2] In this case we will assume that: (1) cost of deferred revenues amounts to payoffs that are only 83 per cent of the payoffs under the no-delay case; (2) the anticipated market share would drop to only 50 per cent of the market; (3) market survey costs increase to $300,000; but (4) the reliability of the resultant information increases to 90 per cent.

Figure 2 summarizes this second analysis. The upper main branch of

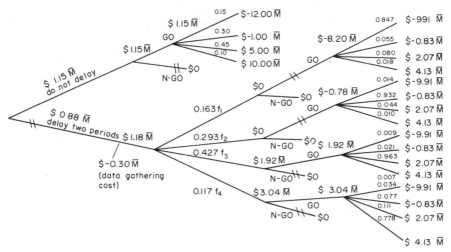

FIGURE 2. Build semiworks—terminate project now vs two-period delay.

the decision tree, covering the no-delay case, is exactly the same as that in Fig. 1. All payoffs and probabilities in the lower main branch, however, are adjusted in accordance with the changed assumptions just enumerated by developing tables analogous to Tables 2 and 3. Solution of the problem again proceeds from right to left, always choosing the best alternative for each subbranch of the tree.

[2]Numerous other combinations could be evaluated ranging from the case where construction of the semiworks and start of the marketing studies are begun simultaneously through various degrees of overlap in timing. No new principles would be involved. Payoffs would, of course, reflect the cost of project "takedown and salvage" if the marketing survey results were to indicate a change in action from go to no-go after construction had already been started.

The upshot of this analysis is that the two-year delay option produces a lower expected payoff than the no-delay option. In other words, the costs associated with delaying the venture more than outweigh the gains expected through increased reliability of the sales information. For this reason the lower branch of the tree is blocked off in Fig. 2.

In summary, it has been shown, via the preceding simplified examples, how costs associated with delay can be balanced against the costs associated with the higher costs of uncertainty related to moving a development along too quickly.

The preceding illustrative case has touched upon some aspects of Bayesian decision theory but has by no means exhausted the many facets of this approach. As could be inferred from our preceding illustration, the Bayesian approach to decision making under uncertainty provides a framework for explicitly working with the economic costs of alternative courses of action, the prior knowledge or judgments of the decision maker regarding the occurrence of states of nature affecting payoffs, and the conditional probabilities of observing specific events, given each state of nature.

Coupled with ancillary techniques such as computer simulation and sensitivity analyses, it seems fair to say that this set of tools constitutes the most powerful analytical apparatus of its class currently available to the product development manager.

3

Maximin Programming: An Approach to Farm Planning Under Uncertainty*

J. P. McInerney

As conventionally applied to farm planning, linear programming models take little or no formal account of imperfect knowledge in the production environment. The implicit assumption (or hope!) in such applications would seem to be that uncertainties are either not present or not important. Clearly, however, this is unrealistic. To the farmer, faced with making and accepting the consequences of decisions, the presence and importance of uncertainties cannot be assumed, or wished, away. It should therefore be of continuing concern to agricultural economists that their models should specifically consider the vagaries of the farm planning environment. Unfortunately, in a world of imperfect knowledge, there can exist no "best" planning method; there exists a variety of "bests", depending on the subjective attitudes of the decision maker. In many instances the maximisation of some expected income level over a period of years—as linear programming implies—is not a sufficient objective. The consequences of income levels in any particular year must also be considered. This paper assumes such a modified objective in an attempt to make uncertainty at least partially manageable within the framework of the linear programming model, using some of the notions embodied in the theory of games.

GAME THEORY AND GAMES AGAINST NATURE

When it first appeared in 1944, von Neumann and Morgenstern's *Theory of Games*[10] was hailed as a major breakthrough in economic

*From *Journal of Agricultural Economics*, Vol. XVIII, No. 2, May 1967, pp. 279–289. Reproduced by permission. (A list of references is given at the end of this article.)

thought and analysis. Stone[9, p. 185] considered it to be "unquestionably, for economists, ... the most important contribution that has appeared since Keynes' *General Theory*". Since then, despite the undoubted importance in applied economics of the uncertainty that game theory attempted to conquer, and despite various suggested and actual applications, the notions of game theory have not become an established tool on the economist's work bench. Three noted economists wrote in 1958[3, p. 445] "the theory of games ... is still merely a promising and suggestive approach". Final disillusionment was recently expressed by Dillon[2] who, in a classic review of the whole field, concluded that "like Marshall, it has had its day". From this short history, it would appear that the theory of games as an operational concept died after a 20-year life of unfulfilled promise. An attempt at resurrection (or exhumation?) is made in the following pages.

The theory of games provides a framework of analysis for situations of conflict between two or more participants.* The theory is best developed in relation to 2-person games; and the most common examples relate to that class of problems known as zero-sum (or constant-sum) games, in which the gains by one player completely represent the losses by the other. The elements of such a game are the set of alternative possible courses of action, or strategies, available to each player, and a corresponding set of potential outcomes resulting from the implementation of any pair of opposing strategies. Thus, the following might represent a generalised 2-person zero-sum game:

Player II

	S_1	....	S_j	....	S_n
A_1	c_{11}	....	c_{1j}	....	c_{1n}
A_i	c_{i1}	....	c_{ij}	....	c_{in}
A_m	c_{m1}	....	c_{mj}	....	c_{mn}

Player I

Here, the set $\{A_i\}$ represents the alternative choices open to Player I (conventionally the maximising player), and $\{S_j\}$ represents the strategy set open to Player II—the minimising player. The payoff matrix $[c_{ij}]$ indicates the gain (in £, utility, etc.) to Player I, and the loss to Player II,

*An eminently readable exposition of the main ideas in game theory is given by Williams.[11]

resulting from any pair of choices simultaneously selected by the two players.

Several criteria for the selection of a particular alternative have been suggested as applicable to such situations (see 6, chapter 13). We shall be concerned with only one such criterion—that of the *maximin*. This approach assumes that the decision maker is interested in that strategy which secures for him the maximum minimum gain—i.e. that his minimum gain from a play of the game will be as large as possible. (The corresponding strategy for Player II is a *minimax* one, whereby he attempts to minimise the maximum loss he might face.) It is obvious that this class of strategies is inherently conservative, but nevertheless it does constitute a basis for rational action in an environment of complete uncertainty—which our model presupposes.

So far this outline may appear to have little relevance to agriculture. In a pure game, the uncertainty is due entirely to the unknown decisions of the opposing player; and in the model the degree of uncertainty is reduced through the assumption that each player knows the objective of his opponent. For agricultural purposes, however, a more apt description of the problem is a "game against Nature", where Nature represents the spectrum of uncertainties in the biological and institutional complex within which the farmer operates. The farmer (Player I) has a range of possible alternative courses of action—enterprises, resource use levels, etc.; while a set of "states of Nature" characterises conditions of weather, disease, prices, or any other inherent uncertainty phenomenon which the farmer can neither control nor predict. It is obvious from this that Nature cannot be considered a conscious adversary; "she" is, in fact, merely a fictitious Player II with no known objective and no apparent strategy. However, although the farmer need not assume that Nature has any specific desires towards his undoing, he might disregard the worst situation she could produce at his peril. (It might be reasonable, for example, for a beginning farmer with high debt commitments to react in maximin fashion, since other courses of action might lead to his bankruptcy and inability to "play the game" again should one of the worst states of Nature occur.)

A major assumption of the theory applied to agriculture in the form of games against Nature relates to absolute uncertainty* on the part of the

---

*Here perhaps it is relevant to recall the simple distinction between risk and uncertainty.[5] Risk inheres if the set of possible outcomes following a course of action can be characterised by some known probability distribution. If no probabilities can be attached to the outcomes, uncertainty prevails.

decision maker regarding the occurrence of any particular state of Nature. Should he have some (subjective or objective) notion of the probability attaching to any state, he might choose his strategy in order to maximise the expected value of his gains (the "standard" reaction in a risk situation). He might still adopt a maximin strategy, however.

THE "PURE" MAXIMIN STRATEGY

Consider the following simple decision situation.

	S_1	S_2	S_3
A_1	20	30	40
A_2	10	30	60
A_3	20	25	30

The A_i represent alternative farmer courses of action—say, to grow barley, potatoes or oats; the S_j represent possible states of Nature—say, the occurrence of bad, average or good weather conditions respectively. The elements of the pay-off matrix then represent the money gains to the farmer following a particular crop activity and the subsequent occurrence of a particular type of weather in the production season.

How should the farmer select his strategy in this situation? The first thing that one notices is that alternative A_3 is "inferior" to A_1. Under no state of Nature will A_3 yield higher returns than A_1, and generally returns will be lower; hence A_3 can be eliminated as a relevant alternative.*†

Given now a reduced decision problem the decision maker would apply a maximin strategy by searching for the minimum gain he might achieve under each alternative. This is £20 for A_1 and £10 for A_2. The maximin rule merely states that A_1 is the optimal choice, since it assumes the largest minimum gain. In other words, by growing barley the farmer can guarantee that, no matter what weather conditions he experiences, he will never achieve less than £20 per acre—and this is higher than any other production alternative can offer. Perhaps he will achieve more than £20 in

---

*One assumption in game theory is that no utility attaches to the alternatives themselves, only to the returns they can produce; also, that alternatives are independent of one another (e.g. that one does not need to grow oats in order to grow barley). In the later development it will be seen that these assumptions, often invalid in agricultural production, can be ignored.

†Strictly speaking, Nature should never use her choices S_2 or S_3, both of which are inferior to S_1; since we ascribe no personal objectives to Nature, we need not consider this implication, however.

the year ahead, but at least he has the certainty that his returns will not fall below this "security level".

As a competitive player, Nature should adopt her minimax strategy and produce bad weather conditions, S_1. In this way her maximum loss is minimised at £20 per acre. Thus the game reaches a stable solution with a value of £20. Player I achieves his maximin gain and Player II her minimax loss; and there is no incentive for either to change strategy.

The selection of such "pure" (i.e. single) strategies is characteristic of so-called "saddle-point" payoff matrices, in which one element is both the minimum of its row and the maximum of its column. Such are the properties of element c_{11} (£20), and here the value of the game lies.

THE "MIXED" MAXIMIN STRATEGY

In cases where a saddle point does not exist in payoff matrices, the optimal strategy for the farmer would be a "mixed" one—that is, a combination of two or more courses of action.

Consider the following decision situation, where the components have the same meaning as previously described.

	S_1	S_2
A_1	40	20
A_2	10	30

The farmer's best *pure* maximin strategy would be to adopt A_1 and expect a minimum gain of £20. Nature's optimal minimax strategy would be the selection of S_2, with a maximum loss expectation of £30. However, this does not represent a stable solution as before; there is incentive for both players to change their choices. On noticing that Player II is using strategy S_2, Player I will consider altering his choice to A_2 and expect an increased gain of £30. Should he do this, Player II will shift to S_1 and expect a reduced loss of only £10. This will cause Player I to move back to A_1, and so the cycle might continue.

A fundamental, and amazing, theorem of game theory states that, in such unstable situations, there exists some combination of strategies for each player such that a stable solution is reached. In the above example, suppose that Player I uses alternative A_1 with a frequency p, and A_2 with a frequency $1 - p$. He is interested in determining the value of p such that this combination of alternatives assures him some guaranteed minimum level of return, regardless of the alternative used by his opponent. Let this return be V. If the state of Nature S_1 prevails, then:

$$V = 40p + 10(1 - p) = 10 + 30p \tag{i}$$

If the state of Nature S_2 prevails, then:

$$V = 20p + 30(1 - p) = 30 - 10p \tag{ii}$$

Since the minimum gain V is to be the same in either case, then:

$$10 + 30p = 30 - 10p \tag{iii}$$

or $p = \frac{1}{2}$ and $1 - p = \frac{1}{2}$.

The implication of this is that if the farmer adopts A_1 half of the time, and A_2 the other half of the time, then over a series of such decisions he can guarantee himself a higher minimum gain than by using his best pure strategy A_1 alone. By substituting the value of $p = \frac{1}{2}$ into either equation (i) or (ii), it is clear that this minimum gain is £25—regardless of whether Nature consistently uses either S_1 or S_2 or a mixture of both.* This is to be compared with the minimum gain assured under a pure strategy of only £20.

These notions of the maximin and the mixed strategy are of central importance in the theory of 2-person zero-sum games; and it is these concepts which may have useful applications in agricultural economics.

INTERPRETATION OF THE MIXED STRATEGY

As determined above, the farmer's optimal mixed strategy suggests the discrete use of either A_1 or A_2 at every time of decision; the actual selection of whether to use A_1 or A_2 at any point in time should be a random process, each alternative having (in this case) the same probability of being chosen.

In larger games with m farmer alternatives, the solution consists of an m-sized set of probabilities $\{p_i\}$, where any p_i indicates the probability (or the frequency over a long series of plays) with which alternative A_i should be selected. Thus, a repetition of the game is implied. An alternative, and more short run, interpretation of the mixed strategy is perhaps more relevant to agricultural decision making. It is that the $\{p_i\}$

---

*By an identical algebraic process, one can determine Nature's optimal mixed minimax strategy to consist of S_1 and S_2 used in the proportions $\frac{1}{4}:\frac{3}{4}$, thus ensuring a lower maximum loss of £25. Hence the maximin gain and the minimax loss are again equal, as with a saddle point matrix, and a stable solution is reached.

indicate the proportions of resources available that should be allocated to
the production alternatives {A_i} during the production year or planning
period.* Thus, rather than practising a mixed strategy over a long series of
plays, one applies the strategy by using a mixture of production alternatives on one play.†

Thus, one can conceive of a farm planning problem as a farmer game
against Nature, in which all the crop and livestock enterprises and other
farm activities are the farmer's resource use alternatives {A_i}; and the
states of Nature {S_j} are the different possible price or weather conditions, etc. which might obtain in the planning period ahead. The payoff
matrix [c_{ij}] then represents the whole set of possible returns (say, gross
margins per acre) which might follow the adoption of any particular
activity and the subsequent implementation of some particular state of
Nature. The derived mixed strategy in this situation, when interpreted in
terms of proportions of resource allocated to each activity, indicates the
best combination of farm activities to derive some guaranteed minimum
level of income in the uncertainty situation specified. One might call this
an "optimal scheme of diversified production in the face of uncertainty".

SOLUTION PROCEDURES FOR LARGER GAMES

For the simple 2×2 game illustrated above, the maximin strategy can
be solved by simple algebraic manipulation. Some graphical and mechanical methods can be applied for solving somewhat larger games (see 11),
but these soon become most tedious. Eventually, there comes a size of
game when entirely different solution procedures are called for.

It has long been known[1] that every 2-person zero-sum game is formally
equivalent to a well defined linear programming (L.P.) problem. One can
thus employ standard L.P. techniques for solving such games.

Let us take the example of a farmer–Nature game in which the farmer
has m alternative production (resource use) activities, and Nature has n
possible states that might obtain during the production period. The
resulting $m \times n$ payoff matrix contains, for each production alternative
A_i, the vector of n possible gross margins that it might generate during the
production period. The basis of the maximin strategy is that one wishes to
assign a probability (or proportional resource use) level p_i to each A_i such

---

*Or, if the A_i represent alternative resource input levels for a given production process, p_i
may be interpreted as the proportion of the enterprise units that should receive resources at
input level A_i.

†This does not necessarily imply a "bending" of the rules (see 11, p. 103).

that, regardless of which state of Nature holds in practice, the resulting total gross margin will never be less than some minimum value V. Our aim is to determine the values of the p_i which maximise V, the maximin return.

The above maximin conditions are satisfied when:

If S_1 prevails: $c_{11}p_1 + c_{21}p_2 + \cdots + c_{m1}p_m \geqslant V$

If S_j prevails: $c_{1j}p_1 + c_{2j}p_2 + \cdots + c_{mj}p_m \geqslant V$ (System I)

If S_n prevails: $c_{1n}p_1 + c_{2n}p_2 + \cdots + c_{mn}p_m \geqslant V$

Finally, since the individual resource proportions must be non-negative and sum to unity:

$$p_1 + p_2 + \cdots\cdots\cdots + p_m = 1 \tag{1}$$

$$p_i \geqslant 0 \ (\text{for } i = 1, \ldots m) \tag{2}$$

This formulation is already very close to that of an L.P. problem; it lacks only a single explicit objective function (V) to be maximised. Various approaches can be adopted to finalise the formulation; we will use the simple one of introducing "dummy" variables.*

For each of the n relationships in system I, introduce a non-negative "dummy" variable, p_{m+j}, so as to transform each inequation into an equation. The system then becomes:

If S_1 prevails: $c_{11}p_1 + c_{21}p_2 + \cdots + c_{m1}p_m - p_{m+1} \qquad = V$

If S_j prevails: $c_{1j}p_1 + c_{2j}p_2 + \cdots + c_{mj}p_m \qquad - p_{m+j} \qquad = V$ (System II)

If S_n prevails: $c_{1n}p_1 + c_{2n}p_2 + \cdots + c_{mn}p_m \qquad - p_{m+n} = V$

and, as before:

$$p_1 + p_2 + \ldots\ldots\ldots p_m = 1 \tag{1}$$

$$p_i \geqslant 0 \ (\text{for all } i = 1, \ldots m + n) \tag{2}$$

By subtracting the first equation† in system II successively from each

---

*For this and alternative approaches, see (4) chapter 15 or (8) chapter 14. Some writers also use the term "slack" variables. It would seem better to refrain from this terminology, since this term is often used as synonymous with the "disposal" variables utilised in the normal simplex procedure, and which are not specifically introduced in constructing the matrix for computer solution with most computer codes. The dummy variables defined for the procedure above, however, must be explicitly introduced when formulating the problem.

†Or any one of the equations.

of the following equations, the unknown V's are eliminated except for the one remaining in the first equation. This now becomes the objective function, with V to be maximised subject to (a) the equality constraints in the remainder of the system and (b) the summation to unity and non-negativity conditions (1) and (2). In other words, our L.P. formulation is now complete.

Maximise $V = \sum_{i=1}^{m+n} c_{i1} p_i$

Subject to $n - 1$ relationships of the form

$$\sum_{i=1}^{m+n} a_{ij} p_i = 0$$

and also

$$\sum_{i=1}^{m} p_i = 1$$

$$p_i \geqslant 0 \text{ (for } i = 1, \ldots m + n)$$

The standard simplex procedure can now be used to solve for the values of p_i which maximise V. The values of $p_1 \ldots \ldots p_m$ will indicate the proportions of resource that should be allocated to each activity A_i, while the value of V will be the maximum minimum gain attainable under the system.*

THE INTEGRATION WITH FARM PLANNING

We have seen that farm resource allocation problems under uncertainty can be conceived of as a game against Nature. Solving the game for the farmer's optimal mixed strategy indicates the proportions of resource he should allocate to each activity in order to achieve a maximin level of return. In general, however, the farmer is not free to choose levels of activity merely in relation to the levels of gross margin they show under a range of uncertainty conditions. He is further constrained by restrictions on the acreages of certain crops, the capacity of fixed equipment, the availability of labour, and rotational considerations etc.—in fact, all the

---

*As a direct result of the solution procedure, the values assigned to the dummy variables $p_{m+1} \ldots \ldots p_{m+n}$ indicate the extent to which returns will exceed the maximin level (V) under the relevant state of Nature (p_{m+i} relates to state of Nature S). Furthermore, the values in the $Z - C$ row (the "shadow prices") for those dummy variables having zero value in the solution show the composition of Nature's optimal mixed (minimax) strategy.

normal constraints that one would include in a conventional farm planning L.P.

Having already transformed the pure game problem into L.P. form, the additional consideration of these farm constraints is accomplished without difficulty. The original game problem, now in the form of a constrained maximising problem, is merely further constrained by the addition of the "farm restrictions". The net result is, in effect, an L.P. formulation of a game in which the optimal strategy is determined, not only by the requirements of the maximin conditions, but also by various other strategy-selection constraints. Or, alternatively, one might find it more convenient in a farm planning context to view the whole construction as a normal farm L.P. with a few extra constraints which ensure that a *maximin* rather than a *maximum* level of total gross margin is attained. If n states of Nature are considered, these extra constraints will number $n - 1$.

The full model then becomes:

$$\text{Maximise } V = \sum_i c_{i_1} p_i$$

Subject to $n - 1$ constraints of the form

$$\sum_i a_{ij} p_i = 0 \qquad \text{(the "maximin" constraints)}$$

and r constraints of the form

$$\sum_i d_{ik} p_i \leqslant b_k \qquad \text{(the "farm" constraints)}$$

and $p_i \geqslant 0$.

Constraint (1) in the game formulation considers the p_i as being resource proportions whose sum equals unity. Two simple modifications here will result in greater simplicity and realism in the full model.

Firstly, if one defines the activities (farmer alternatives) in terms of acreage units, constraint (1) ensures that the levels of these activities, obtained by solution of the p_i, measure the proportion of total acreage to be allocated to each activity. By merely altering this constraint to read

$$\sum_i p_i = L \qquad (i = 1, \ldots m) \tag{1a}$$

where L represents the total acreage of the farm to be planned, the p_i are solved in terms of actual acreages of the prescribed activities—the normal form for farm planning applications.*

Secondly, since in farm planning one rarely insists that all available acreage is necessarily utilised, one can further modify constraint (1a) to read

$$\sum_i p_i \leqslant L \tag{1b}$$

This now has the normal meaning that the amounts of land resource used must not exceed that available. The analogous constraints on other resources are included in the farm L.P. constraint set. Constraint (1b) is thus "shared" in the combined model by both the farm L.P. sub-model and the game L.P. sub-model.

A PROGRAMMED EXAMPLE

To illustrate the application of the above model, and to give some idea of the nature of the results obtained, consider the following farm planning problem.

A 100-acre farm has the set of possible activities shown in Table 1, together with the rotational and other capacity restrictions on these activities. Table 2 shows the levels of gross margin attained by each activity in each of 5 consecutive years. In order to clarify the procedure, the table is set up in "game form". For our purposes, each activity represents a farmer alternative in the game, whilst each year represents a

TABLE 1. *Activities and restrictions for example farm*

Activity	Farmer alternative	Restrictions
A_1	Spring wheat ⎫	
A_2	Winter wheat ⎬	125 tons storage space available
A_3	Barley ⎭	
A_4	Early potatoes ⎫	$\leqslant 15$ acres ⎫
A_5	Maincrop potatoes ⎬	$\leqslant 20$ acres
A_6	Peas	$\leqslant 10$ acres ⎭
A_7	Clover seed	$\leqslant 15$ acres
A_8	Cows	$\leqslant 30$
A_9	Sheep	

*If the model is thought of as basically a normal farm L.P. with added constraints, there is obviously no reason why all activities should be expressed in acreage terms; nor that non land-using activities (e.g. fattening pigs) cannot be incorporated into the model without complication. Such activities merely have no entry in the $\Sigma p_i = L$ row.

TABLE 2. *Gross margins (£ per acre) over 5 years*

Farmer alternative	States of Nature (years)					Average
	I	II	III	IV	V	
Spring wheat	31.3	28.4	30.2	48.7	31.2	34.0
Winter wheat	47.6	38.8	40.6	51.4	48.3	45.3
Barley	46.1	33.5	33.9	39.6	40.0	38.6
Early potatoes	105.0	61.1	109.8	187.8	98.5	112.4
Maincrop potatoes	50.8	22.9	186.1	104.6	120.2	96.9
Peas	50.3	105.9	99.5	76.1	90.1	84.4
Clover seed	23.2	86.0	41.8	77.7	54.0	56.5
Cows	59.0	51.9	57.0	60.4	58.4	57.3
Sheep	25.8	35.8	25.8	26.5	29.7	28.7

state of Nature which might occur. The object of the exercise is to determine a farm plan which satisfies the constraints in Table 1; and one which, furthermore, ensures that the minimum level of total gross margin attained is as high as possible, considering that any one of the 5 "years" may occur during the planning period.

For comparison with the Maximin model, the example farm was also programmed by conventional L.P. procedures. The objective function was defined using the *average* of the 5 different gross margins for each activity, as might be done in a standard application of a farm L.P.

Comparative farm plans resulting from the exercise are shown in Table 3. The two solutions are quite different, notably in relation to wheat, potatoes and cows. The "Standard plan" appears to offer the (slightly) higher income when this is computed on the basis of average gross margin levels for each activity. This, of course, one would expect, since the Standard plan was specifically determined as that solution which maximises returns under the given average price conditions. However, both of the total gross margins shown under (a) in Table 3 are in a sense entirely hypothetical; they would only be achieved if every activity attained its 5-year average gross margin during the production period.* In practice, actual farm returns would deviate significantly from this level depending on the state of Nature which holds. Thus, when recommending to a farmer a "profit maximising" plan derived by normal linear programming methods, one might be recommending a plan which—in the light of activity returns which will conceivably occur in practice—never maximises profit in any year. Furthermore, one gives him no idea what the minimum level might be in any one season.

*And this would be highly unlikely. As can be seen from Table 2, in not one of the 5 years considered did the actual configuration of average gross margins inhere in practice.

TABLE 3. *Specification and comparative performance of farm plans derived by maximin L.P. and standard L.P. procedures*

	Activity level (acres)	
Activity	Maximin plan	Standard plan
Winter wheat	45.9	38.2
Early potatoes	15.0	10.8
Maincrop potatoes	—	4.1
Peas	5.0	5.0
Clover seed	14.8	15.0
Cows	19.4	26.8
Total Gross Margins Generated:	£	£
(a) Each activity at its 5-year		
average gross margin level	6,135	6,147*
(b) In actual practice—Year I	5,499†	5,341
II	5,499†	5,446
III	5,727	6,152
IV	7,871	7,585
V	6,071	6,227
Mean level over 5 years	6,133	6,150

*Value of objective function from Standard L.P. procedure.
†Value of objective function (i.e. V) from Maximin L.P. procedure.

Section (b) of Table 3 shows how the two plans would have performed under each of the 5 possible gross margin configurations (or states of Nature) considered. From this it can be seen that the Maximin plan achieves its stated aim of ensuring the higher minimum level of return (achieved in Years I and II). A farm plan derived by normal L.P. methods would have generated a lower total gross margin in these two "worst" years. While the difference between £5,499 and £5,341 may not appear very important at first sight, it represents a significant effect on net farm income. If there are £4,500 in fixed costs to be met, the maximin income level is some $17\frac{1}{2}$ per cent higher than the minimum income experienced under the Standard Plan. It so happens that the Maximin Plan also produces the highest level of return in one year (Year IV). This result is quite fortuitous in this case, however, and is not an intentional product of the procedure; the maximin level on the other hand is.*

Over the five-year period, the average annual gross margins that would be generated by the two plans are not particularly different. This enables

*Were Nature a conscious adversary, she should employ her alternatives of Year I and Year II, randomly selected, in the proportions 7:3—thus ensuring that the maximin income level is not exceeded.

one to suggest that, in this simple example, the two farm plans are equally desirable in terms of income maximisation over a period; the Maximin plan has the added advantage of securing a higher minimum level of return. Protagonists of the conventional procedure will note that over the 5 years the Standard Plan would achieve an average annual return similar to that "expected" when planning was based on average gross margins—though with a variation around this level which was, perhaps, not expected.

REFERENCES

1. Dantzig, G. B., "A proof of the equivalence of the programming problem and the game problem". In: Koopmans, T. C. (editor), *Activity Analysis of Production and Allocation*, pp. 330–335, John Wiley, New York, 1951.
2. Dillon, J. L., "Applications of Game Theory in Agricultural Economics: Review and Requiem". *Australian Jour. Agric. Econ.*, Vol. 6, No. 2, pp. 20–35, 1962.
3. Dorfman, R., P. A. Samuelson and R. M. Solow, *Linear Programming and Economic Analysis*. McGraw-Hill, New York, 1958.
4. Heady, E. O. and W. V. Candler, *Linear Programming Methods*. Iowa State University Press, Ames, Iowa, 1958.
5. Knight, F. H., *Risk, Uncertainty and Profit*. Houghton Mifflin Co., New York, 1921.
6. Luce, R. D. and H. Raiffa, *Games and Decisions*. John Wiley, New York, 1957.
7. McInerney, J. P., *Game Theoretic Procedures in relation to Farm Management Decisions*. Unpublished Ph.D. thesis, Iowa State University, Ames, Iowa, 1964.
8. McKinsey, J. C. C., *Introduction to the Theory of Games*. McGraw-Hill, New York, 1952.
9. Stone, R., "The Theory of Games". *Economic Journal*, Vol. 58, pp. 185–201, 1948.
10. von Neumann, J. and O. Morgenstern, *Theory of Games and Economic Behavior*. Princeton University Press, Princeton, New Jersey, 1944 (3rd edition 1953).
11. Williams, J. D., *The Compleat Strategyst*. McGraw-Hill, New York, 1954.

4

Linear Programming and Game Theory Models: Some Extensions *

J. P. McInerney

This is an extension of the author's preceding article showing how the complete range of decision criteria conventionally associated with game theory can be applied in conjunction with a linear programming model. The use of these criteria is demonstrated in relation to the same farm planning problem as was shown earlier in the development of Maximin programming, and a comparison of all the alternative plans resulting from the adoption of a game theoretic decision framework is presented.

The object of this paper is to present a completed account of the application of game theoretic criteria in L.P. models by extending the initial work in this field, and which appeared [in the preceding article].[13] Some of that material is repeated here only to enable a connected account and comparison of all the decision rules to be given.

Agricultural applications of game theory to decision-making under uncertainty have most commonly revolved around the "game against Nature".[1, 2, 3, 12, 14] In what follows we shall utilise the standard format of a game against Nature, which can be represented [as shown on page 55].

The set $\{A_i\}$ denotes the array of production processes and resource use activities such as may form the activity set in a conventional L.P. planning model. The states of Nature represent, without specifically identifying, conditions of weather, disease, prices, or any other inherent uncertainty phenomena which cause returns from any activity to be uncontrollable and unpredictable. The elements of the payoff matrix $[c_{ij}]$ measure the returns to the farmer resulting from his adoption of alterna-

*From *Journal of Agricultural Economics*, Vol. XX, No. 2, May 1969, pp. 269–278. Reproduced by permission.

States of nature

	S_1 .... S_j .... S_n
A_1	c_{11} .... c_{1j} .... c_{1n}
Resource :	: : : :
use $\quad A_i$	c_{i1} .... c_{ij} .... c_n
activities :	: : : :
:	: : : :
A_m	c_{m1} .... c_{mj} .... c_{mn}

tive A_i and the subsequent realisation of state of Nature S_j. Table 2 gives the gross margins of the example planning problem set up in game form; Nature's states are here characterised by vectors of gross margins which were experienced in five consecutive years.

Several criteria for selecting among alternatives have been suggested as applicable to game situations. These are (a) the maximin, (b) the minimax regret, (c) the Laplace, and (d) the Hurwicz decision rules.

We can identify at least two different ways of applying these decision rules to the determination of an "optimal" farm plan under conditions of uncertainty. Firstly, we can incorporate any decision rule into an L.P. model and generate a single programmed solution which satisfies the requirements of both the programming constraints and the decision rule constraints. Or, more simply, we can generate a series of farm plans using the L.P. model alone, and then select among the plans by applying the decision criteria. Both methods are here employed to the simple farm setting portrayed in Table 1. For comparative purposes, a farm plan is

TABLE 1. *Activities and main restrictions for example farm**

Activity (farmer alternative)	Restrictions
A_1 Spring wheat ⎫	
A_2 Winter wheat ⎬	125 tons storage space available
A_3 Barley ⎭	
A_4 Early potatoes ⎫ ≤15 acres ⎫	
A_5 Maincrop potatoes ⎬ ⎬ ≤20 acres	
A_6 Peas ≤10 acres ⎭	
A_7 Clover seed ≤15 acres	
A_8 Cows ≤30	
A_9 Sheep	

*Other constraints on total acreage, seasonal labour use, etc. were also included.

TABLE 2. *Gross margins (£ per acre) over 5 years*

Farmer alternative	States of nature (years)					
	I	III	II	IV	V	Average
Spring wheat	31.3	28.4	30.2	48.7	31.2	34.0
Winter wheat	47.6	38.8	40.6	51.4	48.3	45.3
Barley	46.1	33.5	33.9	39.6	40.0	38.6
Early potatoes	105.0	61.1	109.8	187.8	98.5	112.4
Maincrop potatoes	50.8	22.9	186.1	104.6	120.2	96.9
Peas	50.3	105.9	99.5	76.1	90.1	84.4
Clover seed	23.2	86.0	41.8	77.7	54.0	56.5
Cows	59.0	51.9	57.0	60.4	58.4	57.3
Sheep	25.8	35.8	25.8	26.5	29.7	28.7

derived by conventional L.P., using the simple average of the 5 different gross margin levels for each activity; this is referred to as the Standard Plan.

THE APPLICATION OF THE DECISION RULES

Given the game framework, the problem in applying each decision criterion is to associate with each A_i a value p_i which measures the proportion (or more conveniently the actual level) of resources which should be allocated to that activity.

It will be remembered that any non-saddle-point game can be solved as an L.P. problem. For the maximin objective the problem can be expressed as:

Maximise V.

Subject to n constraints of the form:

$$\sum_{i=1}^{m} c_{ij}p_i - V \geq 0 \quad (j = 1, \ldots, n) \quad \text{and} \quad \sum_{i=1}^{m} p_i \leq L$$

where any p_i is the acreage level of activity A_i and L is the total land acreage. On appending to the above constrained maximising problem the further r constraints of the form

$$\sum_{i=1}^{m} a_{ik}p_i \leq b_k \quad (k = 1, \ldots, r)$$

representing the normal resource use constraints of farm planning, one has the complete Maximin programming model. Table 3 includes the results of this model applied to the example problem.

TABLE 3. *Specification and comparative performance of alternative farm plans*

	Activity level (acres)		
Activity	Maximin plan	Standard plan	Minimax regret
Winter wheat	45.9	38.2	13.2
Barley	—	—	31.2
Early potatoes	15.0	10.8	4.5
Maincrop potatoes	—	4.1	10.5
Peas	5.0	5.0	5.0
Clover	14.8	15.0	15.0
Cows	19.4	26.8	20.6
Total Gross Margin Generated:	£	£	£
(a) Each activity at its 5-year average gross margin level	6,135	6,147*	5,775
(b) In actual practice—Year I	5,499†	5,341	4,888
II	5,499†	5,446	4,961
III	5,727	6,152	6,341
IV	7,871	7,585	6,648
V	6,071	6,227	6,083
Mean level over 5 years	6,133	6,150	5,784
Total "Regret" experienced in each year:			
Year I	4,863	4,998	5,423
II	5,094	7,133	5,629
III	12,896	12,440	12,270‡
IV	10,920	11,176	12,132
V	5,955	5,781	5,966

*Maximised value of objective function from Standard L.P. procedure.

†Maximised value of objective function (i.e. *V*) from Maximin L.P. procedure.

‡Minimised value of objective function (i.e. *V**) from Minimax Regret L.P. procedure.

A MINIMAX REGRET MODEL

The adoption of a minimax regret objective in decision-making implies that the farmer feels a dissatisfaction, equal in magnitude to the difference between the return he actually achieved and the (maximum) return he could have achieved had he correctly predicted the state of Nature which would hold. His concern in decision-making might therefore be to minimise the maximum possible value of this *ex poste* regret. The criterion is applied by reformulating the decision matrix, producing a new "regret matrix" $[r_{ij}]$. This is accomplished by subtracting, for every state of Nature in turn, each payoff from the maximum payoff in that column.

Thus

$$[r_{ij}] = [(\max_i c_{ij}) - c_{ij}].$$

Although such matrices are generally solved for pure strategies, randomisation of selection over alternatives usually can yield lower minimax levels of regret. It is but a short step in logic then to formulate a programming model for determining a constrained mixed strategy of production alternatives, subject to the farm restrictions. The steps are similar in most respects to those elucidated for the Maximin model. The main difference lies in the objectives, which are couched in terms of *ex poste* regrets rather than direct money returns; and the optimal farm plan is one which produces the lowest possible maximum regret (V^*).

Minimise V^*

Subject to: $\left.\begin{array}{l} R'P \leqslant V^* \\ IP = L \end{array}\right\}$(the minimax constraints)

and $\left.\begin{array}{l} AP \leqslant B \\ P \geqslant 0 \end{array}\right\}$ (the farm constraints)

where $\left\{\begin{array}{l} R \text{ is an } m \times n \text{ matrix of regrets} \\ P \text{ is an } m \times 1 \text{ vector of activity levels} \\ I \text{ is a } 1 \times m \text{ unit vector} \\ L \text{ is total acreage} \\ A \text{ is a } k \times m \text{ matrix of input–output coefficients} \\ B \text{ is a } k \times 1 \text{ vector of resource levels, etc.} \end{array}\right.$

Table 4 shows the regret matrix derived from the original payoff matrix of Table 2. The Minimax Regret Plan can be compared with both the

TABLE 4. *Regret matrix derived from initial game payoff matrix in Table 2 (£ per acre)*

Farmer alternative	States of nature (years)				
	I	II	III	IV	V
Spring wheat	73.7	77.5	155.9	139.1	89.0
Winter wheat	57.4	67.1	145.5	136.4	71.9
Barley	58.9	72.4	152.2	148.2	80.2
Early potatoes	0	44.8	76.3	0	21.7
Maincrop potatoes	54.2	83.0	0	83.2	0
Peas	54.7	0	86.6	111.7	30.1
Clover seed	71.8	19.9	144.3	110.1	66.2
Cows	46.0	54.0	129.1	127.4	61.8
Sheep	79.2	70.1	160.3	158.3	90.5

Maximin and Standard Plans in Table 3. We have generated yet another totally different resource allocation pattern, yet one which is also "optimal". Our new farm plan achieves its stated aim of ensuring that the maximum regret is as low as can be attained (this occurs in Year III). But in all other years, and over the five years as a whole, the Minimax Regret Plan is inferior to the other two in achieving low regrets. This inferiority is further observed when comparing the actual income results of the three plans. It is again in Year III that the Minimax Regret Plan does well, but in all other respects it performs poorly in satisfying farm income objectives. However, if minimax regret does form a realistic basis for decision-making under uncertainty there is no gainsaying the superiority of this model in satisfying this simple objective.

LAPLACE AND HURWICZ DECISION MODELS

The Laplace decision rule states that, for lack of any better information, equal probabilities are assigned to each state of nature and selections made to maximise the expected value of return. Without identifying it as such, we have already generated a farm plan incorporating a Laplace approach to uncertain decision making. The Standard Plan of Table 3 has all the characteristics of this decision rule embodied in it—for, by using simple average gross margin figures as coefficients in the objective function we were, in effect, placing an equal probability of occurrence on each of the five possible values for each activity and hence on each state of Nature. The plan maximising an objective in these terms is therefore one which maximises an "expected value" of return. It would appear from this that a Laplace approach to decision making is implicit in much farm planning work.

Similarly, the Hurwicz criterion may be incorporated into an L.P. model without (conceptually, at least) any difficulty—provided a measure of the individual's general pessimistic (α) and optimistic ($1 - \alpha$) attitude is known ($0 \leq \alpha \leq 1$). This decision rule states that the alternative maximising the α^* index, where

$$\alpha_i^* = \alpha m_i + (1 - \alpha)M_i$$

(where m_i and M_i are the minimum and maximum payoffs respectively associated with alternative A_i) will be selected by the decision-maker. In a farm planning context, single alternatives (activities) cannot normally be chosen as constituting a complete farm plan alone, due to the restrictions in "the farm constraint set". But if the coefficients in the L.P. objective function are, in fact, the α_i^* indexes for each activity, the resulting solution is the one representing a (constrained) maximisation of the overall α^* index. Thus:

$$\text{Maximise} \qquad \alpha^{*\prime} P$$
$$\text{Subject to} \quad AP \leqslant B$$
$$\text{and} \qquad\qquad P \geqslant 0$$

(where α^* is an $m \times 1$ vector containing the α_i^* indexes for each activity).

In this sense, the Hurwicz decision rule is seen as no more than a simple model for forming expectations of uncertain outcomes, based on the general pessimistic or optimistic attitudes of the decision maker. The practical application of this approach founders on the difficulty of determining the value of α for any individual.

A "STRAIGHT" GAME THEORETIC APPROACH

This same resource allocation problem can be reformulated in line with the more conventional applications of game theoretic procedures to uncertain decision situations. We base this model on the fact that each year (state of Nature) implies a different alternative farm plan—being the one resource allocation pattern which maximises profits under the vector of returns characterising that year. By computing the performance of each plan under each state of Nature, one generates an $n \times n$ payoff matrix of total gross margins for the farm. Any entry c_{ij} of this matrix will indicate how the plan which is optimal for year i would perform under the conditions of year j. The four decision criteria may then be applied to this "aggregate" payoff matrix in an attempt to determine which of the farm plans is the best to adopt.

Let us designate as Plan I the production pattern which maximises farm income, subject to the "farm constraints" previously considered, under the set of activity returns existing in Year I. Plans II, III, IV and V are defined in like fashion. These plans are shown in Table 5 and demonstrate a remarkable variation in the "optimal" resource allocation pattern, depending upon which set of activity returns one uses as a basis for planning; this merely serves to emphasise the uncertainty inherent in the production environment.

By applying the activity gross margins experienced in each of the 5 years to the activity levels of each Plan, the 5×5 payoff matrix of Table 6 is derived. The application of decision rules to this game formulation

TABLE 5. *Farm plans which are optimal under each state of nature (configuration of gross margins)*

Activity	Activity level (acres)				
	Year I	Year II	Year III	Year IV	Year V
Winter wheat	63.9	29.6	13.2	45.6	30.1
Barley	—	—	31.2	—	—
Early potatoes	15.0	4.1	4.5	15.0	6.6
Maincrop potatoes	—	—	10.5	—	3.4
Peas	5.0	10.0	5.0	5.0	10.0
Clover	—	15.0	15.0	15.0	15.0
Cows	16.1	41.3	20.6	19.4	34.9
"Expected" gross margin (£)	5,818	5,892	6,341	7,879	6,262

TABLE 6. *Payoff matrix of total gross margins, for selecting among farm plans*

	State of nature (year)					Row minimum	Row average
	I	II	III	IV	V		
I	5,818	4,761	5,657	7,454	5,955	4,761	5,929
II	5,127	5,892	5,628	6,712	5,956	5,127	5,863
Plan III	4,887	4,961	6,341	6,648	6,055	4,887	5,778
IV	5,490	5,512	5,729	7,879	6,073	5,490*	6,237†
V	5,209	5,809	6,191	7,177	6,262	5,209	6,130

*Maximum minimum income level—selected by maximin decision rule.
†Maximum "expected value"—selected by Laplace decision rule.

results in the following selections:

(a) Maximin—Plan IV selected; maximin income £5,490.
(b) Minimax regret—Plan IV selected; minimax regret £612.
(c) Laplace—Plan IV selected; "expected" income level £6,137.
(d) Hurwicz—Plan IV selected; (both minimum and maximum payoffs from this plan dominate those of any other: thus this plan is superior, regardless of the level of α).

Clearly, the production pattern suggested by Plan IV is a "good" one from the point of view of reacting to uncertainty, regardless of the decision-making approach one adopts. Interestingly enough, Plan IV is virtually identical to the Maximin Plan. One might even say amazingly enough, in view of the fact that Plan IV and the Maximin Plan were effectively determined by totally different objective functions—the latter in relation to the returns in Years I and II*, and the former in relation to the Year IV returns alone. Were this a real farm situation then, an adviser might have no hesitation in recommending the Maximin/Plan IV production pattern—it being as good as the normal L.P. solution for income maximisation over a 5 year period, and better from the point of view of income uncertainty within this period.

CONCLUSION

The foregoing discussion has demonstrated how all the classical decision rules of game theory can be applied in a constrained choice context, as opposed to the usual unconstrained selection procedure of game theory models. Furthermore, the applications suggested here have concerned themselves with the level of decision-making at which uncertainties are perhaps most important—the level of whole-farm income—and not with the more partial or micro farm decisions often employed in game theoretic applications (see, for example, [3, 12, 17]). Many problems remain, however. Nothing is yet known of how these models perform in general over a wide variety of planning situations. It may be that the Maximin model, for example, while generating a plan which undoubtedly satisfies the objective of attaining a maximin income level, often produces a solution which in all other respects is inferior to the one produced by conventional L.P.

REFERENCES

1. Agrawal, R. C. and Heady, E. O.: "Applications of Game Theory Models in Agriculture". *J. Ag. Econ.* 19, 207–218, 1968.
2. Chacko, G. K.: "Certain Game Situations in Regional Economic Development." *Indian J. Econ.* 37, 167–175, 1956.
3. Dillon, J. L.: "Theoretical and Empirical Approaches to Program Selection within the Feeder Cattle Enterprise". *J. Farm Econ.* 40, 1921–1931, 1958.
4. Dorfman, R., Samuelson, P. A. and Solow, R. M.: *Linear Programming and Economic Analysis.* New York, McGraw-Hill Book Company, Inc., 1958.
5. Guilbaud, G. T.: *What is Cybernetics.* London, William Heinemann Ltd., 1959.
6. Hardaker, J. B.: "The Use of Simulation Techniques in Farm Management Research". *The Farm Economist* XI, 4, 162–171, 1967.
7. Harle, J. T.: "Towards a more Dynamic Approach to Farm Planning". *J. Ag. Econ.* 19, 339–346, 1968.
8. Hildreth, C.: "Problems of Uncertainty in Farm Planning". *J. Farm Econ.* 39: 1430–1441, 1957.

*Nature's "optimal" years, and hence the limiting constraints in the game set.

9. Koo, A. Y. C.: "Recurrent Objections to the Minimax Strategy". *Rev. Econ. and Stat.* 41, 36–41, 1959.
10. Langham, M. R.: "Game Theory applied to a Policy Problem of Rice Farmers". *J. Farm Econ.* 45, 151–162, 1963.
11. Luce, R. D. and Raiffa, H.: *Games and Decisions.* New York, John Wiley and Sons, Inc., 1957.
12. McInerney, J. P.: "Game Theoretic Procedures in relation to Farm Management Decisions". Unpublished Ph.D. thesis, Iowa State University, 1964.
13. McInerney, J. P.: "Maximin Programming—An Approach to Farm Planning under Uncertainty". *J. Ag. Econ.* 18, 279–289, 1967.
14. Moglewer, S.: "A Game Theory Model for Agricultural Crop Selection". *Econometrica* 30, 253–266, 1962.
15. Shackle, G. L. S.: *Expectation in Economics.* Cambridge, Cambridge University Press, 1949.
16. Stovall, J. G.: "Income Variation and the Selection of Enterprises". *J. Farm Econ.* 48, 1575–1579, 1966.
17. Walker, O. L. and Heady, E. O.: *Application of Game Theory Models to Decisions on Farm Practices and Resource Use.* Iowa Agr. Exp. Sta. Res. Bul. 488, December, 1960.

5

Risk Evaluation in Farm Planning:
A Statistical Approach*

M. C. Murphy†

Economic planning implies decision-making based on the comparison of alternative courses of action, viewed against a background (in the real world at any rate) of uncertainty and imperfect knowledge. Successful planning is thus heavily dependent on the reliability of prediction which leads inevitably to the domain of probability theory and its application to planning models. In spite of the considerable attention given to the application of mathematical models in farm management research work in recent times[1] to [9] and [15] there is still a paucity of applied work with respect to evaluating the nature of risk associated with planning projects at the individual farm level. In addition, very little published data is available on either a regional or production-type basis that gives a clear understanding of the nature of probability distributions for planning variables. This paper formulates a simple model which can be used in practical planning exercises and also demonstrates that with a new generation of statistically-processed planning data the application of the classical concepts of probability to routine economic planning is both practicable and worthwhile.

INTRODUCTION

Recently[10] and [11] there has been growing concern amongst agricultural production economists that many forward-planning exercises fail to achieve the expected ends. Although it may be contested that the quality of available information is very often so weak that it offers only the most meagre opportunities for prediction, it is in just such circumstances that the economic planner needs to include probability estimates on future

*From *Journal of Agricultural Economics*, Vol. XXII, No. 1, January 1971, pp. 61–74. Reproduced by permission.

†The author is deeply indebted to C. S. Barnard and G. B. Aneuryn Evans for valuable criticisms and advice given during the preparation of this paper. Errors in logic are the responsibility of the author.

performance. In the field of farm management the latter is hindered not so much by the lack of raw data but by the fact that analysis is orientated deterministically rather than stochastically which limits the scope and application of the processed data.

PRINCIPLES OF A RISK EVALUATION MODEL (R.E.M.)

Farm Planning decisions commonly have to be based on uncertain data largely because of the inconsistency of natural phenomena which tend to elude the farmer's control. Rather than treat this variability qualitatively it can be incorporated in planning models and thus handled quantitatively. This generally can be accomplished if the natural phenomena exhibit some degree of regularity so that their variation can be described by a probability model.

The presence of these variations introduces a lack of precision into calculations and the theory of probability is a means of discussing the degree of error to which his estimates may be subject.

This is the basis on which risk (in the *a priori* sense) may be quantified in the statistical sense, where both the mean (central tendency in the behaviour of a random variable) and the variance (dispersion around the mean) form the two basic parameters from which a probability distribution (known as the Normal Distribution) can be developed. An individual's approach to probability[13] depends on the nature of his interest in the subject. The pure mathematician usually prefers to treat probability from the axiomatic point of view, just as he does, say, the study of geometry. The applied statistician usually prefers to think of probability as the proportion of times that a certain event will occur. The approach in this paper is a blending of these two points of view.

One way of tackling this problem is to plan the allocation of farm resources using mean expected values and then to test the solution for variation by means of a risk evaluation model. If the degree of variation is unacceptable the solution can be modified to give lower variation, generally at the cost of a lower expected return.

The risk evaluation model (R.E.M.) is based on the following principles:

The mean expected total product (in physical or financial terms) generated by a combination (linear) of activities can be expressed as:

$$E(Z) = \sum_{j=1}^{n} X_j \qquad j = 1 \ldots n \qquad (1)$$

where A_j = activity level; G_j = gross margin of activity j

$$X_j = A_j G_j \quad \text{thus} \quad Z = \sum_{j=1}^{n} A_j G_j$$

and the expected variances of the mean:

$$V(Z) = \sum_{j=1}^{n} V(X)_j \qquad j = 1 \ldots n \qquad (2)$$

However, since by definition the $X_j s$ are not independent, the magnitude of the variance is also influenced by correlation between them, which can be appropriately measured by the use of covariances. In short, the total variance of a combination of enterprises can be measured using variances of individual enterprises and the covariances between enterprises, as is expressed by equation (3) (which now replaces equation (2)).

$$V(Z) = \sum_{j=1}^{n} A_i^2 V_i + 2 \sum_{i=1}^{n-1} \sum_{j>i}^{n} A_i A_j C_{ij} \qquad (3)$$

where A_i = activity or enterprise level.
   V_i = variance per unit of activity i established empirically from time-series or cross-sectional analysis or a combination of both.
   C_{ij} = covariance between activities i and j $(i \neq j)$.

Equation (3) can be identified algebraically as the quadratic form $A'CA$ where A is the column vector of activity levels, C the symmetric matrix of variance–covariance coefficients, and A' the transpose of A, thus transforming it to a row vector. This, in effect, means that the total variance of a linear combination of enterprises can be estimated by first taking the sum of the individual variances of each enterprise and subsequently adding the sum of twice the covariances for each pair of activities.

   The variance–covariance matrix forms the nucleus of the model in the form of the symmetrical matrix C. If we now consider a cropping plan with enterprises A_i $(i = 1 \ldots 4)$ expressed as a column vector, we can construct the following matrix notation to satisfy $A'CA$.

Variance–Covariance matrix

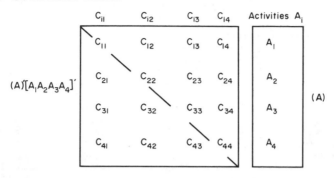

The main diagonal contains the variances of individual activities with the remaining coefficients representing the covariances.

PRACTICAL EXAMPLE OF A RISK EVALUATION MODEL

A practical example may be taken to illustrate the procedure in constructing a risk evaluation model. Table 1 shows, for a 300-acre mixed-cropping farm, the cropping combination that maximises gross margin (£14,511) but which takes no account of risk. The additional data that is required in order to calculate the total variance of this cropping combination is shown in Table 2. The variances calculated for the individual crops in 2a together with the correlation matrix in 2b enable the construction of the variance–covariance matrix in 2c. In turn, the latter is fed into the R.E.M. in Table 3, in columns 2, 4, 6 and 8. Col 1 (A_i) is the

TABLE 1. *Mean expected gross margin for 300-acre mixed-cropping farm (Linear programmed optimal solution)*

Activity	Acres	Mean gross margin per acre	Total gross margin	Per cent of total gross margin
		£s	£s	
Winter wheat	100	34.58	3,458.0	23.8
Spring barley	100	30.97	3,097.0	21.3
Sugar beets	50	66.27	3,323.5	22.9
Potatoes	50	92.65	4,632.5	32.0
	300		£14,511.0	100.0

Mean gross margin per acre = £48.37.

TABLE 2. *Stochastic planning data—mixed-cropping farm (Eastern Counties, 1964–66: 123 observations)*

a *Gross margin per acre*

	Mean	Standard deviation	Variance	Coefficient of variation*
	£	£	£	%
Wheat	34.58	7.12	50.69	20.59
Barley	30.97	5.71	32.60	18.44
Beans	25.50	14.51	210.54	56.90
Sugar beets	66.27	19.52	381.03	29.47
Potatoes	92.65	53.88	2,903.05	58.17

b *Correlation matrix†*

	Wheat	Barley	Beans	Sugar beets	Potatoes
Wheat	1				
Barley	0.160	1			
Beans	−0.100	0.174	1		
Sugar beets	0.360	0.131	−0.150	1	
Potatoes	−0.336	0.149	0.345	−0.133	1

c *Variance–covariance matrix—mixed-cropping farm*

	Wheat	Barley	Beans	Sugar beets	Potatoes
Wheat	50.69				
Barley	6.51	32.60			
Beans	−10.33	14.41	210.54		
Sugar beets	50.03	14.60	−42.49	381.03	
Potatoes	−128.90	45.84	269.72	−139.88	2,903.05

*Coefficient of variation $= \dfrac{\text{Standard deviation}}{\text{Mean}} \times 100\%$. This coefficient does not depend on the units involved since both the mean and the standard deviation are linear functions of the units involved.

†Coefficients of 0.148 or over are significantly different from zero at 5 per cent probability of Type 1 error.

cropping combination for the optimal solution (Table 1) and row 6 is its transpose,* while the remaining entries are self-explanatory.

The R.E.M. shows that for the example farm the standard deviation of the mean total gross margin of £14,511 is ±£2,879 (or a mean of £48.37 per acre ±£9.6 standard deviation). At the same time it offers a visual display

*For ease of computation these have been placed as the leading column and penultimate row respectively.

TABLE 3. *Risk evaluation model (REM) computational procedure**

	1	2	3	4	5	6	7	8	9
		Wheat		Barley		Sugar beets		Potatoes	
	A_i	C_{i1}	A_iC_{i1}	C_{i2}	A_iC_{i2}	C_{i3}	A_iC_{i3}	C_{i4}	A_iC_{i4}
1 Wheat $[A_1]$	100	50.69	5,069.00	6.51	651.00	50.03	5,003.00	128.90	12,890.00
2 Barley $[A_2]$	100	6.51	650.50	32.60	3,260.00	14.60	1,460.00	45.84	4,584.00
3 Sugar beets $[A_3]$	50	50.03	2,501.50	14.60	730.00	381.03	19,051.00	139.88	-6,994.00
4 Potatoes $[A_4]$	50	129.90	6,444.90	45.84	2,292.00	139.88	6,994.00	2,093.05	145,152.50
5 Total	300		1,776.0		6,933.0		18,521.0		129,852.5
			A_1		A_2		A_3		A_4
6			100		100		50		50
7 Total variance			177,600		693,300		926,050		6,492,625

Total variance = 8,289,575. Standard deviation £2,879 (+£9.6 per acre).
*This procedure has been developed from the quadratic form $A'CA$.
Any inconsistencies are due to rounding errors.

of the causes of variance in the plan and thus suggests ways of reducing it if it should be deemed excessive. Table 3 shows that potatoes, although reducing the variance arising under wheat and sugar beets (as they are negatively correlated with them), nevertheless contribute largely to the overall variance of the plan due to the size of their own variance. A reduction in potato acreage is thus likely to reduce total variance (as is confirmed later in Table 6).

Thus there is a distribution of possible financial outcomes from this farm plan, having a mean total gross margin of £14,511 and a standard deviation of £2,879, (i.e. a mean of £48.37 per acre and standard deviation of £9.6 per acre).

This probability distribution* can also be expressed graphically in the form of a cumulative density function† (Fig. 1) which provides the planner with a visual aid towards evaluating the probabilities associated with different levels of gross margin. For example, Fig. 1 shows that the

*One of the most important theorems in mathematical statistics, *the central limit theorem*, states in effect that for reasonably large random samples regardless of the shape of the parent population the sampling distribution* of the sample mean ($\bar{X}$) can be approximated with the normal distribution. (A large sample is one of 30 or more observations.) If the sample is limited and there is reason to suspect skewness, then the log-normal distribution may be used (17) and the resultant parameters inserted into R.E.M. As the coefficients will be in logarithmic form the final solution must be converted to natural numbers for interpretation.

$$E(X) = E(X_i) = u_i; \qquad V(X) = V(X_i) = Q_j^2$$

and because of assumed normality the probability of X lying outside $E(X) \pm 3\sqrt{V(X)}$ is approximately 99.72.
†Using the notation $(X_i - \bar{X}_i)/\sqrt{V} = Z$ in conjunction with tables for normal distribution; where V = variance, $\bar{X}_i$ = mean, and X_i = value above or below mean. From this information the curve in Fig. 1 is constructed by calculating the value for P of a given value of X_i.

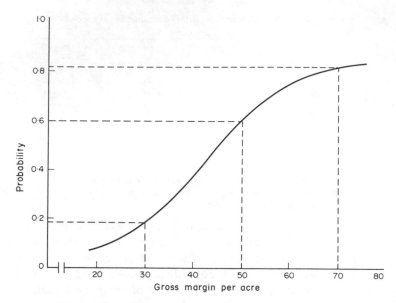

FIGURE 1. Cumulative probability function showing distribution of gross margin for a 300-acre mixed-cropping farm.

probability of obtaining a gross margin of £50 per acre or less is 0.6 or of £30 per acre or less is 0.18.

INCORPORATION OF FIXED COSTS

Thus far fixed costs have been disregarded. Their incorporation into the model permits mean net farm income and its variation to be calculated. In Table 4, this is done for the same 300-acre mixed-cropping farm,* calculating net farm income in two ways. Firstly, by ignoring the standard deviation on fixed costs and the correlation between them and total gross margin (Case 1) and secondly, by including them (Case 2). Case 1 thus represents the common situation when fixed costs are being calculated for a farm, while Case 2 shows, by contrast, the differences that arise assuming stochastic data concerning fixed costs are available. It may be

---

*Taking, for purely illustrative purposes, mean fixed costs per acre of £26.39 with standard deviation £6.19 and with correlation coefficient (r) of 0.575 between total gross margin and fixed costs derived from a sample of 123 mixed-cropping farms in the Eastern Counties for the three years 1964–66 (Appendix III). In specific cases where the precision of fixed costs is high the foregoing may not apply.

TABLE 4. *Net farm income—300-acre mixed-cropping farm (per acre)*

	Case 1		Case 2	
		Standard deviation		Standard deviation
	£	£	£	£	
Mean gross margin	48.37	±9.60	48.37	±9.60 ⎫ $r = 0.575$
Fixed costs	26.39		26.39	±6.19 ⎬
Net farm income	21.98	±9.60	21.98	±7.88 ⎭

noted that, in this example at least, the standard deviation of net farm income is lower in the latter case (£7.88 compared with £9.60). Taking this a stage further, probability distributions reveal that in Case 1 there is a probability of 0.11, that net farm income will be less than £10 an acre, whereas for Case 2 the probability is only 0.06. Or, for example, if £15 per acre is the minimum acceptable net farm income required to meet consumption and reinvestment, then the probability that this level will not be attained is 0.23 and 0.18 respectively.

CALCULATING THE PROBABILITIES OF SUCCESS OR FAILURE OVER A FINITE PLANNING HORIZON

If the probability of an unsuccessful year is designated as P, it follows that the probability of a successful year is $(1 - P)$, which may be denoted as Q. Then by the properties of the Binomial distribution a probabilistic decision table can be drawn up to indicate the expected number of "unsuccessful years" over a finite time period (Table 5).

TABLE 5. *Probability of at least X failures**
in N trials (300-acre mixed-cropping farm)

"$P = 0.23$" Case 1		"$P = 0.18$" Case 2
[(X	$P(0.23)$]	[($P(0.18)$]
1	0.7293	0.6293
2	0.3251	0.2224
3	0.0836	0.0437
4	0.0114	0.0045
5	0.0006	0.0002

(Planning horizon of $N = 5$ years.)
*Failure taken as net farm income $\leq$£15 per acre.

Each row in the table represents the cumulative probability of *at least* X failures (unsuccessful years, net farm income $\leq$£15 per acre) in N trials (years). Thus the probability of at least one failure for each category can be read from the first row of the table, two or more from the second row and so on. The probability of exactly one failure is found by subtracting the probability of two or more failures from Row 1. For example, for Case 1:

$$P(X = 1) = P(X \geq 1) - P(X \geq 2) = .7293 - .3251 = .4042$$

The value of N is purely arbitrary and can be selected to suit the needs or circumstances of a particular case or decision-making problem.

EXTENSIONS TO THE RISK EVALUATION MODEL

The R.E.M. approach is primarily designed to enable a speedy application of probability theory to practical farm planning exercises. Indeed it seems plausible to assume that one of the reasons that the probability approach is not more widely practised is because the relatively sophisticated programming methods that are available[7, 12] may be too expensive, too difficult or too time-consuming to apply at the grass roots of planning exercises. The R.E.M. approach also has the advantage that it can be easily linked up with linear-programming methods. For example, when an optimal combination of activities has been obtained by linear-programming the variance of the solution can easily be found by inserting the relevant activity levels into the activity row and column vectors in the R.E.M. In addition, moving from the optimal solution to some other solution with a lower variance is obviously of interest and this can be carried out by substitution within the planning constraints.[12] Table 6 demonstrates this for the example 300-acre mixed-cropping farm, plans being arranged in order of diminishing variance. It shows that in this case the first plan would normally be acceptable for not only is the mean gross margin higher than for the other plans, but so also is its minimum gross margin.*

CONCLUSION

It has been shown that the introduction of classical probability theory into everyday planning is a relatively simple procedure provided that data

*For example comparing minimum gross margins in the first and second plans. First plan £48.37 − £9.60 = £38.77. Second plan £46.16 − £8.28 = £37.88. This applies throughout, i.e. that in respect of mean and variance margins Plan 1 > Plan 2 > Plan 3 > Plan 4 > Plan 5 > Plan 6.

TABLE 6. *Cropping plans with reducing variance—300-acre mixed-cropping farm (acres)*

Plan	Cereals			Break crops		Root crops			Gross margin (£'s) per farm cropping acre	
	Wheat	Barley	Total	Beans	Total	Sugar beet	Potatoes	Total	Mean	Standard deviation
1	100	100	200	—	—	50	50	100	48.37	9.60
2	90	120	210	—	—	50	40	90	46.16	8.28
3	84	132	216	16	16	50	18	68	41.43	6.09
4	78	143	221	24	24	44	10	54	38.95	5.53
5	70	162	232	31	31	31	6	37	36.30	5.12
6	60	180	240	43	43	17	0	17	32.98	4.92

is readily available and statistically processed. However, in spite of the simplicity of the method the implications are far-reaching, because most of the planning methods currently used by management practitioners are deterministic with all the ensuing shortcomings. As the complexity of the firm grows continually so do the problems of management. In such circumstances it seems reasonable that decision-making at the individual farm level should be given the benefit of mathematical and statistical methods that evaluate the probability of success or failure.

REFERENCES

1. McFarquhar, A. M. M.: "Rational Decision-Making and Risk in Farm Planning". *Journal of Agricultural Economics*, Vol. XIV, No. 4, 1961.
2. Camm, B. M.: "Risk in Vegetable Production on a Fen Farm". *Farm Economist*, Vol. X, No. 2, 1962.
3. McInerney, J. P.: "Maximin Programming—An Approach to Farm Planning Under Uncertainty". *Journal of Agricultural Economics*, Vol. XVIII, No. 2, May 1967.*
4. McInerney, J. P.: "Linear Programming and Game Theory Models—Some Extensions". *Journal of Agricultural Economics*, Vol. XX, No. 2, May 1969.†
5. Harle, J. T.: "Towards a more Dynamic Approach to Farm Planning". *Journal of Agricultural Economics*, Vol. XIX, No. 3, September 1968.
6. Fyfe, M.: "The Importance of Chance in Farm Income". *Journal of Agricultural Economics*, Vol. XVIII, No. 1, January 1967.
7. Hardaker, J. B.: "The Use of Simulation Techniques in Farm Management Research". *Farm Economist*, Vol. XI, No. 4, 1967.
8. Barnard, C. S.: "Farm Models Management Objectives and the Bounded Planning Environment". *Journal of Agricultural Economics*, Vol. XV, No. 4, December 1963.
9. Davies, A. J., Camm, B. M. and Giles, A. K.: "The Future of Farm Management Research". *Journal of Agricultural Economics*, Vol. XIX, No. 1, January 1968.
10. Thomas, W. J.: "Evolution or Revolution in Agricultural Development". *Journal of Agricultural Economics*, Vol. XXI, No. 1, January 1970.
11. MacArthur, J. D.: "Problems of the Multi-Farm Agency in Agricultural Development". *Journal of Agricultural Economics*, Vol. XXI, No. 1, January 1970.
12. Abadie, J. L.: *Non-linear Programming*. North-Holland Publishing Co., Amsterdam, 1967.
13. Murphy, M. C.: "A Stochastic Approach to Investment Appraisal". *Farm Economist*, Vol. XI, No. 7, 1968.
14. Brabb, G. J.: *Introduction to Quantitative Management*. Holt, Rinehart and Winston, Inc., New York, 1968.
15. Bennett Jones, R.: "Stability in Farm Income". *Journal of Agricultural Economics*, Vol. XX, No. 1, January 1969.
16. Davies, G. R.: "The Analysis of Frequency Distributions". *Journal of American Statistical Association*, Vol. 24, December 1929, pp. 349–366.
17. Cochran, W. G.: *Sampling Techniques*. Wiley, New York, 1963.
18. Yates, F.: *Sampling Methods for Censuses and Surveys*. Griffin, London, 1960.
19. Kendall, M. G. and Stuart, A.: *The Advanced Theory of Statistics*, Vol. 1, Distribution Theory. Griffin, London, 1969.

---

*Article 3 in this part.   †Article 4 in this part.

6

Business Simulation and Management Decisions*

J. Niedereichholz

DEVELOPMENT OF BUSINESS SIMULATION

The application of simulation studies in engineering and scientific areas has a relatively long history, whereas the use of simulation in business and economics is a fairly recent development, which is strongly related to the growing availability of digital computers since the mid-1950's. Due to the fact that manual digital simulation could not solve the volume of computations required by simulation models in business and economics the interest in digital simulation techniques was not great prior to this date. Sometimes analog simulation devices were used to solve some minor problems of mostly academic interest but the difficulty of finding suitable analog devices prohibited the development of analog simulation techniques for management decisions.

By the development of high-speed computers and by the supply of specific application software packages simulation models of large-scale systems in business and economics could be tackled. The implementation of general purpose simulation languages such as DYNAMO, SIMSCRIPT or GPSS was a further step necessary for the reduction of time and costs of simulation studies. Economists and operations researchers got powerful tools to simulate economic systems of great complexity as total models instead of partial models.

Of course there are still many practical limitations on the construction of large-scale dynamic models of the firm or of a whole economy but it is very interesting to look at some aspects of these compact simulation

*From *Management International Review*, Vol. 11, No. 1, January 1971, pp. 47–52. Reproduced by permission.

methods especially at those of Industrial Dynamics with DYNAMO and the General Purpose Simulation System GPSS.

TIME-ORIENTED SIMULATION OF LARGE-SCALE SYSTEMS BY INDUSTRIAL DYNAMICS

Basic Conception of Industrial Dynamics

There are two fundamental possibilities to construct a simulation model and to build a simulation language: the time-oriented approach and the event-oriented approach.

The time-oriented simulation (fixed time increment simulation) can be compared with sampled data systems used in cybernetics and systems engineering. There are many cybernetic or control theoretical models of economic problems using simulation, but only Industrial Dynamics can be viewed as a conception to deal with total dynamic models. Industrial Dynamics was developed by Jay W. Forrester[1] of the M.I.T. to analyze particularly the effects of managerial decision processes on highly interdependent organizations with dynamic conditions and information feedbacks of many orders.

The computations are facilitated by the use of the simulation language DYNAMO[2] a time-oriented simulation language especially adapted to the philosophy of Industrial Dynamics. The focus of this philosophy is the proposal that management should recognize the character of industrial organizations as a highly interconnected network of information and material feedback processes. The high level of practicability reached by Industrial Dynamics is due to the fact that Forrester offers a general approach to the construction of dynamic models, not unlike the approaches used by control engineers, rather than a single model to represent industrial activities.

Decision Processes in an Industrial Dynamics World

Let us now look at the basic components used by Industrial Dynamics. There are two fundamental variables: rates and levels.

The rates of flow represent the activities and decisions in the organization and may be viewed as payments, movements of goods, arrival or

---

[1] Forrester, Jay W.: *Industrial Dynamics*, Cambridge 1965.
[2] Pugh, Alexander L., III: *DYNAMO User's Manual*, Cambridge 1963.

departure of work force, orders and materials or the acquisition of capital equipment. The regulation of these flows is caused by managerial decisions expressed by decision functions. The varying rates of flow result in changes of levels of variables in the system. The levels represent accumulations of resources such as inventories, cash balances, number of orders on hand, back-logs etc. There are levels in the information flows as well as in the physical flows of real organizations.

Industrial Dynamics uses a special flow chart technique preceding the construction of the model as a system of equations. Figure 1 shows the symbols representing the different types of flows and decisions.

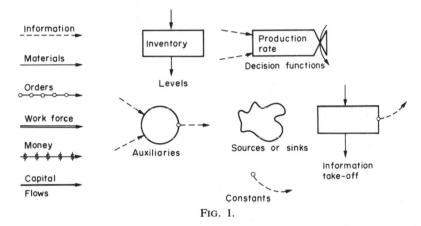

FIG. 1.

Levels are represented as blocks, decision functions as valves controlling the different "pipelines". Sometimes it is necessary to introduce auxiliary variables which are represented by circles. If the origin and/or the future of some controlled flow lie outside the model under research, this may be taken into account by sources or sinks represented by irregular closed shapes.

Information flows interconnect many variables in the system and the take-off of an information at some place in a flow chart is represented by a small circle and a dashed arrow positively incident of this circle. Constant parameters are shown as independent information take-offs.

A small example may illustrate the construction of an Industrial Dynamics model. Consider a retailer inventory (Figure 2) in a multiloop decision-making model of a production–distribution organization with several factories, factory warehouse, distributors, retailers and dealers.

The warehouse shipping rate may be viewed as dependent on the number of unfilled orders and the amount of goods in inventory. To

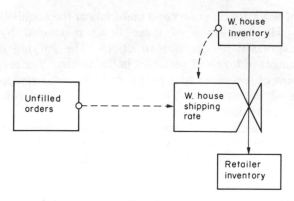

express this the Industrial Dynamics researcher must use the form of equations contained in a DYNAMO-catalog of possible equation forms. DYNAMO permits names with five alphabetic and numeric characters chosen for their mnemonic significance. The level-equation for the retailer inventory may be the following:

RINV.K = RINV.J + (DT)(WSHPR.JK——RSHPR.JK)
RINV   = Retailer *inv*entory (units)
DT   = *D*elta *t*ime (weeks), the time interval used
WSHPR = *W*arehouse *ship*ping *r*ate (units per week)
RSHPR = *R*etailer *ship*ping *r*ate (units per week).

The time notation used is known from difference equations.

The present amount of inventory units at time K equals the amount at time J (last point on the time-axis) plus the sum of changes in inventory after the time interval JK from J to K has passed. In order to construct a complex total model consisting of various partial models, feedbacks, sectors etc. the Industrial Dynamics equations are joined together like building-stones following the DYNAMO-language. Then the model can be simulated as often as needed to get informations for management decisions by the variation of parameters, policies, stochastic influences etc.

There exist many practical investigations in different fields using the Industrial Dynamics simulation technique. Some of the most famous are the study by Forrester of the Sprague Electric Company[3], the simulation of the production and distribution system of a tufted carpet mill[4] and the analysis of the management of the commercial salmon fisheries along the Western rim of North America[5].

EVENT-ORIENTED SIMULATION MODELS

Fixed Time Versus Variable Time Increments

A fixed time-increment model requires the user to specify the size of the time increment DT. This choice is very artificial in the sense that the size of DT can be very important for the conduct of the simulation and the validity of the results as a basis for management decisions. All events (e.g. arrivals of orders, changes in inventory) happening in the time interval DT are treated as if happening all simultaneously at the upper bound of the interval. Therefore the change of the size of DT can radically change the logical interrelationships of the occurring events and the user must take the choice of the time increment of its model very carefully.

A variable time-increment model processes the event occurrences by the next-event mode. After the processing of an event simulation time is advanced to the time of the nearest future occurrence of a coming event. The correct choice of the next processing time-point is done by a so called sequencing set, which is a major part of an event oriented simulation language.

The General Purpose System Simulator GPSS

There is a lot of next-event simulation languages available, but we will look at the General Purpose System Simulator for the sake of its simplicity of learning this language[6].

The simulated system must first be described as a block diagram where the blocks represent the subroutines of the activities and the lines linking the blocks indicate the logical sequence for the execution of the activities.

[3]Forrester, Jay W.: *Industrial Dynamics*, Cambridge 1965, chapters 17 and 18.

[4]Jerome A. Yurow: Analysis and Computer Simulation of the Production and Distribution System of a Tufted Carpet Mill, *The Journal of Industrial Engineering*, vol. 18, Jan. 1967.

[5]G. J. Paulik and J. W. Greenough, Jr.: Management Analysis for a Salmon Resource System, in: *Systems Analysis in Ecology*, ed. by Kenneth E. F. Watt, New York 1966.

[6]IBM Application Program: *General Purpose Simulation System/360 User's Manual*, H 20-0326-2, White Plains 1968.

The user must use only GPSS-blocks in this block diagram. GPSS possesses some forty block types, each of which has a specific, alterable meaning that must be known by the user.

To illustrate the features of the construction of a GPSS-model, consider the following little example:

A job shop produces parts with an average production rate of 1/5, one part every five time units. These parts must finally go through the quality control-section, where they are examined for 4 ± 3 time units. The average rejection rate is 10%. These simple facts can be represented by the following GPSS-diagram Fig. 3, using six GPSS-block types[7]:

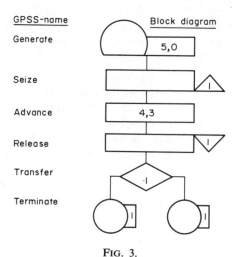

FIG. 3.

The GENERATE-block creates the temporary elements of the GPSS-simulation model, the so-called transactions. Every five time units a transaction is fed into the simulation model. It arrives immediately at the SEIZE-block which represents the occupation of the inspection-facility no. 1 if it is free. The inspection-facility is viewed as being able to inspect only one part at a time. After the occupation of the facility 1 the transaction passes to the ADVANCE-block which represents the inspection delay. The mean 4 and the modifier 3 of the ADVANCE-block indicate that the transaction will be delayed for 1, 2, 3, 4, 5, 6 or 7 time units. Each value has equal probability to be chosen for the delay. After the delay the transaction passes to the RELEASE-block where it com-

[7]G. Gordon: *System Simulation*, Englewood Cliffs 1969.

pletes the inspection of facility 1 and gives this facility free for further occupation. The transaction then moves to the TRANSFER-block where the selection factor of 0.1 indicates that 90% of the inspected part go to exit 1, called ACC (accepted) and 10% go to exit 2 called REJ (rejected). The transactions then move to the TERMINATE-blocks where they are destroyed. The termination count which has to be specified by the user and indicates the number of desired runs is diminished by one. When it has reached the value of zero the simulation will end. At the end of a simulation GPSS automatically prints the interesting statistic results.

There exist many other features and blocks of GPSS to build very complex models of real systems. The application field is very large: Airport systems are simulated by GPSS as well as operating systems of time-sharing computers, assembly lines of large factories or complex priority rules for job shops.

7

PERT Simulation:
A Dynamic Approach to the PERT Technique*

CLIFFORD F. GRAY and ROBERT E. REIMAN

The PERT simulation approach allows management to cope with the uncertainty and instability of time estimates used in the early planning stages of project management. By simulating the PERT network, the PS model reveals the likelihood of shifting critical paths while the project is still in the planning or bidding stages. The method and two applications are discussed in this article.

Today PERT is a familiar acronym used by managers around the world. Since its introduction in 1958 by the special projects office of the U.S. Navy for use in military support projects, several important refinements and extensions have enhanced the value and expanded the application of the technique; e.g., PERT Cost,[1] Critical Path Method[2] and PERT/IOB.[3]

The basic framework or model for the PERT method is a closed system network of activities and events that represent a project from its inception to its completion. The network model depicts events and activities in their chronological sequences and in their explicit interrelationships as conceived and scheduled within the project by its designers and managers. Standard PERT and CPM analyses are deterministic in their solution and static in their scope.

This presentation describes a relatively new technique called PERT Simulation (PS), which injects a neglected but vital dimension into the

*From *Journal of Systems Management*, Vol. 20, No. 3, March 1969, pp. 18–23. Reproduced by permission.

[1] Hilliard W. Paige, "How PERT-Cost Helps the General Manager," *Harvard Business Review*. November–December 1963, p. 87.

[2] Ferdinand K. Levy, Gerald L. Thompson and Jerome D. Wiest, "The ABCs of the Critical Path Method," *Harvard Business Review*, November–December 1963, p. 98.

[3] Peter P. Schoderbek and Lester A. Digman, "Third Generation, PERT/LOB," *Harvard Business Review*, September–October 1967, p. 100.

PERT model and makes it a more powerful and flexible management tool. This dimension is *dynamics*, which is transfused into the closed system model by simulation using Monte Carlo methods.*

In this article, the PERT problem or desirability and need for the dynamic approach to PERT is explored in detail. This discussion is followed by a nontechnical description of the method used to transform the standard PERT model to PS. Next, some of the key points of network analysis under the PS system are noted. Two examples of actual applications are illustrated. The presentation is concluded with a list of the advantages of PS and some observations regarding its use.

THE PERT PROBLEM

The standard PERT approach does not adequately cope with the uncertainty and instability associated with estimates of activity times and the resultant determination of project completion time. For example, in the standard PERT analysis an activity time estimate may be described by optimistic (a), most likely (m), and pessimistic (b) values of 10, 15, and 26. The mean of the activity duration time is calculated by the PERT method $t = \frac{a+4m+b}{6}$: thus the expected time is 16. The mean value for each activity in the network is calculated by this formula, and the duration time for the total project is ascertained by the addition of the activity times along the longest path through the network. Even though this method uses a *beta* distribution and an expected value, it is a deterministic method since the activity time is treated as a single status value.

Unfortunately, a great deal of uncertainty surrounds activity duration time estimates in an actual project portrayed by a PERT network. In the activity example above (10, 15, 26), the actual activity duration time may be expected to occur at some value between 10 and 26 (and in rare cases may actually go beyond these extremes). As the activity time varies within this range, it may have an effect on the entire network of interrelated activities, even to the extent of completely altering the critical path configuration. Each activity in the network may have just such a potential effect. In a large, complex network with several paths having project duration times that are nearly the same length, the probability of the critical path shifting to other paths is high. In a real project situation that has several closely timed critical paths, the actual critical path may

---

*The term dynamics is used here to mean the analysis or examination of numerous duration times within a range—optimistic to pessimistic; it does not include the changing of the parameters of the network.

swing back and forth between the several paths many times during the actual course of the project work. It would be especially useful to know this in the planning and bidding stages of the project.

INTRODUCTION TO PS

PS accounts for the actual duration time associated with each activity being some value lying within optimistic-to-pessimistic time estimates but with some form of probability distribution over the range, rather than being simply a specified deterministic time. PS incorporates this variance or element of uncertainty dynamically into the analysis. By simulating this variance the PS model reveals the likelihood of shifting critical paths in advance by determining the relative probabilities of each network activity and of each alternative path becoming critical.

Thus planning can be refined in advance to reduce the incidence of bottlenecks not detected by the standard PERT analysis. PS can greatly expand the application of management by exception in project management and can reduce brushfire situations to a minimum.

The accuracy of PS is greater than that of PERT. The standard PERT assumes a *beta* distribution, but the true distribution is unknown. PS allows a manager to select the distribution that he judges to fit the situation best—for example, *beta*, normal, triangular, rectangular, or even specially programmed empirical distributions for special jobs.[4] The manager can select any mix of distributions.

Although the PERT network configuration clearly and concisely depicts the interrelationships of all the project activities and events, the PERT analysis, being a deterministic solution using a static model, does not take into account the interaction inherent in these interrelated activities. PS, by converting the PERT network into a dynamic model of the project activities, reflects the interaction within the network as well as the interrelationships, thus accurately modeling the real project situation.

---

[4]For more detail on the mathematical developments see: Kenneth R. MacCrimmon and Charles A. Ryavec, "An Analytical Study of the PERT Assumptions," *Operations Research*, January–February 1964, Vol. 12, No. 1, pp. 16–37; Richard M. Van Slyke, "Monte Carlo Methods and the PERT Problem," *Operations Research*, September–October 1963, Vol. 11, No. 5, pp. 839–860; R. Lowell Wine, *Statistics for Scientists and Engineers*, Prentice-Hall, Englewood Cliffs, N.J., 1964, pp. 71–73; Thomas H. Naylor, Joseph L. Balintey, Donald S. Burdick and Kong Cha, *Computer Simulation Techniques*, John Wiley, New York, 1967, pp. 77–80.

PS USES THE MONTE CARLO METHOD

The conversion of the static PERT model into a dynamic one is done by applying the Monte Carlo (simulated sampling) method. This method makes it possible to manipulate the PERT model of the project and predict how the real system might behave. The method uses random numbers to generate simulated activity times for each activity in the network.

For each simulation trial, the generated activity time for each activity will be early, on schedule or late relative to the expected duration time (t_e) for the activity. The particular time selected will be dependent on the random number and the selected probability distribution. With these factors given for each activity, the model should come up with about the same relative frequency of activity duration times as would occur in the real world. However, the duration times in the model would be "randomized."

By simulating the network several hundred times, each time randomly selecting an activity time from within its estimated range for each activity, one can find the probability of an activity being on any critical path that might occur and the probability of any particular critical path occurring. These probability or criticality indices are very useful, (1) as an indication of the degree of management attention an activity should receive, and (2) in allocation of resources to assure completion of an activity on schedule.

COMPUTER

The PS system requires a computer to execute the simulation, and more time is required to run PS than to run standard PERT. This limitation is less serious as more and faster computer facilities and hardware become available through computer service centers and through remote access to time-sharing groups. With only a few minor exceptions the information needed for PS is identical to that needed for the standard PERT calculations. Most library PS computer programs provide the standard PERT output if desired—critical path, slack times and bar charts—plus other valuable information that comes from a Monte Carlo simulation of the PERT network several hundred times.

AN EXAMPLE OF MONTE CARLO APPLIED

A simple example will illustrate how the Monte Carlo simulation method operates and will demonstrate what the computer program does to simulate a network. Figure 1 is a simple PERT network. The optimistic, most likely and pessimistic times are given for each activity. Assume for simplicity of demonstration that the probability distribution describing the possible time durations for the completion of an activity is a normal

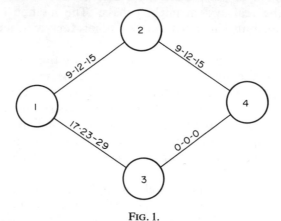

FIG. 1.

distribution and the range is finite.* A graphic representation of the normal distribution form for the two specified ranges of activity time estimates is presented in Fig. 2. With the range of the activity time estimates specified, and assuming the area under the curve to be equal to one, the probability of completing a job by a particular day can be determined by using standard statistical tables for the normal distribution.

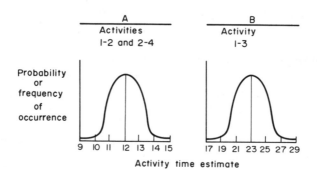

FIG. 2.

---

*Standard PERT assumes a beta distribution. In the strictest sense normal distributions are not finite.

For example, in Fig. 2A the probability of completing the activity in 10 days or less is $p = .02$; of completing it in 11 days or less, $p = .16$. The same procedure applies to Fig. 2B. This information has been plotted for both Figs. 2A and 2B in Fig. 3. Figure 3 is a cumulative presentation of the distribution with 50 percent of the curve being above and 50 percent below the mean value of 12 or 23. With the cumulative probability distributions established for each activity as in Fig. 3, the network can be simulated by hand.

For PS the hand simulation procedure can be broken into five steps:

1. Generate a random number for each activity. (This can be done by randomly drawing chips numbered between 00 and 99—representing probabilities—from a box, or by using a table of random digits.)
2. Sample the specific cumulative distribution to determine a simulated activity duration time for each activity.
3. Record the simulated duration time for each activity.
4. Determine the critical path when the duration times for all activities in the network have been simulated.
5. Record critical activities and critical path.

Assume the first random numbers drawn for activity 1–2 is 16 (see Fig. 3A). Find the cumulative probability on the vertical scale that corresponds to the random number; this number is $p = .16$. Follow across the graph horizontally until intersecting the curve; then move down to the horizontal scale and read the activity duration time—the duration time for activity 1–2 is 11.0 weeks. Record the duration time and follow the same procedure for the other activities in the network. The results of three simulations are given in Table 1. The path taking the longest time for completion is labeled critical.

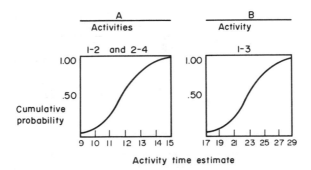

FIG. 3.

TABLE 1. *Network simulation*

	Simulation 1			Simulation 2			Simulation 3		
Activity	Random No.	Activ. dur.	Crit.	Random No.	Activ. dur.	Crit.	Random No.	Activ. dur.	Crit.
1–2	16	11.0		65	12.4	*	6	10.5	*
1–3	84	25.00	*	5	19.8		24	21.6	
2–4	69	12.5		59	12.2	*	55	12.1	*
3–4	—	0.0	*	—	0.0		—	0.0	

*Critical activity

The information in Table 1 is the basic information the computer generates and stores in memory—for possibly 2000 simulations or more. From this information a criticality index for each possible critical path and each activity is calculated. Figure 1 shows that the network contains only two possible critical paths—1–2–4 and 1–3–4. Table 1 indicates that in three simulations, path 1–3–4 was critical once, and 1–2–4 twice. Thus, after three simulations, the criticality index or probability of path 1–2–4 being critical is $p = .67$ or 67 percent, while for path 1–3–4 it is $p = .33$ or 33 percent.

The same process is used to calculate the criticality index for each activity, or the probability that a given activity will be on a critical path. The criticality index for each activity and path is listed in Table 2 for the example with three simulations. Since three simulations would not generally yield reliable information, Table 2 also contains the same information from a computer run when the network was simulated 2500 times.

Of course, if the network were larger and more complex, the indices for

TABLE 2. *Criticality indices*

Activity	Critical index 3 simulations (by hand)	Critical index 2500 simulations (by computer)
1–2	.67	.627
1–3	.33	.373
2–4	.67	.627
3–4	.33	.373
Path		
1–2–4	.67	.627
1–3–4	.33	.373

the paths probably would be different from those found for most activities.

NETWORK ANALYSIS

Figure 4 shows the original simple network with the probability of the activities becoming critical listed also. Using the PERT procedure, the critical path is clearly 1–2–4. However, when the variance element of the activity is incorporated by PS and a criticality index is determined for each activity, management's feeling about the critical path is probably tempered.

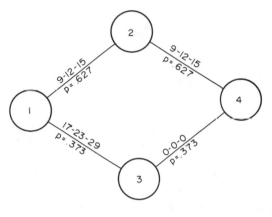

FIG. 4.

It is likely that management would now direct more attention to activity 1–3 since the likelihood of its being on the critical path is $p = .373$ or a 37 percent chance. In a large, complex project with management attention directed primarily to the critical path, and with firm resources—money, manpower, and materials—devoted to activities on the critical path, some very costly mistakes can occur. The criticality index concept is exceedingly useful in directing attention to areas where bottlenecks might occur *before* the project begins and in allocating scarce resources.

The criticality concept alerts management to potential bottlenecks that are not apparent when using PERT and its resulting critical path. An activity with a relatively high criticality index possibly may not appear on the PERT critical path. Activity 1–2 in Fig. 5 with a probability of $p = .360$

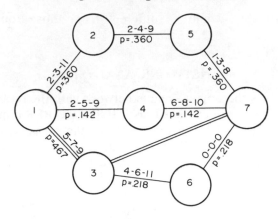

FIG. 5.

is more critical than activity 3–7 (which is on the critical path).* Such weaknesses in the PERT-calculated critical path concept make the case for the criticality concept even stronger.

PS identifies those activities that cannot become critical or are almost never critical. This information is not revealed in PERT, although it can be determined.

One word of caution is necessary for those who choose the criticality index concept to analyze PERT networks. A relatively low activity criticality index such as $p = .20$ does not necessarily mean it is unimportant. If we assume the simple network in Fig. 6, the point is obvious. It should be clear that each activity has one chance in five of being critical; hence $p = .20$. Since each activity is equally important, all should probably receive equal attention. In large, complex networks the greater the number of parallel paths with similar project duration times, the smaller will be the probability of activities occurring on these related paths. Thus the criticality indices should be viewed as relative to all the other probabilities in the network in order to evaluate their importance as critical elements in the project.

---

*Since there is no strong empirical base for using the beta distribution, the authors used the triangular distribution to simulate the network discussed in this article. The simulation results for the beta and triangular distributions are similar.

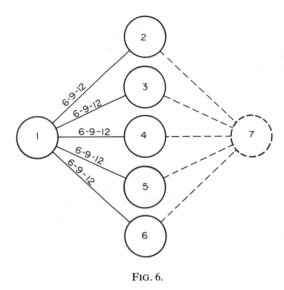

FIG. 6.

PS APPLICATION

Two examples of PS application provide insight into the latent power of PS in developing a wealth of information to guide management in the planning stages of a project.

HIGHWAY DESIGN

An engineering firm used standard PERT for planning a large highway design project. In addition to the most likely time, the estimators provided the minimum possible completion time and the maximum time for completion.

The standard PERT network established sequences and related the 94 activities of the project. The critical path or longest path for the network was found by the standard technique.

These same highway design project data were run through the PS model. Criticality or probability of occurrence for both the activities and the critical paths was calculated. Results of the simulation of this project network were particularly revealing in that a total of 88 unique, critical paths resulted! Thus an apparently insensitive network was revealed to be highly sensitive. The particular path having the highest criticality index was, indeed, the path calculated by the standard PERT technique. But its probability of being the critical path was only 11.5 percent.

The above results of the PS analysis for this design project are meaningful mainly in revealing the relative sensitivity of a given project network schedule. They also illustrate the inadequacy of the static PERT and CPM methods in detecting sensitivity and accounting for variances and uncertainty. But these results, by themselves, do not provide sufficient information to guide management in implementing specific planning action to anticipate critical problem areas in the project network. Further information is generated by the PS model to identify specific critical points for management attention. This is accomplished by the concept of a criticality or probability index for each activity in the network.

In the highway design project, 51 of the 94 scheduled activities of the network were never on the critical path and nine were always critical. The remaining 34 had criticality indices varying from .001 to .999. Management is here provided with a powerful analytical evaluation with specific quantitative data of the critical points in the project schedule.

PRODUCT AND PROCESS DEVELOPMENT

The second example of PS application is the complete development of a company structure—beginning with the decision to produce a balanced line of high-quality, dehydrated food ingredients for manufacturers of consumer food products.

The standard Pert network for the project was designed, and times were assigned to the activities. When these time estimates were run through the PS model, the results indicated that the network was insensitive; that is, the actual path calculated by the standard PERT technique occurred in 84.8 percent of the total computer simulations of the network. Only two other unique paths occurred, and they occurred in only 12.2 percent and 3.0 percent of the total network simulations. In every case delivery of production equipment turned out to be the bottleneck area. But also in every case the PS model identified the bottlenecks with a relatively high criticality index for those troublesome activities.

In the application of PS, the results regarding the critical path were similar to those found by the standard PERT method. However, the depth of the analysis attained by PS provided valuable insight into the planning schedules and greatly increased the confidence level in implementing the project work. The fact that the project was relatively insensitive to variances in activities not on the main critical path allowed more intensive concentration on the critical activities. The criticality index also revealed those activities that were never critical.

ADVANTAGES

PS offers many advantages. Some of the main ones are summarized as follows:

1. PS uses essentially the same input data as does standard PERT but also provides a means to incorporate subjective or intuitive factors into the data.
2. It tests the network to identify what paths are sensitive to delays or early completion of activities.
3. It copes with the uncertainty associated with activity duration times and the dynamic interaction between the activities of the closed network.
4. The criticality indices for the activities reveal the likelihood of activities becoming critical *before* the project begins. The indices also serve as an indication of the degree of management attention an activity should receive.
5. Accuracy and flexibility are increased since any probability distribution or mix of distributions may be used by the estimator.
6. It identifies those activities that will rarely or never occur on any of the possible critical paths.

CONCLUSIONS

The criticality concept is more useful for management by exception than the single critical path concept used in network analysis. The criticality indices provide information to assist in the allocation of scarce resources such as manpower, money, materials and equipment. The information derived from PS is valuable to management whether or not the network is sensitive or insensitive to changes in activity duration times. Since PS fully utilizes the manager's experience and subjective feelings concerning the work of the project, more accurate results are obtained. All of this adds up to improved opportunity for better time and cost performance.

8

*Quicken the Queue**

ROBERT C. WEISSELBERG and JOSEPH G. COWLEY

The typical waiting line exists because it is usually cheaper to have such a line than not to have it. And the length of the line (or the amount of time each unit may have to wait to be serviced) that is most economical can be determined by operations-research techniques. This article deals with methods of handling the waiting customer faster and better by concentrating on the application of scientific decision tools to management problems rather than on the techniques themselves.

Waiting lines, as you are well aware, are everywhere. And everyone, no matter how prestigious, has at one time or another waited in some line, for *some* service. Customers arrive, and demand service. Depending upon the service available, either the customers wait or the facilities are idle. The trick is to balance demand against service, thus minimizing total cost (the cost of having a line versus the cost of idle time).

Basically, waiting lines are an organizational device, a discipline invented by either the organization or the customers to define the order of service.

Typical waiting lines include not just people but trucks waiting to be loaded, papers in an "In" basket waiting to be processed, items on magnetic tape waiting to be read by a computer, semifinished items awaiting a final finishing step, etc.

In most waiting-line situations, the arrivals are *not* subject to control, but the service facilities *are*. This has the pattern of a typical operations research problem. The effectiveness of any system is a function of the variables subject to control and the variables not subject to control. In most waiting-line situations, the variables subject to our control are the service facilities.

*From *The Executive Strategist* by Weisselberg and Cowley, copyright © 1969 by McGraw-Hill; and *Journal of Systems Management*, Vol. 20, No. 10, October 1969, pp. 30–35. Reproduced with permission.

WHY A WAITING LINE?

Although waiting lines may serve other purposes, they exist (and their existence is justified) in most normal situations for one very important reason: it is usually cheaper to have a line than *not* to have a line. And the length of the line (or the amount of time each unit may have to wait to be serviced) that is most economical can be determined by operations research (OR) and regulated by the facilities provided to service the line. Let's look at a typical queuing situation, describing it in OR terminology.

JOE THE BARBER: ORGANIZED FOR SERVICE

When Joe first opened for business, he put in three barber chairs (anticipating future growth), although *he* provided the only service. (On a busy day he might have a customer in the chair and three others waiting.) His shop was an example of the most elementary queue: a single waiting line with a first-come, first-served discipline and a *single-channel, single-phase* operation. Diagrammed, it looks like this:

```
        Waiting line           Channel      Service
    O      O      O      O    ───────────────▶ D (Joe)
```

As business grew, Joe hired another barber (Tony), and the shop now offered a *multichannel* service as diagrammed below:

```
        Waiting              Channels     Service
    O     O     O     O    ─────────────▶ D (Joe)
                                       ▶ D (Tony)
```

Finally, business was so good that Joe was able to hire a second barber (Nick) to take over the third chair. At the same time, it occurred to Joe that maybe he could run a more efficient operation if each of the barbers specialized (he would give the shaves, Tony the haircuts, and Nick the shampoos). Organized this way, his shop became a *three-phase, sequential* operation (because the customers were serviced in sequence), with a single channel and waiting still on a first-come, first-served basis:

```
   Waiting line   Channel       Service
                              Phase I    Phase 2    Phase 3
                              (shave)    (haircut)  (shampoo)
   O   O   O   O  ─────────▶ D ───────▶ D ───────▶ D
                              (Joe)      (Tony)     (Nick)
```

However, it quickly became obvious that this wouldn't work—for the simple reason that not all customers wanted or needed all three services, and thus units (customers) were kept waiting needlessly at service facilities they didn't intend to utilize. And even if all the arrivals required all three phases of the service, the average service time for each phase was different, with the result that one barber might be very busy while another was idle, and the waiting lines would then be inefficient (either too long or too short). Allowing the customers to determine their own sequence (order of service) alleviated the problem somewhat, but obviously failed to provide an optimum solution because of inequality in the demand for each phase of the service.

Joe therefore went back to a single-phase operation, with each barber offering each customer from a single line any or all services. This solution seemed to satisfy Joe, but whether it is optimum or not we don't know. We've made no attempt at an OR solution, and we doubt if Joe has even considered all the strategies available to him that might provide a "good enough" solution to his (or to any) waiting-line problem. Let's look at some of these before considering a queuing problem that is more useful for our purposes in illustrating the application of OR.

WAITING-LINE STRATEGIES: THE SERVICE FACILITIES

Since, in any waiting-line situation, the variable most subject to our control is the service we provide, this is obviously the first (and frequently the only) place to look for a solution. Here are some questions you might ask before calling in an analyst:

• *Can you reduce the service time?*   When a waiting line gets long, a slight cut in average service time can bring dramatic improvement, particularly when arrivals are random. But speeding up service, if it means a decline in quality or a pace that cannot be maintained, can only be a temporary solution (but it may be that the *problem* is only temporary).

• *Can you reduce the variation in service time?*   On the other hand, when arrivals have an even rate (as on an assembly line), variations in service will frequently prove to be inefficient. For example, if units arrive for service every five minutes and it takes $4\frac{1}{2}$ minutes to service each unit on the average, wide variations in service time can get you hopelessly behind.

• *Can you increase the number of service channels?*   If the line at one service facility gets too long, can you switch the customers to another facility via a second channel? The efficiency of Joe the Barber's final solution, for example, lay mostly in the fact that it provided for three channels from a single line.

• *Can you reduce the number of phases?* Occasionally a multiphase operation will be more efficient than a single-phase one (and often it's not possible to avoid them), but as a general rule the fewer the phases, the more efficient it will be—witness Joe's attempt at a multiphase operation.

WAITING-LINE STRATEGIES:
THE CUSTOMERS

The second place to look for a solution is in the arrivals. We have said that this is the variable *not* subject to our control—but that is not always strictly so. Strictly speaking, we really have a queuing problem only to the extent that the arrivals *are* random and uncontrollable. Here, then, are questions you might ask concerning the customer when faced with a waiting-line situation:

• *Can you reduce the arrival rate?* Can you persuade the customer to accept a different service, perhaps even discouraging his arrival?

• *Can you vary the arrival times?* Can you stagger the incoming units, or shift customers to an off-peak period? A store, for example, can do this by having sale days; a barber shop does this by charging more for a haircut on Saturdays.

• *Can you vary the batch size?* If customers arrive in batches, can you break them up (send incoming mail to the various departments, for example, before opening it), or discourage large batching (a restaurant can do this, for example, by insisting upon reservations *for groups* above a certain size).

• *Can you predict and therefore prepare for the arrival rate?* In many businesses it's possible to predict peak demand. The maternity ward in a hospital, for example, gets an advance indication of the need for its services through the obstetricians connected with it.

TYPICAL WAITING-LINE PROBLEM

In short, there are many strategies you can try before deciding that you have a waiting-line problem that calls for the application of OR techniques. Typically, the problem requiring OR will involve a single waiting line on a first-come, first-served basis, the customers will arrive at random, the service time will vary, and the service rate will be greater than the arrival rate. In many cases, the arrival rate will slow as the waiting line increases. For example, every customer who comes to the door of Joe's barber shop will enter for service if there is no one waiting. Eventually you reach a point where the waiting line is so long that no new arrivals will enter the shop for service.

In many instances, also, the service rate will increase with an increase in the line (less time will be spent servicing each unit so that more units can be serviced). For example, if Joe has no waiting line in his shop, he may spend 20 minutes giving a customer a haircut; but if there is a line, he may be able to decrease the service time as the line increases.

ARRIVAL RATES AND SERVICE RATES

The ratio between the arrival rate and the service rate is an essential consideration in solving queuing problems, and their variability can complicate what might otherwise be a rather more simple problem. But as a general rule, when the ratio of arrival rate to service rate (often called the *traffic intensity*, or *load factor*) is very low, so is the waiting line; and, in most cases, when the ratio reaches about 0.7 to 0.8, the waiting line begins to rise sharply, approaching infinity (theoretically, at least) as the ratio approaches 1.

Here are the formulas that tell us the average length of the waiting line and the average time each customer must wait to be serviced—if we know the average arrival rate and the service rate for the operation under study. (However, they apply only to a single-service facility; there are other formulas for parallel-service facilities, or for service facilities in series.) These formulas will be applied below:

$$\text{Average waiting-line length} = \frac{(\text{average arrival rate})^2}{\text{service rate}\left(\text{service rate} - \text{arrival rate}\right)}$$

$$\text{Average waiting time} = \frac{\text{average arrival rate}}{\text{service rate}\left(\text{service rate} - \text{arrival rate}\right)}$$

ELLA, THE TELEPHONE GIRL

At the Little Wonder Manufacturing Company, orders are frequently telephoned in to a special order clerk named Ella. Recently, customers have complained that they can't get orders through, and the switchboard operator claims that Ella's line is always busy. Ella's boss, Sam Smith, thinks she should be able to handle ten incoming calls an hour (since each one averages only six minutes).

Sam happens to mention the problem to Oliver Randall, a young OR analyst who has recently joined the company, and Ollie immediately comes to Ella's rescue. He points out that if she *did* get 10 calls an hour, the waiting line would stretch to infinity (at least in theory). As it is, with eight incoming calls an hour (according to records kept by the switchboard operator), Ollie figures (using the formulas above) that better than three calls (3.2, to be exact) will be waiting for Ella at any one time, and that the average customer will have to wait 24 minutes before getting through to Ella. Add the six minutes of service time to that, and it takes the average customer a half-hour to place a telephone order with Little Wonder.

"Ridiculous!" Sam snorts. "No customer will spend half an hour to place an order with us. And I don't think there's any such thing as an *infinite* waiting line."

"You're right," Ollie agrees. "The queue never really gets very big, because many of your customers undoubtedly just give up and either try again or order from the competition. In other words, the line is self-limiting."

"Let's get the facts," Sam says, and Ollie starts keeping track of the number of incoming calls, how long each waits, and how long it takes for service. He develops a frequency distribution showing the pattern of incoming call rates and another pattern of service-time variations. He then figures what the waiting-line length and average waiting time would be for varying incoming phone-call rates, and prepares a table like the one on page 100.

Of course, this is purely theoretical, since, as Ollie found out through monitoring the incoming calls, some customers refused to wait at all, few were willing to wait beyond six minutes, and none were willing to wait more than 10 minutes. The practical result of this self-limiting factor was that, while the switch-board operator received eight calls on an average for Ella each hour, only five of the customers actually reached Ella for servicing. And since (to keep the problem simple) none of these customers ever called back, the company was losing three orders per hour, each of which would have meant an average profit of $10. This queuing problem, therefore, was costing the company $30 an hour, or $1,200 a week.

Average number of incoming calls per hr	Average potential service rate per hr	Traffic intensity	Expected number of calls waiting to be connected	Expected waiting time of average customer before being connected, min
2	10	0.2	0.05	1.5
3	10	0.3	0.13	2.6
4	10	0.4	0.27	4.1
5	10	0.5	0.50	6.0
6	10	0.6	0.90	9.0
7	10	0.7	1.63	14.0
8	10	0.8	3.20	24.0
9	10	0.9	8.10	54.0
10	10	1.0	∞	∞

SHOULD THEY HIRE ANOTHER GIRL?

Since the cost of adding another special order clerk would be only $120 a week (this includes salary, fringe benefits, office space, etc.), the logic of the situation seemed to dictate doing so. But Ollie wasn't about to advise that yet—not, that is, until they had considered some of the other strategies available to them. So, Ollie sat down with Sam, and together they went over the service facility to see what they should do about improving it.

Instead of writing up the customer's name and address for each order, couldn't Ella keep a file of prestenciled order forms? And couldn't Ella use the production department's code numbers for the make and model of each product ordered (they put the code numbers on in production, anyway—the next step in the process)? They tried the idea and found that the new form enabled Ella to take a telephone order in *three* minutes on the average, a theoretical service rate of 20 orders an hour. By doubling the rate, Sam figured, the waiting time should be cut in half. But he is in for a surprise.

When service time is cut in half (from six minutes to three), waiting time is cut even more. For eight incoming calls an hour, waiting time drops from 25 minutes to only 2, one-twelfth of what it was before. Sam is delighted. But business picks up, and inside of a year better than 15 calls an hour are coming through the switchboard for Ella, and the waiting line (waiting time, too) has grown to the point where it is costing them a considerable amount of business. Ollie takes another look at the situation (see table on page 101).

Average number of incoming calls per hr	Average potential service rate per hr	Traffic intensity	Expected number of calls waiting to be connected	Expected waiting time of average customer before being connected, min
2	20	0.10	0.01	0.33
4	20	0.20	0.05	0.75
6	20	0.30	0.13	1.29
8	20	0.40	0.27	2.00
10	20	0.50	0.50	3.00
12	20	0.60	0.90	4.50
14	20	0.70	1.63	7.00
15	20	0.75	2.25	9.00
16	20	0.80	3.20	12.00
18	20	0.90	8.10	27.00
20	20	1.00	∞	∞

WHAT ABOUT THE ARRIVALS?

There didn't seem to be anything more they could do about the service, so this time Ollie and Sam tackle the arrival problem. "Why can't some of the customers fill in the order form themselves?"

It seemed worth a try, and (surprise!) the new approach eliminates about one-half the incoming calls, which are more than compensated for by postcard orders. Again, everything is fine . . . for about six months. But gradually business doubles. Postcard orders are still coming in at the same rate, but telephone calls for Ella have climbed back up to an arrival rate of about 15 per hour. What to do? It appears that the time has come to hire that extra girl. But no . . .

Ollie notices that telephone congestion occurs during only three hours of the day, in the morning from 11:00 to 12:00 and in the afternoon from 3:00 to 5:00. Out goes a notice to customers that incoming phone orders will be subject to a 1 percent discount if made before 10:30 a.m. or between 1:00 and 2:30 p.m. This smoothing out of the arrival rate cuts the waiting time again, and things are fine for another few months. But with the next spurt in business, Ollie finally gives up, and tells Sam to hire another girl.

QUEUING COMPLICATIONS AND OTHER CONSIDERATIONS

The example above has probably left you with the impression that waiting-line problems are fairly simple and easy to solve. In some cases they are. Many problems, however, involve more than one service facility (in either a parallel or series arrangement), as in Joe's barber shop after he hired help, and the formulas that apply are slightly more complicated.

But there are other complications we haven't discussed much: *last-come, first-served disciplines* (such as letters in an "In" box, goods stacked in a warehouse, etc.), *impatient customers* (who may even *add* to delay by complaining about service), *batching problems* (the girl's club that descends on the soda fountain at one time), *unstable queues* (where the service rate is less than the arrival rate and the crowd gets restive—in a delay at a tunnel exit, for example, where they can't leave the line), and other considerations that make the problem so mathematically complex that some other approach toward a solution is sought.

Also, we've concerned ourselves with waiting lines where it has been assumed that the potential arrivals are infinite. That is, we assume that there is no limit to the people or work or materials that may arrive for service, while in actual practice many waiting lines are finite. That is, the possible customers who *could* show up for service are limited.

Finite waiting lines, as you can imagine, complicate the queuing formulas even more, and the OR analyst may have to turn to finite queuing tables to determine first (in any particular situation) whether the line he is dealing with is to be considered finite or infinite before trying to "solve" the problem. The formulas usually produce results that have to be interpreted in the light of the *measure of effectiveness* (lowest overall cost, minimal customer wait, etc.) previously agreed upon, and this in itself may involve considerable judgment and experience.

PART II

Forecasting and Demand Analysis

Introduction

Businessmen operate in a world of uncertainty, and almost every business decision is based on some form of forecasting. Activities such as sales, production, research, and development must be forecasted so that policies such as marketing, pricing, and investment can be rationally formulated. To put forecasting in its proper perspective one has to emphasize that it cannot, and is not intended to, eliminate uncertainty. Forecasting is aimed at reducing uncertainty and thus the cost associated with it.

Managerial economics is concerned with economic forecasting, which deals with general economic activities such as GNP components, and with business forecasting, which applies to the activities of a particular firm or maybe a particular industry. The distinction between these two types of activities is not always clear, and they are usually interrelated. In addition, the same forecasting techniques are used for both types of activities, although some techniques may be more suitable for one type than for the other. For instance, econometric models may be more appropriate for general economic forecasting than they are for business forecasting.

In the art of forecasting, wide variations exist in the behavioral pattern of the series to be forecasted, in the conditions under which the forecast is being made, and in the backgrounds and philosophies of those who make the forecast.

Such a diversity in what to forecast and who forecasts is bound to produce a similar diversity in how to forecast, and there are a large number of methods that are used to forecast economic and business behavior with different degrees of success. These methods range from simple extrapolation techniques and rules of thumb to highly sophisticated econometric models. It is characteristic of forecasting that a higher degree of sophistication in a particular approach does not always seem to lead to a higher degree of forecasting accuracy. It would be folly to attempt to rank these approaches according to their forecasting performance. In addition to the extreme difficulty involved, such a task may not be meaningful, since each approach may outperform the others in a certain situation. Moreover, some of these techniques complement each other, and the use of two or more may improve the overall forecast in many instances.

Economic and business forecasting methods may be conveniently grouped according to the means of identifying the model and the degree of its specification. (Specification in this context is used to mean *a priori* identification.) It should be emphasized that grouping forecasting approaches according to the above criterion is for illustrative purposes only and not to draw sharp border lines between approaches.

1. The relevant variables affecting the series to be forecasted.
2. The nature of the relationship between these variables and the series forecasted.
3. The signs and the values of the coefficients of the variables.

Five groups of forecasting methods can be recognized:

A. *Automatic forecasting approach.* The models used in this approach are usually simple such as

$$Y_{t \cdot 1} = Y_t, \quad \text{or} \quad Y_{t \cdot 1} = Y_t - Y_{t-1}, \quad \text{or} \quad Y_t = a + bT,$$

where $Y_{t \cdot 1}$ is the forecast at time t for one period ahead, Y_t is the current observations, and T stands for the time variable. In certain instances the models may be fairly sophisticated such as the exponentially weighted average which can be written as

$$Y_{t \cdot 1} = Y_{t-1.1} + \lambda(Y_t - Y_{t-1.1}).$$

This model states that the forecast at time t for one period ahead is a function of the forecast level in the preceding period and the deviation between this forecast and the current observation. The source of specifying the models in this approach is not always clear even though in general it is based on a simple assumption concerning the behavior of the series. The degree of specification, on the other hand, is very strong. Take the model $Y_{t \cdot 1} = Y_t - Y_{t-1}$ as an example. It identifies *a priori* that Y_t and Y_{t-1} are the only relevant variables, that the coefficient of Y_t is one and of Y_{t-1} is minus one, and that the relationship is linear.

B. *Econometric approach.* This approach attempts to depict the economy as a system of stochastic equations and estimates the coefficients of the explanatory variables. The forecasts of the explained variables are generated by solving the equations. A single equation may be used in investigations with a narrow scope, such as forecasting the demand deposit of a certain bank, or tourism in a particular region. The source of model specification is economic theory and the degree of specification is supposed to be fairly strong. Usually *a priori* identification is made concerning the relevant variables to be included in the model and the signs of their coefficients. When it comes to specifying the nature of the relationship, economic theory is not as useful and thus the *a priori* identification in this case is fairly weak.

C. *Box–Jenkins approach.* This approach assumes that a class of models which is a mix of autoregressive and moving average processes is sufficient to explain the behavior of most stationary series. The specific model that describes the series is derived by analyzing the estimated autocorrelation and partial correlation functions of the data. This approach has two distinctive characteristics: the first is that time series models cannot be identified *a priori*. Rather each series is identified from the sample observations. The second is that it offers systematic steps toward identifying the model that best describes the series.

D. *Survey methods.* An implicit assumption in this approach is that forecasting models cannot be specified nor can they be identified from past data. Forecasting the series is made by polling those who affect the series. For example, to forecast investment simply ask some of those who make the investment decisions about their future plans and infer future investments from that. In this approach observations are aggregated rather than relationships. In other words, a model to forecast the series is not constructed.

E. *Judgmental approach.* Many factors that affect the series to be forecasted cannot be quantified and the forecaster's or the decision maker's judgment becomes very important. This approach varies from a simple educated guess to incorporating Bayesian analysis with some of the above techniques. In a sense this is not an independent approach since each forecasting technique may require some form of judgmental forecast. For instance, judgmental forecast is needed to determine the magnitudes of the exogenous variables included in econometric models or a subjective corrective factor may be included in any of the above techniques.

In selecting the articles for this part, care was taken to provide the student with more than a simple description of the standard forecasting approaches. For instance, in article 1 the sales forecast is presented as a probability distribution and not as a single number. In article 2 a single equation regression model is combined with the exponentially weighted average model. In article 3 an attempt is made to incorporate Bayesian analysis and the judgmental forecasting with other forecasting approaches.

SUMMARIES OF ARTICLES IN PART II AND COMMENTS

Article 1

In "How good is your sales forecasting?" J. M. Cummings is concerned with the way sales forecasts are presented and how the assumptions underlying them are expressed. The traditional practice of presenting forecasts as a single number is both deceiving and not very useful. Single-number forecasts are always wrong and thus require specifying the degree of the acceptable errors. In addition most forecasts are plans for action and a single number forecast may not enable management to choose among the various alternatives available.

The assumptions on which the forecast is based must be explicitly stated so that the cause of significant errors in the forecast can be detected. Each of these assumptions may have different degrees of uncertainty, and a forecasting procedure that considers these degrees improves the forecast. The author recommends presenting sales forecasts as a probability distribution derived by combining the probability distributions of the assumptions made. These probabilities have to be subjective because many factors that affect sales cannot be quantified. The subjective probability distribution of each assumption (explanatory variable) is assessed by a simple question and answer approach. The feelings of the decision maker toward the behavior of a certain variable are deduced and translated into probabilities.* This can be achieved by asking the decision maker a few questions such as: In your opinion, what is the value that 99% of the time the demand for the product cannot exceed? What is the value that will be higher than the demand 50% of the time and lower 50%?

In the above technique normality does not have to be assumed in describing the distribution of any of the relevant variables since it can accommodate any kind of distribution. However, combining different kinds of probability distributions into one distribution could be a very complicated task. To circumvent this problem Cummings recommends that the Monte Carlo method be used to derive an approximate probability distribution.

A case study based on an actual problem concerning a firm's sales forecast of electrical devices is presented. This forecast is assumed to be a function of six variables and the relationship among them is assumed to be multiplicative. The subjective probability distribution of each of the six variables is assessed and presented in the form of cumulative distribution. The values of each variable are divided into twenty equally likely groups. This is done by reading the values that correspond to each of twenty midpoints of the cumulative probabilities with width 0.05. Through the use of random numbers one value for each of the six variables is selected and the corresponding sales are computed by multiplying these variables according to the formula introduced in the article. The process is repeated 500 times so that enough information is accumulated concerning the frequency distribution of sales which are divided into groups with one million dollar width. This frequency distribution is an approximation of the probability distribution of sales, though a good one, since 500 iterations are performed.

The above technique is no doubt very useful in sales forecasting where assumptions have different degrees of uncertainty and where the decisions made would be based on different sales possibilities and not on a single value. In addition it is flexible, since it allows for the use of various forecasting techniques, including judgmental forecasting, when assessing the probability distribution of each relevant variable. However, an assumption is made that the variables are independent, and great care

*For a better understanding of the assessment of subjective probabilities the student is referred to article 2 in Part I.

must be taken when selecting them so that they are not highly interrelated. Being acquainted with the following concepts would help in understanding this article:

Probability distribution   Frequency distribution
Subjective probability distribution   The Monte Carlo technique
Objective probability distribution   Random numbers
Cumulative probability distribution

When discussing this article an experiment generating some values of sales for the case given may be performed. This may help the student understand the Monte Carlo technique and illustrate the use of random numbers in this particular case.

Article 2

As was mentioned above, there exist a large number of forecasting techniques, and each has its own strengths and weaknesses. In "A two-stage forecasting model: exponential smoothing and multiple regression", Dwight B. Crane and James R. Crotty combine time series analysis with multiple regression to get a more accurate forecast. The forecasted demand deposit, using the exponentially weighted average model, is introduced as an explanatory variable in a multiple regression explaining the demand deposit of a commercial bank as follows:

$$D_t = f(\bar{D}_{t-1.1}, L_{t-1}, i_{t-1}),$$

where D_t is the demand deposit at time t, $\bar{D}_{t-1.1}$ the forecasted time deposit for time t at time $t-1$, L_{t-1} the lagged business loans value, and i_{t-1} the lagged interest rate. This treatment is assumed to bring about the points of strength in both techniques. The exponentially weighted average model adjusts for a change in the time series but does not predict this change, while an adequate regression model is supposed to predict the change but not adjust for it. To understand this article the student may need some background material on the exponentially weighted moving average. Below we introduce some explanation and illustrations concerning this model.

In its simplest form the forecast equation of this model can be expressed as a function of the forecast of the current period at the previous period and the current observation. The equation may be written (using the terms of this article):

$$\bar{D}_{t.1} = \lambda D_t + (1 - \lambda)\bar{D}_{t-1.1}, \tag{1}$$

where λ is a constant which determines the weights given to past data. This model is called exponentially weighted because eqn. (1) can be expressed as a function of past observations as follows:

$$\bar{D}_{t.1} = \lambda \sum_{i=0}^{n} (1 - \lambda)^i D_{t-1} + (1 - \lambda)^{n+1}\bar{D}_0, \tag{2}$$

where $\bar{D}_0$ is the initial forecast. Equation (2) can be written:

$$\bar{D}_{t.1} = \lambda D_t + \lambda(1 - \lambda)D_{t-1} + \lambda(1 - \lambda)^2 D_{t-2} + \cdots (1 - \lambda)^{n+1}\bar{D}_0. \tag{3}$$

Given that λ is less than 1, the weight assigned to each observation would decay exponentially with time.

The model in the present paper is a little more complicated since it accommodates seasonal variations and time trend even though the principle would be the same. The trend variable is included in the model as an additive component while seasonality is a multiplicative component.

The use of the EWA (exponentially weighted average) employed in this article requires:

1. That the initial values of P, S, and C which are needed to generate the model be found. This can be achieved by selecting an initial period, say, two or three years, and applying any acceptable traditional method.
2. That the weights W, W_s, W_c be chosen. This may be done by selecting the values that minimize the variance of the forecast error for one period ahead.

When combining both techniques the authors found that the average forecasting error was smaller than that which resulted when the EWA model was used alone. This procedure avoided one of the pitfalls of the EWA which is the failure to predict the change. The EWA predicted only 55% of the time that the demand deposit 12 months ahead is higher or lower than the current level, while the combined model was correct 79% of the time. The main problem that may be encountered in this approach is multicollinearity. Using the forecasted dependent variable as an independent variable creates collinearity with the other independent variables since the former is bound to contain information on the latter. However, it should be emphasized that if the model is to be used for

forecasting purposes only, multicollinearity may not be a serious problem. Also great care in selecting the explanatory variables would reduce
its magnitude.

An example of computing the initial values for the EWA model is given
below:

TABLE 1. *The values of sales in the initial periods*

	Quartered data			
	I	II	III	IV
Year I	19	25	26	18
Year II	28	33	34	25

Let us define the following: V_i is the average sale per period for year i;
P_0 the initial permanent component; C_0 the initial trend value; and S_{01},
S_{02}, S_{03}, S_{04} are initial values of the seasonal component.

Recommended methods of computation:

$$V_1 = \sum_{j=1}^{4} \frac{D_{1j}}{4} = \frac{19 + 25 + 26 + 18}{4} = 22,$$

$$V_2 = \sum_{j=1}^{4} \frac{D_{2j}}{4} = \frac{28 + 33 + 34 + 25}{4} = 30.$$

1. $P_0 = V_1 = 22$.

2. $C_0 = (V_{(H/L)} - V_1)/(H - L)$, where H is the total number of periods and L is the number of seasons in a year

$$= (V_{(8/4)} - V_1)/(8 - 4)$$
$$= (30 - 22)/4 = 2.$$

3. $S_{ij} = \dfrac{D_{ij}}{V_i - \left(\dfrac{L+1}{2} - j\right)C_0}$.

Thus

$$S_{11} = \frac{19}{22 - \left(\frac{5}{2} - 1\right)2} = 1.$$

In a similar way we get the rest of S_{ij} and these values are introduced in
Table 2.

TABLE 2

	I	II	III	IV
S_{1j}	1.00	1.19	1.13	0.72
S_{2j}	1.04	1.14	1.10	0.76
Total	2.04	2.33	2.23	1.48
Average	1.02	1.165	1.115	0.74
S_{0j}	1.02	1.165	1.115	0.74

Notice that the sum of the above averages is almost 4 (4.04) and thus normalization is not needed.

The student is advised to be acquainted with the following concepts and techniques:

Time series forecasts   Lagged variable
Multiple regression forecasts   Causal relationship
Dependent variable   Multicollinearity
Independent variable (explanatory variable)

Article 3

James E. Reinmuth and Michael D. Geurts attempt to incorporate management judgments into traditional forecasting in their article, "A Baycsian approach to forecasting the effects of atypical situations".

Most forecasting models are based on past activities and their forecasting accuracies consequently depend on the regularity of the behavior observed. However, impulses (shocks) that are not recurrent may affect the series observed, even if their behavior is normally regular. Sales forecasting models in these atypical instances would be plagued by large forecasting errors. Atypical situations occur because firms have little control over the actions of government, competitors, suppliers, etc. In addition a firm's own practices, such as new promotion campaigns or new pricing policies, may introduce shocks into the sales series. Regardless of the source, traditional forecasting techniques fail to make use of the subjective information available to management which may improve the forecast made under the above conditions.

The effect of the impulse is included as a proportion of the regular forecast. If this effect is $f_{t+T} \times Y_{t+T}$ the adjusted forecast (traditional forecast) becomes

$$Y_{t+T} + f_{t+T} \times Y_{t+T} = (1 + f_{t+T})Y_{t+T}. \tag{1}$$

Equation (1) is correct given that f_{t+T} is known with certainty. However, in most cases this factor is a random variable and thus its expected value should be used instead. Assuming the random variable f_{t+T} to be continuous leads to a more realistic assessment of its subjective probability distribution. This distribution is derived so it reflects the manager's judgment concerning the effect of the impulse on future sales.*

Deriving the continuous probability distribution is not an end by itself. It is recommended so that the assessment of f_{t+T} distribution becomes simple and realistic. The authors suggest the probability distribution be made discrete after being derived to compute the expected value of f_{t+T}.

A further improvement of the forecast of atypical situations can be made by including sample data to revise the prior probability distribution of f_{t+T}.

An interesting case concerning the use of this technique is presented. In this case the atypical situation is caused by price promotion. Including the subjective probability of the decision maker and then revising it by sample information proved very useful. A limitation of the conditioning technique is that it is only useful for atypical situations where management has some knowledge of its effect.

Being acquainted with the following concepts is useful:

Expected value	Prior and posterior
Random variable (discrete,	probability distributions
continuous)	Conditional probability
Probability distribution	Joint probability
Subjective probability	
distribution	

The instructor may wish to discuss the Bayesian approach of deriving the posterior probability distribution from the prior. In this respect it would be helpful to note that column IV of Table 2 represents the heights of the standardized normal curve for the values of column III. To get the conditional probability a further step of multiplying column IV by the widths is needed. However, including this step would not have any effect on the posterior probabilities derived, so it was omitted.

---

*The student is referred to article 1 (Cummings) where the problem is discussed in more detail.

Article 4

The demand function in its theoretical forms, and more so in its empirical forms, cannot be separated from forecasting. An empirical demand model is supposed to enable management to predict sales and measure consumers' response to such variables as price, advertisement, and income. The ability of management to adopt optimal production, marketing, and pricing policies thus may depend on the reliability of such a model. In the remainder of Part II we present two articles on demand analysis. The first is theoretical and the second is empirical.

R. G. Golledge discusses equilibrium solutions to spatial problems in his article "Some equilibrium models of consumer behavior". These solutions are sought because they provide a norm against which practical solutions are measured. In addition they are useful in constructing meaningful spatial systems such as cities or industrial plants. This article emphasizes the models of consumer behavior that produce spatial equilibrium outputs. Thus equilibrium is defined in relation to the location of the producer and is based on the action of the consumer. Models of consumer behavior are numerous and each may result in a different spatial solution.

It would be reasonable to assume that a seller's locational and marketing strategies depend on his perception of customer behavior. If the seller conceives of his customer as a Marshallian "economic man" then he has to choose a location that enables him to follow an aggressive price competition policy. If the seller conceives of the consumer as a Freudian man he may have to choose an attractive location and emphasize the appearance of the product.

The author summarizes some of the models of consumer behavior and their implications on the location of the producer and on marketing strategies. He concludes that there seems to be little success in using behavioral models to arrive at spatial solutions. The real challenge is to determine what spatial pattern results from each model of consumer behavior and what portion of the population can be explained by each model.

Being acquainted with the following concepts may be useful in reading this article:

Vector	Spatial equilibrium
Matrix	Asymptotic value
A first-order-difference equation	Stochastic models
A first-order Markov model	

Article 5

In "New product demand estimation in the pharmaceutical industry" Stuart A. Samuels attempts to estimate the demand for a new product so it can be used to forecast sales a year from introducing the product. The author explains the steps followed to achieve this end.

(a) *The problem.* Developing a new product is an expensive process, and accurate information on the prospect of the product as early as possible is needed so management can make timely decisions. The pharmaceutical industry has abundant data but in many cases they may seem contradictory and thus become confusing unless properly and adequately analyzed.

(b) *The methodology.* Three questions are raised in this respect. What is the analytical tool? What is the type of data? What are the elementary units? The author used regression analysis as the analytical tool and decided on cross-section data rather than on time series data. As far as the elementary units are concerned, various alternatives were available. These are to include, within a period of time,

1. All new products that were introduced by the client company.
2. All new products in the class of the product investigated that were introduced by the industry.
3. All new products that were introduced by the industry.

The last alternative was chosen based on practical considerations discussed in the article.

(c) *The variables to be included.* Including the relevant variables represents a sizable problem to practitioners and researchers. In most cases theory has to be supplemented with specific information concerning the problem investigated. The author being faced with this problem divided the explanatory variables into three categories—market generating variables, actual market activity variables, and attitude and awareness variables. This enabled him to list a set of variables to be considered as candidates. Stepwise regression was used to select the significant variables out of this set. This technique selects the variables according to their contribution to R^2 without paying attention to any other consideration. For this reason such an approach is frowned upon by econometricians who believe that the selection of the relevant variables must be based on theoretical considerations and not on mechanical ones. The author argues that his approach is not a mechanical one. The set of variables (from which the subset of explanatory variables to be included in the regression is chosen) is selected according to theory and/or to prior knowledge of the working variables in the industry. Two criteria are used to keep a variable in the regression. The first is that the sign of the coefficient be in accordance with expectation and the second is that the *t* value be equal to one or more.

In addition to constructing the model for the demand of the new product, a diagnostic system is suggested. This is to benefit from further information available after the third month at which the model is built. The system can be established by building separate forecasting models at months 5, 7, and 9 which employ the same technique used at month 3. Furthermore, the author recommends utilizing the system for corrective actions. This can be done by establishing control limits for forecasting the fourth quarter based on the first quarter data. If the forecasts of the models built at the fifth month and later fall above or below these limits, a corrective source of action based on a careful analysis of the causes of variation is needed.

This paper is very useful in introducing the steps that a researcher may follow to build a forecasting model based on the demand for a new product. In addition it raises some of the problems encountered when estimating this demand.

Students are advised to acquaint themselves with the following concepts:

Time series data
Cross-section data
Regression models
Dependent (explained) variable

Independent (explanatory) variable
Stepwise regression
R^2 (coefficient of multiple determination)

The instructor may wish to discuss the following problems.

1. Multicollinearity. What is it? How does it affect determining the separate effect of the independent variable on the dependent variable? How does it affect forecasting?
2. Criteria for retaining an explanatory variable. The *t* ratio vs. the degree of prior belief. The contribution of the variable to R^2. The effect of leaving out a significant variable. The effect of including a superfluous variable.

1

*How Good Is Your Sales Forecasting?**

J. M. CUMMINGS

THIS paper reviews the traditional method of presenting forecasts—single number forecasts—and goes on to propose an alternative method, using subjective probabilities.

DISADVANTAGES OF SINGLE NUMBER FORECASTS

The simplest way of presenting a sales forecast is in terms such as "We expect sales in 1980 to reach X million". Few companies would now take such a simple approach as this. In most cases, the assumptions underlying the forecast are detailed, if only in such general terms as these:

"Taking into account a past growth rate higher than that for commercial construction and a moderate price increase, we have forecast demand for office furniture at $X\%$ annually through 1975."

This statement shows what factors have been taken into account, but it does not reveal what weighting has been given to them. When it comes to reassessing it, therefore, it could well happen that the price assumption turns out to be correct, but the assumption that growth in sales of office furniture will be faster than that of construction of offices turns out to have been true of the past but not of the future. The company will not know this and may assume both assumptions to have been incorrect.

The most effective way a point forecast can be presented is with all assumptions spelled out. For example, a sales manager might forecast sales of X million next year, assuming:

a. the economy grows at $7\frac{1}{2}\%$.

*From *The Business Quarterly*, Vol. 36, No. 1, Spring 1971, pp. 54–63. Reproduced by permission.

b. the industry grows 2% faster than the economy.
c. the company retains its 12% share of the national market by hiring a new salesman and by negotiating a deal worth $X thousand with customer A to replace customer B's account which was lost last year.
d. that the company adds a further 4% of the market with a new product due out this year.

The effect on the forecast if one of these assumptions were to prove false could then be calculated. The forecast could also be adjusted to take account of the new assumption. A further advantage is that if the forecast turned out to be right, but only because two of the assumptions had been wrong and had cancelled each other out, the assumptions could be changed, and the possibility of error creeping in later eliminated.

Single number forecasts have the advantage that they are easy to understand, and for this reason are still probably the most widely used. However, they have serious disadvantages. In the first place, they are always wrong. Most forecasters would accept an error of, say, ±5% as falling within the bounds of a "correct" forecast. The degree of error acceptable in any single number forecast needs to be specified, though. Without some kind of qualification, a single number makes a spurious claim to accuracy.

Another disadvantage of single number forecasts is that, as stated earlier, most forecasts are plans for action. Now in nearly all real-life situations, the management of a company has a number of options open to it. A single number forecast enables it to choose one of these options. But what if two alternative courses of action could be taken, depending on two different sales forecast?

To take a simplified example, suppose that a company has the alternative of expanding its present 8,000 unit factory to a capacity of 10,000 units or building a new factory with a capacity of 20,000 units. The single number forecast shows demand rising to 12,000 units over 10 years, reaching 10,000 after 7 years. The company is now vitally interested in knowing how accurate the forecast of 12,000 units is likely to be. If the forecast has a fair degree of uncertainty attached to it and the company wishes to play safe, then it will go for the extension to the existing factory. If the forecast is thought to be a conservative estimate, which the company has a good chance of exceeding, then management will probably opt for the new factory.

Of course in most situations management has not two, but a wide spectrum of different alternatives open to it. The sales forecast itself is only one of a series of numbers which could have been produced using different assumptions. In the past, the complexity of handling anything more than a single number sales forecast as an input to a planning programme has inhibited the use of more sophisticated techniques. The advent of large, fast computers, however, means that this barrier has now disappeared. On looking more closely at management's needs, it becomes apparent that what is really required is a range of forecasts against which to match the range of options. The range needs to be expressed in terms of the degree of uncertainty which the forecasters would attach to the numbers.

THE USE OF SUBJECTIVE PROBABILITIES

Most forecasts are built up by working through a progression of assumptions. Since the future is uncertain, all assumptions made in forecasting are arbitrary to some degree. But there are great variations in the amount of uncertainty that can be attached to them.

For example, a company sales forecast may begin with a forecast of population between the ages of 20 and 60 in 1975, and end with a projection of the company's market share of outboard motor sales to that age-group in that year. If the company wants to find out both what the most likely estimate of its sales in 1975 is, and also the probability that other values will be achieved, it needs a method of combining the probabilities attaching to each assumption involved in its forecasts.

Why Subjective?

Probabilities are normally thought of in objective terms e.g. there is a probability of 0.5 that a coin when tossed will come down heads. In the case of an assumption about a company's market share, however, there is a subjective element which cannot be formally quantified. The only way of dealing with this problem is by setting up a kind of question and answer procedure which will elicit from the company's marketing manager his subjective feelings about the chances of getting certain market shares. Schlaifer[1] has given the clearest description of this method:

a. First, the decision maker should divide all possible values of demand into two equally likely halves. To do so he should look for, and ultimately decide on, some value of demand such that he would be just as ready to bet demand will be below this value as he would be to bet that demand will be above. By way of example, we shall suppose that our marketing manager decides that he would be just as ready to bet there will be a demand for less than 500 units as he would be to bet that there will be a demand for more than 500 and it then follows that 500 is the *median* of his distribution of demand.

b. The decision maker's next step should probably be to assess upper and lower limits between which demand will in his opinion almost certainly lie. Our marketing manager might assess an upper limit of this sort by looking, for example, for the value that demand seems 99 times more likely to fall short of than to exceed; and if he decides that demand is about 99 times more likely to fall short of than to exceed 1,100, say, then 1,100 is the *.99 fractile* of his distribution of demand. Without describing the exactly analogous problem of selecting a lower limit, we shall assume that he decides on 200 as the *.01 fractile* of his distribution.

c. Having located the middle of his distribution and roughly located its ends, the decision maker can now go on to subdivide it into quarters by assessing his upper and lower *quartiles*. To assess his upper quartile (i.e. his .75 fractile), our marketing manager can focus his attention on those values of the [distribution] that lie above his assessed median and decide on a value that divides them into two equally likely halves; in what follows we shall assume that he decides on 650 as the upper quartile of his distribution, and we shall further assume that by an analogous procedure he decides on 400 as his lower quartile. (Chapter 8.1.4.)

In companies that have used this technique, it has been found that marketing managers gradually develop an expertise in translating their expectations into probabilities in this way.

The same method can be used to build up a probability distribution for each of the assumptions being made to arrive at the forecast. The problem then is to find a way of combining these distributions to produce a distribution for the final forecast itself.

A Case Study

The best way of illustrating one method of making a forecast using subjective probabilities is to introduce a case study at this point. The study is based on an actual situation. It has only been slightly altered so that the complexities of the real life situation would be preserved, but the numbers quoted are not the real ones.

Turnon Ltee makes electrical devices. Market research has shown that demand for the company's product is determined by:

a. growth in non-residential construction
b. price of product range
c. the more intense use of the product
d. the growth of a competitive product
e. other firms making the same electrical device

a. Growth in Non-residential Construction

A forecast was first made for the growth of expenditure on non-residential construction. The main types of construction to be considered were: industrial, commercial (mainly office buildings) and institutional (mainly schools). A separate forecast was made for each category using regression analysis. The schools forecast was then modified downwards in the light of the forecast fall in the rate of increase in school enrolments. The total forecast was expressed as a range of $4.3–$4.8 billion in the terminal year, 1973.

The next step was to translate this forecast into a probability distribution. We decided not to use conventional bell-shaped distributions, but the cumulative distribution method described earlier by Schlaifer. In Fig. 1 is shown the distribution for non-residential construction in 1973. As the mid-point of our range, with a 0.5 probability of occurrence, we selected $4.5 billion. As the two ends, with a 0.01 and 0.99 probability respectively, we decided on $2.5 billion (below the current level) and $7.0 billion (the

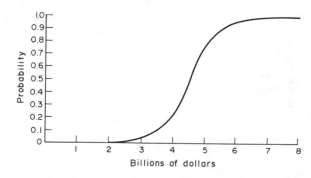

FIG. 1. Cumulative probability distribution for non-residential construction forecast, 1973.

most optimistic forecast we could possibly justify from our regression analysis). We then considered the $4.3 to $4.8 billion range to constitute our 0.25 to 0.75 probability range. Finally, we "faired in" a curve between the five points on our graph using a flexible ruler.

b. Price of the Product Range

The price factor is more difficult to forecast because there is conflicting evidence about the proportion of the product forms of total construction costs. The D.B.S. data for consumption of the products (domestic shipments plus imports less exports) show products as around 1.6% of total non-residential construction costs. Market research evidence, on the other hand, puts the proportion nearer to 1.9%, which compares well with 2.1% in the U.S. Accordingly we have shown 1.9% as the mid-point of our cumulative probability range but with a skewed distribution around it (Fig. 2). On the low side, we have taken account of the chance that the D.B.S. data may prove to be more valid than the market research evidence by skewing the tail of the distribution down in a steady progression to 1.4%; while on the high side we show a 0.75 probability of 2.0% and 0.9 probability of 2.1%.

It is known that the proportion the product forms of construction is falling, because other costs (mainly labour) are rising faster and because there has been fierce price competition among manufacturers of the product. Forecasting this trend requires a high degree of intuitive judgment. The market research evidence points strongly in the direction of continued price erosion, though at a slowing pace, and it is clearly necessary for the outcome of this trend to be taken into account. In Fig. 3 we have shown the probability distribution for the negative effect on the

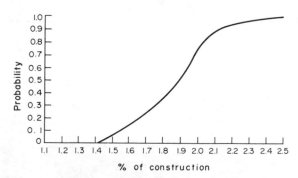

FIG. 2. Cumulative probability distribution for the product as a proportion of construction, 1968.

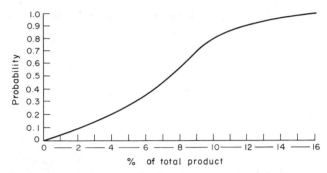

FIG. 3. Cumulative probability distribution of effect of price reductions on market.

1973 market of price erosion in terms of a percentage reduction of the total market.

c. Intensity of Use

In many types of building, Turnon's market intelligence has shown that a plateau has been reached in terms of the product's use. There are still some building types e.g. factories where it is felt that more of the product will be asked for in future. This factor will increase the market for the product but will not be very significant, it is thought. We show the probability distribution for its effect on the market in Fig. 4.

d. Growth of a Competitive Product

Turnon Ltee does not expect that the competitive product will impinge greatly on the market by 1973. However, the possibility needs to be taken into account. Again we have drawn a skewed distribution of the probability of this possibility, with the longer tail showing the low but nevertheless

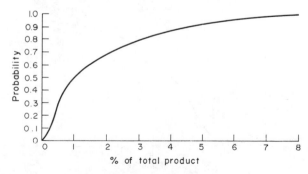

FIG. 4. Intensity assumption.

existing chance of a sizeable loss of sales to the competitive product
(Figure 5).

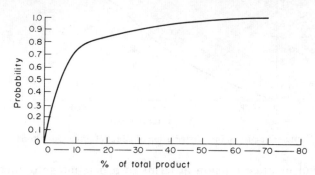

FIG. 5. Cumulative probability distribution for the competitive product's effect on market,
1973.

e. *Turnon Ltee Market Share*

Finally, Turnon's marketing manager was interviewed about the company's probable market share position in 1973, and his comments were
translated into Fig. 6.

The problem now is to find a way of combining the six probability
distributions. This can be done using the Monte Carlo technique on a
computer. The Monte Carlo technique has been defined by Magee and
Boodmann[3] as "Any procedure that involves random-sampling to obtain a
probabilistic approximation to the solution of a mathematical or physical
problem". (For a further description see Churchman, Ackoff and Arnott,[2]
pp. 180–2.)

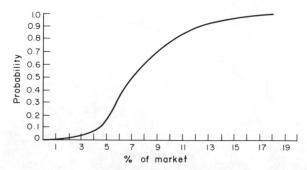

FIG. 6. Cumulative probability distribution for Turnon market share, 1973.

First the probability values on the six graphs are arbitrarily divided into 20 groups: 0.00–0.05 probability, 0.05–0.10 probability and so on to 0.95–1.00 probability. The values opposite the mid-points of these 20 ranges are then read off the six graphs and a table of 20 rows and 6 columns is fed into the computer.

An assumption now has to be made about the way the six factors are related to each other. In this case we assumed that the various factors affecting the market were all independent of each other and that the equation linking them was therefore a multiplicative one:

$$F = a \times b \times (100 - c) \times (100 + d) \times (100 - e) \times f$$

Where F = forecast of Turnon's sales in 1973

a = expenditure on non-residential construction in billions of dollars

b = product range as a % of construction

c = effect of falling price of products (%)

d = gain due to more intense use of product (%)

e = loss due to the competitive market (%)

f = Turnon's market share (%)

This assumption is clearly too simple a description of the real life situation, since some of the factors are almost certainly interrelated. We recognized that further analysis of the six factors affecting the forecast would improve the model. Unfortunately, however, the data necessary to perform the analysis did not exist in most cases.

In order to combine the distributions, the computer generates random numbers, using a standard routine, which are used to select one of the values in the first column of figures, and within the group of probabilities thus selected, one particular probability. It then repeats the procedure for the second column and so on for all six. Finally it multiplies the six values together in accordance with the equation. This sampling procedure can be reiterated any number of times in accordance with the accuracy required of the sample. In this case 500 iterations were made. The computer then calculates and prints out the final distribution of the company's sales prospects in the forecast year in the form of grouped data: $0–1 million, $1–2 million, etc. and also the mean and standard error of the distribution. We can now draw a histogram of Turnon's sales in 1973 as in Fig. 7. As can be seen, the modal (most frequently occurring) sales value is $4 million. Since the distribution is skewed towards the higher end, the mean sales value is $4.9 million.

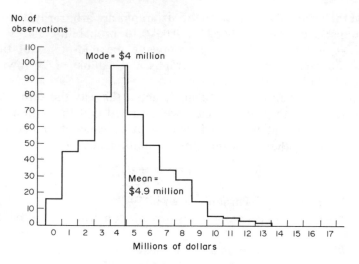

No. of
observations

FIG. 7. Histogram of Turnon sales, 1973.

ADVANTAGES OF PROBABILITY FORECASTING

In order to illustrate the advantages of forecasting using subjective probabilities, we will return to the type of example given previously in which a firm has to choose between two or more rival investments. Let us suppose that it has made a forecast by the method described in the previous section and has transformed the resulting histogram into a cumulative probability distribution. It has to choose between an extension to the old plant which would bring its maximum output in terms of sales to $5 million, and a new plant whose maximum output would be $12 million. Using the modal forecast of $4 million, the firm would have selected the extension to the old plant. However, it is clear from the distribution that it is only 58% certain that sales will be below $5 million. There is a 42% chance that sales will in fact exceed the capacity of the extension. The company's management may well want to make provision for this possibility. In this case, the degree of skewness of the distribution is of great interest to the company, as well as the single number forecast.

In another case, a company might be interested in the spread of the distribution as well as its shape. That is, it might want to know not only the modal point, but also the expected sales at the 0.1 and 0.9 levels of probability. Frequently, it is the low end of the probability scale that interests management, since it wants to be able to assess the chance of low sales volumes and hence the possible failure of a plant expansion programme. On other occasions, it is the high end of the scale, since management may be interested in seeing what its most optimistic performance might be in order to make contingency plans.

Strong objections will be raised to probability forecasting on the grounds that it is less easy for management to understand and use than simpler techniques. But forecasting the future is an inherently uncertain process. And modern computers mean that large masses of data can now be handled with ease. Any method which minimizes, and at the same time measures, this uncertainty has great advantages over methods which give a false sense of certainty. Furthermore, forecasting is primarily a basis for action and secondarily an education process. Management seldom has one course only open to it. Usually it is making a forecast in order to choose between two or more alternatives. Therefore any forecasting system which enables it to match the full range of options open to it against the full range and probability of occurrence of future events, is superior to a system which restricts its view. Also, a system which makes crystal clear the method by which the forecast is produced and enables management to re-work and learn from it, is preferable to a system which leaves the method obscure. On both these criteria probability forecasting is a superior method to the single number forecast.

REFERENCES

1. Schlaifer, Robert: *The Analysis of Decisions Under Uncertainty* (McGraw-Hill, 1967).
2. Churchman, C. W., Ackoff, R. L., and Arnott, E. L.: *Introduction to Operations Research* (John Wiley & Son, 1957).
3. Magee, J. F. and Boodman, D. M.: *Production Planning and Inventory Control* (McGraw-Hill, 1958).

2

A Two-stage Forecasting Model: Exponential Smoothing and Multiple Regression*

DWIGHT B. CRANE and JAMES R. CROTTY

This paper presents a forecasting technique which attempts to combine the advantages of both time series analysis and multiple regression. In this two-stage technique, an exponentially smoothed moving average model is used to forecast values of the dependent variable and/or selected independent variables as desired. These forecasts, along with data for other (lagged) independent variables, are then used as inputs to a multiple regression program. The observations are selected sequentially by the regression model so that each equation is based only upon data which would have been available at the time of the forecast, and the coefficients of the equation are updated as new information becomes available. The final section of the paper describes a successful application of the two-stage model to a demand deposit forecasting problem.

1. INTRODUCTION

The forecasting approach presented in this paper combines two techniques usually applied separately: time series analysis, and multiple regression. The characteristics of these forecasting techniques are complementary in several respects. Time series models such as exponential smoothing provide procedures for detecting and adjusting to changes in the forecast series, but cannot predict these changes.[1] In appropriate cases, the addition of other explanatory variables through regression will aid in the prediction of major changes in the trend of the forecast variable. Multiple regression models, on the other hand, frequently do not use information contained in the historical movement pattern of the forecast, or dependent, variable itself; whereas the use of such information is the

*From *Management Science*, Vol. 13, No. 8, April 1967, pp. B501–B507. Reproduced by permission.
[1]Numerous examples of time series models are provided in [2].

essence of time series analysis. In addition, if the regression model utilizes non-lagged values of the independent variables, exogenous forecasts of these variables are required. Such forecasts may be supplied by time series analysis.

The two-stage forecasting model utilizes an exponentially weighted moving average procedure to forecast the variable of interest and selected independent or related variables. These forecasts are used as input to a multiple regression model which relates actual values of the variable of interest to these forecasts, and other lagged variables if desired. The regression analysis includes tests of the model with past data to select that form of the model which would have provided the best "true" forecasts over the data sample. This analysis entails the revision of the regression coefficients as new data become available.

The two-stage forecasting procedure is most applicable to time series which possess a trend determined by other causally related variables, and a significant cyclical and/or seasonal pattern.

2. DESCRIPTION OF THE TWO-STAGE MODEL

1. Exponentially Weighted Moving Average Forecast Model

There are a number of alternative time series models which could be used to make forecasts of the dependent and/or selected independent variables. We have used an approach presented by P. R. Winters and others which forecasts trends and seasonals using exponentially weighted moving averages. [6, 8] In this approach, the time series to be forecast is assumed to have a permanent component and a multiplicative seasonal component. The model also allows for a linear trend in the permanent component. Current values for these components of the time series are calculated each time period by correcting for the observed errors in the preceding forecast. Forecasts are then based upon these current values.

The approach can be illustrated most easily by considering the basic exponential model, assuming no definite seasonal pattern and no long-run trend. In this situation, fluctuations in the time series are caused by two kinds of components, one permanent and one transitory. The object of the forecasting procedure is to estimate the permanent component, since the forecast for T periods ahead is simply this permanent value. As actual data for each period become available, the estimate of the permanent component is changed by an amount proportional to the most recently observed error. That is,

$$P_t = P_{t-1} + w_p(D_t - P_{t-1}) \qquad (1)$$

where

P_t = permanent component in period t
D_t = actual data
w_p = a number between 0 and 1.

This equation can be restated as:

$$P_t = w_p D_t + (1 - w_p)P_{t-1} \qquad (2)$$

so that w_p is viewed as the proportion of weight to be given to the current actual value. If changes in the permanent component are small relative to the random variations each period, then w_p should be small so that little weight is given to the random noise. If, on the other hand, changes in the permanent component are large, then w_p should be close to one so that recent information, which is a good indicator of the future, is weighted heavily.

The simple model represented by equation (2) can be expanded into one which allows for seasonal movement and a linear trend. In this case, not only is the permanent component updated each period, but the seasonal factor and trend component are also changed in an analogous manner. The permanent component is now calculated as:

$$P_t = w_p(D_t/S_{t-L}) + (1 - w_p)(P_{t-1} + C_{t-1}) \qquad (3)$$

where L = periodicity of the seasonal effect, e.g., 12 months or four quarters.
S_{t-L} = most recent seasonal factor calculated for this part of the seasonal cycle.
C_{t-1} = estimated growth or decline in the permanent component.

Thus, P_t is a weighted average of the current seasonally adjusted value and the past permanent component value, adjusted by the estimated trend growth or decline per period.

Following the estimate of the permanent component, the new seasonal factor is obtained as follows:

$$S_t = w_s(D_t/P_t) + (1 - w_s)S_{t-L} \qquad (4)$$

And, the new value of the change in the permanent component will be:

$$C_t = w_c(P_t - P_{t-1}) + (1 - w_c)C_{t-1} \qquad (5)$$

Forecasts of the data series for T periods in the future are then obtained by projecting the trend of the permanent component and multiplying it by the seasonal factor as in equation (6) below:

$$\bar{D}_{t,T} = (P_t + TC_t)S_{t-L+T}. \tag{6}$$

Two important aspects of the model are the procedures used to obtain initial values of the components and to search for the optimal weights.[2] The first part of the data series is used to obtain the initial values of P, S, and C in the following way: (1) P_1 is the average of the observations for the first year; (2) C_1 is the average change per period between the first and last year used for initialization; and (3) seasonal factors are computed for each period as the ratio of the actual data for the period to the average value for that year, further adjusted by the estimated trend. Seasonal factors for corresponding periods in each of the initial years are averaged to obtain one seasonal factor per period. For example, the S's for each January are averaged to get a single January seasonal factor.

Having thus obtained the initial values of P, C, and S, the exponential system can be used with a given set of weights, w_p, w_s, and w_c to calculate forecast values for observations in the second portion of the data series, i.e., that portion not utilized for initialization. The problem then is to determine the appropriate values for the weights. In this model, the approach used was to select a grid of values for each of the weights. Each set of values in the grid was used to calculate forecasts for the second portion of the data series. The set of weights finally selected was that which minimized the variance of the forecast error.

One problem with the above procedure is that "true" forecasts are not obtained for each of the years of data. For example, assume that the complete series includes data for the years 1953–65, and that years 1953 and 1954 are used in the initialization procedure. Thus, forecasts are desired for each of the years 1955–1965. If this whole time span were used to calculate the optimal weights, then information would be used to obtain forecasts for 1960, for example, which would not have actually been available at that time. To obtain "true" forecasts for 1960, only data through 1959 should have been used to search for optimal weights.

While this problem may not be significant for many uses of exponentially smoothed forecasts, it does lead to an underestimate of the average forecast error and variance of the errors. To avoid this problem in the application of the model discussed later, a true forecasting procedure was

[2]A detailed flowchart of the exponential forecasting procedure is provided in [8].

used which re-selected optimal weights with each new year of data. The forecasts obtained in this manner were then taken as an input to the second stage of the forecast model.

2. Multiple Regression Model

The second stage of the model contains the multiple regression analysis. As discussed in the introduction, the primary purpose of this stage is the specification of a model or framework which will predict changes in the trend of the forecast variable. In any time series multiple regression, the choice of independent variables should be made with great care because of technical problems caused by the general co-movement of variables over time. Such co-movement will often exist apart from any true causal relationship among variables, a phenomenon generally referred to as spurious correlation. It is therefore important that series which may be presumed to be causally related to the forecast variable be selected for the regression stage of the model.

A second problem associated with time series regression analysis is that of multicollinearity. Even assuming that the independent variables are in fact causally related to the forecast variable, it is difficult to separate the degree of variation of the forecast variable caused by changes in each of the individual independent variables if they move together over time. However, confidence in the predictive accuracy of the regression model will not be affected by multicollinearity among the independent variables, provided their pattern of co-movement is reasonably consistent over time.[3]

A final note of caution on the use of this second stage is required. If the independent variables take on values outside the range they exhibited in the regression analyses, forecasts made with the estimated regression equation should be accepted with much less confidence than historical accuracy of the regression model would indicate.

In the second stage of the forecasting model, the input from stage one is a data matrix consisting of the forecasted values of the dependent variable and those explanatory variables which have been transformed through exponential smoothing. Observations of the unsmoothed dependent variable and the other explanatory variables are added to this data matrix in the second stage.

In order to obtain an estimate of the true forecasting ability of the

[3]See [7], p. 207.

regression model, the second stage handles the data sequentially over time.[4] This sequential procedure insures that all forecasts generated by the regression model could have been produced by the model at the time in which the forecast would have been required. That is, the estimation of the regression equation would have been possible at the time the forecast would have been made. This is accomplished as follows. Assume that the model tested is required to forecast one year ahead and that, as a result, lagged independent variables must be lagged at least one year. To generate a forecast for year t, only data available in year $t - 1$ may be used. The regression will thus relate values of the dependent variables observed no more recently than year $t - 1$ with values of the lagged variables observed no more recently than year $t - 2$. Insertion of the lagged independent variables of year $t - 1$ into this equation will yield a true prediction of the dependent variable in period t. A new regression is run and a new forecasting equation estimated to generate a forecast for period $t + 1$. Thus, the sequential regression procedure involves one regression for each forecast desired.

The sequential regression procedure provides two different ways of utilizing the available data. If the structure of the equation relating the dependent variable to the explanatory variables is very stable over time, then the maximum amount of past data available should be used in the equation estimation. However, if the equation structure is changing over time it is better to use only the more recent data observations in the regression. That is, each time a new data observation is added to compute a new equation, the oldest observation used in the previous regression should be deleted. Determination of the optimal number of observations to be included in each regression is essentially a trial and error process unless the analyst has reason to believe that the equation structure is quite stable.

3. APPLICATION TO DEMAND DEPOSIT FORECASTING

The two-stage model has been successfully applied to a problem important to asset management in banks, the forecasting of demand deposits. In the bank studied, the demand deposit series had both characteristics which make it amenable to the two-stage forecasting procedure. The series itself contained important information for forecast-

[4]The sequential regression model was developed in conjunction with previous work by one of the authors and A. H. Meltzer, which appeared in [3].

ing purposes, since it had a significant and relatively stable seasonal pattern. This is illustrated by the fact that the exponential smoothing model alone forecasts deposits quite well for one, two, and three months ahead. For forecasts of longer spans, however, changes in the longer run direction of demand deposits exert a more important influence on predictive accuracy. Since the exponential smoothing model simply assumes a continuation of the recent past growth or decline of the data series, it is helpful to expand the forecast model to include a more realistic explanation and prediction of changes in direction.

For some banks, the level of demand deposits is greatly influenced by local economic conditions. For larger banks, however, the local economy is much less significant. Instead, most of the demand deposit behavior is explained by movements in the deposits of large corporations. Because of this importance of business firm deposits, the framework adopted for the second stage of the forecast model was based partly upon an earlier study of corporate deposit behavior. [4, 5]

This investigation suggested that the general level of deposits of a large corporation at a single bank depends somewhat on the general pace of economic activity, but more importantly on the volume of services provided by the bank. These services take a number of forms including mechanical services concerned with handling and maintaining the demand deposit account, professional and consultative services, and financial services such as the providing of credit. They are important because of the traditional practice followed by banks and business firms in which demand deposit balances are used to compensate banks for services provided to the firm.

It was not necessary to include measures of all these services in the multiple regression model of the second stage. Since an exponentially smoothed forecast of deposits is already included as an independent variable, service variables which change relatively slowly over time add little information to the regression model. Such services appear to include the mechanical services and the less tangible consultative services. The providing of credit, however, does have an important positive influence on the general direction of demand deposits. An increase in the volume of business loans frequently causes a closer "customer relationship" between the bank and the corporations who borrowed, leading to larger balances. On the other hand, as the corporations' need for borrowing declines, there is a tendency for deposit balances to decrease.

Deviations from the trend projected by the moving average model could also be caused by a change in monetary policy. For example, as interest rates rise, it becomes profitable for corporations to shift out of demand deposits into interest-bearing assets, and vice-versa. To include this effect, the corporate Aaa bond rate was added to the regression model as an independent variable.

Thus, the final regression model included three independent variables: a forecast of demand deposits; business loan volume, lagged; and the corporate Aaa bond rate, lagged. The loan volume and interest rate series were lagged not only to maintain a true forecasting procedure, but also because there is some evidence that corporate adjustments of their demand deposit holdings lag behind changes in credit needs and monetary conditions. [4] Since the particular forecast results to be discussed here are 12-month projections of demand deposits, the lagged variables were lagged 12 months behind the dependent variable.

The results from stage 1 of the forecast model, the exponentially weighted moving average projections, indicated that the seasonal pattern of the demand deposit series was relatively stable. The average absolute error of these projections during the period 1959–1965 was a comparatively small 2.09% and the standard deviation of the forecast errors was 2.84%. When these 12-month forecasts were utilized in stage 2 of the model as an independent variable, the average error of the 12-month forecast was reduced to 1.82% with a standard error of 2.32%. While this reduction in average error and variability of errors does not appear to be large in percentage terms, its effect on the average error in dollar terms is several million dollars for the bank studied.

One of the reasons for combining stages 1 and 2 of the forecast model is that the exponentially weighted moving average forecast employs a very naive projection of the trend of the data series. When the exponential model was used alone in the application presented here, it correctly predicted whether the demand deposit level 12 months ahead would be higher or lower than the current level only 55% of the time. The complete model did much better, correctly predicting the direction of 79% of the changes.

Increased confidence in the forecasts of the regression model is obtained from an analysis of the coefficients of the independent variables. The theoretical framework of the model implies that both the exponential forecasts of demand deposits and the business loan variable should appear with positive signs, while the interest rate should have a negative influence. This pattern was in fact obtained in the regressions calculated for each of the 84 monthly forecasts.

Exponential smoothing is, of course, not the only time series analysis which could be used as input to the multiple regression stage. In this particular case, however, it appeared to provide the best time series forecast. Two alternatives were also investigated, a regression model which used demand deposits lagged 12 months as the independent variable, and a similar model with a time trend added as the independent variable. Both of these were inferior forecasting procedures. The lagged demand deposit model had an average error of 2.6% and a standard error of 2.7%. With the time trend added, the forecast error was reduced to 2.5%, but the standard error increased to 3.2%.

4. CONCLUSION

The two-stage forecasting model provides a useful method of combining information contained in past patterns of the dependent variable and information provided by causally related variables. While some caution must be used in selecting and evaluating the independent variables, there are a number of forecasting areas where it is possible to develop a theoretical framework to aid in the selection process. Such a framework helps to assure a proper causal relationship between the dependent and explanatory variables, as illustrated by the demand deposit forecasting model presented in Section 3. Examples of other potential applications are company and industry sales forecasts of products significantly influenced by economic trends, cost and profit forecasting within a firm, security price forecasting,[5] and forecasts of cash inflow by financial institutions.

REFERENCES

1. Ahlers, D. M., "SEM: A Security Evaluation Model," in Cohen, K. J. and F. S. Hammer (Eds.), *Analytical Methods in Banking*, Homewood: Richard D. Irwin, Inc., 1966.
2. Brown, R. G., *Smoothing, Forecasting, and Prediction of Discrete Time Series*, Englewood Cliffs: Prentice-Hall, Inc., 1963.
3. Brunner, K., and A. H. Meltzer, "Predicting Velocity: Implications for Theory and Policy," *Journal of Finance*, Vol. XVIII, No. 2, May, 1963, pp. 319–354.
4. Crane, D. B., "A Simulation Model of Corporation Demand Deposits," in Cohen, K. J. and F. S. Hammer (Eds.), *Analytical Methods in Banking*, Homewood: Richard D. Irwin, Inc., 1966.
5. Crane, D. B., "The Commercial Banking Market and the Demand Deposits of Business Firms," Unpublished Ph.D. Dissertation, Carnegie Institute of Technology, 1965.
6. Holt, C. C., F. Modigliani, J. F. Muth, and H. A. Simon, *Planning Production, Inventories, and Work Force*, Englewood Cliffs: Prentice-Hall, Inc., 1960.
7. Johnston, J., *Econometric Methods*, New York: McGraw-Hill Book Co., Inc., 1963.
8. Winters, P. R., "Forecasting Sales by Exponentially Weighted Moving Averages," *Management Science*, Vol. 6, 1960, pp. 324–342.

---

[5]An approach similar to the two-stage forecasting is presently being used in the development of a security evaluation model. See [1].

3

A Bayesian Approach to Forecasting the Effects of Atypical Situations*

JAMES E. REINMUTH and MICHAEL D. GEURTS

A model is offered for conditioning a forecast during periods when a time series exhibits atypical behavior. The model is based on a Bayesian approach, requiring the assessment of a probability distribution to the proportionate change believed to result from the impending atypical situation.

INTRODUCTION

Traditional mathematical forecasting models are of little or no use when a time series exhibits atypical behavior. Such models tend to be extrapolations of past trends and economic behavior and are inappropriate when current time series activity no longer mirrors past activity. Decision models which ignore unexpected situations are of limited value, for in practice models are evaluated on the basis of infrequency of failures rather than frequency of successes.

Atypical behavior in a time series may be characterized as an impulse from some normal pattern. The impulse is assumed to be nonrecursive and not to follow a discernible pattern over time. When an impulse is induced by promotional campaigns, price adjustments, and mergers, short-term warning is necessary so that management can accommodate the effect of the atypical behavior. Even with warning, however, traditional forecasting methods may prove unresponsive to characteristics of the impending impulse and fail to make use of subjective information available to management regarding its impact.

Under conditions of uncertainty, atypical events occur because firms

*From *Journal of Marketing Research*, Vol. IX, August 1972, pp. 292–297. Reproduced by permission.

operate with limited control over their environments, and unique situations will continue to arise. Actions by government or the firm's competitors, suppliers, or customers and acts of nature are potential causes of atypical situations.

A FORECAST CONDITIONING MODEL

There is perhaps more uncertainty associated with marketing decisions than with those in other areas of business. Marketing decision makers are often faced with problems which have never previously arisen and are unlikely to occur again [5]. Therefore, management's subjective judgments about atypical occurrences may provide worthwhile information for decision models. If the decision maker is unable to predict the exact outcome of such situations, he may find it convenient to view the outcome as a *chance event* and to assign a probability distribution to possible outcomes.

Let y^*_{t+T} be the forecast of the process value of a time series that is T time periods ahead of available data through period t. The type of forecasting model employed to generate y^*_{t+T} is not specified [1, 2, 15, 16]. It is assumed that the forecaster knows that some outside influence will be in effect during the period $t + T$, but the exact magnitude of the effect or impulse on the time series is assumed unknown.

The Multiplicative Correction Factor

The forecaster conditions y^*_{t+T} to reflect uncertainty about the impending impulse by multiplying y^*_{t+T} by the *proportionate change*, f_{t+T}, expected to result from the impulse during the period $t + T$. Then the *conditioned* forecast is:

$$y'_{t+T} = (1 + f_{t+T})y^*_{t+T}. \tag{1}$$

If the impact of the impulse is known for certain, f_{t+T} will be known. In the *otherwise more realistic* case, f_{t+T} must be regarded as a random variable representing the various assumed likely levels of proportionate change. Then one would replace f_{t+T} in (1) by its expected value, $E(f_{t+T})$, obtaining as the conditioned forecast:

$$y'_{t+T} = (1 + E(f_{t+T}))y^*_{t+T}. \tag{2}$$

The random variable f_{t+T} can be discrete or continuous. If assumed discrete, the decision maker must list the set of possible values for f_{t+T}

and assign probabilities of their occurrence. However, assuming f_{t+T} as discrete frequently complicates the analysis and leads to unrealistic results. If it is believed to assume many possible values, it is difficult to effectively assess individual probabilities and hence internal consistency among the probabilities becomes impossible to monitor. Furthermore, it may not be realistic to assume that f_{t+T} will be one of the preselected, discretely spaced values [12].

An alternative approach is to assign a continuous, cumulative probability distribution over a range of values for f_{t+T}; see [9, 13, 19]. If f_{t+T} is assumed continuous, one would plot the cumulative probability against various values within the range of f_{t+T}. That is, one would assess the probability that the proportionate gain over the forecast value y^*_{t+T} is less than or equal to some value within the range of possible values of f_{t+T}. This process would be repeated for different values of f_{t+T} until one is able to construct a smooth, continuous curve through the plot of assessed points.

Although the technique's success is dependent on the precise development of a probability distribution on f_{t+T}, this dependency should not decrease its usefulness. The development of more precise probability distributions is a function of experience with the technique, probability assessments, and the effects of atypical situations.

One valuable method for increasing precision of probability distributions is keeping a journal of atypical events and their effects. The journal should include such information as the causes of a situation, when it was first recognized that the situation would arise, alternative actions available, how long the situation lasted, its effects, and the action taken. The journal will be an aid in assessing effects of subsequent situations.

The Grouped Approximation Approach

The assessment of a continuous probability distribution to f_{t+T} is not an end in itself in the problem at hand. In order to estimate the expected proportionate gain, $E(f_{t+T})$, one must first discretize the continuous probability distribution, as with the grouped approximation approach [12, 13].

This approach first identifies a set of 10 equally likely representative values from the probability distribution. The cumulative probability axis is divided into ten mutually exclusive, collectively exhaustive intervals of equal width; then the median of each interval is found. Thus the representative values are the medians of the 10 equally likely intervals—

the values of f_{t+T} associated with the 10 values .05, .15, .25, . . . , .95 on the cumulative probability axis. The analysis then proceeds as if the 10 values constitute a collectively exhaustive set of values of f_{t+T} each with an associated probability of .10.

If the ith representative value of the random variable f_{t+T} is denoted as $f_{t+T,i}$, then the expected value of the discretized distribution is found by computing:

$$E(f_{t+T}) = (.1) \sum_{i=1}^{10} f_{t+T,i}. \tag{3}$$

The term $E(f_{t+T})$ is not necessarily equal to the true expected value of f_{t+T}. However, the approximation should be sufficiently close to allow use of $E(f_{t+T})$ as computed in (3).

EXAMPLE

The product used in this study was a variety of frozen food sold in all sections of the United States. The product is perishable and expensive to store. The manufacturer makes other food products, but this study concentrated on the one frozen food.

The monthly sales of the product under study from 1965 to 1970 are shown in Fig. 1. Sales followed a seasonal pattern, with peaks during the winter months and troughs during the summer. Notice that sales more than doubled; average annual growth was 23%. This dynamic growth and large volume led management to seek a forecasting system which would allow it to better control raw material and finished product inventories.

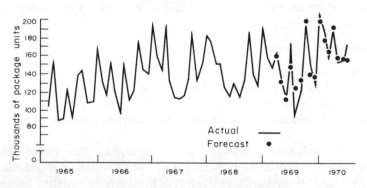

FIG. 1. Monthly sales of frozen foods, 1965–1970.

To take advantage of the seasonality of the product sales, a method similar to Winters' exponentially weighted moving average model [20] was adopted to generate monthly forecasts for the product beginning in April 1969. These forecasts were "exploded" to obtain component requirements.

Atypical Occurrences

The company recorded three atypical situations caused by price promotions of 10 cents per dozen from July 1 to August 1, 1969, November 1 to December 1, 1969, and July 1 to August 1, 1970. The price promotions were not offered to all markets; some receiving a promotion in July also received one in October and the following July, whereas others received only one in July 1969 or October or July 1970.

Glancing at Fig. 1, it appears that the promotions caused customers to stockpile the product at the expense of the period following the promotion. Perhaps customers felt that higher storage costs were offset by the lower purchase price; if so, the company did not increase its total sales volume. The shifting reduced income by 10 cents per dozen during the promotional months. Thus the firm sold the same volume of the product for the two periods, but at a lower margin of profit, so the appropriateness of the promotions must be questioned. One problem with this type of promotion is that stores might not pass on the lower cost to their customers, thereby creating a higher margin for themselves. Under such circumstances, retail demand would obviously not be influenced by the manufacturer's promotion.

Conditioning the Sales Forecast

Disregarding the reasonableness of the promotions, the company wished to adopt some method for revising their sales forecast to consider their effect. Nothing was done to condition the forecasts around the first two promotions, with an underforecast resulting during the month of the forecast and an overforecast the following month. The company was greatly concerned, since underforecasting results in stock depletion, customer dissatisfaction, and expensive raw material purchases. Over-forecasting brings about high warehouse costs for finished goods and raw materials. The results on sales were as follows:

R.I.M.E.—F

Month	Actual sales	Forecast	Percentage error
July 1969	173,724	153,390	−11
August 1969	96,851	130,558	+34
November 1969	157,005	145,003	−8
December 1969	127,027	146,286	+15
July 1970	173,733	154,961	−11

The Bayesian approach previously described was employed early in July 1970 to modify that forecast to accommodate the promotion. The company's Director of Marketing, with his staff, was led through the task of assessing a cumulative probability distribution to the assumed proportionate change in sales.

He established a range of increases in sales for July 1970 from 0% to 30%. The estimates were influenced by the increase in sales after the previous two promotions, and noting which markets were involved in all three promotions assisted the Director. He was then able to assess the probability that the percentage increase in sales for July 1970 caused by promotion would not be greater than values selected from his range. This process was repeated for different values of proportionate increase, f_{t+1}, until a smooth curve could easily be constructed through his assessed points.

The Director's assessed cumulative probability distribution for proportionate change is in Fig. 2. The distribution was then discretized by

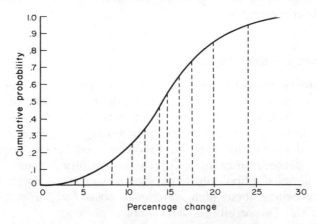

FIG. 2. The assessed cumulative probability of proportionate change, showing representative values.

dividing the cumulative probability axis into 10 mutually exclusive, collectively exhaustive, equiprobable intervals and identifying the median of each.

TABLE 1. *Representative values for the probability distribution in Fig. 2*

Probability interval	Representative value	Associated probability	Expected value
.00–.10	.040	.1	.0040
.11–.20	.081	.1	.0081
.21–.30	.104	.1	.0104
.31–.40	.120	.1	.0120
.41–.50	.135	.1	.0135
.51–.60	.148	.1	.0148
.61–.70	.160	.1	.0160
.71–.80	.175	.1	.0175
.81–.90	.200	.1	.0200
.91–1.00	.240	.1	.0240
Total			.1403

Table 1 lists the 10 representative values of Fig. 2. By considering the representative values as a mutually exclusive, collectively exhaustive set of discrete proportionate change values, each with an associated probability of .1, the expected proportionate change was .1403. Thus from (2) the forecast of sales during July 1970 was "conditioned" to reflect the Director's assumed impact of the sales promotion giving:

$$y'_{t+1} = (1.1403)y^*_{t+1}$$
$$= (1.1403)(154,961) \qquad (4)$$
$$= 176,702$$

where $y^*_{t+1} = 154,961$ is the sales forecast before conditioning for the effect of the sales promotion.

The Director concluded that sales for July 1970 could be *expected* to increase by about 14%. The revised forecast, (4), was, in an ex post facto analysis, much closer to actual sales for July 1970; it is the value the Director would use, in the absence of other relevant information, in place of his original forecast for budgeting, planning, and control.

THE INCORPORATION OF SAMPLE INFORMATION

In many instances, empirical information may be available on the impact of an impending atypical situation. For example, regular buyers from a wholesaler could be canvassed to assess their behavior if a price-cutting program were initiated; buyers of domestically manufactured radio and television equipment could be asked if they would have purchased foreign-made equipment in the absence of an import surcharge. Such sample information can be used in conjunction with management's subjective probability assessment of proportionate change to give an expected change reflecting both management's expectations and buyers' intentions.

Subjective assessments are updated with Bayes' Law to reflect sample information. As applied to this problem, if $f_{t+T,k}$ represents the kth representative value from the subjective distribution of proportionate charge, then the posterior likelihood of $f_{t+T,k}$ in light of the sample information $\bar{x}$ is:

$$P(f_{t+T,k}|\bar{x}) = \frac{P(f_{t+T,k})g^*(z_k)}{\sum\limits_{i=1}^{10} P(f_{t+T,i})g^*(z_i)} \tag{5}$$

where $g^*(z_i)$ is the Gaussian density function evaluated at $z_i = \sqrt{n}(\bar{x} - f_{t+T,i})/\sigma_x$, n is the number of customers supplying sample information, $\bar{x}$ is the mean proportionate change obtained from the customer interviews, and σ_x is the standard deviation of customer responses.

In relation to the example, regular buyers from the manufacturer were the large national grocery chains and some national wholesalers. These were easy to identify and sample. They had dealt previously with the manufacturer's promotions.

Nine prime customers were contacted; the impending sales promotion was described to them. From each, the Director obtained an estimate of the proportionate increase in the purchase order for July 1970. The mean proportionate increase was found to be 10.76%, with a standard deviation of 6.15%. (Suppose s is sufficiently close to σ_x to allow for its use in (5), even though, in this case, n was rather small.)

Table 2 shows how Bayes' Law, (5), was employed to compute a probability distribution on proportionate change reflecting management's evaluations and certain buyers' intentions. The posterior expected proportionate change was:

$$E(f_{t+T}|\bar{x}) = \sum_{i=1}^{10} (f_{t+T,i})P(f_{t+T,i}|\bar{x}) = 11.23959. \tag{6}$$

What did this analysis tell management? Management expectations exceeded buyer intentions, and the sample information served to revise

TABLE 2. *Posterior distribution to reflect the sample information*

Representative value, $f_{t+T,i}$	Priors, $P(f_{t+T,i})$	Argument, z_i, $\sqrt{n}(\bar{x} - f_{t+T,i})/\sigma$	Gaussian, $g^*(Z)^a$	Joint, $P(f_{t+T,i})g^*(Z_i)$	Posterior, $P(f_{t+T,i}\|\bar{x})$
.040	.1	3.298	.0018	.00018	.0016
.081	.1	1.293	.1730	.01730	.1520
.104	.1	0.176	.3928	.03928	.3452
.120	.1	-0.605	.3322	.03322	.2919
.135	.1	-1.337	.1640	.01640	.1441
.148	.1	-1.971	.0571	.00571	.0502
.160	.1	-2.556	.0152	.00152	.0134
.175	.1	-3.288	.0018	.00018	.0016
.200	.1	-4.507	.0000	.00000	.0000
.240	.1	-6.459	.0000	.00000	.0000
Total				.11379	1.0000

[a]Proportional to the true likelihood at each level of the representative value. However, the constant of proportionality is the same for all levels and, hence, cancels out when computing the posterior probabilities.

management's assessed value of 14.03% to a (perhaps) more realistic level of 11.24%. Thus the forecast one month following the onset of the sales promotion should be conditioned by an increase of 11.24%. Or, more formally, posterior expectations should condition the forecast by an amount $E(f_{t+1}|\bar{x})$, giving as the revised forecast:

$$y'_{t+1} = (1 + E(f_{t+1}|\bar{x}))y^*_{t+1}$$
$$= (1.1124)y^*_{t+1}$$
$$= (1.1124)(154,961)$$
$$= 172,379.$$

Conditioned forecasts were considerably closer to actual sales than the unconditioned forecast:

	Units	Error
Actual sales	173,733	
Original forecast	154,961	18,772
Forecast conditioned by management's assessments	176,702	2,969
Forecast conditioned by management's assessments and buyers' intentions	172,379	$-1,354$

Management was somewhat optimistic about the impact of the promotion, overforecasting sales by 2,969; but when assessments were revised to reflect buyer intentions, the forecast underestimated actual sales by 1,354. Both forecasts were well within the company's assumed acceptable limits of accuracy, 10% of sales. The original forecast error was 11%.

A residual benefit of using this method is that those within an organization knowledgeable about the impact of an atypical situation usually work together. Bayesian analysis is efficient for quantifying and evaluating divergent information and converting it to a single entity to relate to the decision problem. When sample information related to the problem is also available, it, too, can be incorporated into the model. Of course it is not always possible to gather such sample information. If buyers and regular customers are not readily identifiable, the decision maker will probably have to rely entirely upon his own subjective assessments.

CONCLUSIONS

This article has introduced a model which conditions a forecast in light of subjective or qualitative information, although problems of subjective probability assessment have not been treated here.

Atypical situations which can be effectively analyzed by this technique cover a broad spectrum. With a sales promotion, for example, the analysis is useful in assessing benefits and costs, perhaps based on the effects of previous promotions.

In addition to use in forecasting and promotional analysis, conditioning calls attention to unique profit opportunities or opportunities to avoid serious losses. The concept of conditioning forecasts in exceptional situations accords with the principle of management by exception.

There is still room for research and study related to atypical situations and their influence on models and model development. Marketing science needs to provide models that perform well in both atypical and typical environments. Further research must also be undertaken to study the effects of atypical influences on performance of forecasting models. It would be most valuable to study the effects of atypical situations in the presence of different trends and seasonal patterns to see how these factors relate to various patterns and volume effects.

REFERENCES

1. Brown, Robert G. *Statistical Forecasting for Inventory Control.* New York: McGraw-Hill, 1959.
2. Brown, Robert G. *Smoothing, Forecasting, and Prediction of Discrete Time Series.* Englewood Cliffs, N.J.: Prentice-Hall, 1963.
3. Buzzell, Robert D. and Charles C. Slater. "Decision Theory and Marketing Management," *Journal of Marketing,* 26 (July 1962), 7–17.
4. Churchman, C. West. *Predictions and Optimal Decisions.* Englewood Cliffs, N.J.: Prentice-Hall, 1961.
5. Enis, Ben M. and Charles L. Broom. *Marketing Decisions: A Bayesian Approach.* Scranton, Pa.: Educational Publishers, 1971.
6. Enrick, Norbert L. *Market and Sales Forecasting: A Quantitative Approach.* San Francisco: Chandler, 1969.
7. Green, Paul E. and Donald S. Tull. *Research for Marketing Decisions.* Englewood Cliffs, N.J.: Prentice-Hall, 1966.
8. Harper, Marion, Jr. "A New Profession to Aid Marketing Management," *Journal of Marketing,* 25 (January 1961), 1–7.
9. Howard, Ronald A. "Decision Analysis: Applied Decision Theory," *Proceedings.* Fourth International Conference on Operational Research, 1966, 2-1–2-18.
10. Howard, Ronald A. "The Science of Decision Making," working paper, Institute in Engineering-Economic Systems, Stanford University, 1968.
11. Mendenhall, William and James E. Reinmuth. *Statistics for Management and Economics.* Belmont, Calif.: Duxbury, 1971.
12. Reinmuth, James E. "Probability Assessment for a Continuous State Variable," working paper, College of Business Administration, University of Oregon, 1970.
13. Schlaifer, Robert. *Analysis of Decisions under Uncertainty.* New York: McGraw-Hill, 1969.
14. Strassman, Paul A. "Forecasting Considerations in Design of Management Information Systems," *Management Accounting,* 46 (February 1965), 27–40.
15. Suits, Daniel B. "Forecasting and Analysis with an Econometric Model," *American Economic Review,* 52 (March 1962), 104–32.
16. Thiel, Henri. *Economic Forecasts and Policy,* second edition. Amsterdam: North-Holland, 1961.
17. Tull, Donald S. and Gerald Albaum. "Decision Processes and the Value of Information," *Oregon Business Review,* 30 (April 1971), 1–3.
18. Whiteman, Irvin R. "Improved Forecasting Through Feedback," *Journal of Marketing,* 30 (April 1966), 45–51.
19. Winkler, Robert L. "The Assessment of Prior Distributions in Bayesian Analysis," *Journal of the American Statistical Association,* 62 (September 1967), 776–800.
20. Winters, Peter R. "Forecasting Sales by Exponential Weighted Moving Averages," *Management Science,* 6 (April 1960), 324–42.

4

Some Equilibrium Models of Consumer Behavior

R. G. GOLLEDGE*

The search for equilibrium solutions for spatial problems has been an active one for obvious reasons. Not only do they provide theoretical norms against which departures are measured, but they generally provide unique solutions to problems—solutions which are objectively derived and provide a mathematical terminating point for some iterative processes. Equilibrium solutions are also sought because they allow the construction of meaningful spatial systems, whether the systems be of cities, industrial plants, or urban functions. Once an equilibrium solution is obtained, and its spatial manifestations noted, it is possible to make generalizations or construct spatial theory about the phenomena being examined.

The emphasis of this paper will be on a selection of behavioral models which can produce spatial equilibrium outputs. Since this is itself a wide area covering many of the behavioral sciences, emphasis is placed on consumer behavior and its equilibrium situations.

BEHAVIORAL EQUILIBRIUM AND SPATIAL EQUILIBRIUM

It is as well at this point to define the two basic concepts around which the paper is built. The concept of equilibrium implies a balance of forces which produces a stable state in a system. Behavioral equilibrium implies that a condition of homeostasis exists, and that behavior is repetitive and invariant within some set of limits; that is, at successive periods of observation there is no net change of behavior. Of course the problem inherent in this definition is to define the extent of the "periods of observation"; in fact this is a key point in distinguishing between static and dynamic behavior, and between equilibrium and nonequilibrium behavior.

Spatial equilibrium is also a condition of balance or stability typified by

*From *Economic Geography*, Vol. 46, No. 2 (Supplement), 1970, pp. 417–424. Reproduced by permission.

no net change between successive observation periods. It has been defined with respect to the location of producers,* for flows between regions [7, 28], for patterns of urban places [29], and for the actions of individuals [36, 21]. This paper focuses on the latter situation.

TYPES OF EQUILIBRIUM BEHAVIOR

Kotler [25] has summarized a number of different types of behavior that typify consumers. He also points out that the way producers classify consumers influences their marketing strategies. Since the types of behavior with which geographers have generally dealt have been limited, some comment on these behaviors and their equilibrium positions are relevant.

The most extensively used behavior type according to Kotler is *Marshallian*. This consumer is regarded as an "economic calculating machine" who reacts instantaneously to changes in quantity and price. This is economic man in all his glory. Equilibrium behavior is obtained when maximum utility is gained from a limited set of resources given fixed quantities, qualities, and prices of goods. Spatially this equilibrium is represented by a system of discrete market areas.

Another type of behavior, little used in geography, is *Pavlovian*. This consumer is stimulus prone, is conditioned to respond to cues such as advertising, and his behavior responds to positive reinforcement (reward) by developing habits, and to negative reinforcement (nonreward) by extinguishing responses. Equilibrium behavior in this case occurs when the consumer becomes a creature of habit, whose stereotyped responses are rigid, repetitive, and complacent. The spatial development of this type of behavior has been summarized by Golledge [12].

Motivational research in marketing has unearthed the *Freudian* consumer. This individual is fantasy prone and relies heavily on stimuli such as the packaging of goods and methods of advertising in selecting places of patronage. It is more difficult to define an equilibrium behavior for this consumer, for his reliance on stimuli which vary constantly can produce only short-run regularities in his spatial behavior.

Social psychologists have produced abundant evidence that factors such as peer-group pressures, attitude, residence location, occupation, and life-cycle stage exert their greatest influence on a group of consumers that Kotler calls *Veblenian.*This type of individual is an extremely useful

---

*Many references are summarized in B. H. Stevens and C. A. Brackett [39].

one for geographers to study. He patronizes places that others in his "group" patronize, and he buys a mix of goods which is common to the whole class to which he belongs. His equilibrium behavior is tied in with his aspiration level and group membership. Behavior attributed to such an individual can represent the behavior expected of a substantial group of people—which of course is most useful for model building purposes.

Perhaps another type of behavior that can be added to this list is that discussed by Festinger [10]. This type of consumer selects patronage patterns that minimize the amount of dissonant feeling following specific acts. In a sense this parallels the idea of minimum regret in game theory. Equilibrium behavior occurs when the courses of action that minimize dissonance are discovered.

In addition to these types of behavior we can add *spatially rational man.* This individual has some credence as a behaving organism—he selects paths of least effort or minimum aggregate distance, he can hold a hierarchy of preferences for routes and move down his preference ranking as barriers occur in his most preferred route. In moving through space this individual may use combinations of transportation types. The selection of paths of movement is always rational because he always patronizes those places which are *perceived* to be nearest, or perceived to involve least effort. Changes in behavior occur only after learning has taken place, i.e., as more information is dispensed to him. Changes of behavior are deliberate attempts to eliminate spatially irrational acts. Equilibrium behavior may be a strict compliance with real-world least effort principles. This consumer may exhibit Lösch's single choice syndrome, or he may become a creature of habit but a multiple patronizer.

It should be apparent by now that different types of behavior will produce different types of spatial equilibria. The patterns produced by a Veblenian consumer may bear little relation to that produced by economic or spatially rational man. It is also reasonable to assume that locational and marketing strategies of sellers will vary depending on how they perceive their consumers. For example the seller who regards his buyers as Marshallian calculating machines will be price conscious, will seek locations which allow him to compete favorably, and will manipulate prices at his location in order to penetrate adjacent marketing areas. However, if he views buyers as creatures of habit, he may accept a less than economically optimum location, attract spatially rational customers, and not engage in aggressive marketing policies. The equilibrium situation for producers will therefore depend partly on the consumer attitude that they adopt.

Quite obviously the range of models that could be used to produce one or another of these spatial equilibrium outputs is large. Some of these are explained below.

BEHAVIORAL MODELS WITH SPATIAL EQUILIBRIUM OUTPUTS

Place-loyalty Model

The place-loyalty model typifies classic market area analysis. In this model consumers scattered in space develop a strong preference or habit for patronizing one place to the exclusion of others. Generally consumers are both economically and spatially rational men who operate under conditions of least effort movement, where "effort" is measured in terms of additions to the base price of goods occasioned by movement. A market situation of place-loyal buyers is essentially what is described by Fetter, Hyson, Reilly, Ackley, Smithies, Cournot, and others. Given a three market situation (with places *A*, *B*, and *C*), the patronage vector would be one of the following: (1.0, 0.0, 0.0); (0.0, 1.0, 0.0); or (0.0, 0.0, 1.0). For multiple market situations, the spatial models of Christaller [6], Lösch [29], Isard [20], and Mills and Lav [32] describe the equilibrium situations that result.

Market-share Models

Single Vector Model

The essence of a market-share model is that it acknowledges that both response uncertainty and response change can occur in an equilibrium situation, so it uses probabilities to specify the proportion of times each feasible alternative is patronized. These models can be constructed for individuals by examining the frequency of selection of alternative places, or they can be constructed for groups of people by averaging the proportion of times people patronize places. If behavioral information is not available, surrogate information, such as characteristics of the stores themselves, are used to allocate patronage. The output from such models is a constant probability vector of the form (.75, .20, .05).

Huff has provided a variety of spatial interpretations of this type of model, calculating gradients of probability about centers, and specifying points of equal probability as market area boundaries [18]. In this model it is assumed that any individual has the possibility of sharing his patronage among markets, but that he complies with the notions of mathematical transitivity, i.e., his preferences are $A > B > C$, but this preference ordering is subject to random fluctuations on individual trips as long as the fluctuations do not violate the constant probability vector. The principal shortcoming of this type of model is that it rarely examines how the market-sharing principle was established, and it presents an equilibrium solution without knowing if the consumers *are* in equilibrium. That is, its vector elements are produced by cross-sectional data which may or may not be a true indication of spatial equilibrium conditions.

Switching and Staying (Markov) Models

Habit-persistence models of equilibrium behavior are based on the assumption that places are patronized more out of habit than by any conscious preference behavior, and that the patronage habit evolves as a result of learning. In this type of model, initial behavior is modified by the strength of rewards associated with trial and error responses. Rewarded responses are strengthened, nonrewarded responses are extinguished. In its simplest format this is similar to the single vector model except that the equilibrium vector is justified by reference to changes in responses through time. Gould's study of wheat growing on Kilimanjaro is an example of this type of behavioral model [*14*].

The more general form of this model is a first-order Markov model in which the state of equilibrium is described by stable-state proportions. The model attempts to summarize the "switching and staying" tendencies either of individuals or populations for successive time intervals. A matrix of transition probabilities for any two time periods might be as follows:

$$
\begin{array}{c c c c}
 & A_{t+1} & B_{t+1} & C_{t+1} \\
A_t & \begin{bmatrix} .75 \\ .48 \\ .55 \end{bmatrix} & \begin{matrix} .20 \\ .40 \\ .25 \end{matrix} & \begin{matrix} .05 \\ .12 \\ .20 \end{matrix} \\
B_t & & & \\
C_t & & &
\end{array}
$$

This would allow us to infer that if A was chosen at time t, the probability of choosing B or C at $t + 1$ would be .20 and .05, respectively. However, if say C was chosen at t_1 the choice would be repeated with a probability of .20 at $t + 1$, and A and B's probabilities would be revised to .55 and .25, respectively. The advantage of this type of market-share procedure is that an equilibrium situation *evolves* from some initial patronage configuration, and by analyzing this evolution, comments can be made on the speed of convergence towards equilibrium, the number of trials before equilibrium, the mean first passage times, and so on [8]. By concentrating on the effect of last patronage on next patronage probabilities, implicit recognition is given to the role of learning and experience as factors producing a state of equilibrium. Spatially, this equilibrium is difficult to portray except in the form of desire lines or directed graphs with magnitude values attached to the links.

Learning Models

Beginning with the work of psychologists Bush and Mosteller, linear operator learning models have received an increasing amount of attention as models which can produce spatial equilibrium conditions of behavior [4]. These models include one-element and two-element linear models. In the one-element case, reward and nonreward (or punishment) are presumed to have the same effects on behavior, and changes in behavior are described in terms of a first-order-difference equation of the form:

$$p_{n+1} = p_n + (1 - \alpha)(1 - p_n)$$

where p_{n+1} = probability of selecting alternative i on trial $n + 1$

α = a fraction representing the rate at which "error" probability is reduced on successive trials.

This model assumes that the probability of a response i on trial $n + 1$ is the sum of the probability of response i on trial n, and an increment proportional to the maximum possible increase $(1 - p_{i,n})$.

In this model $p_{i,n}$ is established either by empirical observation of the number of trials on which place i is patronized by members of a sample group at time n, or is preset using Bayesian estimators. The learning parameter α governs the increment value between time periods, i.e., it determines the rate of approach to asymptotic (equilibrium) behavior. In learning models this is generally defined as a function of the number of trials before a "successful" reply. In the Bush and Mosteller cases, values of α are tabled [4, p. 339].

A more comprehensive model of this type is the two-element model which argues that different results occur with reward (success) and nonreward (failure). The general form of the two-element model is:

$$p_{n+1} = \begin{cases} \alpha_1 p_n + (1 - \alpha_1)\lambda_1 \\ \alpha_2 p_n + (1 - \alpha_2)\lambda_2 \end{cases}$$

where p_{n+1} is the probability of patronizing a place on trial $n + 1$

 α_1 is a parameter describing the rate at which p_n is incremented if a trip is successful (i.e., if any penalty is "avoided")

 α_2 is a parameter describing the rate at which p_n is incremented if a trip is unsuccessful (i.e., if a penalty occurs)

 λ is an asymptotic value for success probability.

As summarized by Kuehn, the application of this model results in an upper and lower limit being placed on the probabilities of patronizing place i such that the calculated probabilities will reach some maximum value, or tend towards a minimum value which approaches but never reaches zero [27]. Kotler has reproduced a diagram of Kuehn's which summarizes this tendency [26]. In this case (Fig. 1) the two operators are labeled "purchase" (λ_1) and "rejection" (λ_2). The upper limit of $p_i(\lambda_i)$ is given by the point at which the "purchase" operator and a line showing a one-to-one correspondence between (p_n) and (p_{n+1}) intersect. This diagram infers that learning is "incomplete," i.e., that no matter how frequently i is patronized, some small probability of going elsewhere is retained. It can be noted that the lines representing the effects of the two operators are parallel and linear; parallel so that the operator probabilities sum to one, and linear so that the estimation of their path is simplified.

Perhaps the single largest problem with this type of model is that it is

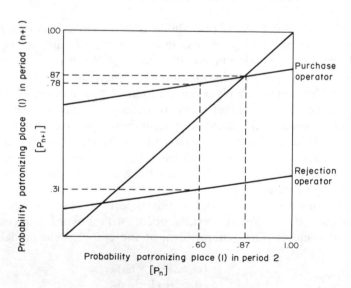

FIG. 1.

one directional with respect to patronage, i.e., patronage always increases the habit of going to place *i*, and only nonpatronage limits this habit formation. In other words a patronage trip that is "unsatisfactory" still increases the probability of patronizing a place.

The spatial manifestations of these behaviors are again difficult to represent. Golledge has previously argued that for any given area it is highly unlikely that a *single* map or spatial diagram can be compiled, because it is probable that in the resident population there will be some individuals in the initial search phases of behavior, some with partly formed behavior (i.e., those not at an equilibrium stage), and others with well-formed habits that represent equilibrium [12]. Thus these models for the most part describe individual behaviors and as Harvey and King have pointed out, the problems have not been solved [16, 23]. In a sense then, given patronage data over time, such models could determine those persons in a population who have reached an equilibrium state, and the spatial manifestations of these states could be examined. This appears to be an area of spatial equilibrium analysis which is as yet underdeveloped.

Stochastic Perceptual Models

Research in the field of marketing has produced a stochastic perceptual model which can produce a short-term equilibrium state of behavior based on the average market perception of places [26]. Basically for any selection of places (*A*, *B*, *C*) information is derived concerning the dimensions which influence choice of a place. The information is generally collected using a rating scale, and the rating of each place for groups of people is summed and normalized. For example, Table 1 reports variables listed as the dominant ones influencing the choice of shopping centers in Columbus, Ohio.

TABLE 1. *Shopping center utilities in North Columbus, June 1967*

Variable	Proportion of times ranked first
Closeness	35.7
Variety of stores	28.7
Quality of products	10.2
Parking	8.9
Price comparability	4.8
Quality of service	2.0
Freeway access	1.7
Others	8.0

The relative frequencies with which each "dimension" (variable) occurs defines a response vector for a population which remains stable through all operations. Each place considered a feasible alternative for the population is then rated on the basis of each dimension, and a matrix of rating scores is compiled. By normalizing each row, we define the relative attraction of each place on each dimension—the greater the attraction a place has on any dimension, the greater is this score, Table 2.

TABLE 2. *Hypothetical attraction*

	North-land	East-land	West-land
Distance from home	.39	.27	.34
Number of stores	.34	.33	.33
Parking	.35	.33	.32
Quality of service	.33	.34	.33
Proximity to freeway	.36	.33	.31
Frequency of bus service	.22	.45	.33
Prices	.50	.30	.20

To operate this model, the response row vector and the transformed rating scale matrix are multiplied, giving a vector output which specifies the probabilities of going to each of the three centers.

In a sense the output from a manipulation of this type represents a market-share output, and this might be regarded as a short-run equilibrium solution. The output is interpreted as specifying the proportions of a given *population* which will patronize each center, but it does not specify *which people* will patronize which center unless the original individual rating scales are manipulated for each person. In this way a map similar to that produced by Huff-type models would result.

Interpreting the model in this way, however, imposes an equilibrium situation which may be *very* temporary. The purpose of the model is to allow the "mix-matrix" to vary at each time period. In this way temporal variations of things such as prices and service quality can be reappraised at each period. The result may be an alteration of the vector output for each time period analyzed.

SUMMARY

The volume of research into general equilibrium models continues to be large in all fields of the social and behavioral sciences. The search for spatial equilibrium models is no less active. Some small success seems promised with continued use of behavioral models. Any success in this area will complement the successes already achieved using econometric models.

This paper has concentrated on only a few of the types of models being used to examine the development of equilibrium behaviors. No mention has been made of the rather extensive applications of gaming and choice models in analyzing the decision processes which produce equilibrium behaviors; this could warrant a completely separate paper. I have also neglected the voluminous literature in statistics and economics which has been concerned with defining and stabilizing the utilities associated with decision making. Some of these approaches—notably those using Bayesian methods—have been summarized elsewhere [24].

The examination of different types of behavior has indicated that most equilibrium models can only be expected to explain a small part of the actual behavior of populations. Herein lies a challenge for the geographer—to determine the spatial patterns of different types of behavior, to build appropriate models, and to state explicitly what proportion of a randomly sampled population's behavior can be explained by the model.

LITERATURE CITED

1. Arrow, K. J. and L. Hurwicz. "On the Stability of the Competitive Equilibrium I and II," *Econometrica*, 26 (1958), pp. 522–54; and 27 (1959), pp. 82–109.
2. Arrow, K. J. and M. McManus. "A Note on Dynamic Stability," *Econometrica*, 26 (1958), pp. 448–54.
3. Atkinson, R., Bowers, and Crothers. *An Introduction to Mathematical Learning Theory.* New York: John Wiley & Sons, 1965.
4. Bush, R. R. and F. Mosteller. *Stochastic Models for Learning.* New York: John Wiley & Sons, 1954.
5. Chamberlin, E. *The Theory of Monopolistic Competition.* Cambridge, Mass.: Harvard University Press, 1962.
6. Christaller, W. *Central Places in Southern Germany.* Translated by C. Baskin. Englewood Cliffs: Prentice-Hall, 1966.
7. Enke, S. "Equilibrium Among Spatially Separated Markets: Solution by Electric Analog," *Econometrica*, 19 (1951), pp. 40–67.
8. Feller, W. *An Introduction to Probability Theory and Its Applications.* New York: John Wiley & Sons, 1950.
9. Ferguson, C. E. and R. W. Pfouts. "Learning and Expectations in Dynamic Duopoly Behavior," *Behavioral Science*, 7 (April, 1962).
10. Festinger, L., *et al. Conflict, Decision and Dissonance.* Stanford: Stanford University Press, 1964.
11. Fetter, F. A. "The Economic Law of Market Areas." *Quarterly Journal of Economics*, 38 (1924).
12. Golledge, R. G. "Conceptualizing The Market Decision Process," *Journal of Regional Science*, 7 (Supplement) (Winter, 1967), pp. 239–58.

13. Golledge, R. G. and L. Brown. "Search, Learning, and the Market Decision Process," *Geografiska Annaler* (1968).
14. Gould, P. "Wheat on Kilimanjaro: the Perception of Choice within Game and Learning Model Frameworks," *General Systems Yearbook*, 10 (1965), pp. 157–66.
15. Haines, G. H., Jr. "A Theory of Market Behavior After Innovation," *Management Science*, 10 (1964).
16. Harvey, David. "Behavioral Postulates and the Construction of Theory in Human Geography." Department of Geography, Bristol University, Seminar Paper No. 6, 1967.
17. Hotelling, H. "Stability in Competition," *Economic Journal*, 39 (1929), pp. 41–57.
18. Huff, D. "A Probabilistic Analysis of Shopping Center Trade Areas." *Land Economics* (February, 1963), pp. 81–96.
19. Hyson, W. P. and C. D. "The Economic Law of Market Areas," *Quarterly Journal of Economics*, 44 (1950), pp. 319–27.
20. Isard, W. *Location and Space Economy.* Cambridge: MIT Press, 1956.
21. Isard, W. and M. Dacey. "On the Projections of Individual Behavior Part I," *Journal of Regional Science*, 4 (1962).
22. Johnson, H. L. and A. M. Cohen, "Experiments in Behavioral Economics: Siegel and Fourker Revisited," *Behavioral Science*, 12 (September, 1967), pp. 353–72.
23. King, L. J. "The Analysis of Spatial Form and its Relation to Geographic Theory," *Annals, Association of American Geographers*, 59 (1969), pp. 573–95.
24. King, L. J. and R. G. Golledge. *Bayesian Analysis and Models in Geographic Research.* University of Iowa, Department of Geography, Discussion Paper No. 12, 1969.
25. Kotler, P. "Behavioral Models for Analyzing Buyers," *Journal of Marketing*, 29 (1965), pp. 37–45.
26. Kotler, P. "Mathematical Models of Individual Buyer Behavior," *Behavioral Science*, 13 (1968), pp. 247–87.
27. Kuehn, A. A. "A Model for Budget Advertising," *Mathematical Models and Methods in Marketing.* Edited by F. M. Bass. Homewood, Ill.: R. D. Irwin, 1961. pp. 302–56.
28. Lefeber, L. "General Equilibrium Analysis of Production, Transportation, and the Choice of Industrial Location," *Papers and Proceedings of the Regional Science Association*, 4 (1958), pp. 77–85.
29. Lösch, A. *The Economics of Location.* New Haven: Yale University Press, 1954.
30. Machlup, F. "Theories of the Firm: Marginalist, Behavioral, Managerial," *American Economic Review*, 57 (1967), pp. 1–33.
31. Mayberry, J. P., J. N. Nash, and M. Shubek. "A Comparison of Treatments of a Duopoly Situation," *Econometrica*, 21 (1953), pp. 141–54.
32. Mills, E. and Lav. "A Model of Market Areas with Free Entry," *Journal of Political Economy* (June, 1964), pp. 278–88.
33. Pfouts, R. W. and C. E. Fergusen. "Learning and Expectations in Dynamic Duopoly Behavior," *Behavioral Science*, 7 (1962), pp. 223–37.
34. Pred, A. *Behavior and Location: Foundations for a Geographic and Dynamic Location Theory, Part I.* Lund Studies in Geography, Ser. B, Human Geography, No. 27 (1967).
35. Pred, A. *Behavior and Location: Foundations for a Geographic and Dynamic Location Theory, Part II.* Lund Studies in Geography, Ser. B, Human Geography, No. 28 (1969).
36. Rumkel, P. J. and D. P. Peizer. "Two-Valued Orientation of Current Equilibrium Theory," *Behavioral Science*, 13 (January, 1968).
37. Smithies, A. and L. J. Savage. "A Dynamic Problem in Duopoly," *Econometrica*, 13 (1940), pp. 130–43.
38. Smithies, A. and L. J. Savage. "Optimum Location in Spatial Competition," *Journal of Political Economy*, 44 (June, 1941), pp. 423–39.
39. Stevens, B. H. and C. A. Brackett. *Industrial Location Bibliography.* Philadelphia, Regional Science Research Institute, 1967.

5

New Product Demand Estimation in the Pharmaceutical Industry*

Stuart A. Samuels

THE PHARMACEUTICAL INDUSTRY

The pharmaceutical industry consists of two rather distinct, heterogeneous segments: 1) An ethical segment and 2) A proprietary segment. The average consumer comes in frequent contact with both segments of the industry without usually realizing the differences, which are significant. The ethical segment is so named and defined because of the manner in which its products are promoted (rather than the way in which the products are used). Ethical pharmaceutical products, which usually but do not necessarily require a prescription, are promoted exclusively to the physician through the media of direct mail, journal advertising in medical books, and personal selling. The proprietary portion of the industry, many times larger in dollar volume, is characterized by products which are promoted to the general public through the so-called mass media of television and radio and do not require a prescription. This paper will concentrate exclusively on a problem in the ethical segment of the industry and future references to the pharmaceutical industry will assume this orientation.

The industry is fortunate in having an abundance of data available. Yet in many cases, this wealth of information can be more of a detriment than an aid to good management decision-making. Unless properly analyzed, these data can be overwhelming and confusing.

For the very good or extremely poor products, the necessary decisions will usually be apparent. However, most products tend to fall in the "grey

*From American Statistical Association, *1969 Proceedings of the Business and Economic Statistics Section*, pp. 334–340. Reproduced by permission.

159

area" between boom and bust where the required courses of action are much more difficult to assess. It is in these cases that the data available tend to be conflicting and inconclusive. Wholesale sales may be increasing while retail prescriptions are decreasing. Doctors' awareness of the product may be high but new patients starting on the product are lower than expected. With information also being received from district and regional sales management, the likelihood of a definite pattern being perceived is small.

It is within this framework that the development of a new product forecasting model was initiated. The basic objective was to construct a model for predicting prescription levels of new pharmaceutical products one year after introduction. These forecasts were to be based on data available from the market research services during the first three months following product introduction. The likelihood of achieving this objective was initially investigated during a feasibility study, since there was no prior empirical evidence that the types of predictions required could indeed be made. As a result of the feasibility study, it was decided to proceed with fullscale development of the model.

METHODOLOGY

Several alternate methodologies were evaluated for constructing the forecasting model with least squares multiple regression analysis ultimately chosen. The particular type of regression analysis employed was cross-sectional rather than aggregative time series, with the unit of association being the product rather than time. Obviously, the latter type of regression analysis would have been inappropriate with only one, two, or three months' data available as a base for projection.

Within this cross-sectional framework, several alternate methods were available for constructing a data base. A forecasting model could have been developed predicated on all new products introduced by the client company over the past several years or on all products introduced in a given therapeutic or product class with a prespecified time period.

Another method for developing a data base would have been to use all new products introduced in the industry over a specified period of time, regardless of the company or product class involved.

After careful evaluation of each approach and a thorough investigation of available data, the third alternative was selected for creating the data base.

This alternative offers several advantages. First, a sufficient number of products would be available to provide statistical significance for the regression analysis. Secondly, since many different product classes would be represented, the forecasting model ultimately developed could be utilized for virtually any kind of product the client company contemplated introducing. Finally, the forecasting model would have the valuable advantage of being able to predict the future demand of competing products as well.

After consultation with the client company, it was decided to use all new pharmaceutical products introduced between January, 1961, and August, 1963. It was estimated that there were approximately 90 new products introduced during this period. However, because of data limitations and the decision to include only "major introductions" in the study, the final data base consisted of 49 new products.

VARIABLES

Once the decisions regarding the data base had been finalized, it was possible to begin gathering information on the basic variables which would ultimately be investigated with least squares multiple regression analysis. As was mentioned at the outset, there is a great deal of accessible data in the pharmaceutical industry. From this abundance of information and after some preliminary computer analysis, it was determined that two basic variables would be employed as dependent variables: 1) Fourth Quarter Product New Prescriptions—Prescriptions written by physicians and audited in drug stores during the tenth to twelfth month after introduction of the product, and 2) Annual Product New Prescriptions—Prescriptions defined as above but occurring between month 4 and month 15 after product introduction.

The many possible independent variables can be classified into several general categories:

1. Demand Generation Variables
2. Actual Market Activity Variables
3. Attitude and Awareness Variables

DEVELOPMENT OF THE FINAL MODEL

Construction of the final model for predicting both Fourth Quarter Product New *Rx*'s and Annual Product.

New *Rx*'s was accomplished by successive experimentation with sets of the independent variables. In effect, a large number of different least squares multiple regression equations were investigated. However, it should be noted that in no instance was this experimentation performed in a purely mechanistic fashion. The sets of independent variables chosen for evaluation were determined by detailed analysis of prior computer runs and by specification of known or suspected relationships between the variable in question and the quantity being estimated.

The major criterion for the retention of an independent variable in the final models was its ability to explain residual variance in the variable to be predicted.

This procedure was facilitated by the use of a step-wise regression approach. In general, the criterion for evaluating the many regression equations investigated was the coefficient of multiple determination. Equations which exhibited a high R^2 were considered good candidates for further analysis and modification.

Other criteria were also employed. The signs of the regression coefficients were examined to insure that they were not illogical and that the indicated relationships could be expected to persist in the future. The significance of the regression coefficients was also evaluated. (Various interpretations of significance have been adopted by different authors. A recent article by Hartovsky indicated that maximization of "R^2" is associated with the retention of variables whose associated t-statistic is greater than 1.[1] In retrospect, this procedure was adopted in almost every case.)

Through the process of experimentation, an evaluation of the three categories of marketing research data with respect to their ability to forecast the dependent variable was provided. In general, actual market activity variables were better predictors of future demand than were demand generation and attitude and awareness data.

However, because of the high degree of multicollinearity between many of the market activity variables, the final models contained variables other than these.

THE FINAL MODELS

After exhaustive experimentation the final models, consisting of six independent variables each, were formulated, with the same six indepen-

---

[1]Hartovsky, Joel. "A Note on the Maximization of R^2," *The American Statistician*, 23, No. 1, February, 1969.

dent variables being employed with both models. An illustration of the form of these models is indicated in Tables 1 and 2.

TABLE 1. *Month 3 model for estimating Fourth Quarter New Rx's*

Variables

Y = Fourth Quarter New Rx's

Market activity variables

X_1 = Product New Rx's—Month 3
X_2 = Market Share of New Rx's—Month 3
X_3 = Market Share of Product Appearances—Month 3
X_4 = Product Class Appearances
X_5 = Change in Market Share of Product New Rx's

Demand generating variable

X_6 = Cumulative Direct Mail Expenditures
$Y = -83.059 + 1.349X_1 + 1.386X_2 + 58.382X_3 + 0.969X_4 + 31.598X_5 + 0.614X_6$
$R^2 = 0.84$

TABLE 2. *Month 3 model for estimating annual new Rx's*

Variables

Y = Annual New Rx's
$X_1, \ldots X_6$ = Same Variables as in Table 1
$Y = -239.863 + 8.468X_1 + 3.810X_2 + 122.422X_3 + 2.049X_4 + 98.347X_5 + 0.417X_6$
$R^2 = 0.91$

A DIAGNOSTIC SYSTEM

In any forecasting situation there exists the condition that an initial estimate is made of a variable activity (in this case prescriptions of a new product) *at* some point in time (three months after introduction) *of* some future point in time (twelve months). At the the time this forecast is made, it represents the best estimate of the future event. Such a forecast is, however, static in nature; it does not contain any mechanism for re-evaluation as further information becomes available between the third and twelfth months. This period between the time at which the forecast is made and for which the forecast is made should not be considered a vacuum. As time evolves, the initial forecast should be constantly re-evaluated in light of any new information available and current circumstances.

It is for this reason that a diagnostic system was developed as an extension to and an integral part of the basic Month 3 models. Two alternate approaches were investigated for constructing the diagnostic system. The first consisted of analyzing the deviations between actual product new prescriptions at periods of 5, 7 and 9 months and predictions of these quantities rendered as a part of the basic Month 3 models. It was hoped that from this analysis a correction factor could be derived to modify the Month 3 forecast of Fourth Quarter Product New *Rx*'s. However, the deviations between actual and predicted prescriptions at the intermediate time points exhibited virtually no correlation with the deviations between the Month 3 prediction and actual Fourth Quarter Product New *Rx*'s. Therefore, this orientation was abandoned in favor of another method.

In the second approach, separate forecasting models were constructed for predicting Fourth Quarter Product New *Rx*'s at Month 5, 7, and Month 9. In each case, the same basic methodology was employed as was utilized in developing the Month 3 models. An illustration of the type of model which evolved from this analysis is given in Table 3.

TABLE 3. *Month 7 model for estimating Fourth Quarter New Rx's*

Variables

Y = Fourth Quarter New *Rx*'s
X_1 = Cumulative Direct Mail
X_2 = Cumulative Product New *Rx*'s
X_3 = Market Share of New *Rx*'s—Month 7
X_4 = Change in Market Share of Product Appearances
$Y = -35.620 + 0.311X_1 + 0.651X_2 + 3.484X_3 + 1.86X_4$
$R^2 = 0.84$

USE OF THE FORECASTING SYSTEM

The fundamental purposes of any forecasting system are to provide management with the basis for constructing sound future plans for making timely decisions.

It is important to note that forecasts such as these (Fourth Quarter Product New *Rx*'s and Annual Product New *Rx*'s), or any forecasts, are based on an assumption of persistence in the historical relationship between these variables and factors observable in the early months after a new product's introduction. If these relationships do indeed persist, the predictions *would* prove to be accurate. For a prediction 12 months hence, the basic purpose of a forecasting model is for management planning rather than for day-to-day operating decisions. This type of appraisal of future prospects, if accurate, and *if it is used*, has obvious value in such areas as financial planning, capital appropriations, timing purchases, setting production and inventory levels and directing various types of marketing effort.

Further, the models provide, as an auxiliary benefit, an evaluation of the various data sources available to marketing management regarding new pharmaceutical products. As an illustration, the study demonstrated that actual market activity variables were the most relevant in predicting future product success or failure.

The basic Month 3 forecasts can be considered as an "early warning system", designed primarily to alert management very early in the life of a new product to the longer range prospects for that product.

If a forecast generated by the model indicates that sales will be significantly lower or higher than management's prior anticipation of sales, then what should be done? Obviously, it would be very naive to suggest that marketing plans based on extensive collective judgment should be radically changed because of this single prediction. This is where the concept of a new product forecasting *system* is particularly relevant.

For operational decision-making, it may be advisable to establish control limits for predicted Fourth Quarter Product New *Rx*'s based on third month data (plus or minus 20%, say). Then in the fifth or seventh month, actions would be based upon where the reforecasted sales fell relative to these control limits. For example, if in the third month the Fourth Quarter Product New *Rx*'s forecasts placed the product in a size class which agreed with marketing management's prior judgments, no particular departures from current operating procedures would be indicated. On the other hand, if in the fifth month, the forecasts dropped below the lower control limit for Fourth Quarter Prescriptions, the inference would be that if present courses of action were continued, a lower-than-initially-predicted level of demand would be achieved. Points falling above or below established control limits would indicate so-called "assignable causes of variation". Returning to the situation where the fifth month prediction fell below the lower control limit, various remedial courses of action might be considered *depending upon a careful diagnosis of the cause or causes of variation.* These might include a change in advertising emphasis toward a different product characteristic, an attempt to reach a somewhat different group of physicians, increases or decreases in promotional dollars predicated on revised assessments of product potential, changes in advertising copy, revisions in the amount of personal selling time allocated to the product, and so forth.

Analogously, if a point falls above control limits, a diagnosis of the reasons for this unusually good variation might indicate that an unexpectedly good product has been introduced. If this can be properly diagnosed, the reasons for increased sales would be spotlighted, and even more intensified activity might be given in the appropriate directions. The main point is that a forecasting system could function as the basis for a comprehensive marketing control, diagnosis, and decision system.

In addition, the ability to forecast the sales of competitors' products offers marketing management a valuable decision-making tool. An early indication of competitor market penetration can be a significant aid in planning retaliatory marketing strategies and in assessing the value of competing promotional tactics for new products.

CONCLUSION

Although the new product forecasting model was never intended to identify the "assignable causes of variation", it can at the very least signal the need for additional market and product analysis. The system cannot tell marketing management *what to do*. However, *it can deliver considerable insight into current courses of action* and would aid in instituting a management exception system—indicating when changes in present programs might be advisable because of either unusually high or low estimates of future sales. Thus the model may be viewed as a valuable supplement to existing forecasting and evaluation procedures—a tool for use in "confirming" or "casting doubt" on existing or prior intuitive judgment. It provides a more systematic and objective analysis of data already in existence and is designed to reduce, to as great a degree as possible, the uncertainty associated with these various information sources. The model can therefore furnish marketing management with a more concise and accurate interpretation of future product worth.

PART III

Production and Cost

Introduction

From his first principles course, any economics student worth his supply and demand will find, especially in microeconomic theory, that a fundamental area of inquiry of the discipline is that which is involved with weighing the benefits of an action against the costs incurred in achieving these benefits. The "economic man" assumption, based on the maximization of utility, has its counterpart in the production process; specifically, to maximize output net of the costs of producing that output.

The net benefit thereby derived provides an indicator of the productivity and efficiency of the production process, the latter criterion more accurately being indicative of the degree to which costs are being minimized "net" of benefits. Accordingly, the output of a firm and the costs incurred in producing that output are complementary aspects of the production process; a discussion of one suffers from the exclusion of the other.

In the last quarter of the eighteenth century, when the Industrial Revolution was gaining momentum in England, production theory as we know it today was in its infancy. Although Adam Smith extended the concept of production to the factory system, production was viewed largely in terms of agricultural output. It was not a happy subject. Its study by Ricardo and Malthus and their resultant pessimistic conclusions prompted Carlyle to brand the whole of economics "the dismal science."

SUMMARIES OF ARTICLES IN PART III
AND COMMENTS

Article 1

Peter J. Lloyd, in "Elementary geometric/arithmetic series and early production theory," believes that there is an oversight in the history of economic thought concerning the precise form of the marginal product and average product function implied by early statements of the Law of Diminishing Returns. Malthus's Law of Population and von Thünen's version of the Law of Diminishing Returns illustrate the use of geometric and algebraic series to explain these economic principles.

Malthus's innovation lies in his statements, "Population, when unchecked, increases in a geometric ratio. Subsistence increases only in an arithmetic ratio." In his formula he assumes:

1. An initial population at time $t = 1$ of $x_1 = a$.
2. An initial supply of the means of subsistence of $y_1 = b$.
3. An increase in population that is geometric; while a subsistence increase is arithmetic; that is, the latter increases by a constant quantity c per period.

Thus $$x_t = a^t$$
and $$y_t = b + c(t - 1), \text{ where } t = 1, 2, 3, 4 \ldots. \tag{1}$$

We may interpret the above formula as follows:

1. Both the geometric and arithmetic series represent two series that occur simultaneously, but independently, over time.
2. Solving for x in terms of y, and vice versa:

$$x = a^{[(y-b)/c]+1}, \text{ where } (y - b)/c = 1, 2, 3, \ldots, \tag{2}$$

$$y = (b - c) + [c(\log_e x / \log_e a)]. \tag{3}$$

Equation (3) may be interpreted as a functional relationship in which population x is the independent variable and the means of subsistence y is the dependent variable. If the general population is regarded as a proxy for labor, equation (3) describes a total product curve relating the input of labor to the output of the means of subsistence.

Lloyd has several objections to Malthus's ratios:

1. They did not link the theory to these terms.

2. They did not attribute increases in output, or any part thereof, directly to the labor force as population increased.

3. They did not separate the contributions to increased output due to more intensive cultivation of existing lands, the cultivation of more land of inferior quality, and the use of improved methods of agricultural production, all of which Malthus mentioned in his discussion of the arithmetic ratio.

von Thünen, in discussing the marginal product function, said: "It is in the nature of agriculture—and this is a circumstance that must be stressed—that the additional yield is not in direct proportion to the number of additional laborers, but every additional laborer brings an additional product lower than the preceding."

Specifically, total product of the nth unit is the sum of a geometric series of n terms, such that $\lim_{x \to \infty} A(1 - r^x) = A$. This geometric series is the "law of the soil" of Spillman and Mitscherlich. The total product curve has monotonically decreasing marginal and average products because it is concave from below. It also has the property that all positive inputs of the variable factor yield positive outputs. Indeed, both the Malthusian and von Thünen total product curves represent contours of the production function, not the production functions themselves.

From this discussion of Malthus and von Thünen, Lloyd concludes that:

1. Although there are objections to his theory, Malthus must be credited with having some notion of the principle later known as the Law of Diminishing Returns.

2. von Thünen's contributions to production theory have yet to be properly acknowledged.

Students should acquaint themselves with these concepts from Lloyd's article:

Arithmetic series	Law of population
Average product	Law of the soil
Concavity vs. convexity	Marginal product
Functional relationships	Monotonic function
Geometric series	Production contours
History of economic thought	Production theory
Labor input	Subsistence
Law of diminishing returns	Total product curve

Article 2

R. J. Ball, in "Classical demand curves and the optimum relationship between selling costs and output," begins his paper by noting that Hieser and Soper's paper evaluating the relationship between output and optimal selling cost outlays in an imperfectly competitive model criticizes:

1. Chamberlin—they hold that Chamberlin's treatment of selling costs, as aggregated with production costs rather than as a deduction from revenue, is in error.
2. Hahn—although commended for treating selling costs as deductions from revenue, Hahn is criticized in that "... he fails to take the second step and abandon the idea of a given demand curve ...".
3. The notion of a necessarily preexisting demand curve, the shape or position of which may be deliberately manipulated by selling expenditures, is rejected.

Ball refutes Hieser and Soper's propositions as follows:

1. *To defend* Hahn's assumption of a given demand curve, not only in principle but in detail, Ball analytically shows that all of the Hieser and Soper's principal propositions can be derived from the assumption of a constant elasticity independently given demand function of the form $q = Ap - \alpha s\beta$. Furthermore, in their own analysis, Hieser and Soper consider the economies of scale effect in terms of alternative fixed elasticities. Since, for the study of equilibrium conditions, values in the neighborhood of equilibrium are of interest, the constant elasticity assumption becomes a useful device.

2. *To argue* that Hieser and Soper have not made clear the crucial difference between their analysis and Hahn's, which affects the optimal pricing conditions.

(a) The issue is not concerned with the existence or nonexistence of an independent demand curve.
(b) Hieser and Soper's conclusions about equilibrium conditions do not prove the point that they wish to make. It is easily shown that the Hieser and Soper propositions are quite incorrect and that their approach leads exactly to the Hahn result.

3. *To argue* that the analysis of selling costs and output cannot be adequately treated without distinguishing between different types of selling costs. Failure to consider such distinctions gives rise to problems and differences. Both the Hieser and Soper analysis and the Hahn

analysis fail to distinguish between discretionary and variable selling costs. Hieser and Soper and Hahn both treat all costs as discretionary.

In conclusion, having proven the fallacies of the Hieser and Soper propositions, Ball notes that treatment of selling costs remains open to some extent. To him, Chamberlin is half right, for variable selling costs can be conveniently aggregated with production costs.

The following concepts are of interest to the reader:

Constant elasticity
Demand curve
Discretionary vs. variable selling costs
Economies of scale
Equilibrium conditions
Imperfectly competitive model

Optimal selling cost out-
lays
Revenue
Selling costs vs. produc-
tion costs
Variable selling costs

Article 3

A. Ross Shepherd, in "A note on the firm's long-run average cost curve," elucidates the distinction between the optimum output for a given plant size and the optimum input ratio for producing that output when all factors are variable. He also shows that the standard textbook representation of the relationship between the firm's short-run average cost (SAC) curves and the firm's long-run average cost (LAC) curve is valid.

These arguments are presented in response to Chen Fu Chang's criticism that "with few exceptions there seems to be no reason for the least-cost points of the SAC curves to be standing off the LAC curve, and the normal case of the LAC curve should consist of a series of the least-cost points of the SAC curves."

The production homogeneity assumption used by Shepherd makes it strictly correct to explain the behavior of long-run costs solely by reference to the concept of returns to scale. In order to rationalize the U-shaped LAC, it is assumed that marginal returns to scale decline continuously with increases in output. Thus, the LAC curve is "... the cost–output space equivalent of the expansion path." Once that the justification of the asserted relationships between the expansion path and the locus is established, argues Shepherd, it is clear that Chang's concern for maintaining optimum proportions between factors should lead him away from the SAC minima and back to the LAC envelope curve.

Shepherd undertakes the proof that, under increasing, constant, and decreasing returns to scale, the labor intensities of the SAC minima are, respectively, greater than, equal to or less than the optima given by the expansion path. Specifically,

(1) $P_K(K/Q) + P_L(L/Q) = P_L(1/MP_2) \Rightarrow$
$P_K/P_L = (Q/MP_L - L)/K^*$.

(2) $MP_K K + MP_L L = rQ \Rightarrow$
$MP_K/MP_L \gtreqless (Q/MP_L - L)/K$.

(3) $(MP_K)/(MP_L) \gtreqless (Q/MP_L - L)/K$
$= P_K/P_L (K = K^*)$.

Intuitively, as the scale increases and capital is fixed (in the short run) at higher levels, it is necessary in seeking SAC minima to reduce the relative usage of the variable factor, labor. His argument also holds in the case of labor being fixed and capital being treated as the variable factor.

The following concepts from Shepherd's article should be studied by the reader:

Envelope curves	Minima
Expansion path	Optima
Fixed factors of production	Optimum input
Labor intensity	Optimum output
Least-cost combinations	Production homogeneity
Long-run average costs	Returns to scale
Marginal returns to scale	Short-run average costs
Maxima	Variable factors of production

Article 4

In "Cost–effectiveness analysis: implications for accountants" Barry G. King discusses the application of a systematic, analytical approach to problems of choice. His purpose is to describe and illustrate the methodology of cost–effectiveness analysis in a nontechnical manner by avoiding most aspects of the mathematics of maximization, and to specify some implications that the maximization approach has for accountants. The author has selected the term "cost–effectiveness" analysis for his presentation. Other similar terms include (1) systems analysis, (2) operations analysis, (3) cost–benefit analysis, (4) cost–utility analysis, and (5) planning, programming, and budgeting systems (PPBS).

In its narrowest sense, cost–effectiveness analysis may be defined as a technique for choosing among given alternative courses of action in terms of their cost and their effectiveness in the attainment of specified objectives. In a broader sense, cost–effectiveness analysis has been defined as simply a "technique for evaluating broad management and economic implications of alternative choices of actions, with the objective of assisting in the identification of the preferred choice."

Most of the more interesting problems arise in this broader context, and King pursues this view in his discussion. Before continuing, it is necessary to emphasize that cost–effectiveness analysis is output-oriented, and that the approach stresses effectiveness as opposed to technical economic efficiency in the allocation of resources.

Because cost–effectiveness analysis is designed to yield solutions that are uniquely responsive to problems which are ill-structured, and which have objectives that are less precisely defined, a sequence of general steps rather than a set of standard procedures constitute its approach. These include:

1. *Definition of objectives.* Since careless selection and specification of objectives can lead to solutions for the wrong problem, the desired goal(s) must be defined as explicitly as possible.
2. *Identification of alternatives.* These represent competing "systems" (strategies, policies, specific actions, or necessary elements) for accomplishing objectives.
3. *Selection of effectiveness measures.* Gauging the effectiveness of each alternative is probably the most difficult and unique problem in the analysis. The challenge is to provide measures that are relevant to the objective sought, and measurable in terms that allow comparisons of effectiveness among alternatives.
4. *Development of cost estimates.* Two issues are involved here: (a) what costs to include, and (b) how to measure them.
5. *Selection of a decision criterion.* This is the standard by which all alternatives are evaluated in terms of cost and effectiveness. Three types of valid criteria from which the analyst must choose are: (a) maximize effectiveness at given cost; (b) minimize cost while attaining a given effectiveness; and (c) some combination of these two which recognizes a tradeoff of cost for effectiveness to maximize a selected utility function of the two factors.
6. *Creation of models relating cost and effectiveness.* Needed are cost models, effectiveness models, and a synthesizing model based on outputs therefrom.

King says that several limitations of cost–effectiveness should be considered:

1. It must be realized that all analytical results are merely inputs to be judged along with other less systematic factors by a higher-level decision-maker.
2. The difficulty in selecting measures of effectiveness is of prime importance.
3. Imperfect information or insufficient input may result in an analysis that is misleading or erroneous.
4. There is a lack of a probability orientation in most cost–effectiveness analysis.

Some implications for the accounting field include the following:

1. *Implications for an expanded concept of organizational objectives.* Accountants must be willing and prepared to provide information about and perform analysis of activities which are not primarily profit-oriented and whose effectiveness cannot be adequately measured in dollars.
2. *Implications for an increased knowledge of quantitative management science.* The accountant must understand the concept of a model and the modeling process, and its uses and limitations. He must have the ability to conceptualize problems in an input–output format; and must have the capacity to express and manipulate relationships in a functional form.
3. *Implications for design and operation of management information (data)systems.* Accountants, because of their interest in information and data processing, should be vitally concerned with the development of systems which improve the quality of input data for decision models.
4. *Implications for more sophistication in cost estimation and forecasting.* Accountants have not developed the capability of analyzing costs in terms of other potential independent variables. Techniques of regression and correlation analysis should be mastered. Also rather than following the traditional "micro" view of cost estimating, King suggests that accountants take a "macro" approach which involves costing the total system in terms of its parameters.

The following concepts are of interest to the reader:

Cost–benefit analysis   Cost–effectiveness analysis

Cost–utility analysis
Efficiency
Macro
Maximization
Micro
Operations analysis
Parameter

Planning, programming, and budget-
ing systems (PPBS)
Probability
Resource allocation
Systems analysis
Utility function

Article 5

One solution to the rapidly rising costs in service industries is based on improved productivity. In "An approach to productivity in two knowledge-based industries" John F. Rockart's examination of two industries—medicine and education—presents four methods of increasing performance and productivity. He adds some useful suggestions for implementing new methods of production and measurement in industries having professional as well as organizational loyalties.

Education and medicine are treated together because of their similarity, which includes domination by professionals. Also:

1. Dominant "employee group" ties to disciplines are usually stronger than ties to organizations.
2. Dual power structures, professional and administrative, exist.
3. In heavily labor-intensive industries it is difficult to measure the value of the product delivered.

The author notes the concern so succinctly expressed by Peter Drucker: "The bulk of tomorrow's employment will be in the service trades, knowledge jobs—in health care, teaching, government, management, research and the like. And no one knows much about the productivity of knowledge work, let alone how to improve it."

Managers in these two industries have seldom pressed for greater productivity, or even for research into it, because of the obstacle that, if productivity increases are forced, not only will it be impossible to measure them, but both the quality of the work and the professional's satisfaction in that work probably will decrease. Rockart feels, however, that increased productivity is compatible with quality or "professional satisfaction" considerations. He notes, however, that additional study is needed to understand what can and cannot be done about productivity in knowledge-based industries.

Methods by which productivity may be increased include:

1. *Revising the content of a particular job by:*
   (a) mechanizing certain job steps (automation); and/or
   (b) turning particular parts of the job over to lower-paid personnel.
2. *Providing more output with the same inputs through improved scheduling by the method of:*

   (a) prospective schedule smoothing; and
   (b) retrospective analysis of productivity leading to changes in future periods.

Having established these four methods, Rockart proceeds with specific examples in medicine and education. In the first general category of job content, reactions of participants were favorable; and the established programs were successful. Participation and involvement on the part of the professionals involved was, perhaps, most significant in leading to acceptance of change.

In conclusion, favorable results have been obtained only where there has been a careful quantitative analysis of the factors involved; and a high continuous participation, and involvement, of the professionals themselves in productivity-increasing changes.

The reader should understand the following concepts:

Knowledge-based industry	Productivity
Labor intensive	Schedule smoothing
Power structure	Service trades

Article 6

In "Medium range aggregate production planning: state of the art" Edward A. Silver describes the medium range production smoothing and work force balancing problem. It is a paper concerning the problem of rationally establishing work force sizes and production rates under seasonal demand conditions; and it is a problem faced by many manufacturing firms.* In addition, several different approaches to its solution are presented.

There are four pure strategies that management may follow in an attempt to absorb fluctuations in demand:

---

*Medium range planning, often called annual planning, is on the order of 6 to 18 months.

1. The size of the labor force can be altered by hiring or laying off. This has the effect of changing the production rate.
2. The production rate can be varied by keeping the size of the labor force constant, and then introducing overtime or idle time adjustments.
3. Management can hold the production rate constant, and allow the fluctuations in demand to be absorbed by changes in the inventory level.
4. In some industries, the fluctuations in demand can be handled by subcontracting.

Because there are costs incurred by each of these pure strategies or any combination thereof, the criterion is to select the combination of the four that minimizes the total relevant costs over a suitable time period. There are essentially six categories of costs to consider:

1. Costs of regular time production.
2. Overtime costs.
3. Costs of change in production rate.
4. Inventory costs (out of pocket expenses and lost opportunity).
5. Costs of insufficient capacity in the short run.
6. Control system costs.

Silver provides a brief discussion of the first five of these above-mentioned costs.

Having established the cost basis, Silver discusses several approaches to the selection of production rates and work force sizes. These can be divided into three fundamental groups. The first is essentially non-mathematical in nature; the second consists of mathematical models for which theoretically optimal solutions are obtainable; the third is where the mathematical model is made more realistic, but an optimal solution is usually no longer guaranteed.

The specific approaches include:

1. *Nonquantitative haggling.* Generally this is not desirable since the policy is usually dictated by the most persuasive individual rather than being set in an objective manner.
2. *Constant turnover ratio.* It would seem appealing to set production rates so as to achieve a constant turnover ratio; but this is fallacious for two reasons: First, such a rule leads to large gyrations in the inventory level for a fluctuating demand pattern; and second, it can

easily be shown that a constant turnover ratio is not the most economical choice.

3. *Adjustment to the previous year's plan.* The danger here lies in the implicit assumption that the previous year's plan was close to optimal.

4. *Linear programming and extensions.* This consists of selecting the values for several nonnegative variables so as to minimize a linear function of these variables subject to several linear constraints on the variables.

5. *Linear decision rule.* When the costs can be approximated by linear and quadratic functions, the decision rules are of a simple linear form.

6. *Management coefficients approach.* This is a partially heuristic approach that assumes that managers behave in a rational manner.

7. *Simulation search procedures.* By a trial and error procedure, the variables are paired until results are obtained that require no further reduction in the total relevant costs.

8. *Other mathematical approaches.* These include dynamic programming, queueing theory, and Pontryagin's maximum principle.

It was found by Silver that most of the decisions for the current period reached by mathematical approaches are very insensitive to forecasts of demand well into the future. Silver also notes that it is possible to adjust some of the "given" conditions by:

1. *Influencing demand.* This is usually accomplished through price and promotion schemes.

2. *Adaptations.* When the demand cannot be influenced, one way of removing seasonality is to combine contracyclical demand patterns.

3. *Coalition efforts.* Two or more companies may share their facilities when their seasonal patterns are different.

Silver concludes that there are at least three other approaches aside from linear programming that potentially promise significant benefits:

1. Extensions to the basic linear programming models that include the effects on the detailed daily scheduling when doing the aggregate production smoothing and work force balancing.

2. The management coefficients approach.

3. Simulation methods.

The reader should note the following concepts:

Capacity

Contra-cyclical demand

Idle time

Inventory costs

Linear programming

Medium range production

Opportunity costs

Production rate

Pure strategies

Seasonal demand

Seasonality

Short run

Subcontracting

Work force or labor force

Article 7

Because some confusion regarding the relation between cost curves and the shape of the firm's production function exists, John W. Rowe, Jr., in "Short-run, long-run, and vector cost curves" explores the relationships between and among short-run, long-run, and vector cost curves derived from a two-input production function. The relationship between short-run and long-run cost curves is well known; but their relationship with vector cost curves has not been specified. Vector cost curves are defined as cost curves constructed for constant input proportions.

Before construction of cost curves, the firm must choose the expansion path along which cost is to be measured. The slope of the firm's short-run expansion path is $(dv_2/dv_1) = 0$, whereas a point along a long-run expansion path is

$$\frac{dv_2}{dv_1} = \frac{f_1 f_{12} - f_2 f_{11}}{f_1 f_{12} - f_1 f_{22}}.$$

Whereas construction of cost curves has traditionally concentrated on short- and long-run expansion paths, returns to scale have been measured along a vector with constant input proportions. It is possible to demonstrate that Bassett's assertion (that there is not a relationship between returns to scale and [long-run] cost curves when the [long-run] expansion path does not coincide with a vector) is incorrect by constructing vector cost curves along a vector expansion path. Since input proportions are constant along such a path, the slope is $(dv_2/dv_1 = v_2/v_1)$.

The relationship between cost curves for the three paths can be evaluated at a point at which all three intersect.

Four elementary conclusions may be noted:

1. SMC = LMC = VMC at the intersection point (SMC, LMC, VMC are short-run, long-run, and vector marginal cost curves, respectively).
2. SAC = LAC = VAC where the three paths cross (SAC, LAC, VAC are short-run, long-run, and vector average cost curves, respectively).
3. Since all three marginal cost levels are equal, and all three average cost levels are equal, the slope of SAC, LAC, and VAC are equal. The slope of LAC gives an unambiguous measure of returns to scale under the assumption of fixed factor prices.
4. The curvature of the average cost curve for one expansion path is greater than, equal to, or less than the curvature of the average cost curve for another expansion path depending on whether the slope of the marginal cost curve for the former path is greater than, equal to, or less than the slope of the marginal cost curve for the latter.

Except for the situation where the long-run expenditure elasticity of v_2 is zero, the slope of the SMC curve exceeds the slope of the LMC curve; and thus, the curvature of SAC exceeds that of LAC. It can thus be concluded that the long-run expansion path (LEP) is the most efficient of all paths. As for a comparison between VAC and LMC curves, when the two paths do not coincide, the slope of VAC exceeds the slope of LMC, and hence the curvature of VAC exceeds the curvature of LAC, again reflecting that LEP is the most efficient path.

Although the slopes of both SMC and VMC are greater than the slope of LMC, except for cases of coinciding paths, it is necessary to determine which of the other two paths is more efficient. Clearly in most cases VEP is more efficient than the short-run expansion path (SEP); however, the higher the output level, the more likely that SEP be more efficient than VEP.

The reader should be familiar with the following terms:

Average cost	Marginal cost
Constant input proportions	Production function
Cost curves	Returns to scale
Efficiency	Short run
Elasticity	Slope
Expansion path	Vector
Long run	Vector cost curves

Article 8

Gary M. Roodman's "The fixed coefficients production process under production uncertainty" develops a generalized theory of the firm under factor uncertainty in the fixed coefficients case. Roodman begins his discussion by developing a production function that explicitly incorporates random elements, and serves as the basis for developing the uncertainty model. The production function that the firm faces under uncertainty is given by

$$Q_e = \frac{F_1}{S_1} E_\alpha^h(u) + \frac{F_2}{S_2} G(h).$$

Since output under conditions of certainty is given therein by

$$Q_e = \min \left(\frac{F_1}{S_1}, \frac{F_2}{S_2} \right),$$

expected output will be less than certainty output for any set of factors acquired; with the discrepancy between the two being measured by either K_1 or K_2.

Following this discussion, Roodman explores in detail the properties of the production and places function, placing particular emphasis on its similarities to the variable proportions production function treated in discussions of the traditional theory of the firm. Concerning the Q production function, he develops measures of returns to scale, marginal productivity, and marginal rates of factor substitution.

This discussion leads directly to a set of production and output optimality conditions developed for the risk-neutral firm. The optimal relationship between the two factors is selected so as to:

Minimize:

$$C = p_1 F_1 + p_2 F_2.$$

Subject to:

$$Q_e^t = \frac{F_1}{S_1} E_\alpha^h(u) + \frac{F_2}{S_2} G(h).$$

It is assumed that the firm is risk-neutral with a defined range; and sells its output at a price P in a purely competitive market. Then the firm will select the values of F_1 and F_2 that maximizes expected profit,

$$\pi_e = PQ_e - C.$$

Thus, at optimum,

$$P \cdot MEP_1 = p_1,$$
$$P \cdot MEP_2 = p_2.$$

This conclusion is illustrated numerically; which, in turn, permits certain additional observations of interest. Having provided this mathematical justification, Roodman discusses the implications of risk aversion of the part of the firm, rather than risk-neutrality, as had been done to this point. The optimal production method here is shown as:

$$\frac{\frac{1}{S_1} \int_\alpha^h U'(\pi_1) u f(u)\, du}{\frac{1}{S_2} \int_h^\beta U'(\pi_2) f(u)\, du} = \frac{p_1}{p_2}.$$

Roodman thus shows that the risk-averse firm will choose to employ proportionately more of factor 1 (the unreliable factor) than it would employ if it were risk-neutral.

The most important idea emerging from Roodman's discussion is that production uncertainty brings a dimension to the fixed coefficients problem that makes it important to speak of choosing the optimal input configuration on an economic basis. Optimal input levels are dependent upon prices of factors and their marginal contributions to output; and, in the case of the risk-averse firm, upon the marginal utility of profit.

The reader should understand the following concepts:

Factors of production	Pure competition
Fixed coefficient production function	Returns to scale
Marginal productivity	Risk aversion
Marginal rate of factor substitution	Risk-neutral firm
Marginal utility	Uncertainty
Optimality	Variable proportions pro-
Production function	duction function

1

*Elementary Geometric/Arithmetic Series and Early Production Theory**

PETER J. LLOYD

ALTHOUGH the evolution of the concept of the law of diminishing returns has now been outlined by historians of economic thought, almost no attention has been paid to the precise form of the marginal and average product functions implied in early statements of the law. Some early exponents—for example, Sir Edward West and David Ricardo—employed arithmetic series to illustrate the law. In the eighteenth and nineteenth centuries geometric and algebraic series were used to illustrate certain economic principles. The most famous of these was Malthus' law of population. His example can be interpreted as a statement of the law of diminishing returns. Von Thünen also employed geometric series in his version of the law of diminishing returns. Curiously, despite the many volumes which have been written about the evolution of this law, it appears that the elementary algebra of Von Thünen's examples has not been examined and that of Malthus has been considered only briefly by one writer (Stigler [1952], pp. 190–92). This is an oversight in the history of economic thought. Both examples turn out to have interesting technical properties.

I

The first and almost simultaneous discoveries of the basic notion of diminishing returns in agriculture are usually credited to Turgot (1844, pp. 420–22) and Steuart (1966), both originally written in 1797, and to Ortes (1774). Of these three, Turgot's version is by far the most commendable.

*From *Journal of Political Economy*, Vol. 77, No. 1, January/February 1969, pp. 21–34.

Turgot was aware of both the extensive and the intensive margin cases, to use the Ricardian terminology, of diminishing returns due to increases in the amounts of the composite factor capital applied to land. He formulated the law in terms of diminishing marginal returns and introduced a range of variable inputs that give rise to increasing returns before the diminishing returns begin to apply. One interesting detail of his concept is his assertion that the total product would approach a maximum.

In 1815 both Malthus (1903) and West (1903) published versions of the law. A discussion of Malthus' treatment of diminishing returns in his *Essay on Population* is deferred for the moment. West's contribution is the foundation of the English Classical tradition on this subject. Although he is criticized for falsely identifying diminishing marginal returns with diminishing average returns, West stressed admirably the general significance of his "principle" and clearly separated diminishing returns with a given technology from the effects of technological change. The most interesting feature of West's exposition in this context is the numerical example he cited. He demonstrated the principle by supposing that equal quantities of capital, £100, bestowed on 10-acre lots of successively inferior quality might yield net profits of £20, 19, 18, 17, etc. (West, 1903, pp. 15, 39).

II

Several eighteenth-century writers before Malthus had believed that human population tended to increase according to the "law of geometric progression," and long before that others had believed that population tended to increase to the limits of human fecundity. Malthus' sensational innovation lay in the juxtaposition of this law with a second concerning the means of subsistence. "Population, when unchecked, increases in a geometrical ratio. Subsistence increases only in an arithmetical ratio" (Malthus, 1798, p. 14). Now, let us assume that a country has an initial population at time $t = 1$ of $x_1 = a$ and an initial supply of the means of subsistence of $y_1 = b$, and that in subsequent periods the population doubles, quadruples, and so on, according to a geometric series, whereas the means of subsistence increases only according to an arithmetic series, that is, by the constant quantity of c per period. Then, in any time period t,

$$x_t = a^t,$$
$$y_t = b + c(t - 1), \qquad t = 1, 2, 3, 4, \ldots \tag{1}$$

The length of the discrete time period t is such that the population exactly doubles during this period. (Malthus, on the basis of some questionable American statistics, adopted a 25-year period.) If $a = b = 2$ and $c = 1$, we have the series which Malthus himself used as an illustration (Malthus, 1798, p. 25):

Population: 2, 4, 8, 16, 32, 64, 128, 256, 512, ... ,
Means of subsistence: 2, 3, 4, 5, 6, 7, 8, 9, 10, ...

The logical necessity of the arithmetic and geometric ratios in Malthus' theory of population has been questioned. In a famous passage John Stuart Mill wrote:

"Some, for instance, have achieved an easy victory over a passing remark of Mr. Malthus, hazarded chiefly by way of illustration, that the increase of food may perhaps be assumed to take place in an arithmetical ratio, while population increases in a geometrical: when every candid reader knows that Mr. Malthus laid no stress on this unlucky attempt to give numerical precision to things which do not admit to it, and every person capable of reasoning must see that it is wholly superfluous to his argument" [Mills, 1848, par. 61].

Malthus could as well, for example, have assumed that the means of subsistence increased as a geometric progression but at a rate slower than that of the increase in population.

There are two distinct ways in which these ratios can be interpreted and discuss their mathematical properties. The first interpretation is that the geometric and arithmetic series represent two series that occur simultaneously but independently over time. According to this interpretation the arithmetic increase in the means of subsistence is not causally related, directly at least, to the concurrent geometric increase in the population. Algebraically, this interpretation is given by the parametric equations with respect to time in equation (1). These equations do, of course, imply that the means of subsistence per head of population progressively diminish. This decline could not continue indefinitely.

The second interpretation is the more interesting. From the parametric equations, we can solve for x in terms of y and vice versa. The general equations relating y and x are

$$x = a^{[(y-b)/c]+1}, \quad \frac{y-b}{c} = 0, 1, 2, 3, \ldots, \tag{2}$$

or

$$y = (b - c) + c \, (\log_e x / \log_e a). \tag{3}$$

If further one allows x and y to vary continuously, these functions are continuous. Equation (3) may be interpreted as a functional relationship in which population x is the independent variable and y, the means of subsistence, the dependent variable. Finally, if population is regarded as a proxy for labor, equation (3) describes a total product curve relating the input of labor to the output of the means of subsistence. If $a = b = 2$ and $c = 1$, as before, the equation of the curve is $x = 2^{y-1}$. Stigler gave the equation of Malthus' implied total product curve as $L = 2^{P-1}$, where L is the labor input and P is the total product. Since he assumed that the labor input is proportional to the population, this is the same equation as mine.

There are major objections to this post-factum reinterpretation of Malthus's ratios as a statement of the law of variable proportions. First, Malthus certainly did not put his theory in these terms. Second, Malthus did not attribute the increase in output, or any part of it, directly to the labor force as the population increased. Third, Malthus did not separate the contributions to increased output due to more intensive cultivation of existing lands, the cultivation of more land of inferior quality, and the use of improved methods of agricultural production, all of which he mentions in his discussion of the arithmetic ratio. (Sir James Steuart [1966] was guilty of the same confusion.) Nevertheless, Malthus in his *Essay* was very much aware of the extensive margin case of diminishing returns, if not of the intensive margin case on which we ordinarily rely today. In the second edition of his *Essay*, Malthus explicitly states the law of diminishing returns to counter some criticisms of his first edition (Malthus, 1803, p. 7). In *An Inquiry into the Nature and Progress of Rent*, Malthus gives a clearer statement of the law of diminishing returns on the intensive and the extensive margins (Malthus, 1903). Most interpreters agree that he "was indeed arguing in the spirit, if not the direct language, of diminishing returns" (Field, 1931, p. 16). Even in the first edition of his *Essay*, Malthus must be credited with at least a fuzzy idea of the principle later known as the law of diminishing returns. Indeed, his entire theory of population in the *Essay* ultimately rests on this principle.

Treating equation (3) as a total product curve, we can now examine its technical properties. In Fig. 1 a graph of the function has been plotted. The curve is just a slightly displaced version of the simple logarithmic function, and it has all the properties of the latter. Positive inputs of $x < a^{1-(b/c)}$ yield negative outputs. This property is untenable economically, and, since it only arises because of the assumption of continuity, we shall disregard this section of the curve. As the input of labor x increases, $y \to \infty$, but the ratio $(y/x) \to 0$. This is shown more clearly by the average

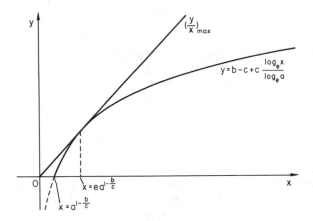

$$\text{FIG. 1.}$$

product curve. This curve has the equation

$$\frac{y}{x} = \frac{b-c}{x} + \frac{c}{\log_e a} \frac{\log_e x}{x}, \quad x \geq a^{1-(b/c)}. \tag{4}$$

This function exhibits continuously diminishing average returns, beyond the initial range $a^{1-(b/c)} < x < ea^{1-(b/c)}$. (The simple logarithmic function $y = \log_e x$ has a maximum value of y/x at $x = e$.) This property is due not to the existence of a convex and a concave region of the total product curve but to the fact that the total product curve, which is concave from below, has a positive intercept with the horizontal axis. This initial range of increasing average product is, however, an accidental result of the particular form of his total product curve, not the result of an awareness of this possibility, as it was with Turgot. Note that marginal product is a monotonically decreasing function of x that, in the limit, tends to zero. The equation for the marginal product is

$$\frac{dy}{dx} = \frac{c}{\log_e a} \frac{1}{x}. \tag{5}$$

Stigler has observed that "if workers received a wage equal to their marginal product, the aggregate wage bill would be independent of the size of the labor force, and the population simply would not grow" (Stigler, 1952, p. 193). This is so because $x(dy/dx) = c/\log_e a$.

III

Von Thünen, unlike Malthus, developed the concept of marginal product explicitly and at length. Von Thünen is usually given an honored place in the history of economic thought because of his location theory and because he was probably the first to develop the marginal productivity theory of pricing for factor prices in general. Little attention has been paid to his particular statement of the marginal product function.

Von Thünen contended that "It is in the nature of agriculture—and this is a circumstance that must be stressed—that the additional yield is not in direct proportion to the number of additional laborers, but every additional laborer brings an additional product lower than the preceding" (Dempsey translation, 1960, p. 203). His agricultural examples refer to the intensive margin because of his assumption of constant and equal fertility of all land in *The Isolated State*. He made a great advance over his predecessors and contemporaries in that he studied the marginal product of labor and capital separately. He extended the law of diminishing returns to the capital factor and to the application of manures and other materials to land (Dempsey translation, 1960, pp. 309, 254–55). Furthermore, Von Thünen extended his "universal" principle to the enterprises and trades outside the agricultural sector (for example, the Dempsey translation, 1960, Vol. II, chaps. viii, ix).

Despite his inclination to express his economic theory in mathematical terms, Von Thünen did not develop the algebraic statement of his special geometric series form of the total product curve. In general, if the marginal product of a unit of a variable factor is a constant proportion of the marginal product of the previous unit and r is the factor of proportionality, the marginal product of the n units is

$$\Delta y_n = ar^{n-1}, \tag{6}$$

where a is the marginal product of the first unit. Since the total product of n units of inputs is, by definition, the sum of the marginal products of all units of inputs, the total product of the nth unit is

$$y_n = \sum_{i=1}^{n} ar^{i-1} = A(1 - r^n), \tag{7}$$

where $A = a/(1 - r)$. The total product of the nth unit is therefore simply the sum of a geometric series of n terms. In terms of the input x, $y = A(1 - r^x)$. As $r < 1$,

$$\lim_{x \to \infty} A(1 - r^x) = A. \tag{8}$$

That is, the total product curve approaches asymptotically a maximum finite limit of $a/(1-r)$.

One should note that Von Thünen's geometric series is precisely the "Law of the Soil" which was rediscovered in the early twentieth century by two agricultural scientists, the American W. J. Spillman and the German E. A. Mitscherlich, independently (see Spillman, 1924). In 1921, while studying the increases in the yield of cotton on an experimental plot which were due to increases in fertilizer, Spillman conjectured that the increments due to the addition of successive units of fertilizer tended to form the terms of a decreasing geometric series. This result was confirmed by other experiments with fertilizer and irrigation water as the variable factor (Spillman, 1924, Part 1). He stated the equation for the total product curve as in equation (7). Meanwhile, working at the Köningsberg Experiment Station, Mitscherlich had discovered the same law, which he called the law of physiological relations. By observing the increases in the quantity of oats grown on fixed plots as increasing quantities of fertilizers were applied, he conjectured that the yield increase was proportional to the quantity by which the current yield falls short of the maximum yield, A. The existence of a finite maximum followed from his belief in the "law of the minimum" which prevailed among German agricultural scientists of the time. We may recall that, over a century before, Turgot had postulated a maximum agricultural output under these conditions. Similarly, Von Thünen's geometric series imply that agricultural output asymptotically approaches a maximum. Mitscherlich derived his "law of the soil" function by seeking an algebraic expression to approximate his experimental results. He considered and rejected linear and logistic curve approximations and was apparently totally unaware of Von Thünen's earlier suppositions concerning diminishing returns.

The differential equation of the change in output according to Mitscherlich's law is

$$\frac{dy}{dx} = k(A - y). \tag{9}$$

By integration, we obtain the formula

$$y = A(1 - e^{-kx}), \quad x \geq 0. \tag{10}$$

This is in fact the continuous form of the Spillman equation. A total product curve given by this equation passes through the origin and in the limit, as $x \to \infty$, asymptotically approaches the maximum A. Marginal product is given by equation (9). It is a monotonically decreasing function of x, like the Malthusian marginal product curve, but it has a further property:

$$\frac{d^2y/dx^2}{dy/dx} = -k.\tag{11}$$

That is, the proportionate rate of decline of marginal product itself is a constant. The constant k of equation (10) is thus the instantaneous rate of decline of marginal product, while e^{-k} is the factor of proportionality over the unit interval. This is true since the ratio of the marginal product of the $(x+1)$th unit of input to the marginal product of the xth unit is

$$\frac{Ake^{-k(x+1)}}{Ake^{-kx}} = e^{-k} = r.\tag{12}$$

The average product curve is

$$\frac{y}{x} = \frac{A(1-e^{-kx})}{x}.\tag{13}$$

Average product continuously diminishes toward zero as the input increases. The Von Thünen–Mitscherlich–Spillman total product curve has monotonically decreasing marginal and average products because it is concave from below, and it also has the property that all positive inputs of the variable factor yield positive outputs.

The Malthusian and the Von Thünen–Mitscherlich–Spillman total product curves above represent merely contours of the production function surfaces, not the production functions themselves. Mitscherlich also believed that his mathematical law correctly described the increase in output from any one variable input if the quantities of all other inputs were held constant. Equation (10) above can be generalized to form a production function that has unusual properties. If there are n factors, the production function can be written as

$$y = A(1 - e^{-k_1x_1})(1 - e^{-k_2x_2})\ldots(1 - e^{-k_nx_n}).\tag{14}$$

Positive output requires positive quantities of all inputs. The maximum output A is approached asymptotically only if the quantities of all n factors are increased indefinitely. This production function is clearly non-homogeneous. The Von Thünen–Mitscherlich–Spillman total product curve is a reduced form of this production function, with $n = 1$. Moreover, the Von Thünen two-factor case, where the marginal products of both factors are a decreasing geometric series, is given by this formula with $n = 2$.

While Von Thünen did not state the production function implied by his numerical examples, he gave a clear and unmistakable verbal statement of the notion of a production function in which output is the joint product of the two factors, labor and capital, that can be combined in variable proportions (Dempsey translation, pp. 270–71, 317, 321). Von Thünen's clear realization of the substitutability of factors was a necessary prelude to the concept of a production function. Furthermore, his definition of product as that part of gross output attributable to capital and labor was unquestionably a fortuitous aid, leading him to regard the product explicitly as a function of the two variables, inputs of capital and labor.

To put his discovery of the production function beyond dispute, we need only note that Von Thünen gives the equation of the production function which he believed described the actual output of his Tellow estate. This is probably the first algebraic formula for a particular production function. The general equation (Dempsey translation, p. 347) is

$$p = h(g + k)^n,\tag{15}$$

where p is the product of a unit of labor, k is the quantity of capital per laborer, g is a positive constant, and n is a constant whose value Von Thünen always took to be less than unity. Capital may be measured in terms of the worker's means of subsistence, or it may be measured in terms of labor, since in Von Thünen's model capital is itself stored-up labor. (When capital is measured in terms of labor, Von Thünen uses the symbol g to represent capital per worker. Thus g has two different meanings in Volume II, Part 2, of *The Isolated State*.) The parameter h is also a constant. Von Thünen noted, "The value of h depends (1) upon the object to which the labor is directed; that is, upon the greater or less fertility of the soil, and (2) upon the strength and diligence of the worker" (Dempsey translation, 1960, p. 344). Multiplying both sides of equation (15) by L, the number of units of labor input, we get

$$P = hL(g + k)^n = hL^{1-n}(gL + k)^n,\tag{16}$$

where P is the total product. This production function is linearly homogeneous, and hence Von Thünen was able to express output per laborer as a function of the capital per laborer, as is commonly done today in such functions. Von Thünen understood the marginal product of capital as the derivative of equation (15),

$$\frac{dp}{dk} = nh(g + k)^{n-1}.\tag{17}$$

This marginal product equation has positive values for all values of k and continuously diminishes as the capital input is increased. The marginal product of labor is positive and will, for normal values of n and g, decrease as the labor input is increased.

As a final measure of Von Thünen's accomplishments, we may note that he considered alternative values of g, including $g = \frac{1}{2}$. In the previous chapter, chapter 2 of Volume II, Part 2, Von Thünen uses hg^n as the expression for the product of a laborer working with g here representing units of capital measured in quantities of labor (Dempsey translation, 1960, p. 334). This example corresponds to the case of the production function in equation (15) with the constant $g = 0$:

$$p = hk^n, \tag{18}$$

where k is the capital:labor ratio. But this is the equation, with the output per unit of labor as the dependent variable, of the linearly homogeneous two-factor Cobb-Douglas production function!

Von Thünen's enormous contributions to production theory, as distinct from his contributions to the marginal productivity theory of factor pricing, have yet to be properly acknowledged. A part of the explanation may lie in the fact that his algebraic production functions are contained in the last fragments of his writings, published 13 years after his death. Moreover, the attention of his nineteenth-century readers was diverted almost exclusively to his celebrated formula for the natural wage. When a writer wanders onto a false track of thought, he not only suffers the justifiable criticism of his errors but also suffers the neglect of his true discoveries.

REFERENCES

1. Dempsey, Bernard W. *The Frontier Wage.* Chicago: Loyola Univ. Press, 1960.
2. Dillon, John L., and Heady, Earl O. *Agricultural Production Functions.* Ames: Iowa Univ. Press, 1960.
3. Douglas, Paul H. "Are There Laws of Production?" *A.E.R.*, XXXVIII (March, 1948), 1–41.
4. Field, James Alfred, *Essays on Population.* Chicago: Univ. of Chicago Press, 1931.
5. Hall, Peter (ed.). *Von Thünen's Isolated State.* Oxford: Oxford Univ. Press, 1966.
6. Malthus, Thomas Robert. *An Essay on the Principle of Population.* 1st ed. London: 1798.
7. Malthus, Thomas Robert. *An Essay on the Principle of Population.* 2nd ed. London: 1803.
8. Malthus, Thomas Robert. *Principles of Political Economy.* London: J. Murray, 1820.
9. Malthus, Thomas Robert. *The Nature and Progress of Rent.* ("A Reprint of Economic Tracts.") Baltimore: Johns Hopkins Univ. Press, 1903.

10. Mill, John Stuart. *Principles of Political Economy.* London: Parker & Co., 1848.
11. Ortes, Giammaria. *Economia Nazionale,* 1774.
12. Ricardo, David. *The Principles of Political Economy and Taxation.* Cambridge: Cambridge Univ. Press, 1951.
13. Schultz, T. W. *Economic Organization of Agriculture.* New York: McGraw-Hill Book Co., 1953.
14. Schumpeter, Joseph A. *History of Economic Analysis.* New York: Oxford Univ. Press, 1954.
15. Smith, Kenneth. *The Malthusian Controversy.* London: Routledge & Paul, 1951.
16. Spillman, W. J. (ed.). *The Law of Diminishing Returns.* Yonkers-on-Hudson, N.Y.: World Book Co., 1924.
17. Steuart, Sir James. *An Inquiry into the Principles of Political Economy.* Vol. I. Chicago: Univ. of Chicago Press, 1966.
18. Stigler, George J. "The Ricardian Theory of Value and Distribution," *J.P.E.,* LX (June, 1952), 187–207.
19. Turgot, Anne Robert Jacques. *Ouvres de Turgot.* Vol. I. Paris: Guillaumin, 1844.
20. Von Thünen, Johann Heinrich. *Der Isolierte Staat in Besiehung auf Landwirtschaft und Nationalokonomie.* Hamburg: Friedrich Perthes, 1826.
21. West, Sir Edward. *The Application of Capital to Land.* ("A Reprint of Economic Tracts.") Baltimore: Johns Hopkins Univ. Press, 1903.

2

Classical Demand Curves and the Optimum Relationship Between Selling Costs and Output*

R. J. BALL

IT IS remarkable how little attention has been paid by the economists in the last twenty years to the relationship between selling costs and output. A recent paper by Messrs Hieser and Soper [4] has reconsidered the relationship between output and optimal selling cost outlays in an imperfectly competitive model. In the course of this paper they focus criticism on the treatment of selling costs by Chamberlin in his seminal work on imperfect competition [1] and on a much later treatment by Hahn [3]. They claim that Chamberlin is in error in treating selling costs as aggregated with production costs rather than as a deduction from revenue. And although Hahn is commended for in their view correctly treating selling costs as a deduction from revenue, they nevertheless argue that "his analysis comes to an immediate dead end because he fails to take the second step and abandon the idea of a given demand curve. Not only does he assert such a curve, but he postulates for it a constant elasticity" (p. 385). They go on to "reject the notion of a necessarily pre-existing demand curve the shape or position of which may be deliberately manipulated by selling expenditures" (p. 387). This is supported by some *ad hoc* argument about the importance of demand creation: ". . . the manufacture of demand is in this day and age, one of our most important industries" (p. 387).

The present paper has a number of objectives. The first is to defend the Hahn assumption of a given demand curve not only in principle but also

*From *The Economic Record*, Vol. 44, No. 107, September 1968, pp. 342–348. Reproduced by permission.

for the most part in detail. The assumption of a constant elasticity demand function is in the first instance a useful tool for establishing results. The second is to argue that Hieser and Soper (H-S) have not made clear the crucial difference between their analysis and Hahn's which certainly affects the optimal pricing conditions. The issue has nothing to do with the existence or non-existence of an independent demand curve. Moreover, it is shown that H-S conclusions with regard to equilibrium conditions do not prove the point they wish to make. Thirdly, it is argued that the analysis of selling costs and output cannot be adequately treated without distinguishing between different types of selling costs. In part some of the differences and problems arise from a failure to consider such distinctions.

THE HIESER–SOPER ANALYSIS RECONSIDERED

In this section it is shown that all the H-S results can be derived from the assumption of a constant elasticity demand function of the form,

$$q = Ap^{-\alpha}S^{\beta} \qquad (1)$$

where q = quantity demanded, p = price, and S = selling cost. Briefly the H-S argument is that for any output level there are an infinite number of combinations of selling costs and price that will dispose of that output. Thus, for any given level of output the businessman's problem is to choose that combination of price and unit selling cost that maximizes net revenue at that output level. Thus net revenue, NR, is equal to

$$NR = pq - S, \qquad (2)$$

which for a given level of output, q, can be expressed as

$$NR = q\left(p - \frac{S}{q}\right) = q(p - \sigma) \qquad (3)$$

where σ is average selling cost per unit. Thus for a given level of output the problem is to choose values of p and σ such that the difference is maximized. Plotting p and σ as in Fig. 1 it is clear that this will occur at F where $\partial p / \partial \sigma = 1$. Having established the optimum combinations for different levels of output, H-S derive a net revenue curve as a function of output and a curve marginal to that which is then equated to marginal production cost to determine the optimum output level. This has the advantage of reducing the optimum analysis to a single diagram. It is argued that where there are constant returns to selling costs, the relation between

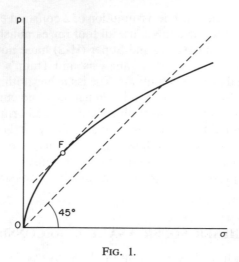

FIG. 1.

price and quantity that maximizes *NR* for a given quantity will be perfectly elastic, but will be positively sloped for increasing and negatively sloping for decreasing returns. It is one of the advantages of the approach developed below that the implicit assumptions that underly their results are made clear. In particular no account is taken of the second order condition for a maximum explicitly with regard to the difference $p - \sigma$ which is sufficient to establish some of their propositions. We consider these propositions in turn.

It will be seen from (1) that we can express unit selling cost in the form

$$\sigma = \frac{p^{\alpha/\beta} q^{(1-\beta)/\beta}}{A^{1/\beta}} \tag{4}$$

For a given level of output this defines the form of the function in Fig. 1. The shape of this curve is defined by the ratio of the price elasticity and the selling cost elasticity. As drawn by them it is implied that $\alpha > \beta$. "This curve will probably converge towards the vertical axis" (p. 388). "Normally one would expect a relationship between price and unit selling cost something like the *PS* curve of Fig. 1" (p. 388). If this is not the case no maximum of course will exist. The net revenue coefficient *NRC* can be defined as

$$NRC = p - \sigma \tag{5}$$

so from (4) we have

$$NRC = p - \frac{p^{\alpha/\beta}q^{(1-\beta)/\beta}}{A^{1/\beta}} \tag{6}$$

Differentiating (6) partially by p and setting it equal to zero we have

$$1 - \frac{\alpha/\beta p^{(\alpha-\beta)/\beta}q^{(1-\beta)/\beta}}{A^{1/\beta}} = 0 \tag{7}$$

and solving for price

$$p = \left(\frac{1}{\alpha/\beta}\right)^{\beta/(\alpha-\beta)} A^{1/(\alpha-\beta)}q^{(\beta-1)/(\alpha-\beta)} \tag{8}$$

Here we note that for (7) to be a maximum it is necessary that $\alpha > \beta$ and that equation (8) defines the "optimal" average revenue curve derived by H-S. Their propositions about the slope of this curve follow immediately from (8). For constant returns to selling cost, $\beta = 1$ and so price and optimal unit selling cost are independent of output. The price-quantity relation will be upward-sloping if $\beta > 1$, and negative if $\beta < 1$. They analyse the increasing returns case as follows. "We must now consider the behaviour of average selling cost (with increasing returns). This is not immediately obvious because there are opposing forces at work. On the one hand increasing returns will operate to reduce σ. On the other hand the resultant rising price will operate to increase σ. *A priori* one would expect the upward pull of a rising price to outweigh the downward pressure of increasing returns, and this turns out to be so." There follows a diagrammatic demonstration. That the proposition is correct in our case follows immediately by substituting (8) into (4) which, after some simplification and a new constant term, can be written

$$\sigma = \frac{K^{\alpha/\beta}}{A^{1/\beta}} q^{(\beta-1)/(\alpha-\beta)} \quad K = \left(\frac{1}{\alpha/\beta}\right)^{\beta/(\alpha-\beta)} A^{1/(\alpha-\beta)} \tag{9}$$

Since the second order condition requires that $\alpha > \beta$, it follows directly that the relation between σ and q is determined by the value of β. For increasing returns the slope will be positive. Their argument with regard to the decreasing cost case is ambiguous although it may be interpreted correctly. "In the face of diminishing returns to selling cost we shall get a continuous translation to lower prices as output is expanded so that the 'optimal' average revenue curve will be falling over this range. Average selling cost will also be falling but at a slower rate than price since the firm must have recourse to successively lower net margins if it wishes to increase its sales" (p. 394). The first statement is of course quite correct.

The second is ambiguous since, while it is true that the net margin falls as output rises, both price and unit selling cost may fall at the same proportionate rate. This follows directly from (8) and (9).

To summarize, all the principal propositions advanced by H-S so far are consistent with a constant-elasticity independently-given demand curve. This formulation in fact allows a more rigorous proof of the results. Nothing so far is dependent on the non-existence of such functions as H-S imply. Moreover, in their own analysis H-S consider the economies of scale effect in terms of alternative fixed elasticities. This as in our case is a quite sensible simplifying device. No one supposes that the relevant elasticities are actually constant over the whole range of output. But for many purposes this is irrelevant. For the study of equilibrium conditions we are interested in values in the neighbourhood of equilibrium and for that purpose the constant elasticity assumption is a useful device.

EQUILIBRIUM CONDITIONS

If this is all there is to the matter there is nothing really to argue about. But it turns out that it is not and there is. We seem to come to the (potential) point of the exercise when we consider the equilibrium conditions for output and price as derived by Hahn and similar conditions derived by Dorfman and Steiner [5]. Hahn states that equilibrium requires equality between marginal gross revenue and marginal production costs. The same conclusion comes from Dorfman and Steiner. But according to H-S this is obviously wrong since, at the margin, revenue must cover the additional costs of selling as well as producing. A Hahn-type result is obtained by writing the profit function for the firm as

$$\pi = Ap^{1-\alpha}S^{\beta} - S - C(q) \tag{10}$$

where $C(q)$ is the cost function. From this it follows that the profit-maximizing price is obtained by solving

$$\frac{\partial \pi}{\partial p} = (1 - \alpha)Ap^{-\alpha}S^{\beta} + (\alpha Ap^{-\alpha-1}S^{\beta})C' = 0 \tag{11}$$

from which we derive the classical proposition that price is determined by

$$p = \frac{\alpha}{\alpha - 1} C' \tag{12}$$

Moreover, in the constant elasticity case we derive the interesting conclusion that the optimal ratio of selling costs to the value of sales is determined solely by the ratio of the two elasticities α and β.

Instead of the Hahn result, say H-S, the approach of Fig. 1 enables us to define an average net revenue curve from which a marginal curve can be obtained and "clearly profit will be a maximum when marginal net revenue is equal to marginal production cost. It may readily be verified that this involves

$$MR = MC + MSC$$

where MR is marginal revenue, MSC is marginal selling cost and MC is marginal production cost" (p. 395). Thus they claim they do not make the "error" of equating gross marginal revenue and production cost. Unfortunately it is easy to show that their proposition is quite incorrect and that their approach leads exactly to the Hahn result.

To see this, consider their net revenue curve, NRC, which can be written in the form

$$NRC = q(p^* - \sigma^*) \tag{13}$$

where the optimal values p^* and σ^* are functions of q as defined by (8) and (9). Thus the profit function can be expressed also as a function of q as

$$\pi = q[p^*(q) - \sigma^*(q)] - cq \tag{14}$$

for constant marginal production cost c. As a necessary condition for maximum profits we have

$$0 = (p^* - \sigma^*) + q\frac{\partial p^*}{\partial q} - \frac{\partial \sigma^*}{\partial q} - c \tag{15}$$

which can be written in the form

$$p^*\left(1 + \frac{1}{e_{qp^*}}\right) - \sigma^*\left(1 + \frac{1}{e_{q\sigma^*}}\right) - c = 0 \tag{16}$$

where the e_{ij} are elasticities. From (8) and (9) it can be seen that these two elasticities are equal and defined by $(\beta - 1/\alpha - \beta)$. Moreover, it is also apparent that in the constant elasticity case the ratio between p^* and σ^* is constant and can be shown to be equal to the ratio of β to α. Putting this together it can be shown almost directly that the equilibrium price is exactly the same as defined by (12).

DISCRETIONARY AND VARIABLE SELLING COSTS

The H-S criticism of Hahn is quite unjustified. However, while their analysis does not establish what they think it does, their intuition raises a point of importance. They state that gross marginal revenue "must surely cover the additional cost of selling that unit as well as the extra cost of producing it" (p. 395). What they have not seen is that both their analysis and the Hahn analysis do not cover the point because they both fail to distinguish between variable and discretionary selling costs. The whole point here is that H-S and Hahn treat all selling costs as discretionary. Mathematically this means that when choosing the optimal values of p and S from the profit function (10), the partial derivative of (10) with respect to p is taken holding S constant. But if we exclude inventories and equate production and sales, there are some selling costs that will be variable with output. The problem here has nothing to do with the demand function as argued by H-S; it has to do with an implausible specification of the sales production function which requires certain costs to be incurred on the selling side in bringing to market, etc. If we specify a requirement that some selling costs (distribution, transport, etc.) are a function of production (sales), then it is easily shown that the optimal price will be partly determined by these costs. In this sense H-S are right that gross marginal revenue should cover the additional costs of selling a unit. But not all selling costs are of this type. In fact advertising broadly interpreted and other demand-shifting expenditures are not so variable and are discretionary. Indeed, since H-S are so keen to note the way in which the problem presents itself to businessmen, it may be observed that there is a clear distinction drawn by businessmen between the variable costs of selling and items like advertising that are usually defined as programmed costs. The theory of programmed costs is closer to the theory of capital and to treat all such costs as variable in the short run and so entering into the determination of short-run price is quite inappropriate—they would certainly not be so regarded by any business-man nor, we suggest, should such a treatment be advocated by any economist.

The critical question of how best to treat selling costs therefore remains open to some extent. It seems that Chamberlin is half right, for variable selling costs in the sense intended here are quite conveniently aggregated with production costs and treated as part of the cost of bringing goods to market. Such costs are unambiguously related to selling volume. They are necessary for any sales to be made at all, and they correctly enter into the determination of short-term price.

REFERENCES

1. Chamberlin, E. H., *The Theory of Monopolistic Competition*. Fifth edition (Harvard University Press, Cambridge, Mass., 1947).
2. Doyle, P., "Economic Aspects of Advertising: A Survey", *Economic Journal*, Vol. LXXVIII, September 1968.
3. Hahn, F. H., "The Theory of Selling Costs", *Economic Journal*, Vol. LXIX, June 1959.
4. Hieser, R. O., and Soper, C. S., "Demand Creation; A Radical Approach to the Theory of Selling Costs", *Economic Record*, Vol. 42, September 1966.
5. Dorfman, R., and Steiner, P. O., "Optimal Advertising and Optimal Quality", *American Economic Review*, XLIV, December 1954.

3

A Note on the Firm's Long-run Average Cost Curve *†

A. Ross Shepherd

RECENTLY, Chen Fu Chang criticized the standard textbook representation of the relationship between the firm's short-run average cost (SAC) curves and the firm's long-run average cost (LAC) curve.[1] The gist of his argument is that "... with few exceptions there seems to be no reason for the least-cost points of the SAC curves to be standing off the LAC curve, and the normal case of the LAC curve should consist of a series of the least-cost points of the SAC curves."[2]

The feature of the standard LAC envelope curve that most·perplexes Chang is the indication that beyond the point of minimum LAC the optimal input ratio for any given output requires a plant to be operated beyond its least-cost point. Chang finds it "inconceivable"[3] and "impossible"[4] that a larger plant operated at its point of minimum SAC could fail to be more efficient in producing that (minimum-cost) output than could a smaller plant operated beyond its point of minimum SAC. The reason he cites for his incredulity is that "It would certainly be cheaper to produce a certain output by adapting the scale so as to maintain [an] optimum proportion among factors than it would be by utilizing a given scale and thus disturbing this optimum proportion."[5]

*From *Quarterly Review of Economics & Business*, Vol. 11, Spring 1971, pp. 77–79. Reproduced by permission.

†The version of the paper which is reprinted here has benefited from the comment by J. Kirker Stephens, Associate Professor of Economics, University of Oklahoma, which appeared in the Autumn 1972 issue of the *Quarterly Review of Economics & Business*.

[1]Chen Fu Chang, "The Firm's Long-run Average Cost Curve," *Quarterly Review of Economics & Business*, Vol. 9 (Winter 1969), pp. 80–84.

[2]*Ibid.*, p. 84.   [3]*Ibid.*, p. 81.

[4]*Ibid.*, p. 83.   [5]*Ibid.*, p. 82.

After arguing that returns to scale normally exceed returns to variable proportions Chang concludes that it would be "...inconsistent...to allow for the least-cost points of the SAC curves lying above other SAC curves."[6]

Fortunately for those accustomed to the standard analysis, Chang's concern is misplaced. He has erroneously identified the optimum input ratios given by the firm's expansion path with the locus of minimum points on the SAC curves. As a result, he fails to distinguish between the optimum output for a given plant size and the optimum input ratio for producing that output when all factors are variable. The purpose of this note is to elucidate this distinction and show that the standard textbook representation is valid.

The standard diagram relating SAC curves and the LAC curve is shown in Chart 1, which is similar to Chang's Chart 1. Chart 2 shows the underlying production function. The firm's expansion path is assumed to be linear, as shown by the ray *OP*. This assumption makes it strictly correct to explain the behavior of long-run costs solely by reference to the concept of returns to scale, and it therefore is implicitly if not explicitly made in the usual textbook discussion. In order to rationalize the U-shaped LAC we assume that marginal returns to scale (i.e., the proportional increase in output divided by an equiproportional increase of all inputs) decline continuously with increases in output. From zero to q_2 output they are greater than one (increasing returns to scale), at q_2 they are equal to one (constant returns to scale), and beyond q_2 they are less than one (decreasing returns to scale). In Chart 2 the tangency points **a**,

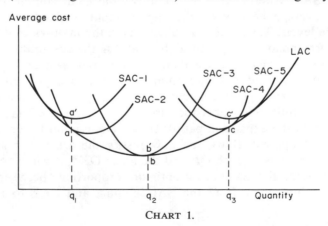

CHART 1.

[6] *Ibid.*

Capital

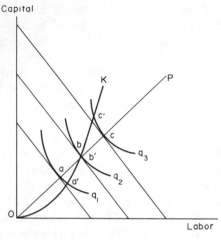

CHART 2.

b, and **c** between isoquants and isocost lines show the optimum input combinations for outputs q_1, q_2, and q_3, respectively. At each of these points ratios of marginal factor products equal ratios of factor prices. These points in the input–output space of Chart 2 correspond to the points **a**, **b**, and **c**, respectively, in the cost–output space of Chart 1. This is simply to say that the LAC curve is "... the cost–output space equivalent of the expansion path."[7]

In Chart 2 the locus OK^* is asserted to show the outputs that produce minimum SAC. Alternatively put, it shows the input combinations that minimize average cost when the capital input is fixed ($K = K^*$) at alternative levels. Thus points **a′**, **b′**, and **c′** in the input–output space of Chart 2 correspond to the points **a′**, **b′**, and **c′** in the cost–output space of Chart 1. In each chart we see that, as compared with optimum input ratios, producing q_1 at SAC minimum **a′** involves overly intense operation of a too small plant whereas producing q_3 at SAC minimum **c′** involves underutilization of a too large plant. Since SAC minimum **b′** coincides with the expansion path-LAC envelope point **b**, the indicated input ratio is optimal. If we can now justify the asserted relationship between the expansion path OP and the locus OK^*, it will be clear that Chang's concern for maintaining optimum proportions between factors should lead him away from the SAC minima and back to the LAC envelope.

[7]C. E. Ferguson, *Microeconomic Theory* (Homewood: Irwin, 1969), p. 205.

I will prove that under increasing, constant, and decreasing returns to scale the labor intensity of the SAC minima are, respectively, greater than, equal to, and less than the optima given by the expansion path, as is asserted by the drawing of Chart 2. Every point on the locus of SAC minima satisfies the condition:

$$P_K(K^*/Q) + P_L(L/Q) = P_L(1/MP_L), \tag{1}$$

where P_K and P_L are the price of capital and labor, respectively, Q is the quantity of output, K^* is the (fixed) capital, L is units of labor, and MP_L is the marginal physical product of labor. The first term on the left side is average fixed cost, the second is average variable cost, and the right-side term is marginal cost. Equation (1) is easily manipulated to yield

$$P_K/P_L = (Q/MP_L - L)/K^*. \tag{1'}$$

Now from the mathematics of production functions we have it that[8]

$$(MP_K)(K/Q) + (MP_L)(L/Q) = r. \tag{2}$$

The terms on the left side of Equation (2) are, respectively, the output elasticity of capital and the output elasticity of labor, whereas r is the marginal returns to scale. Multiplying both sides of (2) by Q yields

$$(MP_K)K + (MP_L)L = rQ. \tag{2'}$$

The left side of Equation (2') will be greater than, equal to, or less than Q as r is greater than, equal to, or less than unity. Thus we may write

$$MP_K/MP_L \gtreqless (Q/MP_L - L)/K, \tag{2''}$$

where one of the inequalities or the equality holds depending on the value of r. So from Equations (1') and (2'') we see that along OK^* of Chart 2:

$$(MP_K)/(MP_L) \gtreqless (Q/MP_L - L)/K = P_K/P_L   (K = K^*). \tag{3}$$

For $r > 1$, as it is below output q_2 in Chart 2, $MP_K/MP_L > P_K/P_L$, and the capital/labor ratios at the SAC minima are suboptimally low. When $r = 1$, as it does at output q_2 in Chart 2, the ratios of marginal products and factor prices are equal and the SAC minimum yields an optimal input ratio. For $r < 1$, as it is assumed to be above output q_2 in Chart 2, $MP_K/MP_L < P_K/P_L$, and the capital/labor ratios at the SAC minima are suboptimally large. Thus we have shown that the relationship between the expansion path, OP, and the locus of SAC minima, OK^*, is correctly drawn in Chart 2.

[8]*Ibid.*, pp. 140–43.

R.I.M.E.—H

An intuitive explanation of the increasing capital intensity of the SAC minima is not far to seek. As the scale of operations expands in the standard textbook model, **r** falls and so does each of the output elasticities. Therefore, as the scale increases and capital is fixed (in the short run) at higher levels, it is necessary in seeking SAC minima to reduce the relative usage of the variable factor, labor.[9]

[9]The argument is symmetrical. If labor is fixed in the short run, SAC minima will require reductions in the relative usage of the variable factor, capital, as the scale of operations expands.

4

Cost–Effectiveness Analysis: Implications for Accountants*

Barry G. King

SELECTION from among alternative uses of sizable, but limited, financial resources in order to meet stipulated, but often vague, objectives is a challenge to modern management of both private and public enterprise. Particularly challenging are those situations in which the immediate objectives of management cannot be conveniently reduced to the profit motive, so that alternative means of meeting these objectives cannot be compared on the basis of relative profitability. Recent years have seen the development and refinement of a number of analytical approaches for meeting this challenge. A family of these approaches has become known under such names as (1) systems analysis, (2) cost–effectiveness analysis, (3) operations analysis, (4) cost–benefit analysis, (5) cost–utility analysis and (6) planning, programming and budgeting system (PPBS). No attempt is made in this article to distinguish the shades of meaning in these terms as they are used in the field and in the literature. All refer to the attempt to apply a systematic, analytical approach to problems of choice. *Cost–effectiveness* analysis has been selected for this discussion, but much of what follows could be said about others of the group.

Cost–effectiveness is a term which has been used in a formal sense only in recent years. Wide publicity was given to the use of the technique in managing the activities of the Department of Defense under Robert McNamara. Many of the top people brought into the Defense Department by McNamara came from the Rand Corporation, where they had been

*From *The Journal of Accountancy*, March 1970, pp. 43–49. Copyright © 1970 by the American Institute of Certified Public Accountants, Inc. Reproduced by permission.

working on problems concerning "the economies of defense,"[1] and where the formal approach had been developed.

In its narrowest sense, cost–effectiveness analysis may be defined as a technique for choosing among *given* alternative courses of action in terms of their cost and their effectiveness in the attainment of *specified* objectives. Treated as given by the analyst are: (1) A specific statement of objectives, (2) a complete listing of the alternative solutions to be considered and (3) acceptable measures of effectiveness in meeting objectives. The decision-maker is viewed as a "higher-order" system who sets these constraints, and for whom the analysis will provide informational inputs for making his choice.

In a broader sense, cost–effectiveness has been defined as simply a "technique for evaluating broad management and economic implications of alternative choices of action with the objective of assisting in the identification of the preferred choice."[2] Here the analyst takes a somewhat more general view of the decision-maker's problem and is concerned with (1) less explicitly stated objectives, (2) undefined alternative solutions and (3) more subjective measures of effectiveness.

For example, cost–effectiveness analysis may be applied in its narrower sense to the problem of deciding among three proposed aircraft systems. The objective may be one of providing capability of transporting personnel, with effectiveness to be measured in terms of the aircrafts' technical characteristics, such as payload, speed and reliability.

On the other hand, the approach may be utilized in its broader sense, in the case where the objective above becomes one of providing personnel at key locations when needed. The alternatives for meeting this objective go far beyond three competing airplanes, and involve strategies of personnel assignment as well as logistical considerations. Most of the more interesting problems arise in this latter, broader context, and it is this view of cost–effectiveness which is pursued in this article.

Two characteristics of the analysis deserve special emphasis. First, cost–effectiveness analysis is output-oriented. As such, decision situations are analyzed from a program, or mission, viewpoint rather than from a functional one. Problems are treated not as production, marketing or financing problems, but as problems in carrying out a specified program.

---

[1] See Hitch, Charles J., and McKean, Roland N., *Economics of Defense in the Nuclear Age* (Cambridge: Harvard Press, 1960).

[2] Heuston, M. C., and Ogawa, G., "Observations on the Theoretical Basis of Cost Effectiveness," *Operations Research*, March–April 1966, pp. 242–266.

Second, the approach emphasizes effectiveness as opposed to technical economic efficiency in the allocation of resources. In a technical sense, resources are allocated efficiently when an increase in one output can be obtained only at a sacrifice of another output or with an increase in input, whereas effectiveness measures, in terms of an objective, the comparative desirability of alternative efficient allocations.

It is the purpose of this article to describe and illustrate the methodology of cost–effectiveness analysis in a nontechnical manner, and to specify some implications that the approach seems to have for accountants.

METHODOLOGY

Although it may include the use of models developed as operations research techniques, cost–effectiveness analysis should not be considered as simply another *OR* tool or technique. Unlike such tools as mathematical programming and queuing theory, which are useful only in solving particular classes of problems which can be structured according to prescribed formats, cost–effectiveness analysis is designed to yield solutions that are uniquely responsive to particular problems. It deals with problems which are ill-structured and which have objectives that are less precisely defined. Thus, the methodology of cost–effectiveness analysis cannot be set forth as a set of standard procedures, but must be outlined as a sequence of general steps which constitute an approach. These include:

1. Definition of objectives.
2. Identification of alternatives.
3. Selection of effectiveness measures.
4. Development of cost estimates.
5. Selection of a decision criterion.
6. Creation of models relating cost and effectiveness.

Objectives

The beginning point for any analysis must be a consideration of objectives. Objectives, the desired goal (or goals) to be attained by the use of resources, must be defined as explicitly as possible. Careless selection and specification of objectives can lead to solution of the wrong problem.

Alternatives

The alternatives represent the competing "systems" for accomplishing objectives. They represent opposing strategies, policies or specific actions as well as the necessary elements, such as materials, men, machines, etc. Even though certain elements or tactics may overlap, each alternative is viewed as a complete system. These alternatives need not be obvious substitutes for each other or perform the same specific function.[3]

Effectiveness Measures

Overall performance must be combined into appropriate measures that gauge the effectiveness of each alternative. Choosing appropriate measures of effectiveness is probably the most difficult unique problem in cost–effectiveness analysis. The challenge is to provide measures that are relevant to the objective sought and measurable in terms that allow comparisons of effectiveness among alternatives.

In order to compare alternatives, a single quantitative indicator of effectiveness would be the ideal. As in the case in most situations, however, such a single measure is not available. Nonetheless, measures tempered with judgment concerning nonquantifiable aspects should lead to satisfactory comparisons of effectiveness of given alternatives.

Cost Estimates

To implement a given alternative, it is anticipated that certain resources must be used. Foregoing the use of these resources elsewhere represents a cost in the economic sense. Estimation of the cost of the alternatives constitutes a very important and difficult step in cost–effectiveness analysis.

Basically, two issues are involved: (1) what costs to include and (2) how to measure them. What is desired, of course, is an estimate of all *relevant* costs of each alternative. The concepts of sunk costs, incremental costs and joint costs, all familiar to accountants, are applicable in the same manner as in traditional accounting analyses.

---

[3]Quade, E. S., "Systems Analysis Techniques for Planning–Programming–Budgeting" in *Systems, Organizations, Analysis, Management: A Book of Readings*, edited by David I. Cleland and William R. King (New York: McGraw-Hill, 1969), p. 195.

Selection of a Decision Criterion

The decision criterion is the standard by which all alternatives are evaluated in terms of cost and effectiveness. Three types of valid criteria from which the analyst must choose are: (1) maximize effectiveness at given cost; (2) minimize cost while attaining a given effectiveness; or (3) some combination of these two which recognizes a tradeoff of cost for effectiveness to maximize a selected utility function of the two factors (e.g., maximize effectiveness minus cost, where the two can be expressed in common terms).

Adoption of an invalid criterion can be deceptively easy. For example, the statement "maximize effectiveness at a minimum cost" reflects a criterion that can seldom be met. It is not reasonable to believe that the best alternative from a number of feasible ones in terms of effectiveness will also be the one that costs the least. Also, the criterion—maximize the *ratio* of effectiveness to cost, or "effectiveness per dollar"—can also be seen to be invalid unless the ratio remains constant for all levels of activity.

Creation of Models

Having determined adequate measures of cost and effectiveness, and a criterion by which to compare alternatives, there remains the problem of formulating analytical relationships among costs, effectiveness and environmental factors. Needed are cost models, effectiveness models and a synthesizing model based on outputs from them.

Cost models attempt to describe relationships between the characteristics of a given alternative (system) and its costs. Thus the result of operating a cost model should be an estimate of the cost of each alternative. Effectiveness models attempt to describe relationships between an alternative's characteristics and its effectiveness. The result of operating an effectiveness model should be an estimate of the effectiveness of each alternative. Additionally, and very significantly, these models should provide tradeoff relationships between system costs and characteristics as well as tradeoffs between system effectiveness and characteristics. For example, besides outputting the fact that alternative A has characteristics X, Y and Z with a cost of C, the cost model should provide relationships such as estimated marginal cost of changes in system characteristics. The synthesizing model should provide relationships between cost and effectiveness among alternatives. It should provide aid in answering such questions as: (1) How much effectiveness can be bought with an additional $X spent on alternative A? (2) What is the cost of a given increase in the effectiveness of alternative B?

Model structure depends on how well the analyst knows the relationships which are to be expressed in the model, along with the complexity of the alternatives involved. If relationships are fairly well known, they may be expressed in algebraic terms and solved by use of the calculus. Other well-developed and understood techniques of operations research, such as mathematical programming, and simulation, are available when applicable. Operational gaming may be used to determine less well-known relationships when the human element is crucial. Finally some relationships may be so uncertain that the only acceptable model is verbal.

Figure 1 is an attempt to depict in pictorial form the structure of

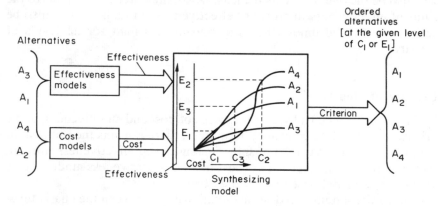

FIG. 1. Structure of cost–effectiveness analysis.

the analysis.[4] In this figure, the curves relating cost and effectiveness permit illustration of both the criterion of maximizing effectiveness with given cost and minimizing cost of given effectiveness. For example, effectiveness is maximized with a given cost of C_1 by using alternative A_1 or with a given cost of C_2 by alternative A_4. Cost is minimized with a given effectiveness of E_3 by choosing alternative A_2. The ordered alternatives shown in the figure are the result of applying either criterion at the level of C_1 or E_1.

[4]This illustration is adapted from one used by Quade, E. S., "Introduction and Overview," in Goldman, *Cost–Effectiveness Analysis, op. cit.,* p. 6.

LIMITATIONS

Several limitations of cost–effectiveness analysis should be considered. First, it must be realized that all results are merely inputs to be judged along with other less systematic factors by a higher-level decision-maker. Quade summarizes this limitation by saying, "No matter how we strive to maintain standards of scientific inquiry or how closely we attempt to follow scientific methods, we cannot turn cost–effectiveness analysis into science. Its objective, in contrast to that of science, is primarily to recommend—or at least to suggest—policy, rather than merely to understand and predict."[5]

A second limitation of the analysis is the difficulty in selecting measures of effectiveness. The best that can be done is to reasonably approximate objectives with measures which can aid in guiding decision-making.

A third limitation results from imperfect information. Insufficient input information in terms of costs and benefits of various alternatives may result in an analysis that is misleading or downright erroneous.

A final limitation which should be mentioned is the lack of a probability orientation in most cost–effectiveness analysis. Whereas several techniques for including probability factors in quantitative models have been developed in an attempt to measure uncertainty, almost no use has been made of these in cost–effectiveness analysis.

IMPLICATIONS FOR ACCOUNTING

The foregoing has been very general and non-technical in an attempt simply to introduce some basic concepts of cost–effectiveness analysis. Avoided were the very relevant, but somewhat technical, aspects of the mathematics of maximization,[6] which is the basis for most of the quantitative models in the analysis. There appear to be some germane implications for accounting. These fall conveniently into four categories:

1. Implications for an expanded concept of organizational objectives.
2. Implications for an increased knowledge of quantitative management science.
3. Implications for design and operation of management information (data) systems.

---

[5]Quade, E. S., "Systems Analysis Techniques for Planning–Programming–Budgeting," *op. cit.*, p. 201.

[6]For a discussion of the "Mathematics of Maximization," see Hitch, Charles J., and McKean, Roland N., *op. cit.*, Appendix A.

4. Implications for more sophistication in cost estimation and forecasting.

Expanded Concept of Organization Objectives

Accountants have been performing a form of cost–effectiveness analysis for some time. Capital budgeting analysis, incremental cost analysis and financial source selection are all decisions to which the basic cost–effectiveness approach is used. All involve evaluation of alternatives for which return is compared with cost as a criterion for selection. The common factor which they exhibit is that effectiveness is measured in terms of return (profitability). Thus cost and effectiveness are stated in terms of a common denominator—dollars.

Modern management must initiate, plan and control activities which are designed to meet objectives which are not primarily profit-oriented and whose effectiveness cannot be adequately measured in dollars. Accountants must be willing and prepared to provide information about and perform analysis of such activities. This includes understanding and helping to define objectives explicitly as well as searching for adequate measures of effectiveness. Perhaps even more significant for accountants than this responsibility to management for aid in their decision-making is an implied responsibility for external reporting of the results of such activities.

Quantitative Management Science

Several concepts of management science are exemplified in cost–effectiveness analysis. These serve to point out areas in which accountants should become knowledgeable. First, the accountant must understand the concept of a model and the modeling process, its uses and limitations. He needs to view models as descriptions or representations of the real world, quantitative or nonquantitative, which are valuable only to the extent that they accurately depict the situation. Also there needs to be the ability to conceptualize problems in an "input–output" format. That is, the accountant must take the approach which takes controllable variables as inputs and manipulates them to learn more about the uncontrollable variables, eventually resulting in an output which optimizes, or at least satisfies, the objectives.

Another valuable aspect of the mathematics in management science is the capacity to express and manipulate relationships in functional form.

Cost-estimating relationships (CERs) are nothing more than functions which treat cost as a dependent variable and other factors as independent variables.

Information and Data Systems

Perhaps the weakest link in cost–effectiveness analysis is the "data gap." Models of cost and effectiveness are no better than the data used in developing them and as input to them. Too often, accurate timely data of the type needed are not available. Brussell has the following comment:

"Today the modeling aspects of cost–effectiveness analysis are firmly entrenched. However, there has been a misallocation of research resources as between model building and data inputting or estimating. The conceptual problem of formulating models is relatively easy but probably more interesting and prestigious than the actual bird-dogging, collection, understanding, and estimation of grubby old numbers. There are undoubtedly increasing returns to analysis by improving the input numbers, both cost and performance data, whereas there are diminishing returns when the aim is at better models, cost models included."[7]

The same data gap exists in the use of most management science models and techniques. Accountants, because of their interest in information and data processing, should be vitally concerned with development of systems which improve the quality of input data for decision models.

Cost Estimation

Cost–effectiveness analysis offers the challenge of estimating costs of activities which are unique and for which past cost data are unavailable. Here unavailability is not caused by the cost system, but the fact that the activity has not been tried before. More sophisticated estimating and forecasting techniques must be used. Effects on cost of many factors must be predicted. Accountants have for a long time realized the value of analytical techniques which employ the concept of variable costs. Thus the effect of volume on cost is well recognized. What has not been developed on the part of many accountants is the capability of analyzing costs in terms of other potential independent variables. Techniques of regression and correlation analysis should be mastered.

[7]Brussell, Eugene R., "Defense Contractor Use of Cost–Effectiveness Analysis," in Goldman, *Cost–Effectiveness Analysis, op. cit.*, p. 114.

A related point involves the approach taken with regard to cost estimation. Accountants have traditionally taken a "micro" or "building block" view of cost estimating, based on the breakdown of cost present in the accounting system. Costs of the smallest elements into which costs can be divided are estimated and total cost is derived by aggregating these elementary costs. Tradeoff relationships between cost and effectiveness and between costs of two or more competing alternatives are difficult and time-consuming to determine. The alternative is to take a "macro" or "broad-brush" approach to estimating costs. This approach involves costing the total system in terms of its parameters, i.e., system characteristics and capabilities. For example, estimating costs of a new airplane may be done in terms of its speed, range, reliability, payload, etc., based on historical data for similar planes, as opposed to a detailed costing of all elements of labor, materials, indirect cost, etc., involved in designing and producing it.

In summary, the framework for cost–effectiveness analysis has been outlined in a nontechnical manner. This form of analysis is being used extensively, although sometimes under other names, in government and will be used more extensively in the future in private enterprise. Therefore, accountants should be aware of it, its uses and limitations.

5

An Approach to Productivity in Two
Knowledge-based Industries*

JOHN F. ROCKART

INTRODUCTION

Traditionally Americans have looked toward an increase in productivity to help create a better life. Despite some periods of fluctuation, productivity in this country has increased steadily and contributed to a rising standard of living from year to year. Recently, however, the proportion of the economy represented by service industries has shown a major increase.[1] Since most service industries are labor-intensive and have shown little evidence of productivity increase, their effect on the overall long-term productivity trend has become subject to increasing scrutiny.[2] Peter Drucker expressed this idea succinctly: "The bulk of tomorrow's employment will be in the service trades, knowledge jobs—in health care, teaching, government, management, research and the like. And no one knows much about the productivity of knowledge work, let alone how to improve it."[3]

The importance of this concern cannot be underrated. The two major knowledge-based industries of education and medicine account for approximately 10 percent of the gross national product. Medicine in 1971 was 7.4 percent of the G.N.P. Education accounted for 2.5 percent.[4] Most observers expect these figures to grow considerably within the next

*From *Sloan Management Review* (Massachusetts Institute of Technology), Vol. 15, No. 1, Fall 1973, pp. 23–33. Copyright © 1973 by the Industrial Management Review Association, all rights reserved. Reproduced by permission.

[1]See Fuchs [5], pp. 19–24, and Reynolds [11], pp. 61–66.
[2]See [10], and Bowen [2], p. 65.
[3]See Drucker [3].
[4]See [19].

decade. Yet, as Drucker points out, there has been very little analysis concerning productivity in these vital industries.

Education and medicine are treated together here because of their similarity. Both industries are dominated by professionals—faculty and physicians respectively. Among these dominant "employee-groups," ties to disciplines are usually stronger than ties to organizations. Dual power structures, professional and administrative, exist within the organizations in each industry. Both industries are heavily labor-intensive. In each it is difficult to measure clearly the value of the product delivered. Although there are differences between the two industries, the similarities are striking.

For health services, studies differ regarding the direction of productivity changes. One set of studies suggests a decline of 0.3 percent per year between 1947 and 1965, followed thereafter by a slight increase of 0.6 percent per year.[5] Barzel, on the other hand, found that productivity per physician visit rose 0.6 percent per year between 1949 and 1964.[6] At any rate, the increases and decreases in productivity in the industry are not very significant, nor are they in education.

Three stated reasons for this paucity of reported productivity gains, or even attempts to increase productivity in these two industries, are easily identified. First, it is difficult to measure effectively the output of either the medical or teaching process since the products are not clearly definable.[7] Second, if output is raised, it is argued that quality probably will be reduced. Finally, it is suggested that measures to increase output will destroy the creative urge of the professional involved. In sum, if productivity increases are forced, not only will it be impossible to measure them, but both the quality of the work and the professional's satisfaction in that work probably will decrease. Faced with these obstacles and other considerations primarily raised by the professionals themselves, managers in these two industries seldom have pressed for greater productivity or even for research into it.[8]

Increased productivity is, however, *not* incompatible with quality or "professional satisfaction" considerations. Given certain conditions, which are noted below, it is possible to move in a positive direction with respect to all variables. One thing that is clear with regard to productivity

[5]See Spengler [18].
[6]See Barzel [1].
[7]See Kershaw and Mood [8].
[8]This tendency has been strengthened by the fact that in both industries costs have been, until very recently, merely passed on to the consumer.

in knowledge-based industries is that the work environment is different from the typical production shop. Most significantly, professional manpower is the key resource which must be made productive. Human interaction is the primary mode of "business." It is also true that the end product, "output", of the production processes in these industries is rarely well-defined. To deal effectively with productivity in these industries, one must account for this different set of circumstances.

Additional study is needed to understand what can and cannot be done about productivity in knowledge-based industries. The immeasurability problem can be dismissed, at least temporarily. Assuming that the overall product of the processes under investigation cannot be measured (it is difficult, for example, to know what a student *really* has learned), there are secondary measures which will suffice, at least for the present time. These secondary measures include such things as relative examination performance in education or changed input time to achieve the same *perceived* output in medicine.[9]

METHODS OF INCREASING PRODUCTIVITY

Productivity gains usually have been developed by either revising the content of a particular job or providing more output with the same inputs through improved scheduling. Job content can be changed either by mechanizing certain job steps (i.e., automation, the popular view of *the* way to increase productivity) or, alternatively, by turning particular parts of the job over to lower-paid human resources. Improved scheduling can be used to increase resource utilization either through *prospective* schedule smoothing or through *retrospective* analysis of productivity leading to changes in future periods. There are thus four major approaches to increasing productivity. The examples below illustrate how each can be applied in knowledge-based industries.

Changing Medical Job Content by Automation

In one effort to increase physician productivity through the revision of job content, an automated medical history questionnaire (AMHQ) has been developed at the Lahey Clinic in Boston. This 160 item questionnaire is mailed to the patient approximately two weeks before he registers initially at the clinic. The patient completes the form in the quiet of his

---

[9]See Enthoven [4], and Keller [7].

home with his own medical and family records available for reference. The form, which takes about forty-five minutes to complete, is then mailed back to the clinic where it is optically scanned and computer processed to edit the output into relatively terse medical terminology. The physician annotates this patient history record with additional findings. The considerable amount of patient information available is very important to the physician as he begins his own history-taking process. Moreover the process of writing in the record is reduced. Each questionnaire costs approximately $1.50, and with a mean physician-reported time savings of approximately four minutes, the benefits outweigh the cost in dollar terms by a factor of three.

Physician acceptance of the system is good and has improved with time. Yet the questionnaire is not perfect. Physicians still must check the history which it provides. Its primary value has been as a data base for more intensive medical evaluations. There is evidence that productivity has risen, while quality at least has remained constant (many physicians believe it has risen), and acceptance of this method change by the professionals is good.

There are two major reasons why this productivity-increasing automation of job content has been successful with respect to all variables. First, a respected professional, then the chairman of the Department of Internal Medicine at the Lahey Clinic, took the leading role in developing the content of the questionnaire. Many other physicians also were involved heavily in developing the questionnaire. Second, in determining the needs and methods of system development, a significant amount of analysis was performed by computer and other systems experts who served as staff to the physicians. A study of the factors leading to acceptance of the AMHQ by the physicians has shown clearly that *participation* in its development is by far the most significant factor in professional acceptance and use.[10]

Changing Medical Job Content by Substitution

The other approach to changing job content, substituting the labor of less well-trained and less well-paid para-professionals for that of professionals, is being carried out in several places today. Notable in the medical field are the efforts of the Medex program and the ambulatory care project at Beth Israel Hospital.[11] Both of these programs are aimed at developing para-medical personnel who can satisfactorily deal with

[10]See McLean [9].
[11]See Smith [17], and Sherman and Reiferi [16].

patient complaints which do not require the expertise of a physician. Although large-scale tests have not yet been completed, it appears that both programs are effective. Indications are that the Beth Israel paramedics (who have only four weeks of training and work from structured questionnaires and detailed instructions) will be able to save physicians from seeing a large percentage of routine complaints.

Changing Job Content in Education through Automation and Substitution

Productivity in higher education has changed little over the past two thousand years. The traditional lecture method and class discussions have continued throughout time. More recently the case method has grown as a method of instruction, but has done little for productivity. Some gains have been made through televising an instructor's lecture to multiple classrooms at some loss in quality. Video tape also has had a minor impact. There has been a continuing substitution in education of lower cost factors in the form of doctoral fellows as teachers but this is neither new nor will it be a major source of productivity increases in the future. What is most significant is the continuing heavy dependence on the teacher-resource as the predominant actor in a learning process that remains focused around the classroom setting.

Recently computer technology has been discovered and used. The student himself has been identified as a resource in the learning process, and self-paced, self-study courses have been developed.[12] Unfortunately in most cases this "new technology" has been viewed as the total answer to presentation considerations for the entire course. There rarely has been an integration of methods so that the student is made to adapt to this "all or nothing" approach with varying results.

In a recent attempt to maximize teacher productivity while at the same time increasing student satisfaction and professional acceptance of the method, the author adopted an approach of fitting the methods to the task at hand at the Sloan School of Management at M.I.T.[13] First, the *learning objectives* of the course were developed. Second, the *material* which could be used to enable the students to meet these learning objectives was selected. Third, the best *method of learning* for each type of material was selected. Finally, the *learning resource* (professor, student, or technology) appropriate for the particular material and method of learning was chosen.

[12]See Keller [6].
[13]See Rockart [12].

From this groundwork the course was conducted using three distinct resources. One set of eight sessions was termed *professor-intensive*. In these sessions the professor either lectured or led class discussions to expose and transmit material which motivated the student towards the course; discussed in depth "gray areas" of the material; or delivered new material which had not yet been sufficiently committed to written form. However a majority of the material in this course is well understood and has been more than adequately described in textbooks. This written material formed the basis for a set of fifteen *student-intensive* sessions. Basically these were self-study periods. For these sessions students learned by themselves from textbooks following directions presented in study modules developed especially for the course. For those students having trouble with segments of the material or desiring deeper knowledge about any part of it, the professor was available during the regularly scheduled classroom periods for question-answer sessions in which the students initiated the lines of discussion. Student attendance at these sessions varied from fifteen to fifty percent of the class.

Finally, computer technology was used for one *technology-intensive* session. As he performs traditional homework, the student is never sure whether he is right. Fragmented homework assignments often prevent the student from grasping the essentials in an integrated way, while long turn-around times for corrected papers provide corrections only after the student has lost interest in the material. Interactive computer homework, therefore, has several advantages. Each mistake can be corrected through "tutoring" on the spot. Tedious extraneous writing and small arithmetic mistakes are avoided as these functions are performed by the computer. In this way, the speed of working through a computer assisted problem set is greater. This speed coupled with dynamic graphic displays can enable the student to better visualize the entire process he is working through. It is this combination of learning methods and resources (each method utilized for the material it fits best) which can best lead to increased productivity as well as satisfaction on the part of both teacher and student.

The possibility of putting several sections together for question-answer sessions (since less than half of the students attend these sessions) allows increased professor productivity.[14] In addition the quality of output in terms of grades and student acceptance, at least in this case, was

---

[14]Only the students who sincerely need help or who want a deeper coverage of the material attend. The majority of the class for whom the textbook and the instructional modules provide a satisfactory self-study method of learning stays away.

increased by this manner of teaching. Faculty acceptance was good, but once again it should be noted that the professionals involved had been instrumental in developing the new method. Similar results were found in the summer of 1972 with a second repetition of the course.

In the short run it is clear that measurably greater productivity is possible in education with a concomitant increase in quality. A detailed, tedious but systematic *analysis* of course objectives and material lead to a workable "new product" design. In this case, too, *participation* and *involvement* on the part of the professionals involved was perhaps most significant in leading to acceptance of change. The results attainable by other professionals with lower levels of participation and involvement in the development of the new methodology are at present uncertain.

Prospective Scheduling in the Medical Setting

The second major way of increasing professional productivity is to improve the utilization of professional time through more effective scheduling. This can be done either *prospectively* or *retrospectively*. In this section the prospective scheduling of physicians is discussed. Retrospective analysis of the scheduling of university faculty is examined in the next section.

Multiple-specialist group medical practices today are moving out of the cottage industry stage into an era in which there is a need for probing analysis of the coordinated use of physician and other resources in the delivery of medical care. The primary asset of these medical practices is a highly perishable inventory of available physician time which must be effectively and efficiently utilized if medical care costs are to be contained.

The major misuse of this primary asset occurs through daily variations in the demand for and use of each of the physician resources. There are multiple reasons for this variability in demand, some of which can be controlled. The author's research group at the Lahey Clinic in Boston currently is attempting to reduce the effects of several sources of this variability.

The effects of this variability of resource demand are clear. On a given day, a specialist who is fully scheduled for a three hour morning clinic may have the following occur. His first patient may be a "no-show." The next three, all scheduled for thirty minutes each, may take an average of ten minutes apiece. His fifth patient, originally given an appointment by the scheduling office, might be cancelled through a previous physician's decision that an appointment with the specialist is unnecessary. Although the rest of his patients are seen for approximately the amount of time scheduled, the physician will have had an under-scheduled morning and the physician resources of the Clinic will have been under utilized.

On the other hand, the opposite can happen. Patients can take more time than scheduled. Additional patients can be sent to the specialist by other physicians who believe these patients must be seen on an emergency basis. The scheduling office may, through clerical error, have "double-booked" the specialist for one or more appointment times. As a result on *this* morning the physician is actually heavily overscheduled, hurried, and late in seeing each patient. This example illustrates how both the physician and his patients could become quite distressed.

In an early study of this problem the author isolated more than a dozen possible sources of variability in demand for physician resources. These may be reduced into four major solution areas. These are the improvement of:

1. The routing of patients to physician specialists
2. The estimation of service time or the time a patient will spend with a physician
3. The clerical scheduling process
4. Management control of the overall scheduling process through analysis and system change.

Efforts at reducing variability in the first, second, and fourth areas have been reported extensively elsewhere.[15] The improvement of clerical processes and management control of the scheduling system will be used here to illustrate the potential inherent in reducing or eliminating some of the causes of schedule variation. Concomitant increases in productivity also will be noted.

The primary tool in these areas has been the construction of an on-line computer scheduling system. The system provides the appointment coordinators with files containing patient data and physician schedules enabling them to schedule each patient using more accessible information than they had in the past. As a result, the appointment coordinators can make more effective use of the physician time available for scheduling.

---

[15]See Rockart *et al.* [13], Rockart and Herzog [15], and Rockart *et al.* [14].

Using Retrospective Data for Scheduling Purposes in the Educational Environment

A multi-specialist medical group practice approximates an industrial production shop where effective prescheduling can influence resource utilization. The "production" schedule of professional activities, however, is less apparent, the scheduling period is much longer, and the schedules are apt to change drastically, often at the will of the professional himself. This scenario also applies, it is clear, to the conditions under which a university faculty works.

The best balanced set of prescheduled loads for the faculty of a school can be drastically changed during the three to four month period of these schedules. The professional himself can affect drastically his load on the positive side, for example, by volunteering to take additional sections of courses where student demand is high, taking on a heavy load of thesis students, or responding to other demands on faculty time so that he heavily over schedules himself during the term. Other faculty members may follow a reverse strategy and be underloaded. Even the most far-sighted prescheduling method can not anticipate these circumstances.

As a result there is a need to apply retrospective analysis as a scheduling aid. This involves assessing the loads that professionals have taken on themselves in previous periods and recognizing these self-loading tendencies when scheduling future activities. Professionals who have had light loads for previous periods can be more heavily prescheduled in the future and vice versa. Increasing the loads of professionals with lighter loads will increase overall productivity since their more motivated colleagues will continue to find productive outlets for their time.

REFERENCES

1. Barzel, Y. "Productivity and the Price of Medical Services." *Economy*, 77 (1969): 1014–1027.
2. Bowen, W. G. "The Economics of the Major Private Universities." The Carnegie Commission on the Future of Higher Education, Berkeley, California, 1968.
3. Drucker, P. "The Surprising Seventies." *Harper's Magazine*, July, 1971, pp. 35–39.
4. Enthoven, A. C. "Measures of the Outputs of Higher Education: Some Practical Suggestions for Their Development and Use." Office of the Vice President for Planning and Analysis, University of California, May, 1970.
5. Fuchs, V. R. *The Service Economy.* New York: National Bureau of Economic Research, 1968.
6. Keller, F. S. "Goodbye Teacher." *Journal of Applied Behavior Analysis*, 1 (1968): 78–89.

7. Keller, J. K. "Higher Education Objectives: Measures of Performance and Effectiveness." Western Interstate Commission for Higher Education. Boulder, Colorado, July 1970.
8. Kershaw, J. A. and Mood, A. M. "Resource Allocation in Higher Education." *Monthly Labor Review*, March 1970, pp. 46–48.
9. McLean, E. R. "A Computer-Based Medical History System: Factors Affecting Its Acceptance and Use by Physicians." Ph.D. dissertation, Massachusetts Institute of Technology, 1970.
10. "Productivity: Industry Isn't the Only Place Where It's a Problem." *Forbes*, February 1, 1971, pp. 43–45.
11. Reynolds, L. G. *Labor Economics and Labor Relations.* Englewood Cliffs: Prentice–Hall, 1970.
12. Rockart, J. F. "An Integrated Use of Available Resources (Student, Professor, and Technology) in the Learning Process." Sloan School of Management Working Paper, Massachusetts Institute of Technology, 1972.
13. Rockart, J. F. *et al.* "A Symptom Scoring Technique for Scheduling Patients in a Group Practice." *Proceedings of the IEEE*, 57 (1969): 1926–1933.
14. Rockart, J. F. *et al.* "Interim Results of an Ambulatory Scheduling Project." *Lahey Clinic Foundation Bulletin*, January–March 1973, pp. 5–16.
15. Rockart, J. F. and Herzog, E. L. "A Predictive Model for Ambulatory Patient Service Time." Sloan School of Management Working Paper, Massachusetts Institute of Technology, 1972.
16. Sherman, H. and Reiferi, B. "Ambulatory Care Project Reports 1–24." Beth Israel Hospital and Harvard Medical School, Boston, Mass., 1971–1972.
17. Smith, R. A. "Medex." *J.A.M.A.*, 211 (1970): 1843–1845.
18. Spengler, J. J. "Cost of Specialization in a Service Economy." *Social Science Quarterly*, 51 (1970): 237–262.
19. U.S., Bureau of the Census, *Statistical Abstract of the U.S.*, 93rd Edition (Washington, D.C.: Government Printing Office, 1972).

6

Medium Range Aggregate Production Planning: State of the Art*

EDWARD A. SILVER

I. INTRODUCTION

In this paper we are concerned with a problem that faces the majority of manufacturing concerns, namely how, under seasonal demand conditions, to rationally set work force sizes and production rates. The production supervisor desires long runs of individual items so as to reduce production costs; the marketing personnel wish to have a substantial inventory of a wide range of finished goods; those concerned with labor relations desire a stable work force size; finally, the comptroller generally wants as low an inventory level as possible. It is clear that these objectives are conflicting in nature. Therefore, a cross-departmental (or systems) approach to the solution of the problem is essential.

In 1966 the author presented an invited tutorial paper on this subject. The current writeup differs from the earlier publication [42] in several respects, particularly in terms of including the significant developments in the area during the last few years. An excellent recent reference on the subject is a publication by Buffa [7]. His discussion is illustrated by an earlier study performed by Gordon [13].

In the next section we more carefully define the medium range production planning problem. This is followed, in Section III, by a discussion of the relevant costs involved. Section IV presents a brief

*From *Production and Inventory Management*, First Quarter 1972, March 1972, pp. 15–40. Reproduced by permission. An expanded version of this article is presented in, R. Peterson and E. A. Silver, *Decision Systems for Inventory Management and Production Planning*, New York, John Wiley and Sons, 1975.

description of the different basic approaches to the problem. Some of these are amplified in Sections V through VIII. Section IX deals with an important finding of several of the approaches. Section X broadens the scope of the study; we look at ways of changing the "givens" of the earlier problem.

II. PROBLEM DEFINITION

We are restricting our attention to medium range planning, on the order of six to eighteen months. This type of planning is often called annual planning. It is preceded by long range planning which fixes the production capacities period by period. The capacity may be purposely reduced in certain periods for such reasons as vacation shutdowns and preventive maintenance.

The medium range planning precedes the detailed weekly, daily or shift scheduling. In fact, the medium range plans impose constraints on the shorter term, detailed scheduling in the form of aggregate work force sizes and production rates that should be altered only under unusual circumstances. This type of constraining action provides a needed stability, in an aggregate sense, over time.

We assume that demand forecasts are given period by period out to the planning horizon (e.g. month by month out to a horizon of one year). An important consideration is the accuracy of these forecasts. As we shall see, some of the approaches to medium range planning depend upon accurate forecasts of future demand while others are relatively insensitive to the amount of uncertainty in the forecast values.[1]

Figure 1 displays graphically cumulative requirements as a function of time. Also shown is the cumulative production for a particular production plan (production rate as a function of time). The slope of the cumulative production graph represents the production rate at the particular point in time. The difference between the cumulative production and the cumulative requirements at a particular point represents the inventory (or backorder) at that time.

If demand is perfect by constant with time, it might make sense to keep a

[1]Unless otherwise noted, we shall restrict attention to a single production facility. In such a situation it is usually necessary to do some aggregation of products. Basically what is required is a reduction to common units, such as hours of production. In the more complicated models, where more than one production facility is allowed, the aggregation may be into several groups.

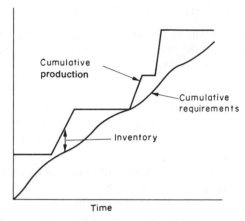

FIG. 1. A typical production plan.

uniform production rate. In any event, normally there are fluctuations in the demand pattern. There are four pure strategies (aside from altering the demand itself) that management may follow in an attempt to absorb the fluctuations:

1. The size of the labor force can be altered by hiring or laying off. This has the effect of changing the production rate.
2. A second way of varying the production rate is to keep the size of the labor force constant but introduce overtime or idle time.
3. Management can hold the production rate constant and allow the fluctuations in demand to be absorbed by changes in the inventory level.
4. In some industries the fluctuations in demand can be handled by subcontracting.

There are costs incurred by each of these pure strategies or any combination thereof. The criterion we use is to select the combination of the four strategies that minimizes the total relevant costs over a suitable time horizon. When we neglect subcontracting our problem boils down to selecting the appropriate work force sizes and production rates period by period.

III. COSTS INVOLVED

Two excellent references for discussions of the relevant costs are McGarrah[33] and Orr[38]. There are essentially six categories of costs (again, ignoring subcontracting):

A. *Costs of regular time production*: These are the basic costs of producing a quantity x with only regular time production in a period. They are composed of labor, material and facility components.

B. *Overtime costs*: These are the costs associated with using manpower on an overtime basis.

C. *Costs of changes in production rate*: There is an expense incurred in altering the production rate substantially.

D. *Inventory costs*: As in any production scheduling or inventory control model there are costs associated with carrying inventory. There is a wealth of literature on this topic, hence we will only briefly mention the components of inventory carrying costs. They can be conveniently divided into two subcategories.

1. Out of pocket expenses: These include the cost of running the warehouse, depreciation, taxes, insurance, etc.
2. Lost opportunity: There is the cost of tying up the capital in inventory. The capital could be invested elsewhere if the inventory were not present.

E. *Costs of insufficient capacity in the short run*: These include the costs incurred when demands occur while an item is out of stock. Such costs are a result of backordering, lost sales revenue and loss of good will. Also included in this category are the costs of actions initiated to prevent shortages, e.g. split lots and expediting.

F. *Control system costs*: These are the costs associated with operating the control system. They include the costs of acquiring the input data (required for the decision rules), the costs of the computational effort involved per time period, and any implementation costs which depend upon the particular control system in use.

We now look at the first five categories of costs in more detail.

A. Costs of Regular Time Production

A typical relation of the costs versus the production rate is shown in Fig. 2. Different models make different assumptions about the shape of the curve. Usually, some form of monotonic increasing behavior is assumed

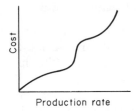

FIG. 2. Typical costs of regular time production.

(i.e., the costs associated with any production rate must be at least as high as those associated with any lower production rate). The vertical type rise in Fig. 2 can occur because of a requirement for an additional piece of equipment. The shape of the curve may depend upon the particular time period under consideration.

B. Overtime Costs

The general graphical form of overtime costs is illustrated in Fig. 3. The production rate is at first increased beyond the regular time capacity at

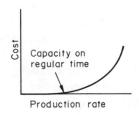

FIG. 3. Typical shape of overtime costs for a given work force size.

little extra cost. This is because only the bottleneck operations need to run on overtime. However, with continued increase of the production rate more and more of the operation must be run at overtime premium rates. It is clear that a single overtime cost curve versus production rate is appropriate only for a single size of work force, i.e. there really are a whole set of curves for different work force sizes.

C. Costs of Changes in the Production Rate

Here we are thinking primarily of production rate changes brought on by changes in the size of the work force. Such changes incur the costs of training, reorganization, terminal pay, "bumping," loss of morale, and decreased productivity. Decreased productivity results from a type of learning process when new labor and/or equipment is started up. "Bumping" is a common union requirement that specifies that when a man is laid off, his place cannot be left vacant, but rather there is required a whole chain of changes of positions.

A typical behavior of the costs as a function of the change in rates is shown in Fig. 4. Two points are worth mentioning. First, the curve is

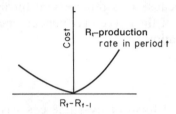

FIG. 4. Cost of production rate changes.

usually asymmetric about the vertical axis, i.e., a unit increase does not necessarily cost the same as a unit decrease. Second, ideally there should be a separate curve for each starting rate R_{t-1}. This is because going from 90 percent to 95 percent capacity may have an appreciably different cost than going from 30 percent to 35 percent.

Some models do include a cost for changing production rates. Instead they may specify that the change from one period to the next can be no greater than a certain value or simply that the rate iself must stay within certain bounds.

D. Inventory Costs

As discussed above, these are the costs of actually carrying the inventory. The standard approach is to say that the costs for T periods are given by

$$\text{Costs for } T \text{ periods} = \bar{I}_1 r + \bar{I}_2 r + \bar{I}_3 r + \cdots + \bar{I}_T r$$

$$= r \sum_{k=1}^{T} \bar{I}_k, \tag{1}$$

where $\bar{I}_k$ is the average inventory (in dollars) in period k, often approximated by the starting or ending inventory, and r is the carrying rate in $/$/period. The parameter r reflects all the aforementioned costs of carrying inventory. Typically its value lies in the range 0.05/year to 0.35/year.

E. Costs of Insufficient Capacity in the Short Run

When a shortage actually occurs the costs can be expressed in a number of different ways; which to use is a function of the environment of the particular stocking point under consideration. The possibilities include

(i)   a fixed cost each time that a shortage occurs, independent of the size or duration of the shortage;
(ii) a cost that is proportional to the number of units short;
(iii) a cost that is proportional to the time duration of the shortage; and
(iv) combinations of (i), (ii), and (iii).

In general, the actual costs of a shortage, as well as those associated with avoiding a stockout, are quite difficult to estimate. An entirely different approach proposed by Schwartz[40] is to not explicitly place a cost on shortages but rather have them influence long run profits by reducing the future demand rate.

An Alternate Way of Looking at Costs Associated
with the Average Inventory Level

Some organizations look at the combined costs of inventory and insufficient short run capacity in a slightly different and more aggregate fashion. From fundamental economic arguments the best inventory level in period t is proportional to the square root of S_t, where S_t is the forecasted sales for period t. Over a narrow range the square root can be approximated by a straight line, i.e.,

$$\text{Optimal inventory in period } t \simeq a + bS_t, \tag{2}$$

where a and b are constants.

Deviations from the optimal inventory result in extra costs; too high an inventory results in excessive carrying costs, too low an inventory leads to inordinate shortage costs. For a given value of S_t the typical curve of costs versus inventory is shown in Fig. 5. There is a whole set of such curves, one for each value of S_t.

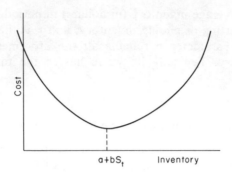

FIG. 5. Inventory and shortage costs.

IV. BASIC APPROACHES

There are several approaches to the selection of production rates and work force sizes. However, they can really be divided into three fundamental groups.

The first group is essentially non-mathematical in nature. The philosophy here is that the decision maker is either unaware of mathematical solutions to his problem or he does not believe that the mathematical models are representative enough of the actual situation.

The second category consists of mathematical models for which theoretically optimal solutions are obtainable. Usually however, such models have built in assumptions that may not be realistic.

When one attempts to make the mathematical model more realistic an optimal solution is usually no longer guaranteed. This is the situation in the third category. Basically, the costs are modeled as accurately as possible. Then various heuristic (or plausible) decision rules are tested out until a reasonably good solution is obtained. Quite often a computer search routine is used to home in on a good set of parameter values.

We now will take a brief look at each of several approaches. Some will be discussed in more detail in later sections.

A. Nonquantitative Haggling

As discussed in the Introduction, there are conflicting objectives held by different departments of an organization when it comes to production smoothing and work force balancing. One way to achieve a compromise of the conflicting desires is to bargain in a noneconomic manner. In general, this is not desirable. The policy usually is dictated by the most persuasive individual rather than being set in an objective manner.

B. Constant Turnover Ratio

A simple concept used in inventory control is that of the turnover ratio, defined by

$$\text{Turnover Ratio} = \text{Total Sales}/\text{Average Inventory}. \tag{3}$$

Managers' performances are often, in part, measured by the turnover ratios that they achieve. Therefore, it would seem appealing to set production rates so as to achieve a constant turnover ratio. This is fallacious for two reasons. First of all, such a rule leads to large gyrations in the inventory level for a fluctuating demand pattern. Second, it can easily be shown that a constant turnover ratio is not the most economical choice, viz:

To simplify the argument let us ignore the costs of production rate changes. Then, basic economic order quantity theory gives (as discussed earlier):

$$\text{Optimum inventory} = k\sqrt{S_t}, \tag{4}$$

where k is a constant.

Therefore, the best turnover ratio is

$$\text{Optimum turnover ratio} = S_t/k\sqrt{S_t} = \sqrt{S_t}/k. \tag{5}$$

This shows that the best turnover ratio is not a constant, but depends upon the sales forecast.

C. Adjust Last Year's Plan

An approach often used in industry is to take the previous plan and adjust it slightly so as to meet this year's conditions. The danger here is the implicit assumption that the previous plan was close to optimal; in this way management can get locked into a series of poor plans. This is not to say that one should never arrive at the new plan by adapting the old one. On the contrary, when the use of an appropriate mathematical model guarantees a close to optimal plan and when the computational procedure is iterative in nature, it makes good sense to use the old plan as an initial solution for the new plan.

D. Linear Programming and Extensions

Under certain assumptions the setting of production rates and work force sizes can be viewed as a linear programming problem. A linear programming problem consists of selecting the values for several nonnegative variables (the production rates and work force sizes in the different periods) so as to minimize a linear function (the total relevant costs) of these variables subject to several linear constraints on the variables (e.g. production and inventory capacities). More will be said on this subject in Section V.

E. Linear Decision Rule

When the various costs discussed earlier can be approximated by linear and quadratic (i.e., U-shaped) functions it turns out (through a rigorous mathematical analysis) that the decision rules for setting the work force sizes and production rates are of simple linear form. We will take a closer look at this approach in Section VI.

F. Management Coefficients Approach

This is a partially heuristic approach that assumes that managers behave in a rational fashion. Past behavior of managers is used to estimate the unknown coefficients in plausible decision rules. We will deal with this approach in more detail in Section VII.

G. Simulation Search Procedures

As discussed previously, the philosophy here is that a closed-form mathematical solution cannot be obtained when the model is made truly representative of the prototype situation. Therefore, a mathematical model is developed that represents quite accurately the actual cost functions and constraints. Then, by a trial and error procedure the variables (production rates and work force sizes) are varied until there results no further reduction in the total relevant costs. A computer is often used to facilitate this search procedure. More will be said on this topic in Section VIII.

H. Other Mathematical Approaches

Attempts have been made to use various other mathematical techniques in analyzing the production smoothing and work force balancing problem. These include dynamic programming[2, 30, 31, 43, 46], queueing theory[12, 38], and Pontryagin's maximum principle[20]. In general, the primary value of these theoretically oriented approaches has been in finding general properties of the optimal solutions. The determination of a usable solution is usually not feasible; either the calculations are too complex or the assumptions are too severe to be practical.

V. LINEAR PROGRAMMING MODELS

Linear programming is the technique of operations research that has probably received the most attention in both theoretical and computational development. One of the first published articles relating linear programming to production planning used a special form of linear programming model known as the transportation model. (Earlier work by Hoffman and Jacobs[15] and Johnson and Dantzig[21] assumed a very special demand pattern.)

A. The Transportation Model

The assumptions of Bowman's model[5] are:

(i) Demand is deterministic

$$S_t \text{ in period } t \quad (t = 1, 2, \ldots, T).$$

This may be unrealistic. However, there is no further assumption such as nondecreasing demand (which is required by certain other models).

(ii) Each period i is split into subperiods, e.g., regular, overtime, and third shift.

(iii) The cost of producing each unit in the jth subperiod of period i is given by f_{ij}, i.e., the marginal cost is constant for a subperiod.

(iv) The inventory carrying cost is given by r_i $/$ for period i.

Note that this allows the flexibility of having a different holding rate in each period.

(v) There are restrictions on the total amount that can be produced in each subperiod. This is a desirable feature.

(vi) There is no cost for a change in the production rate.

(vii) The model may give a solution that puts the inventory at a higher than physically allowable level, i.e., there is no simple way to include a bound on the inventory level.

Under the above assumptions the production planning problem is identical to the classical transportation problem of producing a commodity at a number of plants and shipping it to a number of warehouses. The analogy is apparent with the following definitions:

jth subperiod of period $i \equiv$ plant ij, period $k \equiv$ warehouse k,

and

$$c_{ijk} = f_{ij} + r_i + r_{i+1} + \cdots + r_{k-1}, \tag{6}$$

where c_{ijk} is the cost of producing and transporting one unit of commodity from plant ij to warehouse k. Specialized efficient techniques have been developed for obtaining solutions to transportation problems.

B. General Linear Programming Models

Some of the assumptions made in the transportation model are rather restrictive. The more general linear programming models relax some of them but at the cost of increased computational complexity.

1. *Assumptions*

(i) Again the demand is taken as deterministic

$$S_t \text{ in period } t \quad (t = 1, 2, \ldots, T).$$

(ii) The costs of regular time production in period t are described by a piecewise linear, convex function as shown in Fig. 6 (here convex merely means that the slopes of the linear segments become larger and larger, i.e., the marginal cost is increasing).

(iii) The cost of a change in the production rate is also piecewise linear as shown in Fig. 7. Note that the cost function need not be symmetrical about the vertical axis. An alternate approach in some linear programming formulations is to not assign costs for changes

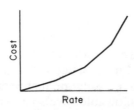

FIG. 6. The costs of regular time production in the linear programming model.

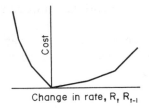

FIG. 7. Costs of changes in the production rate in the linear programming model.

in production rates, but rather to limit the size of the change or, alternatively, to simply put upper and lower bounds on the allowable production rates in any particular period.

(iv) As mentioned in the previous assumption one can introduce bounds on the production rates. A similar statement holds for the inventory level.

(v) As in the transportation model there can be a different inventory carrying rate for each period.

(vi) In most linear programming models it is assumed that there is a single production facility serving a given market.

(vii) In general, backorders or lost sales are not allowed. (This is possible to achieve mathematically because of the earlier assumption of deterministic demand.)

2. *Method of Solution*

We will not go into the details of the solution procedure because it is lengthy and several references have already done so (see, for example, Hanssmann and Hess[14]). The piecewise linearity (rather than straight linearity) complicates the situation somewhat. It necessitates defining for each production period several variables related to the production in that period (one variable is required for each straight line segment in Fig. 6) and several other variables related to the work force size in that period. The change in work force size from one period to the next can be expressed in terms of the basic work force variables. The constraints on the production rates are simple inequalities. Generally, additional variables, representing the inventory levels, are defined. Besides the possible maximum level constraints on inventory there are conservation of material constraints, namely that the inventory at the end of a period must equal the inventory at the start of the period plus the production minus the sales during the period. The requirement that no demand must be backordered or lost leads to nonnegative constraints on the inventory. The cost function turns out to be a linear function of the aforementioned production rate, work force, and inventory variables.

Once the problem has been formulated as above any of a number of standard linear programming techniques, such as the Simplex method, can be used to obtain the solution.

3. *Strengths and Weaknesses*

One of the basic weaknesses of the linear programming approach is the assumption of deterministic demand; in most applications there is considerable uncertainty in the forecasts of demand. However, tests have been done (see, for example Dzielinski *et al.*[9]) where a deterministic model was used under stochastic conditions and the results were quite favorable.

Another shortcoming of linear programming models is the requirement of linear cost functions. However, the possibility of piecewise linearity improves the validity (at a cost of additional computational effort).

An important benefit of a linear programming model is the potential use of the dual solution to obtain the implicit costs of constraints such as the maximum allowable inventory level. Also parametric methods allow a simple determination of the production plan for conditions somewhat different from those for which the primary solution is obtained. This last property is useful for two purposes; first, for sensitivity tests; second, in case one or more of the conditions change slightly.

Another approach that we will discuss at length is the linear decision rule. As contrasted with the linear decision rule, the parameters of a linear programming model are relatively easy to obtain. However, the computation required each time the model is used is considerably larger in the case of the linear programming model.

4. *Extensions*

There are several extensions that have been made to the basic linear programming model discussed above. In general these result from attempts to make the model a better representation of the physical situation. Unfortunately, the improved representation often necessitates considerably more computational effort.

(a) Removal of convexity and/or inclusion of a setup type cost—as mentioned earlier and as shown in Fig. 6, the basic production costs are normally taken as convex piecewise linear. However, in some situations the true costs have one of the forms shown in Fig. 8. Either form of Fig. 8 complicates the model. One or more integer variables are required to

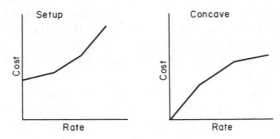

FIG. 8. Setup and concave production costs.

include the setup cost and/or the concave cost. The reason for the integer variable in the case of the setup cost is because of the discontinuity in the cost function. When production is zero, the cost is zero; however, a very small production incurs the entire setup cost. The need for the integer variable in the case of the concave function is not as obvious. To illustrate the need let us consider a simple example:

Consider a product whose concave production costs are as follows

Rate range (pieces/period)	Cost per additional piece produced
0–10	2
11 and higher	1

The basic linear programming model would select production units only from the 11 and higher range because they are less expensive than those in the 0 to 10 range. Of course, this is physically impossible. The integer variable forces the use of all of the 0 to 10 range before any production can be taken from the next higher range. The integer variable can take on only the values 0 or 1. The 11 and higher range can only be used when the integer variable is 1. However, the logic is arranged such that it is 1 only when the entire 0 to 10 range is used.

The presence of integer variables drastically increases the computational time. Thousands of continuous variables can be handled in a regular linear program, whereas only problems with less than 100 0–1 variables can be solved in a reasonable length of time.

(b) Inclusion of many products—there is no problem in making this extension. Now separate inventory equations are required for each product.

(c) Production at several locations—a former colleague, N. J. Driebeck (in unpublished work), has extended the linear programming model to the case of production of several products at more than one location. His model takes account of transhipment costs in computing the production rates at the various facilities.

(d) Worker productivity and wages—Orrbeck *et al.*[39] have extended the basic Hanssmann–Hess model to include the situation where worker productivity and wages both increase with experience. Effectively, they divide the labor force into several experience categories.

(e) Inclusion of effects of the detailed scheduling that will follow in the short run—as mentioned at the beginning of this paper production planning and work force balancing are normally done before the detailed daily or shift scheduling; in fact, they place constraints on the detailed scheduling in the form of aggregate production rates. Recently considerable research effort has been devoted to attempting to include the effects on the detailed scheduling when doing the production planning and work force balancing. A model formulated by Dzielinski *et al.*[9, 10] includes individual lot sizes and their associated setup costs. The output dictates when to make each setup of each product. The method uses the decomposition principle and other new mathematical techniques to keep the computation time from becoming prohibitive. O'Malley *et al.*[37] have developed a similar type of model that takes account of the economic order quantities of the individual products.

VI. THE LINEAR DECISION RULE

In the mid-1950s the linear decision rule was developed by Holt, Modigliani, Muth, and Simon [16, 17] at the Carnegie Institute of Technology. In 1960 they wrote a textbook [18] that also briefly discusses other approaches to production planning and work force balancing.

In contrast to linear programming models the demand is not assumed to be deterministic. However, aggregation across all products is now mandatory.

As we discussed earlier in this paper the planner can react to fluctuating demand in one or more of three ways (ignoring the possibility of subcontracting):

(i)   change the size of the labor force;
(ii) work overtime or idle; or
(iii) let inventories increase or decrease.

Really there are only two independent controllable variables. Holt *et al.*[16, 17] select the work force size and the production rate. For a given size of demand, setting values to these two automatically specifies the change in the inventory level.

A. Costs

As discussed earlier the costs (other than those of the control system itself) are divided into five categories. To understand the assumptions of the model it is instructive to run through a brief discussion of the mathematical forms of the costs.

1. *Regular Payroll Costs, $K_a(t)$*

The approach here is slightly different than in the earlier discussion on costs. Rather than showing costs of regular time production versus production rate (as was done in Fig. 2) here instead we relate payroll costs in period t to the size of the work force (independent of the production rate) in that period. In fact, as indicated in Fig. 9, a simple linear

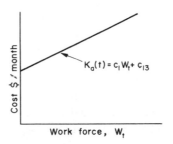

FIG. 9. Regular payroll costs.

relationship is assumed:

$$K_a(t) = c_1 W_t + c_{13}, \tag{7}$$

where W_t is the labor force size and the c's are constant.*

2. *Hiring and Layoff Costs, $K_b(t)$*

These are analogous to the earlier mentioned costs of changing the production rate. As shown in Fig. 10 the costs are approximated by a

*The subscripts on the c's are not numbered sequentially. This is because we are retaining the same numbers as in the original writeups of the model.

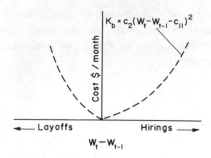

FIG. 10. Hiring and layoff costs.

quadratic (i.e., U-shaped) function

$$K_b(t) = c_2(W_t - W_{t-1} - c_{11})^2, \tag{8}$$

where W_t and W_{t-1} are the labor force sizes in periods t and $t-1$ respectively and the c's are again constants.

3. *Overtime–Undertime Costs, $K_c(t)$*

For a given work force size W_t there is a maximum production rate on regular hours (the regular time capacity). The model assumes that this capacity is proportional to the work force size, i.e. it is denoted by $c'W_t$ where c' is a constant. Use of a higher rate than $c'W_t$ means that overtime is required. As indicated in Fig. 11 a quadratic function is again fitted to these costs. However, note that this causes extra costs for running below the maximum rate $c'W_t$. This is not really valid because we have already included the cost of the labor (whether it idles or not) in the K_a expression.

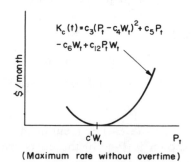

(Maximum rate without overtime)

FIG. 11. Overtime–undertime costs.

The quadratic expression

$$K_c(t) = c_3(P_t - c_4 W_t)^2 + c_5 P_t - c_6 W_t + c_{12} P_t W_t, \qquad (9)$$

where W_t is the size of the labor force, P_t is the production rate, and the c's are constants. Equation (9) is a general form of a quadratic in P_t and W_t. It should be noted that there are a whole family of curves, one for each value of W_t.

4. Inventory and Shortage Costs, $K_d(t)$

Here they use the method discussed earlier and illustrated in Fig. 5.

$$K_d(t) = c_7[I_t - (c_8 + c_9 S_t)]^2, \qquad (10)$$

where I_t is the inventory level, S_t is the sales forecast, and the c's are constants. Again, there is an entire family of curves, one for each value of S_t.

B. The Mathematical Problem

The production planning and work force balancing problem can be expressed mathematically as:

Find the work force (W_t's) and production rate (P_t's) levels that minimize the expected value of C_T:

$$\text{where } C_T = K(1) + K(2) + K(3) + \cdots\cdots + K(T-1) + K(T) \quad (11)$$

with $K(t) = K_a(t) + K_b(t) + K_c(t) + K_d(t)$

(the total relevant costs of period t).

T is the total number of periods that we are attempting to schedule. The decisions at the different values of t cannot be and are not treated independently; e.g., the size of the labor force in a near future period could be significantly affected by whether or not we change the size during the present period.

It is important to note that we speak of minimizing the expected costs. Because the demand is not deterministic we cannot know ahead of time the exact costs of making a particular decision; instead we work in terms of the average or expected costs.

The minimization of equation (11) is made, of course, conditional on the satisfying of the conservation of material constraints mentioned in an earlier section. The mathematical minimization, in the form of differentiations, leads to simple linear rules for setting the W_t's and P_t's. (The linearity results from differentiating the quadratic functions.)

C. Application

The first step in an application of the linear decision rule is the estimation of the constants, i.e., the c's of equations (7) through (10). This is a difficult and time-consuming effort that combines statistical estimates from accounting data with subjective estimates from management. Then the demand forecasts and the values of the constants are substituted into the linear decision rules to find the values of work force size and production rate for the first period being scheduled.

D. Form of the Rules

The form of the rules is as shown in the following equations:

$$W_t = a_0 S_t + a_1 S_{t+1} + a_2 S_{t+2} + \cdots + b W_{t-1} + c - d I_{t-1}, \qquad (12)$$

$$P_t = e_0 S_t + e_1 S_{t+1} + e_2 S_{t+2} + \cdots + f W_t + g - h I_{t-1}, \qquad (13)$$

where W_t is the size of the work force for period t, P_t is the production rate for period t, S_j is the forecast of the demand in period j, and the a's, b, c, d, the e's, f, g, and h are constants.

In general the a's and e's drop off rapidly, i.e., very little weight is given to forecasts for periods well into the future. The a's tend to decrease even faster than the e's. f is a positive number which implies that P_t increases with W_t. This says that the desired production rate tends to increase with the size of the work force, a desirable result. Similarly b is positive, resulting in W_t increasing with W_{t-1}, i.e., the work force size in a period is positively correlated with the size in the previous period. The minus signs before d and h say that the work force size and production rate tend to decrease as the starting inventory increases, again desirable.

An important point to note is that only the forecasts themselves, and not the amount of uncertainty in them, appear in the decision rules [equations (12) and (13)]. Therefore, forecast errors do not enter into the selection of P_t and W_t values. This is in contrast to many mathematical models in production and inventory control where the magnitude of the forecast errors influences the values of the decision variables. Again, this is primarily a consequence of the quadratic cost functions.

E. Strengths and Weaknesses

In tests performed [16, 18, 47] the linear decision rule has been shown to lead to costs significantly lower than those encountered under the existing management procedure. Also a detailed study[45] has demonstrated that the behavior of the rule is quite insensitive to errors in estimating the cost coefficients. This is encouraging because, as mentioned earlier, one of the serious problems with the linear decision rule is the difficulty encountered in estimating these coefficients.

Unlike the linear programming models the linear decision rule does not require that the demand pattern be deterministic. This is a favorable property because usually there is some uncertainty in the demand forecasts.

The set up time (estimation of the values of the cost coefficients) is quite lengthy, considerably longer than that required by linear programming models. However, repetitive use is much simpler. At the start of a new period all that one need do is substitute the current estimated values S_t, S_{t+1}, S_{t+2}, ... into equations (12) and (13).

One potential drawback of the linear decision rule is that the costs may not be really quadratic. In this connection the rule tends to lead to frequent (though possibly small) changes in the work force because the costs of small changes are underestimated by the quadratic function. Furthermore, as discussed earlier, the use of a quadratic function for overtime costs introduces a double counting of costs for idling the work force.

Another drawback is that the model does not allow for costs of changing production and work force levels that depend upon the point of departure. Finally there is no easy way of including constraints (minimum or maximum) on the inventory or production levels. Such was not the case in the linear programming models.

VII. THE MANAGEMENT COEFFICIENTS APPROACH

In 1963 Bowman[6] advocated a procedure for modeling management decision making with an illustration in the area of production smoothing and work force balancing. The following quotation from his article portrays the central theme of his approach.

"Managerial decisions might be improved more by making them more consistent from one time to another than by approaches purporting to give 'optimal solutions' to explicit models ... especially for problems where intangibles (run-out costs, delay penalties) must otherwise be estimated or assumed."

Bowman justifies his philosophy by arguing that most managers in any decision situation are aware of the criteria and the factors influencing

them. Over many repetitive decisions their behavior is unbiased, i.e., on
the average, they tend to make the correct decisions. However, their
behavior is more erratic than necessary. Actions such as emergency
phone calls from their superiors tend to produce deviations from their
normal behavior. Therefore, the whole point of the management coefficients approach is to try to keep the managers closer to their average
behavior by removing the erratic actions. Kunreuther[29] and Gordon[13]
have both reported on applications of this approach.

A. Approach

For a given repetitive decision the first step is to express the decision
variable(s) in terms of observable or predictable state variables. For
example, in the production smoothing and work force balancing situation
we might select

$$P_t = aP_{t-1} + b_1 S_t + b_2 S_{t+1} + c ; \qquad (14)$$

i.e., together with management we decide that the production rate in
period $t(P_t)$ is linearly related to the production rate in the previous
period (P_{t-1}) and the estimated sales in periods $t(S_t)$ and $t + 1(S_{t+1})$.

To determine the values of the constants (here a, b_1, b_2, and c) we do
not perform a cost derivation as in the linear decision rule. Instead use
is made of actual historical values of P_t and S_t's to estimate the constants,
i.e., the values of the constants are obtained from management's own past
behavior. The actual mathematical procedure used is what is called least
squares estimation. The values of the unknown constants are selected so
as to minimize the sum of the squares of the differences between the
predicted P_t's or W_t's and the corresponding actual production rates or
work force sizes.

B. Strengths and Weaknesses

A strong point of Bowman's method is that it has intuitive appeal to
management. This makes implementation considerably easier than in the
case of a sophisticated mathematical decision model where the involved
manager has to accept a great deal on faith. Furthermore, cost data are
not required for implementation.

Tests with actual company data[6, 29] have shown that costs can be
significantly reduced through the use of the management coefficients

approach. In fact, in some situations costs are lower than those resulting from use of the linear decision rule. (This is because the actual costs are not really quadratic in nature.)

A serious drawback of the procedure is the essentially subjective selection of the form of the rule. It very easily can be selected incorrectly. For example, instead of equation (14), the correct form of the rule for selecting the production rate could be

$$P_t = a(P_{t-1})2 + b_1 S_t^{3/2} + b_2 S_{t+5} - c_1 W_{t-1}. \tag{15}$$

Obviously, in this case the use of equation (14) would lead to less than ideal results.

Implicit in Bowman's approach is the assumption that the past is a good description of the future. This historical orientation may prevent the manager from quickly adapting to new conditions in a rapidly changing competitive environment.

Kunreuther[29] explains that the erratic behavior of a manager is caused by his receiving selective cues from the environment. As he points out, if these cues indeed represent reliable information about the future, their effect should not be smoothed out as is done in the Bowman approach.

VIII. SIMULATION SEARCH PROCEDURES

The philosophy here, first proposed by Vergin[47], is that in many cases the current state of the art does not allow the analytical solution of a mathematical model that is representative of the prototype situation. Therefore, a possibly better approach is to model the actual cost functions accurately in mathematical or tabular form (so that functions more complex than those allowed in such approaches as linear programming and the linear decision rule can be included). For a horizon of T months this cost function, in general terms, is

$$C(T) = f(W_1, P_1, W_2, P_2, \ldots, W_T, P_T) \tag{16}$$

As in any simulation the approach is to systematically vary the variables (e.g., the work force sizes and production rates) until a reasonable (and hopefully near optimal) solution is obtained. Normally a computer is required to make the approach feasible, even under the assumption of no uncertainty in the forecasts of demand.

A. Taubert's Search Decision Rule

Taubert[44] uses the above philosophy in his approach. He has investigated several different heuristics for searching the $C(T)$ surface in the $2T + 1$ dimensional space (there are $2T$ variables on the right hand side of equation (16); $C(T)$ itself contributes the one other dimension). The idea is to get reasonably close to the global minimum of $C(T)$. Taubert reports that the best performance (including computational effort) is achieved through the use of a pattern search procedure. He explains the logic of the procedure and provides a literature reference.

Both Vergin and Taubert have found that simulation search procedures perform extremely well. When the true cost structure closely resembles that assumed by one of the optimizing procedures (e.g., linear programming) the search procedures do essentially as well as the true optimizing procedure. When the true costs structure differs from that assumed by the optimizing procedure, the simulation search approach generally outperforms the optimization strategy.

It is clear that the number of controllable variables (namely $2T$) in the cost function of equation (16) goes up linearly with the time horizon, T. The solution time required in simulation search increases rapidly with the number of variables. As Taubert has pointed out, a potential tool for a drastic reduction of the required computational effort is the branch-and-bound technique. In essence, branch-and-bound allows us to eliminate many potential solutions without having to test each of them. A future combination of branch-and-bound with simulation search should allow us to obtain good solutions to even more realistic (i.e., more complicated) models.

B. Parametric Production Planning

Jones[23] in his "Parametric Production Planning" avoids the aforementioned dimensionality difficulty by postulating the existence of two linear feed-back rules, one for the work force, the second for the production rate. Each rule contains two parameters. For a likely sequence of forecasts and sales the rules are applied with a particular set of the four parameters, thus generating a series of work force levels and production rates. The relevant costs are evaluated using the actual cost structure of the firm under consideration. By a suitable search technique the best set of parameters is determined. Again, the results are quite encouraging.

C. A Manual Simulation Approach

Close[8] has suggested an approach which, in a sense, bridges the gap between the sophisticated optimization models on the one hand and the computerized simulation search techniques on the other. The cost structure assumed closely resembles that in the linear programming model (i.e., essentially linear costs). However, Close suggests a manual heuristic approach for homing in on a good solution. The approach makes use of a basic graph illustrated early in this paper as Fig. 1.

IX. THE PLANNING HORIZON CONCEPT

A finding common to most of the mathematical approaches to production smoothing and work force balancing is that the decisions concerning work force size and production rate for the current period are very insensitive to forecasts of demand well out in the future, i.e., only the forecasts for the first few periods are important. We have already seen this in the results of the linear decision rule. This type of result is encouraging because of the generally high uncertainty in the forecasts of demand in distant periods. Where there is a significant seasonal peak in the demand pattern it is usually sufficient to consider the horizon as the low point in the demand pattern beyond the next peak.

X. THE LARGER PROBLEM

All of our discussion so far has assumed that the demand pattern, the various constraints and the various costs are given and we must do our best within these conditions. Galbraith[11], in an interesting article, has suggested various possibilities for adjusting these "given" conditions. These include:

(i) Influencing demand—The usual means here are pricing and promotion. A good example is afforded by the commercial airlines who attempt to influence patterns within a single day, during the week, and on an annual seasonal basis.

(ii) Adaptations—When the demand cannot be influenced, one way of removing seasonality is to combine contracyclical demand patterns. To illustrate, snow blowers and lawn mowers are a good combination. Another possible adaptation is to locate a plant in an area where a seasonal or part-time labor force is more readily available.

(iii) Coalition efforts—Two or more companies may share their facilities when their seasonal patterns are different. For example, Trans World Airlines and Eastern Airlines have decided to share jumbo jets because TWA has heavy summer traffic (across the Atlantic) while Eastern's peak is in the winter (north–south movement).

XI. SUMMARY

In this paper we have defined the production smoothing and work force balancing problem and have discussed several different approaches to its solution. Although the mathematical development work has been in progress since the early 1950's, until recently, only linear programming has found significant practical application. In the 1967 article by the author[42] it was stated: "However, there are at least three other approaches that potentially promise significant benefits. These are:

(i) Extensions to the basic linear programming models that include the effects on the detailed daily (or shift) scheduling when doing the aggregate production smoothing and work force balancing.
(ii) The management coefficients approach that uses a methodology that is appealing to management and relatively easy to implement.
(iii) Simulation methods that allow more realistic, tailor-made models to be used."

The developments of the past three years have not changed these conclusions. In particular, the latter two have been reinforced by the findings of Kunreuther[29] and Taubert[44].

REFERENCES

1. H. Antosiewicz and A. J. Hoffman, "A Remark on the Smoothing Problem," *Management Sci.* 1, 92–95 (1954).
2. M. J. Beckmann, "Production Smoothing and Inventory Control," *Opns. Res.* 9, 456–467 (1961).
3. D. A. Bly, "Production Rate Variations Resulting from Forecast Errors," *Proc. of 2nd International Conf. on OR*, pp. 195–213, Wiley, N.Y., 1960.
4. J. de Boer and J. van der Sloot, "Een Systeem van Kostenbeheersende Productieplanning," *Statistica Neerlandica* 16, 99–112 (1962).
5. E. H. Bowman, "Production Scheduling by the Transportation Method of Linear Programming," *Opns. Res.* 4, 100–103 (1956).

6. E. H. Bowman, "Consistency and Optimality in Managerial Decision Making," *Management Sci.* 9, 310–321 (1963).
7. E. S. Buffa, *Production-Inventory Systems: Planning and Control*, Irwin, Homewood, Illinois, 1968, Chapters 5–7.
8. J. Close, "A Simplified Planning Scheme for the Manufacturer with Seasonal Demand," *J. Indust. Eng.*, Vol. XIX, No. 9, 454–462 (1968).
9. B. Dzielinski, C. Baker, and A. Manne, "Simulation Tests of Lot-Size Programming," *Management Sci.* 9, 229–253 (1963).
10. B. Dzielinski and R. Gomory, "Optimal Programming of Lot Sizes, Inventory and Labor Allocations," *Management Sci.* 11, 874–890 (1965).
11. J. R. Galbraith, "Solving Production Smoothing Problems," *Management Sci.* 15, 665–674 (1969).
12. D. P. Gaver, "Operating Characteristics of a Simple Production-Inventory Control Model," *Opns Res.* 9, 635–649 (1961).
13. J. R. M. Gordon, "A Multi-Model Analysis of an Aggregate Scheduling Decision," unpublished Ph.D. dissertation, Sloan School of Management, Massachusetts Institute of Technology, 1966.
14. F. Hanssmann and S. Hess, "A Linear Programming Approach to Production and Employment Scheduling," *Management Tech.*, Monograph No. 1, 46–51 (Jan. 1960).
15. A. J. Hoffman and Walter Jacobs, "Smooth Patterns of Production," *Management Sci.* 1, 86–91 (1954).
16. C. Holt, F. Modigliani, and H. Simon, "A Linear Decision Rule for Production and Employment Scheduling," *Management Sci.* 2, 1–30 (1955).
17. C. Holt, F. Modigliani, and J. Muth, "Derivation of a Linear Decision Rule for Production and Employment," *Management Sci.* 2, 159–177 (1956).
18. C. Holt, F. Modigliani, J. Muth, and H. Simon, *Planning Production, Inventories and Work Force*. Prentice-Hall, New York, 1960.
19. T. Hu and W. Prager, "Network Analysis of Production Smoothing," *Naval Res. Log. Quart.* 6, 17–23 (1959).
20. C. L. Hwang, L. T. Fan, and L. E. Erickson, "Optimum Production Planning by the Maximum Principle," *Management Sci.* 13, 751–755 (1967).
21. S. Johnson and G. Dantzig, "A Production Smoothing Problem," *Proc. of 2nd Symp. in L.P.* 1, 151–176 (1955).
22. S. M. Johnson, "Sequential Planning Over Time at Minimum Cost," *Management Sci.* 3, 435–437 (1957).
23. C. H. Jones, "Parametric Production Planning," *Management Sci.* 13, 843–867 (1967).
24. W. G. Jones and C. M. Rope, "Linear Programming Applied to Production Planning," *Opnal Res. Quart.* 15, 293–302 (1964).
25. W. Karush and A. Vazsonyi, "Mathematical Programming and Service Scheduling," *Management Sci.* 3, 142–148 (1957).
26. J. Klecka, "An Application of L.P. for the Determination of the Minimum Cost Labor Mixture Under the Conditions of Varying Production Levels," 13 Annual Conference American Institute of Industrial Engineers, May 1962, 151–157.
27. M. Klein, "On Production Smoothing," *Management Sci.* 7, 286–293 (1961).
28. H. Kunreuther, "Scheduling Short-Run Changes in Production to Minimize Long-Run Expected Costs," *Management Sci.* 12, 541–554 (1966).
29. H. Kunreuther, "Extensions of Bowman's Theory on Managerial Decision-Making," *Management Sci.* 15, 415–439 (1969).
30. S. A. Lippman, A. J. Rolfe, H. M. Wagner, and J. S. C. Yuan, "Optimal Production Scheduling and Employment Smoothing with Deterministic Demands," *Management Sci.* 14, 127–158 (1967).
31. S. A. Lippman, A. J. Rolfe, H. M. Wagner and J. S. C. Yuan, "Algorithms for Optimal Production Scheduling and Employment Smoothing," *Opns Res.* 15, 1011–1029 (1967).

32. A. S. Manne, "Note on the Modigliani-Hohn Production Smoothing Model," *Management Sci.* 3, 371–379 (1957).
33. R. E. McGarrah, *Production and Logistics Management*, Wiley, New York, 1963.
34. E. S. Mills, "The Theory of Inventory Decisions," *Econometrica* 25, 222–238 (1957).
35. F. Modigliani and F. Hohn, "Production Planning Over Time," *Econometrica* 23, 46–66 (1955).
36. G. Nemhauser and H. Nuttle, "A Quantitative Approach to Employment Planning," *Management Sci.* 11, B155–B165 (1965).
37. R. O'Malley, S. Elmaghraby, and J. Jeske, "An Operational System for Smoothing Batch-Type Production," *Management Sci.* 12, B433–B449 (1966).
38. D. Orr, "A Random Walk Production-Inventory Policy: Rationale and Implementation," *Management Sci.* 9, 108–122 (1962).
39. M. G. Orrbeck, D. R. Schuette, and H. E. Thompson, "The Effect of Worker Productivity on Production Smoothing," *Management Sci.* 14, 332–342 (1968).
40. B. L. Schwartz, "A New Approach to Stockout Penalties," *Management Sci.* 12, 538–544 (1966).
41. H. A. Simon and C. C. Holt, "The Control of Inventories and Production Rates; A Survey," *Opns Res.* 2, 289–301 (1954).
42. E. A. Silver, "A Tutorial on Production Smoothing and Work Force Balancing," *Opns Res.* 15, 985–1010 (1967).
43. G. H. Symonds, "Stochastic Scheduling by the Horizon Method," *Management Sci.* 8, 138–167 (1962).
44. W. H. Taubert, "A Search Decision Rule for the Aggregate Scheduling Problem," *Management Sci.* 14, 343–359 (1968).
45. C. Van de Panne and P. Bose, "Sensitivity Analysis of Cost Coefficient Estimates: The Case of Linear Decision Rules for Employment and Production," *Management Sci.* 9, 82–107 (1962).
46. A. F. Veinott, "Production Planning with Convex Costs," *Management Sci.* 10, 441–460 (1964).
47. R. C. Vergin, "Production Scheduling Under Seasonal Demand," *J. Indust. Eng.* 260–266 (May 1966).
48. P. R. Winters, "Constrained Rules for Production Smoothing," *Management Sci.* 8, 470–481 (1962).

7

Short-run, Long-run, and Vector Cost Curves *

John W. Rowe, Jr.

There still seems to be some confusion regarding the relation between cost curves and the shape of the firm's production function. The purpose of this note is to explore the relation between short-run, long-run, and vector cost curves derived from a two-input production function. The relation between the first two of these cost curves is well known, but their relation with vector cost curves (cost curves constructed for constant input proportions) has not been specified.

Before cost curves can be constructed, the firm must choose the *expansion* path along which cost is to be measured. Let the firm's one output, two-input production function be

$$x = f(v_1, v_2), \tag{1}$$

where x is output, and v_1 and v_2 are input quantities. For the short run one of the inputs is assumed to be fixed in quantity. If v_2 is the fixed input, the slope of the firm's short-run expansion path is:

$$\frac{dv_2}{dv_1} = 0. \tag{2}$$

For the long run both inputs are variable, and the firm chooses the input combination that minimizes the cost of producing each potential level of output. This requires

$$w_1 = \lambda x_1, \tag{3}$$

*From *The Southern Economic Journal*, Vol. XXXVII, No. 3, January 1971, pp. 245–250, Chapel Hill, North Carolina. Reproduced by permission.

$$w_2 = \lambda x_2, \tag{4}$$

where w_1 and w_2 are the prices of the two inputs, λ is long-run marginal cost, and f_1 and f_2 are the marginal productivities of the two inputs. To determine the slope of a long-run expansion path, (3) and (4) are differentiated to form

$$f_1 d\lambda + \lambda f_{11} dv_1 + \lambda f_{12} dv_2 = 0, \tag{5}$$

$$f_2 d\lambda + \lambda f_{12} dv_1 + \lambda f_{22} dv_2 = 0. \tag{6}$$

Elimination of $d\lambda$ from (5) and (6) yields

$$\frac{dv_2}{dv_1} = \frac{f_1 f_{12} - f_2 f_{11}}{f_2 f_{12} - f_1 f_{22}} \tag{7}$$

at a point along a long-run expansion path.

While cost curves have traditionally been constructed along short- and long-run expansion paths, returns to scale have been measured along a vector with constant input proportions. Bassett [1, 189–90] asserts that there is no relation between returns to scale and (long-run) cost curves when the (long-run) expansion path does not coincide with a vector. It is possible to demonstrate that this assertion is incorrect by constructing vector cost curves along a vector expansion path. Since input proportions are constant along such a path, its slope at any point is defined by

$$\frac{dv_2}{dv_1} = \frac{v_2}{v_1}. \tag{8}$$

Figure 1 depicts a possible set of expansion paths: *SEP*, *LEP*, and *VEP* being, respectively, short-run, long-run, and vector paths. The relation between cost curves for the three paths will be examined at a point at which all three cross, such as point *A* in Figure 1.

Along any *expansion* path:

$$c = w_1 v_1 + w_2 v_2, \tag{9}$$

where c is total cost. Treating v_1 and v_2 as independent variables, the level and slope of a marginal cost curve are

$$MC = \frac{dc}{dx} = \frac{w_1 + w_2 \dfrac{dv_2}{dv_1}}{f_1 + f_2 \dfrac{dv_2}{dv_1}}, \tag{10}$$

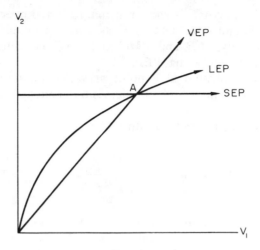

and

$$\frac{dMC}{dx} = -\frac{\left(w_1 + w_2 \frac{dv_2}{dv_1}\right)\left(f_{11} + 2f_{12}\frac{dv_2}{dv_1} + f_{22}\left(\frac{dv_2}{dv_1}\right)^2\right)}{\left(f_1 + f_2 \frac{dv_2}{dv_1}\right)^2}. \tag{11}$$

At a point at which all three paths cross, conditions (3) and (4) hold, and thus (11) becomes

$$\frac{dMC}{dx} = -\frac{\lambda \left(f_{11} + f_{12}\frac{dv_2}{dv_1} + f_{22}\left(\frac{dv_2}{dv_1}\right)^2\right)}{\left(f_1 + f_2 \frac{dv_2}{dv_1}\right)^2}. \tag{12}$$

Along any expansion path, the level, slope, and curvature of an average cost curve are

$$AC = \frac{c}{x} = \frac{w_1v_1 + w_2v_2}{x}, \tag{13}$$

$$\frac{dAC}{dx} = \frac{1}{x}(MC - AC), \tag{14}$$

and

$$\frac{d^2AC}{dx^2} = \frac{1}{x}\left(\frac{dMC}{dx} - \frac{dAC}{dx}\right) - \frac{1}{x^2}(MC - AC). \tag{15}$$

Define *SMC* and *SAC* as short-run marginal and average cost measured along *SEP*, and *LMC* and *LAC* as long-run marginal and average
cost measured along *LEP*, and *VMC* and *VAC* as vector marginal and
average cost measured along *VEP*.

Since cost is evaluated at a point at which all three paths cross,
conditions (3) and (4) hold, and four elementary conclusions may be noted
at this point.

1. Substitution of (3) and (4) into (10) yields

$$MC = \frac{\lambda f_1 + \lambda f_2 \dfrac{dv_2}{dv_1}}{f_1 + f_2 \dfrac{dv_2}{dv_1}} = \lambda. \tag{16}$$

Thus *SMC* = *LMC* = *VMC* at the intersection point.

2. Since v_1, v_2, and x are equal where the three paths cross, (13)
indicates *SAC* = *LAC* = *VAC*.

3. Since all three marginal cost levels are equal, and all three average
cost levels are equal, (14) indicates that the slopes of *SAC*, *LAC*, and
VAC are equal. Since the slope of the vector average cost curve is
positive, zero, or negative according as returns to scale are increasing,
constant, or decreasing, and since the slope of *VAC* equals the slope of
LAC at a point where the paths intersect, the slope of the long-run
average cost curve gives an unambiguous measure of returns to scale
under the assumption of fixed factor prices.

4. Because of 1, 2, and 3 above, (15) indicates that the curvature of the
average cost curve for one expansion path is greater than, equal to, or less
than the curvature of the average cost curve for another expansion path
according as the slope of the marginal cost curve for the former path is
greater than, equal to, or less than the slope of the marginal cost curve for
the latter.

To determine the slopes of the three *MC* curves at an intersection
point, insert (2), (7), and (8) in (12) to yield

$$\frac{dSMC}{dx} = -\frac{\lambda f_{11}}{f_1^2}, \tag{17}$$

and

$$\frac{dLMC}{dx} = \frac{\lambda (f_{11}f_{22} - f_{12}^2)}{-f_1^2 f_{22} + 2f_1 f_2 f_{12} - f_2^2 f_{11}}, \tag{18}$$

$$\frac{dVMC}{dx} = \frac{\lambda (v_1^2 f_{11} + 2v_1 v_2 f_{12} + v_2^2 f_{22})}{(v_1 f_1 + v_2 f_2)^2}. \tag{19}$$

First compare the slopes of the short-run and long-run MC curves. The slope of short-run MC is greater than, equal to, or less than the slope of long-run MC according as

$$-\frac{\lambda f_{11}}{f_1^2} \gtreqless \frac{\lambda (f_{11}f_{22} - f_{12}^2)}{-f_1^2 f_{22} + 2f_1 f_2 f_{12} - f_2^2 f_{11}}. \tag{20}$$

Noting that the denominator of the right-hand side of (20) is positive so long as isoquants are concave from above, cross multiplying, and rearranging terms yields $dSMC/dx \gtreqless dLMC/dx$ according as

$$(f_1 f_{12} - f_2 f_{11})^2 \gtreqless 0. \tag{21}$$

Comparison of (21) with (2) and (7) indicates that the short-run MC curve has greater slope than the long-run MC curve except when the slope of the long-run expansion path coincides with the (zero) slope of the short-run expansion path. This is true if, and only if, the long-run expenditure elasticity of v_2 is zero [3,780]. Except for this situation, the slope of the short-run MC curve exceeds the slope of the long-run MC curve, and thus the curvature of SAC exceeds that of LAC. This reflects the well-known conclusion that the long-run expansion path is the most efficient of all paths.

Second, compare the slopes of vector and long-run marginal cost curves. The slope of VMC is greater than, equal to, or less than the slope of LMC according as

$$\frac{-\lambda (v_1^2 f_{11} + 2v_1 v_2 f_{12} + v_2^2 f_{22})}{(v_1 f_1 + v_2 f_2)^2} \gtreqless \frac{\lambda (f_{11}f_{22} - f_{12}^2)}{-f_1^2 f_{22} + 2f_1 f_2 f_{12} - f_2^2 f_{11}}. \tag{22}$$

Noting that both denominators are positive, rearrangement yields

$$\left[\frac{(f_1 f_{12} - f_2 f_{11})}{(f_2 f_{12} - f_1 f_{22})} - \frac{v_2}{v_1}\right]^2 \gtreqless 0. \tag{23}$$

Comparison of (23) with (7) and (8) indicates that vector MC has greater slope than long-run MC, except in the case where the slope of the long-run expansion path coincides with the slope of the vector expansion path. When isoquants are homothetic and long-run expansion paths are vectors, $LAC = VAC$. When the two paths do not coincide, the slope of VAC exceeds the slope of LMC, and hence the curvature of VAC exceeds the curvature of LAC, again reflecting that LEP is the most efficient path.

Except for cases of coinciding paths, the slopes of both SMC and VMC are greater than the slope of LMC. But which of the other two paths is

more efficient? This question has relevance when isoquants are assumed
to be homothetic when, in fact, they are not. In this case the firm believes
VEP is the long-run expansion path and is unaware of the true *LEP*.
Would it be possible in this case for the firm to adjust output more
efficiently using *SEP* rather than *VEP*?

The slope of *SMC* is greater than, equal to, or less than the slope of
VMC according as

$$\frac{-\lambda f_{11}}{f_1^2} \gtreqless \frac{-\lambda(v_1^2 f_{11} + 2v_1 v_2 f_{12} + v_2^2 f_{22})}{(v_1 f_1 + v_2 f_2)^2}. \tag{24}$$

Since both denominators are positive, rearrangement yields

$$(f_1 f_{12} - f_2 f_{11})(v_2 f_2 + 2v_1 f_1) \gtreqless v_2 f_1 (f_2 f_{12} - f_1 f_{22}). \tag{25}$$

Assume v_1 is not inferior. Thus $(f_2 f_{12} - f_1 f_{22}) > 0$, and (25) may be
rearranged to form

$$\frac{(f_1 f_{12} - f_2 f_{11})}{(f_2 f_{12} - f_1 f_{22})} \bigg/ \frac{v_2}{v_1} \gtreqless \frac{1}{2 + \dfrac{1}{\dfrac{f_1}{f_2} \big/ \dfrac{v_2}{v_1}}}. \tag{26}$$

Define e_L as the *elasticity* of the long-run expansion path at the
intersection point. Thus noting (7):

$$e_L = \frac{dv_2}{dv_1} \bigg/ \frac{v_2}{v_1} = \frac{(f_1 f_{12} - f_2 f_{11})}{(f_2 f_{12} - f_1 f_{22})} \bigg/ \frac{v_2}{v_1}. \tag{27}$$

Further, define e_I as *minus* the elasticity of the isoquant passing through
the intersection point. Then

$$e_I = -\frac{dv_2}{dv_1} \bigg/ \frac{v_2}{v_1} = \frac{f_1}{f_2} \bigg/ \frac{v_2}{v_1}. \tag{28}$$

Substitution of (27) and (28) into (26) yields

$$e_L \gtreqless \frac{1}{2 + \dfrac{1}{e_I}}. \tag{29}$$

A preliminary inference may be drawn at this point. Since e_I cannot be
negative if the prices of the two inputs are positive, a sufficient condition
for the vector expansion path being more efficient than the short-run
expansion path is that e_L exceed one-half. A geometric interpretation may
be given in the case in which e_L is less than one-half.

In Figure 2 *LEP* is a long-run expansion path and *II'* is the isoquant passing through *A*, the point of intersection of all three paths. The elasticity of *LEP* at *A* is $AC/BC/AC/EC$, or EC/BC. The elasticity of *II'* at *A* is $AC/CD/AC/EC$, or EC/CD. Thus (29) may be written as

$$\frac{EC}{BC} \gtreqless \frac{1}{2 + \dfrac{1}{\dfrac{EC}{CD}}}. \tag{30}$$

Rearrangement of (30) yields

$$ED \gtreqless BE. \tag{31}$$

The short-run expansion path is less, equally, or more efficient than the vector expansion path according as $ED \gtreqless BE$. For the case depicted in Figure 2 the short-run expansion path is more efficient.

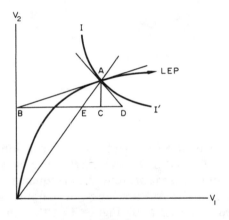

FIG. 2.

Clearly in most cases *VEP* is more efficient than *SEP*. Is it more likely that the reverse might be the case at high or low levels of output? As noted, the elasticity of *LEP* must be less than one-half for this phenomenon to occur. In this case v_2/v_1 declines as output increases. Thus e_I increases as output increases since x_1/x_2 is constant along *LEP*. This being the case, the higher the output level the more likely the right-hand side of (29) might exceed e_L and *SEP* be more efficient than *VEP*.

The conclusions of this note are summarized in Figures 3 and 4. In Figure 3 *LEP* is a long-run expansion path crossed at three points (A_1, A_2,

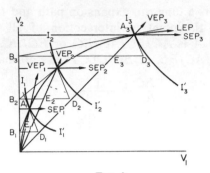

FIG. 3.

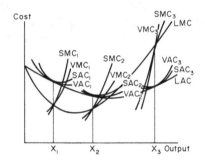

FIG. 4.

and A_3) by three sets of short-run and vector expansion paths (SEP_1 and VEP_1, SEP_2 and VEP_2, and SEP_3 and VEP_3). The output levels at these three intersections points are represented by isoquants I_1I_1', I_2I_2', and I_3I_3'.

In Figure 4 *LMC* and *LAC* are long-run marginal and average cost curves constructed along *LEP* of Figure 3. Although in this paper the precise shape of the production function has nowhere been discussed, it is assumed here that the long-run marginal and average cost curves have "U" shapes. Output levels x_1, x_2, and x_3 are the output levels for isoquants I_1I_1', I_2I_2', and I_3I_3' respectively.

At output levels x_1, x_2, and x_3, all three *MC levels* are equal, and hence the *levels* and *slopes* of all three *AC* curves are equal. At all three output levels, the slopes of both *SMC* and *VMC* exceed the slope of *LMC*, and hence the curvatures of *SAC* and *VAC* exceed that of *LAC*. For points A_1 and A_2 of Figure 3, $E_1D_1 > B_1E_1$ and $E_2D_2 > B_2E_2$. Thus in both cases *VEP* is more efficient than *SEP*. However for A_3, $E_3D_3 < B_3E_3$, and *SEP* is more efficient than *VEP* at this highest of the three output levels.

REFERENCES

1. Bassett, Lowell, "Returns to Scale and Cost Curves," *Southern Economic Journal*, October 1969, 189–90.
2. Ferguson, C. E., *Microeconomic Theory*, Homewood, Ill.: Richard D. Irwin, 1969.
3. Ferguson, C. E. and Saving, T. R., "Long-Run Scale Adjustments of a Perfectly Competitive Firm and Industry," *American Economic Review*, December 1969, 774–83.

8

The Fixed Coefficients Production Process Under Production Uncertainty*

GARY M. ROODMAN

I

NEOCLASSICAL microeconomic theory assumes that the firm converts the services of factors of production into units of output in a deterministic world where technological conditions and factor input prices are known with certainty. Although frequently not explicitly stated, the assumption is ordinarily made that the quantity of each factor acquired for current use need not be distinguished from the quantity of factor services actually channeled into the production process. Thus, the acquisition of K pieces of equipment and L men is generally presumed to uniquely determine the quantity of capital and labor services that will be available to put into production. No recognition is given to the fact that labor productivity may fluctuate from day to day (for a multitude of reasons—illness, personal circumstances, the weather, etc.), or that pieces of equipment may fail according to some random pattern.

In 1960 A. A. Walters[5] made some initial probes into the implications of relaxing this assumption. Walters's basic premise was that the firm generally "*controls* the quantity of *factors* [that it purchases], but it does not, and usually cannot, control the quantity of factor *services*". Treating the latter quantity as a random variable and assuming a fixed coefficients production function, Walters develops several important observations

*From *The Journal of Industrial Economics*, Vol. XX, No. 3, July 1972, pp. 273–286. Reproduced by permission.

about the effects of factor uncertainty on certain classical theorems, particularly those concerning the importance of factor substitution.[1]

The purpose of the present study is to develop a more general theory of the firm under factor uncertainty in the fixed coefficients case. This, in turn, will lead to an extension of Walters's original observations. In Section II a production function is developed which explicitly incorporates random elements and serves as the basis for developing the uncertainty model. In Section III the properties of this function are explored in some detail, with particular emphasis on its similarities to the variable proportions production function found in the traditional theory of the firm. This discussion leads directly to a set of production and output optimality conditions, developed in Section IV for the risk-neutral firm. Section V offers a numerical example illustrating the preceding conclusions and also permitting certain additional observations of interest. Finally, in Section VI the implications of risk-aversion on the part of the firm are briefly explored.

II

Consider a two-factor fixed coefficients production process, in which technical or other considerations dictate that exactly S_1 units of factor 1 must be combined with S_2 units of factor 2 in order to produce one unit of output. The production of holes in the ground via the combination of laborers and spades is a classic example. If a formal distinction is drawn between the quantity of each factor *acquired* for current use, denoted by F_1 and F_2, and the quantity of factor *services* actually rendered by each input, $\hat{F}_1$ and $\hat{F}_2$, then for a specified set of factor services, $(\hat{F}_1, \hat{F}_2)$, output, Q, may be written

$$Q = \min\left\{\frac{\hat{F}_1}{S_1}, \frac{\hat{F}_2}{S_2}\right\}. \tag{1}$$

[1]Other authors have treated production uncertainty in a fixed coefficients model. Smith[4, pp. 55–61] develops a production function for a trucking firm using concepts from queuing theory. While this approach to the problem is somewhat different from the one employed by Walters and the one that will be used here, the theme that production uncertainty gives rise to a meaningful form of substitution among factors is central to both treatments.

Also, see Hurter and Moses[2], who study the fixed coefficients problem via chance-constrained programming.

Finally, the interested reader may wish to refer to Georgescu-Roegen[1, pp. 279–99], which presents a rigorous analysis of a production process containing fixed coefficients under conditions of certainty.

Assume that $\hat{F}_2 = F_2$, so that the supply of factor 2 services may be termed *reliable*, but that the supply of factor 1 services is *unreliable*, in the sense that $\hat{F}_1 = g(F_1, u)$, where u is a random variable having a known density function $f(u)$ on the interval $[\alpha, \beta]$. Thus, we assume that the services of factor 1 actually delivered into the production process are a function of the amount of factor 1 acquired, F_1, as perturbed by a random disturbance, u. Specifically, we shall assume that $g(F_1, u) = F_1 u$, so that u might be interpreted, for example, to reflect proportional fluctuations about some measure of standard factor productivity. A further assumption that $E(u) = 1$ implies that $E(\hat{F}_1) = F_1$ for all F_1. This last assumption will facilitate comparison to the certainty case.

For specified values of F_1 and F_2 and for any value of u such that $\hat{F}_1/S_1 < \hat{F}_2/S_2$, or

$$\frac{F_1 u}{S_1} < \frac{F_2}{S_2}, \tag{2}$$

factor 1 is the factor constraining output and thus $Q = F_1 u / S_1$. If the inequality in (2) is reversed, then $Q = F_2/S_2$. Equivalently, if h is the value of u such that $F_1 h / S_1 = F_2/S_2$, i.e.,

$$h = \frac{S_1 F_2}{S_2 F_1},$$

then for specified F_1 and F_2,

$$Q = \frac{F_1 u}{S_1} \quad \text{for } u < h \tag{3a}$$

$$Q = \frac{F_2}{S_2} \quad \text{for } u \geq h. \tag{3b}$$

Hence, expected output, $Q_e = E(Q)$, takes the form

$$Q_e = \int_\alpha^h \frac{F_1 u}{S_1} f(u) du + \int_h^\beta \frac{F_2}{S_2} f(u) du \tag{4}$$

or

$$Q_e = \frac{F_1}{S_1} E_\alpha^h(u) + \frac{F_2}{S_2} G(h), \tag{5}$$

where $E_\alpha^h(u)$ is the partial expectation of u over $[\alpha, h]$ and $G(h)$ is the cumulative density of $f(u)$ over $[h, \beta]$. Expression (5) may now be viewed as the production function that the firm faces under uncertainty. It specifies *expected* output, Q_e, in terms of the two factor inputs the firm controls, F_1 and F_2.

It follows immediately from (4) that the expected output generated by an (F_1, F_2)-set will be smaller than the output the set would yield under certainty. For (4) may be rewritten as either

$$Q_e = \frac{F_1}{S_1} - K_1(F_1, F_2)$$

or

$$Q_e = \frac{F_2}{S_2} - K_2(F_1, F_2),$$

where

$$K_1(F_1, F_2) = \int_h^\beta \left[\frac{\hat{F}_1}{S_1} - \frac{\hat{F}_2}{S_2}\right] f(u)\,du$$

and

$$K_2(F_1, F_2) = \int_\alpha^h \left[\frac{\hat{F}_2}{S_2} - \frac{\hat{F}_1}{S_1}\right] f(u)\,du.$$

By the definition of h, K_1 and K_2 will always be positive [except, of course, in those extreme cases when $h \le \alpha$ (and $K_2 = 0$) or $h \ge \beta$ (and $K_1 = 0$)]. Consequently, $Q_e < F_1/S_1$ and $Q_e < F_2/S_2$. Since output under conditions of certainty is given by $Q_c = \min\{F_1/S_1,\ F_2/S_2\}$, *expected output will be less than certainty output for any set of factors acquired*, with the discrepancy between the two being measured by either K_1 or K_2. Thus, for example, when $Q_c = F_1/S_1$, K_1 measures the expected number of units not produced due to the presence of the factor uncertainty.

III

In terms of the Q_e production function, it is meaningful to develop measures of returns to scale, marginal productivity, marginal rates of factor substitution and to employ other economic concepts that are ordinarily encountered only in more traditional theory of the firm. Indeed, it is this fact that lends theoretical importance to the presence of uncertainty in the fixed coefficients model.

Consider first the effect of changing the levels of all inputs acquired by a factor of λ. From (5) the resulting expected output, Q_e^+, is given by

$$Q_e^+ = \frac{\lambda F_1}{S_1} E_\alpha^{h^+}(u) + \frac{\lambda F_2}{S_2} G(h^+). \tag{6}$$

But $h^+ = S_1(\lambda F_2)/S_2(\lambda F_1) = S_1 F_2/S_2 F_1 = h$, so that $h^+ = h$ and, from (6), $Q_e^+ = \lambda Q_e$. Thus, *the Q_e function exhibits constant returns to scale, in the* sense that changing all inputs acquired by a factor of λ changes expected output by a proportionate amount.

Next, it is easily verified from (5) that

$$\frac{\partial Q_e}{\partial F_1} = \frac{1}{S_1} E_\alpha^h(u) \tag{7a}$$

and

$$\frac{\partial Q_e}{\partial F_2} = \frac{1}{S_2} G(h). \tag{7b}$$

We shall refer to these quantities as the marginal expected productivities of factors 1 and 2, respectively (MEP_1 and MEP_2).

Both of these expressions may be given useful interpretations. Considering MEP_2 first, expression (7b) states that for any F_1 and F_2 yielding a value of h such that the likelihood of $u \geq h$ is positive, MEP_2 is positive. Since a value of $u > h$ indicates a shortage of factor 2 services relative to the factor 1 services available, (7b) implies simply that the marginal unit acquired of factor 2 will make a positive contribution to expected output, as long as there is some probability of having enough factor 1 services to utilize it. By a comparable line of reasoning in (7a), whenever there is some likelihood that factor 1 services will be in short supply relative to factor 2 services, the acquisition of an additional unit of factor 1 will make a positive contribution to expected output and MEP_1 will be positive. Hence, it is in a *probabilistic* sense that MEP_1 and MEP_2 are measures of marginal productivity.

Now forming

$$\frac{\partial^2 Q_e}{\partial F_1^2} = -\frac{h^2}{S_1 F_1} f(h) \tag{8a}$$

and

$$\frac{\partial^2 Q_e}{\partial F_2^2} = -\frac{h}{S_2 F_2} f(h), \tag{8b}$$

it may be observed that *both factors of production exhibit* DIMINISHING *marginal expected productivity*, since both (8a) and (8b) are negative. This is a reflection of the fact that as more and more of one factor of production is acquired (the level of the other being held constant), the likelihood of employing the marginal unit of that factor must be decreasing. In the case of MEP_2, for example, as F_2 is increased, h becomes larger and, as a result, $G(h)$ and MEP_2 must become smaller.

It is also interesting to note that

$$\frac{\partial^2 Q_e}{\partial F_1 \partial F_2} = \frac{h}{S_2 F_1} f(h),$$

which is always non-negative and implies a form of *complementarity* between the two factors of production, i.e., increasing the acquisitions of one factor increases the marginal expected productivity of the other. Again, this is due to changes in the associated likelihoods. For as the acquisitions of one factor of production increase, so does the probability that an additional unit of the other factor will be used.

This definition of marginal productivity leads directly to a related measure of the marginal rate of factor substitution, since, in theory, *there now exists a whole continuum of production methods from which to choose.* At the extremes, a specified expected output, Q_e^+ can be generated by:

A. Acquiring an extremely large amount of the reliable factor, F_2, so as to be prepared to fully exploit any supply of unreliable factor services, $\hat{F}_1$, that may arise; or

B. Acquiring an extremely large amount of the unreliable factor, F_1, so as to make it a virtual certainty that any quantity of factor 1 services available will be more than adequate to use all of the reliable factor, F_2, held.

At any point between these extremes, it will be possible to maintain Q_e^+ by exchanging, for example, a decrease in the likelihood that all of factor 2 will be used (i.e., a decrease in F_1) for an increase in the likelihood that all of factor 1 will be used (i.e., an increase in F_2).

IV

The optimal relationship between the two factors will be selected so as to

$$\text{Minimize:} \quad C = p_1 F_1 + p_2 F_2$$

$$\text{Subject to:} \quad Q_e^+ = \frac{F_1}{S_1} E_\alpha^h(u) + \frac{F_2}{S_2} G(h),$$

where F_1 and F_2 are purchased in purely competitive markets at prices p_1 and p_2, respectively. The first-order conditions of the appropriate

Lagrangean function then specify that

$$\frac{\frac{1}{S_1} E_\alpha^h(u)}{\frac{1}{S_2} G(h)} = \frac{MEP_1}{MEP_2} = \frac{p_1}{p_2} \tag{9}$$

for the optimal production method. For some purposes, it is useful to write (9) in the form

$$\frac{E_\alpha^h(u)}{G(h)} = \frac{p_1 S_1}{p_2 S_2}. \tag{9'}$$

The optimal relationship between the two factors of production is being determined here jointly by the cost and technological components of the problem. The numerator and denominator on the right side of (9') represent the contributions of factors 1 and 2, respectively, to the cost of one unit of output under certainty. One can easily verify (using the definition of h) that the larger the contribution of factor 1 relative to factor 2, the lower will be its utilization level relative to that of factor 2.

The immediate implication of these observations is that *it will generally not be optimal to acquire factors of production in proportion to their fixed coefficients.* Suppose, for example, that $h^+ = S_1 F_2^+ / S_2 F_1^+ < 1$ satisfies expression (9'). Then the optimal production method is such that $F_1^+ / S_1 > F_2^+ / S_2$; or rewriting this inequality in the form $E(\hat{F}_1^+)/S_1 > F_2^+/S_2$ an amount of factor 1 equal to $[E(F_1^+) - S_1 F_2^+/S_2] > 0$ will be wasted on the average. It is, in effect, optimal to program an excess capacity of factor 1, in the sense that the best production method calls for more of factor 1 than will, on the average, be utilized in the production process.

If it is now assumed that the firm is *risk-neutral* in the relevant range and sells its output at a price P in a purely competitive market, then the firm will select the F_1 and F_2 that maximize expected profit,

$$\pi_e = PQ_e - C.$$

Thus, at the optimum,

$$P \cdot MEP_1 = p_1 \tag{10a}$$

$$P \cdot MEP_2 = p_2. \tag{10b}$$

When the available factor 2 is fixed at $F_2 = F_2^+$, the optimal value of F_1, F_1^*, will be such that

$$\frac{P}{S_1} E_\alpha^h(u) = p_1 \tag{11a}$$

or

$$E^h_\alpha(u) = \frac{p_1 S_1}{P}.$$ (11b)

The left side of (11a) specifies the marginal expected revenue product of factor 1 and, as such, it defines a demand curve for that factor when F_2 is fixed. In the alternative form (11b), the firm chooses $h^* = S_1 F^+_2 / S_2 F^*_1$ to be the $p_1 S_1 / P$ "expectile" of the probability distribution of u. Note that in general, F^*_1 / S_1 will not equal F^+_2 / S_2, so that a surplus of one factor or the other will exist on the average.

It is interesting to further note, however, that regardless of whether or not a surplus of F_1 is acquired, *optimal expected output, Q^*_e, and profit, π^*_e, will be less than they would be under certainty.* It has already been observed that $Q_e < Q_c$ for any F_1 and F_2 (including F^*_1 and F^+_2). Thus, $Q^*_e < \min\{F^*_1 / S_1, F^+_2 / S_2\}$, so that if optimal certainty output is $Q^*_c = F^+_2 / S_2$, it follows that $Q^*_e < Q^*_c$. Furthermore, it must also be true that the cost of producing a specified level of expected output will be larger than the cost of producing an equal amount of output under certainty, i.e., if $Q^{++}_e = Q^{++}_c$, then $C(Q^{++}_e) > C(Q^{++}_c)$, where $C(\cdot)$ denotes the minimal cost functions. Hence, $\pi^{++}_e < \pi^{++}_c$. Since, by definition, optimal profit under certainty, π^*_c, is such that $\pi^{++}_c \leq \pi^*_c$ for all π^{++}_c, it follows that $\pi^{++}_e < \pi^*_c$ for all π^{++}_e (including $\pi^{++}_e = \pi^*_e$). Thus, $\pi^*_e < \pi^*_c$.

V

For purposes of illustration, assume that the production process is characterized by fixed coefficients $S_1 = 0.4$ and $S_2 = 0.2$ and that the random variable u is uniformly distributed on the interval $[0.75, 1.25]$. Thus,

$$f(u) = \frac{1}{0.5} = 2,$$
$$E^h_\alpha(u) = (h^2 - 0.5625),$$
$$G(h) = (2.5 - 2h),$$

and Q_e, MEP_1 and MEP_2 may be written, from (5), (7a), and (7b),

$$Q_e = 2.5 F_1 \cdot (h^2 - 0.5625) + 5 F_2 \cdot (2.5 - 2h),$$
$$MEP_1 = 2.5(h^2 - 0.5625),$$
$$MEP_2 = 5(2.5 - 2h).$$

Figures 1a and 1b depict these three curves as functions of F_1, with F_2 fixed at 10. The diminishing marginal productivity of F_1 and its complementary relationship to F_2 are apparent from the diagrams.

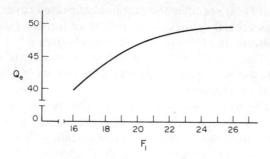

FIG. 1a.

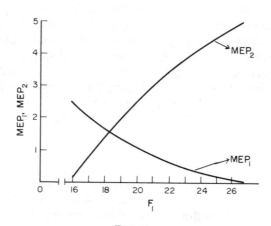

FIG. 1b.

Much as in the traditional theory of the firm, the Q_e function may be used to trace out a set of isoquants for alternative levels of expected output. Figure 2 depicts such a set. The expansion path AB demonstrates the constant returns to scale property attributed earlier to Q_e.

The optimal method for producing a specified expected output, Q_e^+, will be given by the h^+ satisfying

$$\frac{MEP_1}{MEP_2} = \frac{h^{+2} - 0.5625}{5 - 4h^+} = \frac{p_1}{p_2}.$$

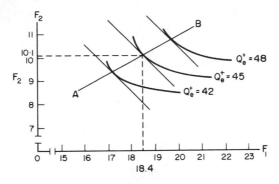

Fig. 2.

If $p_1 = p_2 = 10$, so that $p_1/p_2 = 1$, and $Q_e^+ = 45$ then, from Figure 2, the optimal combination of inputs will fall at $F_1^+ = 18.4$ and $F_2^+ = 10.1$ (with $h^+ = 1.10$), and the minimal cost will be $C = 285$. The locus of optimal input combinations, as Q_e^+ varies, will, of course, be AB.

Assuming now that output is sold at a price $P = 20$ and fixing F_2 at 10, the optimal value of F_1, F_1^*, will be chosen so that

$$P \cdot MEP_1 = p_1$$

or

$$50(h^{*2} - 0.5625) = p_1,$$

where $h^* = 0.4(10)/0.2F_1^* = 20/F_1^*$. Thus, the demand for factor 1, as a function of p_1, may be written

$$F_1^* = \frac{20}{\sqrt{(0.02p_1 + 0.5625)}}.$$

This function is diagrammed as the solid curve in Figure 3. If $p_1 = 10$, then $F_1^* = 22.9$, as indicated in the figure. The dotted vertical line at $F_1^* = 20$ simply indicates what F_1^* would be under certainty. Obviously, in the example an amount larger than this is being called for.

Also appearing in Figure 3 are factor demand curves for the cases when $\alpha = 0.6$, $\beta = 1.4$ and $\alpha = 0.9$, $\beta = 1.1$ (dashed lines C and D, respectively). The three curves make clear the fact that, the larger the *degree* of variability in u (as measured by the range of u values), the larger will be the *deviation* of factor demand from its counterpart under certainty. Note, however, that *the* LEVEL *of factor demand itself may rise or fall with a change in variability*. It is apparent from Figure 3 that, when p_1 is

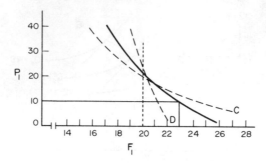

FIG. 3.

relatively small, increased variability implies increased demand for factor 1; while exactly the opposite is true, if p_1 is relatively large.

VI

We now briefly examine the impact of assuming the firm to be risk-averse rather than risk-neutral, as we have done to this point. For this purpose let the firm's utility for profit be specified by a function $U(\pi)$, such that the marginal utility of profit is always positive but declining as the level of profit increases. (Thus, $U'(\pi) > 0$, while $U''(\pi) < 0$.)

It is necessary to distinguish here between two profit functions corresponding to the two output ratios in (3). These are

$$\pi_1 = P\left[\frac{F_1 u}{S_1}\right] - C \quad \text{for } u < h,$$

$$\pi_2 = P\left[\frac{F_2}{S_2}\right] - C \quad \text{for } u \geq h,$$

where $C = p_1 F_1 + p_2 F_2$, as before. The risk-averse firm wishes to choose the F_1 and F_2 that

$$\text{Maximize} \quad E\{U(\pi)\} = \int_\alpha^h U(\pi_1) f(u) du + \int_h^\beta U(\pi_2) f(u) du.$$

The first-order conditions for a maximum are then given by

$$\frac{P}{S_1} \int_\alpha^h U'(\pi_1) u f(u) du = p_1 E\{U'\} \tag{12a}$$

and

$$\frac{P}{S_2}\int_h^\beta U'(\pi_2)f(u)\,du = p_2 \cdot E\{U'\}, \tag{12b}$$

where

$$E\{U'\} = \int_\alpha^h U'(\pi_1)f(u)\,du + \int_h^\beta U'(\pi_2)f(u)\,du.$$

(12a) and (12b) now replace (10a) and (10b) in the original analysis. Taken together they specify the optimal usage of the two factors of production. In addition, implicit in these conditions is the further statement that the optimal production method will be such that

$$\frac{\dfrac{1}{S_1}\displaystyle\int_\alpha^h U'(\pi_1)\cdot uf(u)\,du}{\dfrac{1}{S_2}\displaystyle\int_h^\beta U'(\pi_2)f(u)\,du} = \frac{p_1}{p_2}. \tag{13}$$

(13) now takes the place of (9) in Section IV. It should be noted, however, that the production optimality condition is not stated here entirely in terms of technological parameters and factor prices as it was earlier (and as it is generally stated in the theory of the firm). The marginal utility of profit also plays a role in (13), so that, unlike the usual finding, a change in selling price could change the optimal method of production.

It is interesting to compare the production method decision, as specified by (13), with the one the firm would make if it were risk-neutral. In particular, it can be shown that *the risk-averse firm will choose to employ proportionately more of factor 1 (the unreliable factor) than it would employ if it were risk-neutral.*

Recalling that h is chosen so that $F_1 u/S_1 < F_2/S_2$ for all $u < h$, it is apparent from the definitions of π_1 and π_2 that all permissible values of π_1 must be less than π_2; or we will write simply $\pi_1 < \pi_2$. Since for the risk-averse firm $U'(\pi) > 0$ and $U''(\pi) < 0$, it follows that $U'(\pi_1) > U'(\pi_2)$. If $U'(\pi_2)$ is now substituted for $U'(\pi_1)$ in (13), then

$$\frac{\dfrac{1}{S_1}\displaystyle\int_\alpha^h U'(\pi_2)\cdot uf(u)\,du}{\dfrac{1}{S_2}\displaystyle\int_h^\beta U'(\pi_2)f(u)\,du} < \frac{p_1}{p_2}.$$

Since $U'(\pi_2)$ is a constant with respect to u, this reduces simply to

$$\frac{\dfrac{1}{S_1} E_\alpha^h(u)}{\dfrac{1}{S_2} G(h)} < \frac{p_1}{p_2}. \tag{14}$$

It was shown earlier that the risk-neutral firm will choose a production method that equates the two sides of (14) (again, see (9) in Section IV). The inequality above suggests that the risk-averse firm will prefer a production method yielding a smaller value of h and therefore a proportionately larger amount of factor 1 than it would choose if it were risk-neutral.

Indeed this result is exactly what should be expected. In Section III, the two extremes on the production method continuum were detailed. It will be apparent from that discussion that output will be quite volatile if Method A is employed (extremely large amount of the *reliable* factor) and virtually stable if Method B is employed (extremely large amount of the *unreliable* factor). Hence, the risk-averse firm's preference for utilizing a proportionately larger amount of the unreliable factor simply implies a preference for a production method closer to Method B than it would choose if it were risk-neutral.

VII

The purpose here has been to examine the impact of production uncertainty on a particular type of production function. Perhaps the most important idea emerging from the discussion is the fact that production uncertainty brings a dimension to the fixed coefficients problem that makes it completely meaningful to speak of choosing the optimal input configuration on an economic basis. While input proportions remain *technologically* fixed (in the sense that factors of production can still be combined in one and only one way), they are not at all fixed for purposes of economic decision making in the face of production uncertainty. Rather, the optimal input levels are dependent upon the prices of the factors and their marginal contributions to output (much as in the traditional variable proportions analysis), and, in the case of the risk-averse firm, upon the marginal utility of profit.

REFERENCES

1. Georgescu-Roegen, Nicholas, *Analytical Economics.* Cambridge, Massachusetts: Harvard University Press, 1966.
2. Hurter, Arthur P. and Moses, M. A., "Prices and Productive Uncertainties in Dynamic Planning", *Journal of Regional Science*, VII (Summer, 1967), 33–48.
3. Roodman, G. M., "Production Uncertainty and the Theory of the Firm", Unpublished doctoral dissertation, Indiana University, 1969.
4. Smith, Vernon L., *Investment and Production.* Cambridge, Massachusetts: Harvard University Press, 1961.
5. Walters, A. A., "Marginal Productivity and Probability Distributions of Factor Services", *Economic Journal*, LXX (June 1960), 325–30.

PART IV

Pricing and Market Structure

Introduction

Economic models of competition have traditionally been most acceptable to the profession in those cases where the models have concentrated on the extremes of competition. The classical models of perfect competition at one extreme and perfect monopoly at the other established limits that have proven useful in explaining the competitive tendency of the firm and the market. Economists, however, recognize that these limiting cases are nothing more than that; and, while they are useful as benchmarks in describing competitive behavior, they do not provide the means for a thorough analysis of that broad area in between the limits that includes the cases of monopolistic competition, oligopoly, duopoly, and a host of others, each of which largely requires analyses unique to its type. It is for the "middle range" of the competitive spectrum that some of the more controversial models have been designed, and no one model can yet claim superiority in describing the nebulum of the middle range, at least with the precision enabled by the limiting cases of perfect competition and perfect monopoly described above.

The classical "economic man" assumption—based on the maximization of utility—has as its counterpart at the level of the firm the maximization of profits, the latter being traditionally viewed as the difference between revenues and costs. Depending on the competitive aspects of the market, varying degrees of influence on a firm's revenue position can be exerted by changes in the quantity of output placed on the market or by the pricing of that output. In turn, the greater the tendency of the firm toward a monopoly extreme, the greater the ability of that firm to use pricing policy as a means to enhance profits. Pricing policy, however, has other influences as well, including the allocation of resources, the distribution of finished goods, and the process of inflation.

Just as the degree of competition is a determinant of the ability of a firm to affect prices, so too is the ability of a firm to raise or lower prices determinant of its degree of monopoly power. An example of the interrelationship between these two cases is that of price discrimination.

SUMMARIES OF ARTICLES IN PART IV AND COMMENTS

Article 1

Bruce Yandle, Jr., in "Monopoly-induced third-degree price discrimination," defines third-degree price discrimination as that which occurs when a firm induces other firms to separate their markets. Examples of this method of price discrimination include the cases of:

1. distributors who maintain separate markets;
2. separation of "resale" customers, i.e. those who do not quite qualify as distributors for a particular product but who operate in the market as distributors for other products.

The article concerns itself with yet another pricing method, for a situation in which the distributor finds himself confronted with a chaotic user market; one in which numerous discounts and prices prevail. Yandle attempts to develop an economic model for explaining the actions of distributors in such chaotic markets where numerous prices are charged for the same product to the same class of trade.

In exhausting the possibilities for third-degree price discrimination, certain costs of price discrimination must be considered. These include:

1. internal difficulties such as a high probability that errors will be made in quoting prices, billing customers, and accounting for costs;
2. the expected cost of losing customers who learn that they have been paying "too much" for a product.

For these reasons it is unlikely that a firm will pursue market separation to the fullest possible extent. The rising costs of discriminatory pricing for the distributor causes the ultimate market for the manufacturer–supplier to be limited.

Distributors are offered incentives by manufacturers who wish to sell to as much of the market as possible. Since the distributor may meet competitive prices as low as their costs, the manufacturer establishes a control system in which he can issue a rebate to the distributor. For this plan to be successful, the distributor must be operating in the elastic portion of its demand curve. Otherwise, decreases in price will lead to decreases in total revenue. A distributor might also prefer to select a profit maximizing price in each of several markets. This will always be advantageous to the firm.

In conclusion, for a profit-maximizing firm to move to a non-optimal position successfully, both the manufacturer and the distributor must have monopoly power. Because the rebate plan gives rise to "cheating" distributors and "greedy" manufacturers, perhaps an outright reduction in price might add stability to the market.

The student should acquaint himself with the following concepts:

Discounts	Price elasticity of demand
Discriminatory pricing	Rebates
Expected costs	Third-degree price discrimination
Monopoly	Total revenue
Price discrimination	

Article 2

B. R. Darden, in "An operational approach to product pricing," notes that, despite the various analytical approaches available, the product pricer usually displays "irrational" behavior by basing price on experience, intuition, and cost–plus methods. Such behavior can be accounted for when obstacles to optimal product pricing is examined. These obstacles occur where:

1. The pricer lacks time and interest to analyze the latest pricing literature which is not directly applicable in practice.
2. The objectives differ between those of the pricer and that which is assumed in the literature in order to arrive at optimal price.
3. The volume of products to be priced is great so that the relative time allotted to each product pricing decision is small.

4. There is difficulty in quantifying and measuring the effects of products which are substitutes or complementary.
5. There are problems in determining competitor reactions to price strategies.
6. The pricer lacks methods, time, and money to measure demand curves or other consumer response curves properly.

Because it is undoubtedly true that the product pricer relies on more than just cost and turnover, the article seeks to formalize, heuristically, an operational approach to pricing, given the beliefs of the pricer.

The central concept of the proposed pricing approach concerns profit variance and price limits. The major strength of the "operational approach" lies in its ability to draw on the experience and judgment of marketing specialists in the firm. Furthermore, it provides the product pricer with the formal plan which is used to summarize and integrate his various hypotheses into a clear picture of economic alternatives.

In this framework there are several considerations affecting the pricer:

1. There may be overlapping of quantity estimates for upper and lower price limits.
2. It is not necessary to assume that costs remain constant in determining upper and lower price limits. In this way, the prices can change marketing blends without affecting the usefulness of the approach.
3. Complete agreement is not necessary concerning forecasted sales.
4. Once the upper and lower price limits are "bracketed," a sequential approach may be used to test the expected profitability of immediate prices.
5. The pricer is able to compute and compare profits, quantity, and variances at various prices.

The reader should be aware of the following terms:

Complementary goods	Optimal price
Constant costs	Pricing strategy
Cost-plus pricing	Product volume
Marketing blends	Substitute (competitive) goods
Neutral goods	Turnover

Article 3

Morris L. Mayer, Joseph B. Mason, and Einar A. Orbeck, in "The Borden case: a legal basis for private brand price discrimination," note that careful planning aids in avoiding litigation. Such was not the case discussed at hand in this article since the Borden Company and the FTC went through 10 years of litigation over price differentials in the sale of private brands. Borden had been producing private brand evaporated milk for about 20 years when the FTC issued a complaint charging price discrimination among different purchasers by the selling of milk of "like grade and quality" at lower prices to some of its purchasers than to others. The FTC charged that the effect of the discriminations was to lessen competition or to create a monopoly, or to injure, destroy, or prevent competition. This was in violation of the Clayton Act as amended by the Robinson–Patman Act.

The case route included the following steps:

1. *The FTC hearing.* Borden's first attempt was to prove that the products were not of like grade and quality. FTC rejected this by saying that reaction within the marketplace in no way changes the physical composition of milk. Its attempt at cost differentials was refuted by a former case.

2. *Appeal to the FTC.* In the FTC appeal: (a) Borden questioned the finding that the two products were of just grade and quality; (b) the FTC counsel challenged the finding that Borden had justified the differences in price on the basis of cost and that there had been a failure to prove injury to competition. The appeal decision:

   (i) upheld the opinion that the products were of like grade and quality;
   (ii) charged Borden with competitive injury;
   (iii) determined that the cost analysis was inadequate to justify price differences between Borden and private label brands;
   (iv) determined that the acts and practices of Borden were in violation of the Robinson–Patman Act.

3. *Appeal to a Federal Circuit Court of Appeals.* In the second appeal, the decision was that, because of brand name, the products, though chemically the same, were not of like grade and quality. The petition was set aside, and a cease and desist order was granted.

4. The Circuit Court decision was then appealed to the Supreme Court of the United States, where the Supreme Court decision reversed the Fifth Circuit Court of Appeals decision.

5. The petition was then remanded to the Circuit Court, where the decision was that there was substantial evidence to support the finding

that Borden was not engaged in illegal price discrimination. The court granted the petition to set aside the cease and desist order, and consumer preference for the Borden label was again acknowledged.

Decisions were set aside at each level which finally led to a new precedent being set:

> "The decision, that no competitive advantage is created by a price difference between a brand name and private brand which reflects only the consumer preference for the brand name, is limited in application to manufacturers whose brands are highly promoted and for which there is a consumer preference shown by a willingness to pay more for the brand name."

This indicates that value has been created for a product by promotion.

The reader should be familiar with the following terms:

Brand name vs. private label	Federal Trade Commission
Cease and desist order	Monopoly
Clayton Act	Price differentials
Competitive injury or injury to competition	Price discrimination
Consumer preference	Product Promotion
Cost differentials	Robinson–Patman Act

Article 4

Advertising is a controversial economic topic. Critics claim it abuses consumer confidence; shapes and sometimes vulgarizes tastes; and creates abnormal, unjustified profits. L. G. Telser presents his study, "Some aspects of the economics of advertising," as an aid to protagonists on all sides of the debate on advertising.

There are certain aspects of advertising to consider, says Telser. (1) Advertising has various forms. There are differences in the extent of advertising by commodity, if any at all, and in the media employed for advertising; (2) There is a secular stability of the ratio of total advertising outlays as a percentage of national income. This results from the stability of the determinants of these expenditures. As for its behavior over the business cycle, the percentage tends to rise when business is slack and to fall when business is more active. (3) More money is spent on personal selling, an older method of promoting the sale of goods and services, than for advertising.

Statistics show that, along with research and development, advertising, which began its modern form in England in the middle of the nineteenth century with the popular press, accounts for high profitability as seen in the expenditures of firms with the highest rate of return on invested capital. Profitability, however, is not the only aspect which advances the understanding of advertising; studying the mechanisms of advertising is another means.

In general, advertising budget funds are allocated among the various media so as to obtain the maximum number of potential customers.

It is believed that creation of brand loyalty through advertising can reduce competition; but, this is not necessarily true. A test conducted by Telser showed that some of the large advertising outlays are explained by the rapid introduction of new products; and that advertising, by itself, seems incapable of maintaining consumer acceptance of a product that is found to be unsatisfactory.

Furthermore, empirical data have shown that the hypothesis linking a positive association between advertising and monopoly is weak. Advertising levels are, instead, better explained by such factors as (a) characteristics of the consumers of the product, (b) their number, and (c) the cost of contacting them by various media.

As for consumer protection, argues Telser, advertising cannot be considered dangerous. There are a number of means that provide information to consumers, as well as a number of alternatives for recourse, if necessary.

In conclusion, Telser presents two recent studies of advertising which are of interest—the Reith Report and the Backman study. Neither study presents new positions; but both are valuable for their numerous references to the works of others. Telser also comments, in conclusion, on the effects of the introduction of pay television in terms of improvement in the quality of television entertainment.

The reader should refresh his understanding of the following concepts:

Advertising	National income
Brand loyalty	Pay television
Business cycle	Personal selling
Commodity	Profitability
Consumer protection	Rate of return
Invested capital	Tastes
Media	

Article 5

The Kaldor–Bain hypothesis holds that advertising will result in increasing industry concentration, thereby affecting competition adversely. Because tests by Telser and Mann, Henning, and Meehan have yielded conflicting results, Matityahu Marcos' article on "Advertising and changes in concentration" reevaluates the Kaldor–Bain hypothesis by employing newer data and a more comprehensive test procedure.

Marcos begins the discussion with the Kaldor–Bain theory. To properly evaluate the hypothesis it is necessary to formulate a model of concentration changes and to appraise the effect of advertising within it. Variables to be included in the model are:

1. The influence of industry growth on changes in concentration—it has been suggested that concentration will decrease (or increase less rapidly) in rapidly growing industries.
2. The current level of concentration—the higher the concentration already achieved by the leading firms the smaller is the likelihood of a given further increase in concentration.
3. The effect of advertising on concentration ratios (this is of prime interest in this study)—Kaldor suggested the presence of increasing returns to advertising outlays which would favor the leading and larger firms (with their larger advertising outlays).

Statistical tests of the model were based upon data obtained from the Federal Trade Commission publication, *Industry Classification and Concentration*. The following model was then formulated:

$$d_{i_{t-1}} = \alpha_0 + \alpha_1 g_{i_{t-1}} + \alpha_2 CR_{i_{t-1}} + \alpha_3 MD_i + \alpha_4 HD_i + u.$$

That is, changes in industry concentration $d_{i_{t-1}}$ are a function of the industry growth rate $g_{i_{t-1}}$, the base period concentration ratio $CR_{i_{t-1}}$, and the advertising intensity class into which the industry falls, MD_i or HD_i. The performance of the advertising variables appears to confirm the Kaldor–Bain hypothesis.

Marcos concludes that: "... advertising can be expected to lead to substantial rise in industry concentration. This may raise concern about the long run impact of advertising on the nature and intensity of competitive behavior."

The student should reacquaint himself with the following terms:

Advertising outlays   Growth industries
Base period   Industry concentration
Concentration ratio

Article 6

Colwell argues that (a) the FTC and the Supreme Court consider efficiencies as a primary indicator of anti-competitive results in product-extension mergers, and (b) that this is correct under Section 7 of the Clayton Act concerning Anti-Merger Law.

In "'Antitrust and efficiency: product extension mergers': a comment," Peter Asch points out that Colwell's arguments depend, in part, upon (a) a mistaken definition of efficiencies, and (b) a decision criterion for merger policy that appears irrational if it is extended to public economic policies generally.

To show that the FTC and the Supreme Court will find a product-extension merger illegal because it creates efficiencies, Colwell discusses the Procter and Gamble decisions which primarily concern efficiencies in advertising. In these decisions, the FTC and the Supreme Court concluded that a larger purchaser of advertising holds advantages which might reduce the vigor of competition among smaller established rivals and, thus, discourage the entry of new competitors.

Within the context of the theory of the firm, efficiency refers to a relationship between productive inputs and output. When a firm becomes "more efficient" through merger, internal expansion, or technological improvement, the implication is that the relationship between its inputs and output has changed in some specific way. This is not, however, the implication of increased "efficiency" in advertising.

It must be remembered that the output of advertising is not the same as the output of the firm; hence, it is possible to speak of efficient advertising, but not in a manner such that firms are more efficient in the usual technical sense.

Asch's argument is that the Kaldor proposition cannot be demonstrated with reference to advertising. The *Brown Shoe* decision may have provided for a more compelling discussion.

Colwell's reason for efficiency-creating mergers to be stopped is that they are likely to increase the power of the merged firms. Asch, however, makes clear that such efficiency can be of benefit to society, and that the essence of rational policy making should compare the costs of increased power concentrations and benefits to society.

In conclusion, Asch states that perhaps he has misinterpreted Kaldor's propositions. If such is the case he would wholly agree with the Kaldor hypothesis. It is obvious, however, that there is a need to distinguish more clearly between technical economies and pecuniary gains.

The reader should review the following concepts:

Clayton Act	Merger
Efficiency	Product-extension mergers
FTC	Technological improvement
Kaldor proposition	

Article 7

Since discussion of conglomerates has recently declined, the implications are that conglomerates were either a passing thing or no longer deserving of attention. "Conglomerates revisited" by D. T. Carroll contends that neither implication is, as yet, justified by the facts.

It is not possible to prove that conglomerates have or have not had their heyday, but the prospects favor continued enthusiasm for conglomeration. As for conglomerates no longer deserving attention, perhaps this slack period is most conducive to achieving a balanced view of the managerial skills of conglomerates.

There are three reasons given by Carroll for postulating that conglomerates are actually making contributions to the art of management.

1. Conglomerates have rarely had the time or the resources to apply conventional management solutions to their problems.
2. Conglomerates have been forced by their own ambitions to deal with an unusual mix of business.
3. Conglomerates have had to give greater expression to the ideas and insight of their usually young management.

Some evidence of the changes that conglomerates are bringing about include: (1) methods of profit improvement, (2) use of management consultants, and (3) style of management control.

1. *Methods of profit improvement.* Improvements in purchasing have resulted through the use of such techniques as value analysis, competitive "sourcing," and make/buy analysis. Another profit improvement area has been in salesman work loads. Here, conglomerates have been able to distribute their selling capabilities more equitably; and thereby gain increased sales productivity.

2. *Use of management consultants.* Conglomerates seem to have realized the importance of investing as much of top management's time and money as is necessary to make consulting principals intimately familiar with objectives, practices, personalities, facilities, and products.

3. *Style of management control.* One element of the style of management control could be characterized as total absence or total presence. A conglomerate can be either aware of or unaware of its superstructure. Another element of this style is full centralization of cash management. The conglomerate may be motivated by the desire to activate idle funds and to inject planning into the cash cycle. The final element of style is the conglomerate's continuous involvement in the selection of incentives for management. Given the rising rates of executive mobility, conglomerates may prove to be more foresighted than opportunistic.

The student should be familiar with the following terms:

Cash cycle	Idle funds
Competitive "sourcing"	Make/buy analysis
Conglomerates	Sales productivity
Executive mobility	Value analysis

1

Monopoly-induced Third-degree Price Discrimination*

BRUCE YANDLE, JR.

IN WHAT has now become a classic article on the classification of types of price discrimination, Fritz Machlup describes the firm which induces other firms to separate its market (that is, to practice third-degree price discrimination). "For example, a single firm may participate in a discriminatory scheme by serving different consumer groups through different (subsidiary) distributor firms to whom it sells at a uniform price but whom it induces to resell with different mark-ups" [2, p. 398].

The possibilities suggested by this description may fit the large number of manufacturing firms which sell their products through industrial distributors or jobbers. For example, most industrial bearings, conveyors, electrical controls, gears, and a multitude of other industrial products are marketed in this manner.[1] These independent firms contract with various manufacturers to buy and then resell the manufacturers' products.

There are certain well-established patterns of market separation which have evolved for the industrial jobber, the most significant example being the separation of the purchases of the original equipment manufacturer (hereafter referred to as OEM) from those of the industrial user.

For this purpose there are established user and OEM discounts from list prices. The distributor may sell each account an identical product and incur identical costs but there will be differential prices (usually in favor of the OEM). This case, clearly one of third-degree price discrimination, has been successfully accomplished by those distributors who have been able to maintain separate markets. This established approach to the

---

*From *The Quarterly Review of Economics & Business*, Vol. 11, No. 1, Spring 1971, pp. 71–75. Reproduced by permission.
[1]According to the 1963 Census of Business, there were 7,247 merchant wholesalers selling industrial supplies in the United States. These firms reported a sales volume of $3.6 billion.

market begins to break down as more and more firms become OEM accounts in addition to being users of a product.

A market division of less significance performed by industrial distributors is the separation of the "resale" customer from the OEM and user accounts. "Resale" customers are those which, for various reasons, do not qualify as distributors for a particular product, but who operate in the market as distributors for other products. These accounts have traditionally been given a discount which is somewhat greater than the user discount. Usually there is a reciprocal arrangement such that most distributors obtain a reseller's discount from one another.

In contrast to these institutionalized methods of price discrimination is the case of the distributor who finds himself confronted with a chaotic user market, one in which numerous discounts and prices prevail. In such cases the best interests of the manufacturer may be served by encouraging its distributor to "compete" and by some means to obtain a market share. Such cases may have resulted in another version of induced third-degree price discrimination of the kind described by Machlup. Manufacturers begin to offer additional discounts to their distributors who are willing to "meet the competition."

This article examines such a case. It is an attempt to develop an economic model for explaining the actions of distributors in such chaotic markets.

ANALYSIS

A chaotic user-market may develop for numerous reasons, but that suggested by Eli Clemens appears to be fairly plausible:

> "... it is probably impossible to find in the whole of our economy a single firm that sells a single product at a single price. This is theoretically explainable by the fact that the conventional single-product firm that is presumably in equilibrium when marginal revenue is equal to marginal cost is not in equilibrium if it can serve the remaining portion of the demand curve at a price greater than marginal cost without adversely disturbing its existing market" [1, pp. 262–63].

Such a case is shown in Chart 1. DD' represents the demand for the product sold by the jobber. A marginal revenue curve, MR, has been drawn relative to DD', and marginal cost, MC, is drawn as constant. That is, each unit of the product sold by the firm costs the same; all other costs

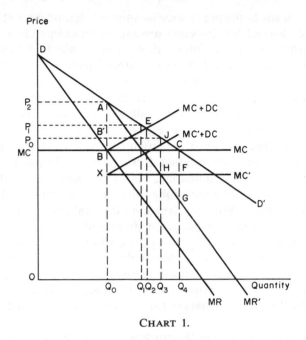

CHART 1.

are assumed to be fixed.[2] Given these relationships and assuming the firm to be a profit maximizer, it would operate at the point at which $MC = MR$ and produce OQ_0 units of product priced at P_2. This would leave a large segment of the product demand unserved, namely the segment AD' of the demand curve.

If the firm views this unserved portion of its market as a separate market we may let Q_0A become an ordinate for further analysis. In this case MR' will be the relevant marginal revenue locus for demand AD'. The firm will again maximize profit and sell $Q_1 - Q_0$ additional units at price P_1. The firm may continue to separate markets in this manner so long as there are marginal units which may be sold at prices greater than or equal to marginal cost. Eventually such division could lead the firm to the intersection of MC with DD', point C, thus exhausting the possibilities for third-degree price discrimination.

[2] The product must be thought of as being standardized units which include all the services offered by the firm. That is, the product sold by the manufacturer-supplier to the distributor has been transformed by the distributor into something else. Time and place utility in addition to other utilities have been given to the product.

This process leads to the previously mentioned chaotic market. Numerous prices are charged for the same product to the same class of trade. The jobber who chooses to follow this strategy will find that chaotic pricing is not costless; there is a cost of discriminating. First, there are internal difficulties for the firm which has numerous discounts on the same product to the same class of trade; there is a high probability that errors will be made in quoting prices, billing customers, and accounting for costs. To these costs of administering a chaotic pricing system must be added the expected cost of losing customers who learn that they have been paying "too much" for a product. Perhaps this is the most significant portion of the cost of discriminating. As more market separations are made there is an increase in the probability that customers will learn of their being "exploited." For these reasons it is unlikely that a firm will pursue market separations to the point described.

The locus $MC + DC$ explicitly brings the cost of discriminatory pricing into the analysis.[3] The logic as previously described would now allow the firm to work toward the intersection E where OQ_2 would be the quantity produced. Thus, the rising cost of discriminatory pricing for the distributor causes the ultimate market for the manufacturer-supplier to be truncated.

In an effort to sell as much of the market as possible many manufacturers have developed incentives to offer their distributors. In practice the distributor may meet competitive prices as low as their cost. In order to accomplish this the manufacturer establishes a control system. Accounts to be sold at jobber cost must be cleared with the supplier and, if possible, evidence of the price being met is submitted to the manufacturer. The manufacturer, in turn, will issue a rebate to the distributor for sales made at distributor cost, MC in the chart.

The effect of this on the previous analysis may be seen in the chart. MC' represents the revised marginal cost to the distributor; XB being the amount of the rebate per unit. Thus, under this system the distributor first sets his profit maximizing price OP_2, sells OQ_0 units, and then goes after the remaining accounts with the price MC (assuming that they can be approved). There is a one-time market separation. The firm sells $Q_4 - Q_0$ additional units and gains a total surplus of price over marginal cost of $XBCF$. If the distributor were allowed to set his own price, given the revised cost MC', and if the distributor chose to make only a single market

---

[3]At this level of analysis the second derivative of the function described by $MC + DC$ is not significant. It is necessary that the function have a positive slope and the foregoing discussion provides this logic.

separation, he would price the additional product at OP_0 and produce $Q_3 - Q_0$ additional units. The single market separation avoids the cost of administering a chaotic market and permits the firm to maximize in the second market by equating MC' with MR'.

When the manufacturer sets the selling price at MC the jobber gains an additional surplus comprised of an amount XAH in marginal profits minus HFG in marginal losses. In a sense the distributor has subsidized the manufacturer by the amount HFG inasmuch as the distributor has been induced to produce beyond the amount he would choose as a profit maximizer with distributor costs given. Under this pricing system the distributor adds a surplus of $XB'JH$, an amount exceeding that acquired with the price set by the manufacturer.

Of course, given the opportunity to set his own price, the jobber might choose to price his product chaotically on the basis of the cost MC'. In such a case the cost of discriminating would again become relevant to the analysis. The locus $MC' + DC$ represents this added cost. Now, the firm would make market separations toward a limit of point J. The first market separation in this case would take place where $MC' + DC$ equals MR'. Additional separations would then take place with each division contributing additions to the firm's surplus.

From all of this it appears that, given the choice, the distributor might prefer to select a profit maximizing price in each of several separate markets. This freedom in planning activities will always be to the firm's advantage.

In order for the rebate plan to be unambiguously successful in extending the manufacturer's market the distributor must be operating in the elastic portion of its demand curve. Otherwise decreases in price will lead to decreases in total revenue. There is also an area where the distributors must consider trade-offs between the surplus to be gained by the rebate plan and revenues to be lost because of movement into the inelastic portion of demand. It quickly becomes apparent that the problem faced by the typical distributor is not a simple one.

SUMMARY

The analysis offered here suggests yet another case of induced price discrimination. It has been shown that under certain circumstances the profit-maximizing firm will move to what might be termed a non-optimal position. For such strategy to be successful it appears that both the manufacturer and the distributor must have monopoly power. Also it appears that the demand for products of such firms must be elastic over a relatively large quantity range.

In the analysis, the costs of market separation have explicitly been taken into account. As a result it has been shown that firms involved in third-degree price discrimination will stop short of what might be termed complete market extension.

The "equilibrium" positions obtained by the firm under the rebate plan are somewhat tenuous. For example, there are opportunities to "cheat" in any system of reporting sales, and, no doubt, all such opportunities have been discovered at one time or another. The distributor may choose to report many sales at price *MG*, under the rebate plan, when in fact none or very few have been sold at that price. By this means the surplus available from the rebate plan may be obtained in addition to any other surplus available to the distributor by selling his product at prices above *MG*. The "honest" distributor may feel that he is subsidizing his supplier. This creates instability in the market. Thus, manufacturers complain about "cheating" distributors, and distributors complain about "greedy" manufacturers. It would appear that an outright reduction in price by the manufacturers might add stability to the equilibrium position obtained by the distributor who "meets competition" in separate markets.

REFERENCES

1. Eli W. Clemens, "Price Discrimination and the Multiple-Product Firm," *Review of Economic Studies*, Vol. 19 (1950–51), pp. 1–11, reprinted in American Economic Association, Richard B. Heflebower and George W. Stocking, eds., *Readings in Industrial Organization and Public Policy* (Homewood: Irwin, 1958), pp. 262–76.
2. Fritz Machlup, "Characteristics and Types of Price Discrimination," in *Business Concentration and Price Policy* (Princeton: Princeton University Press, for the National Bureau of Economic Research, 1955), pp. 397–440.

2

An Operational Approach to Product Pricing *

B. R. DARDEN

THE best brains in the business and academic worlds labor to provide the product pricer with a repertoire of sophisticated techniques and approaches, and he continues pricing products in his usual manner. While the economist expounds use of concepts of demand and marginal analysis, the pricer uses experience, intuition, and cost-plus. While the statistician calls for probability and payoff tables, the pricer uses experience, intuition, and cost-plus. While the professional expounds the use of price elasticity and cross-elasticity concepts, the pricer again uses experience, intuition, and cost-plus.

OBSTACLES TO OPTIMAL PRODUCT-PRICING

Why does the pricer persist in this "irrational" behavior? This question seems to evoke answers from academicians and professionals that are as "irrational" as the pricer's behavior. Actually, the answers are simpler than presupposed and are all in the form of obstacles to "optimal" pricing. Some of these obstacles are:

1. The pricer does not have the time, nor the interest, to read and digest the latest literature on pricing, even if it were directly applicable in practice, which it is not.
2. In many cases the objectives of the pricer may be quite different from the objectives assumed in the literature for arriving at optimal guides to action.
3. The typical pricer usually has many product lines, and in each

*The *Journal of Marketing*, Vol. 32, No. 2, April 1968, pp. 29–33. Reproduced by permission.

product line he may have many products. Thus, the time that he may allot to pricing each product may be very small.

4. Also, while the pricer recognizes that many products are substitutes or complementary to each other, he has no way to quantify or measure these effects properly.

5. The product pricer also has problems in determining competitor reactions to price strategies. The direction and degree of *price* reactions is a prime trouble area.

6. Again, the pricer does not have the methods, time, or money to measure demand curves or other consumer response curves properly. From experience, intuition, and judgment he must make hypotheses about future decision relationships. Future positive feedback increases the belief in these hypotheses, while negative feedback decreases the belief in these hypotheses. With negative feedback, the pricer begins to investigate his "key" hypotheses, sequentially, and these may be revised.

The above "obstacles" do not begin to show the difficulties of the "complete" pricer. The "complete" pricer must deal with all the myriad combinations of price, advertising, sales promotion, personal selling, place, and product. Heuristically, he must hypothesize about the degree to which competitors will react to his price change and in what form this reaction will occur. The product pricer must "guess"—on the basis of his present hypotheses—what blend of marketing decisions will go best with a given price, and he must in turn determine what effect the given price will have on the sales of other products in the product line (both in the short run and in the long run). To continue with the latter thought, the product pricer must coordinate pricing policy with channel decisions, product decisions, and promotion decisions. *This coordination must take place through time*, not only at a point in time (as economic analysis often assumes).

It is not surprising, then, that the product pricer cannot predict the quantity demanded for a given price during a given period. However, it is probable that the product pricer does use an implicit, informal method of determining a sales volume range for a given price. Thus, it is believed that most product pricers *do* consider more than cost and turnover in pricing. It is hypothesized in this paper that many pricers use experience and intuition to arrive operationally at hypotheses which serve as a basis for price making. The purpose of this paper, then, is to formalize, heuristically, an operational approach to pricing, given the beliefs of the pricer.

PROFIT VARIANCE AND PRICE LIMITS

The central concept of the proposed pricing approach is exemplified in Fig. 1. Assuming some given price, P_1, the breakeven chart in Fig. 1 can be easily produced. The typical marketing executive will determine the most likely quantity demanded at P_1—in this case, Q_M. Now the marketing student determines the most likely profit at Q_M, as well as the breakeven quantity, Q_B. This approach is likely to be repeated for several prices, yielding respective profit and breakeven quantities for each price. Actually, the marketer is using repetitive breakeven analysis to feel out demand.

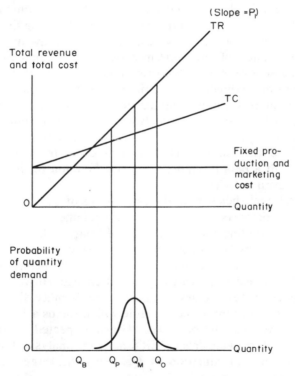

FIG. 1. At a given price (P_1), the use of three volume estimates to fit a beta probability distribution.

In addition, the marketer may determine optimal advertising and sales promotion for each price, which in turn also affects the profit and breakeven quantities received for each price. It is also recognized that the final most likely price is that which reflects judgments about competitive reactions.

Now the price investigator can estimate for a given price a pessimistic quantity demanded and an optimistic quantity demanded. These estimates are Q_P and Q_O, respectively, for price P_1 in Fig. 1. Thus the pricing specialist has three sales volume estimates at a given price, P_1: a most likely estimate (Q_M), a pessimistic estimate (Q_P), and an optimistic estimate (Q_O).

Rationale and Uses of Quantity Estimates

In the Program Evaluation and Review Technique, commonly called PERT, the planner is faced with the problem of estimating times required for accomplishing particular activities. In order to draw upon the judgment and experience of the superintendent or foreman in charge of completing the activity, and at the same time eliminate bias, the planner asks for three time estimates. These time estimates include an optimistic estimate, a pessimistic estimate, and a most likely estimate. In the cases of optimistic and pessimistic estimations, the planner counsels the estimator to choose times that have a chance of 1 in 100 of occurring. The rationale behind this counsel is that such estimates can be used to approximately fit a beta probability density function to the time occurrence of the given activity.

The same rationale lies behind the estimations of Q_P, Q_M, and Q_O at P_1 in Fig. 1. The marketer is unsure what future volume will be generated by the projected marketing mix (including, of course, the price, P_1). For example, the degrees to which competitors may react, the change in marketing environment, and changes in company implementation effectiveness are all subject to varying degrees of change. However, using the three quantity estimates and assuming a beta probability distribution, the price-maker can determine a sales volume which stands a 50-50 chance of occurring. This volume will be called "largest expected volume" and is denoted by Q_E. Borrowing from PERT network analysis, the following formula yields an approximation of Q_E, using the three quantity estimates:

$$Q_E = \frac{Q_P + 4Q_M + Q_O}{6} \qquad (1)$$

An important characteristic of this approach is the flexibility of the beta distribution. It allows the volume estimator to make the extreme volume estimates asymmetrical around the most likely volume, if he so chooses. Thus, the probability distribution fitted to the volume estimates may be positively skewed, negatively skewed, or symmetrically distributed.

VARIANCE OF THE SALES VOLUME

In addition to yielding the "largest expected volume" for a given price, this "operational approach" produces a good estimate of the volume variance. Using again the volume estimates at P_1, the marketer can compute this approximate variance with Equation (2) shown below:

$$\sigma^2 = \frac{(Q_O - Q_P)^2}{36} \tag{2}$$

Price Range and the "Operational Approach"

The major strength of the "operational approach" lies in its ability to draw on the experience and judgment of marketing specialists in the firm. The knowledge in regard to competitor reactions, market changes, consumer behavior, and company implementation effectiveness should to a great degree be reflected in the estimates of volume at a given price. Using a repetitive approach, the same analysis can be made for several prices.

Specifically, the pricer wishes to determine some upper and lower limits for prices that must be investigated. Figure 2 shows a special type of demand curve (or curves). This demand curve actually represents three demand curves: the first (D_O) indicates optimistic quantity estimates at various prices; the second (D_M) shows most likely sales volume at all prices; and the third (D_P) shows pessimistic estimates. These three curves generate three total revenue curves in Fig. 2: the optimistic revenue curve, the most likely revenue curve, and the pessimistic revenue curve.

The marketer begins at a high price level, decreasing the price until at a given price (in this case P_1) the pessimistic quantity estimate generates only enough revenue to just break even (BEP_1). At a higher price P_{1+}, the volume Q_{P1-} will not cover costs and at a lower price P_{1-}, the volume Q_{P1+} will generate profits. The price (P_1) which accompanies Q_{P1} becomes the upper price limit, ensuring the firm that it will do better than break even over 99% of the time at this price.

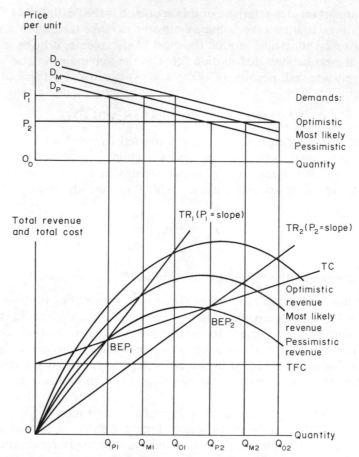

FIG. 2. Determination of feasible price range through the interaction of pessimistic, most
likely, and optimistic demands with cost curves.

In order to establish a lower price limit, in Fig. 2, the marketer lowers
the price past P_1 until a price is reached which allows the pessimistic
revenue curve to break even again (BEP_2). At P_2, such a situation occurs
and this price, again, will generate profits 99% of the time.

The marketer has now "bracketed" the feasible prices available to him.
This price range may be so small that the respective quantity estimates of
the two extreme prices may overlap; however, this seems unlikely in most
cases.

After the upper price limit ($P_1 = P_U$) and the lower price limit ($P_2 = P_L$)
have been determined, the firm may wish to find the largest expected

quantities and the quantity variances at each price limit. From this information, the largest expected profit can be determined at both P_U and P_L as shown below.

$$Q_{E1} = \frac{Q_{P1} + 4Q_{M1} + Q_{O1}}{6}$$

Expected Profit $= PR_E = Q_{E1}(P_U) - TFC - (V)Q_{E1}$

Where V = Average Variable Cost, TFC = Total Fixed Cost

Now the same information can be determined at the lower end of the price bracket.

Implications for Pricing Strategy

The "operational approach" provides the product pricer with a formal vehicle to summarize and integrate his various hypotheses into a clear picture of economical alternatives. Some considerations for the pricer are:

1. The quantity estimates for the upper price limit and the lower price limit may overlap. For example, the upper limit may have an optimistic quantity estimate of 500,000 units, while the lower price limit may have a pessimistic quantity estimate of 499,000.
2. While Fig. 2 assumes that costs remain constant in determining the upper and lower price limits, this assumption is not necessary. Thus, the pricer can change marketing blends to optimize some given objective at each price without changing the usefulness of the operational approach.
3. The use of three quantity estimates for a given price *does not* require that pricing specialists within a firm reach complete agreement as to forecasted sales. Thus, the difficult problem of "consensus" in pricing is largely overcome.
4. Once the product pricer has "bracketed in" the upper and lower price limits, he can use a sequential approach to test the expected profitability of intermediate prices.
5. The product pricer can not only compute and compare expected largest profits, but he can also compute and compare quantity and profit variances at various prices. There is no guarantee that quantity variances will be similar at different prices; therefore, a product pricer may be willing to accept a lower expected largest profit at some price in exchange for a much smaller variance (in other words, the pricer may be willing to trade off expected profit for a greater degree of certainty).

3

The Borden Case: A Legal Basis for Private Brand Price Discrimination*

M. L. MAYER, J. B. MASON, and E. A. ORBECK

This case study provides excellent insight as to how litigation may be avoided through careful planning.

This article describes ten years of litigation, as taken from court records, between the Borden Company and the FTC relative to price differentials in the sale of private brands. It is an excellent case for analysis in that it was heard by the FTC, appealed to the FTC, appealed to a Federal Circuit Court of Appeals, appealed to the Supreme Court of the United States, and remanded to the Circuit Court. At each level decisions were set aside and in the final analysis a new precedent was set.

The Borden Company had been producing private brand evaporated milk for approximately twenty years prior to the subject landmark litigation. However, on April 22, 1958, the FTC issued a complaint against the Borden Company charging that Borden had discriminated in price among different purchasers of its evaporated milk by selling milk of "like grade and quality" at lower prices to some of its purchasers than to others during the period January 1, 1956 to April 22, 1958. This milk was produced at various Borden plants and the price differentials are shown in Table 1 with the prices in effect in July 1957. The FTC charged that the effect of the price discriminations between different purchasers of the product was to lessen competition or to create a monopoly, or to injure, destroy, or prevent competition[1]. These alleged discriminations were charged to be in violation of subsection (a) of Section 2 of the Clayton Act as amended by the Robinson-Patman Act.

*From *MSU Business Topics*, Vol. 18, No. 4, Winter 1970, pp. 56–63. Reproduced by permission.

TABLE 1. *Milk production sites and price differentials*

	Borden Label Per Case	Buyer Label Per Case	Price Differential
Albany, Oreg.	$6.45	$5.59	$ .86
Modesto, Calif.	6.45	5.12	1.33
Ft. Scott, Kans.	6.45	5.26	1.19
Dixon, Ill.	6.45	5.25	1.20
New London, Wis.	6.45	5.32	1.13
Perrinton, Mich.	6.45	5.42	1.03
Wellsboro, Pa.	6.45	5.37	1.08
Lewisburg, Tenn.	6.45	5.01	1.44
Chester, S.C.	6.45	5.01	1.44

The initial decision was rendered December 15, 1961. The following is a summary of events that led to this decision.

Borden responded to the FTC charges and stated that the prices of the two lines of evaporated milk did not differ by more than the difference in the cost thereof and that their pricing practices were not such as to be in violation of the Robinson-Patman Act. Borden further stated that the price of its private label evaporated milk was determined by a special pricing formula used at each individual packing plant and which was applicable to purchases of all private label customers. Included in the formula were all costs of buying and processing the milk plus a profit factor. The price per case could vary from month to month depending on the price Borden paid for the milk.

It was readily admitted that there was no chemical difference between the Borden and private brand labels, and Borden's first approach was to contend that the products were not of like grade and quality because its brand of evaporated milk commanded a substantially higher market price than did private label milk. The reasoning was that if it could be proven that the products were not of like grade and quality because of consumer acceptance, this would in essence reveal that the brands identified were in effect two different products. Such proof would remove the products from the purview of the Robinson-Patman Act, and they could be priced with no relationship to one another. The FTC did not accept this reasoning and stated that reaction within the marketplace in no way changes the physical composition of the milk and that it was of like grade and quality within the meaning of the Robinson-Patman Act[1].

Borden then endeavored to justify its strategy from a cost standpoint. The FTC pointed out that in the case of *FTC* v. *Anheuser-Busch, Inc.*, (363 U.S., 536), the court held that price discrimination was a mathematical difference between two prices without giving any consideration to factors of cost justification which could be offered as defense for a price differential. Thus it was held that the differences in the prices of the evaporated milk were *prima facie* price discriminations within the intent and meaning of the Robinson-Patman Act. Borden responded with an analysis of its costs as shown in Table 2.

It was the hearing examiner's opinion that this cost analysis constituted full justification for the differences in price within the meaning of the Robinson-Patman Act and was therefore an adequate cost justification defense against the complaint. It was further concluded that the differences in price between the Borden brand and the private label evaporated milk did not substantially lessen competition.

TABLE 2. *Analysis of costs (per case)*

	Borden Brand	Private Label	Difference
Gross sales	$6.4046	$5.1743	$1.2303
Less sales deductions			
Damaged goods	.0112	.0027	.0085
Cash discount offered	.1279		.1279
Net sales	$6.2655	$5.1716	$1.0939
Costs			
Labels and cartons	.1789	.1376	.0413
Primary freight	.3684	.0188	.3496
Secondary freight	.0112		.0112
Reserve storage	.0690		.0690
Consignment storage	.0305		.0305
Investment cost	.0972	.0568	.0404
Premium label redemption	.2316		.2316
Advertising	.1247		.1247
Sales department	.3163	.0009	.3154
Brokers' commissions	.0427		.0427
Promotion department	.0189	.0123	.0066
Clerical	.0151	.0062	.0089
Total	$1.5045	$ .2326	$1.2719
Difference in cost			$1.2719
Difference in price			1.0939
Excess of cost difference over price difference			$ .1780

APPEAL TO THE FTC

Both parties appealed to the FTC. Borden contested the hearing examiner's finding that the two products were of like grade and quality, and the FTC counsel challenged the findings that (1) Borden had justified the differences in price on the basis of costs, and (2) that there had been a failure to prove injury to competition. They further requested that Borden be found in violation of the Robinson-Patman Act and be ordered to cease and desist.

The Commission upheld the hearing examiner's opinion that the products were of like grade and quality.

In terms of the injury to competition contention, the FTC counsel presented additional evidence to the Commission showing that there were differences in prices to competing customers. One of the examples given is shown in Table 3[1].

The FTC contended that the data in Table 3 showed that some merchants were required to pay more for like goods than other merchants (competitors). The effect of this type of discrimination was to lessen, or to injure, destroy, or prevent competition between Borden's wholesale and retail customers. Pertinent testimony from several wholesalers and retailers revealed that if they had been able to buy evaporated milk from Borden at the same prices their competitors had bought the milk, they would have been able to meet the prices of their competitors. Since it had been shown that some purchasers paid less than their competitors for purchases of like goods from Borden, Borden was charged with competitive injury as prescribed in the Robinson-Patman Act.

TABLE 3. *Price differences to competing customers*

Customer	Date	Borden Brand Price	Private Label Price
Hartley Grocery Columbia S.C. (wholesaler)	7/18/57		$6.45
Biddle Purchasing Co., Columbia S.C. (wholesaler)	7/18/57		$4.9051
Rawl Distributing Co., Columbia, S.C. (wholesaler)	7/ 8/57	6.45	
Rawl Distributing Co., Columbia, S.C.	3/ 4/58	6.60	
Biddle Purchasing Co., Columbia, S.C.	2/ 4/58		5.0289
Piggly Wiggly Carolina Co., Inc., Columbia, S.C. (chain retailer)	{1/10/58 {3/ 7/58		5.0227} 4.9436}

In the proceedings on the cost justification complaint, the Commission reviewed the material contained in Table 2 and stated that it was an inadequate study of costs because the figures were a result of broad averaging throughout the Borden evaporated milk business. The reasoning was that Borden customers were not faced with the average prices, but with prices as shown for a specific area in Table 3. The Borden cost defense failed to present any customer classifications, even though it sells to retailers, wholesalers, cooperatives, and others. In short, Borden's cost analysis was not sufficiently specific to be acceptable. In addition, the Commission found that several of the costs were not acceptable as part of a cost justification scheme under the Robinson-Patman Amendment— The resultant ruling was that the cost analysis was inadequate to justify the price differences between the Borden and private label brands of milk. The Commission concluded that the acts and practices of Borden were in violation of the Robinson-Patman Act.

APPEAL TO THE CIRCUIT COURT

Borden's next step was to file a petition in the Fifth Circuit Court of Appeals requesting that the cease and desist order be set aside. The court first considered the question of whether products sold at different prices were of like grade and quality. A review of the record showed that retail customers were willing to pay more for a manufacturer's brand of evaporated milk than for a private label.

The court felt it could not ignore the fact that a brand name might command a higher price in the market than a private label because of public acceptance. Therefore it was of the opinion that distinctions affecting market value, whether they be physical or promotional, should be considered when determining like grade and quality[2].

The court was of the opinion that Borden had clearly shown that its brand name had value in the market, and therefore ruled on December 4, 1964, that the products, though chemically the same, were not of like grade and quality within the meaning of the Robinson-Patman Amendment, and the petition to set aside the cease and desist order was granted. The court did not consider arguments concerning injury to competition or cost justification defenses[2].

APPEAL TO THE SUPREME COURT

The FTC appealed this decision to the Supreme Court and because of the importance of the issue, the Supreme Court granted certiorari. The opinion of the Court was delivered on March 23, 1966, and it reversed the decision of the Fifth Circuit Court of Appeals relative to the concept of like grade and quality and remanded the case to that court to determine the remaining issues of injury to competition and cost justification. In reaching a decision that Borden's evaporated milk was of like grade and quality, even though the brand product had more economic value in the marketplace, the Court turned to both precedent and legislative history.

In summary, the Supreme Court stated that the arguments for exempting private brand selling from the provisions of the Robinson-Patman Act would be more appropriately legislated in Congress than addressed in a court.

THE CASE REMANDED TO THE CIRCUIT COURT

The Fifth Circuit Court of Appeals delivered its second opinion on July 4, 1967. The court held that there was not substantial evidence to support the FTC finding that Borden had engaged in illegal price discrimination. For a second time it granted the petition to set aside the cease and desist order.

In reaching this decision, the court had to resolve the legality of an established price difference. Its first action was to see if the FTC finding of competitive injury was supported by substantial evidence in the record. The record showed that there had been testimony in support of the complaint by seven Midwestern canners of private label evaporated milk. They complained they had lost business to Borden. In reality, Borden's processing plants were closer to the buyers who were therefore able to buy cheaper because of the savings in transportation charges. The record also showed that Borden had lost sales to its main competitors, Pet and Carnation, in various parts of the United States for the same reasons. The record further showed that during the period in question Borden's share of the market increased from 9.9 percent to 10.7 percent, while the competitors who had testified against Borden had an increase from 6.3 percent to 6.8 percent. These factors were significant as they did not show the court reason to support a finding of substantial injury to competition. The competitors had lost business in one area, but in the aggregate had bettered their market position in the same proportion as had Borden. The court also found no reason to believe that one customer had been favored over another, as it was Borden policy to sell unbranded milk for private branding to any customer requesting it at the same price being charged to other customers.

The court felt it unnecessary to review the issues of cost justification because of its position on the issue of injury to competition. Thus consumer preference for the Borden label again won in the Court of Appeals. This time it was used to show no injury to competition.

THE PRECEDENT DECISION

The decision, that no competitive advantage is created by a price difference between a brand name and private brand which reflects only the consumer preference for the brand name, is limited in application to manufacturers whose brands are highly promoted and for which there is a consumer preference shown by a willingness to pay more for the brand name. This in effect means that a manufacturer cannot merely attach a different label to his product and then sell it at a different price. It must be demonstrated that a label enjoys a significant consumer acceptance demonstrated through the fact that buyers are willing to pay more because the product is a certain brand.

This case is in the nature of a landmark decision as it recognizes the fact that value has been created for a product by promotion. Though there is no change in the grade or quality, there may be an economic value attached to a brand name product over its private brand counterpart.

The decision is far from being a panacea for all dual brand producers as there are still ways to prove competitive injury. Had the FTC been able to prove that a competing seller had been injured by a loss in sales due to Borden's difference in price, Borden would have had to attempt to justify its position based on cost differences. Thus, manufacturers must be aware of the effect their private brands may have on competition, as the FTC does not have to prove that competition has been injured, but can rule on the probable future impact of a private brand.

REFERENCES

1. The Borden Company, 62 FTC 130 (1962).
2. *The Borden Company* v. *FTC*, 339 F. 2d 133 (5th Cir. 1964).

4

*Some Aspects of the Economics of Advertising**

L. G. TELSER

I. INTRODUCTION

High on the list of controversial economic topics stands advertising. The critics of advertising claim it abuses consumer confidence, shapes and sometimes vulgarizes taste, and creates abnormal, unjustified profits. To these critics advertising is the leading symbol of materialistic Western civilization and of capitalism in particular.

Nowadays there are few defenders of advertisers, and even these speak humbly and possibly without conviction. In intellectual circles it is risky to one's reputation of intelligence and/or honesty to defend advertising. Some aspects of advertising pose problems of considerable intellectual challenge, whose study will aid protagonists on all sides of the debate on advertising.

II. SOME PROBLEMS IN ADVERTISING

Advertising comes in many forms. Not all goods are advertised to the same extent, if at all, and different goods are advertised in different media. A conspicuous form of advertising is on television, and even larger sums in total are spent on advertising in the other media—newspapers, magazines, radio, billboards, and direct mail. Some commodities are more advertised in one medium than in another.

Some commodities are not advertised at all, such as locomotives, contraceptives, and glass eye balls. Consumer goods are much more

*From the *Journal of Business* (*The Graduate School of Business of the University of Chicago*), Vol. 41, No. 2, April 1968, pp. 166–173. Copyright © The University of Chicago Press. Reproduced by permission.

advertised than industrial products. What explains these differences in the usage of advertising by commodity and by media?

Although advertising outlays on a given commodity change over time, total advertising outlays as a percentage of national income show remarkable stability over time. In the United States this ratio has remained between 2 and 3 per cent of national income annually, except for some changes over the business cycle. The percentage rises somewhat when business is slack and falls somewhat when business is more active. What explains the secular stability of this ratio and its behavior over the business cycle?

Advertising is only one means of promoting the sale of goods and services. Personal selling is the older method, and more is spent on salesmen than on advertising. Moreover, one cannot understand the determinants of advertising expenditures without considering the problem of explaining total selling outlays. There are wide differences in personal selling. In supermarkets there are salesmen who are little more than clerks; at auto dealers there are salesmen who are anything but clerks. Industrial-goods salesmen often provide their customers with technical advice, and detail men give physicians considerable information about drugs. Some goods are sold mainly through the efforts of salesmen, while others rely mainly on advertising and still others, notably drugs, depend on both personal selling and advertising. There is a logic to these methods of promotion. This is shown by a comparison between two independent sets of data on advertising in the 1930's, one collected in England by Kaldor and Silverman[4] and the other in the United States by the Federal Trade Commission[10]. Advertising as a percentage of sales for the same products in the two countries is remarkably close. This can be no coincidence. Basic factors inherent in the market, the product, and the tastes of consumers explain these similarities.

III. ADVERTISING AND PROFITS

Study of the problems just cited advances our understanding of the determinants of advertising outlays and throws light on the contention that advertising is a means to abnormally high profits. In its most naive form this belief rests on some easily available statistics. The Fortune list of the five hundred largest companies gives the ten companies with the highest rate of return on invested capital. Other companies among the golden ten are those that spend large sums on research and development. The moral seems clear. The road to riches requires a firm to spend on research and development and advertising.

Alas the figures are fallacious, because they cling to old-fashioned accounting conventions that define capital as consisting only of investments in tangible items such as plant, equipment, and inventories. However, the true capital of a company includes expenditures that yield a return long after the initial outlays. Advertising expenditures together with research and development have this property. Yet the typical balance sheet omits them. The relevant rate of return on the firm's true capital is much lower than the Fortune figures suggest.

IV. A SHORT HISTORY OF ADVERTISING

Advertising is among the oldest of man's activities, probably first appearing in conjunction with the oldest profession. Advertising in its modern form began in England in the middle of the nineteenth century, together with the popular press. This is no accident. The large circulation of the penny newspapers provided a ready audience for advertising messages not long overlooked by businessmen. Proprietary medicines were among the first major advertisers in these newspapers, and more respectable products, such as tea, cocoa, and sewing machines, did not lag far behind.

It is the United States that deserves the credit for the rapid improvement and development of advertising. The modern national advertising campaign can be said to have begun with the introduction of the first domestic blend of cigarettes, Camels, in 1913. Cigarette makers continued to innovate in advertising, particularly by their use of radio in the twenties and thirties.

Important changes in methods of distribution were helped by the emergence of advertising. The local shop and retailer played a smaller role, and self-service stores offering customers packaged, branded, and nationally advertised goods at lower prices grew rapidly. Competition among retailers became keener, because with the new sales methods it was easier for consumers to shop in several stores in search of the lowest price for a standard, branded item. At the same time, manufacturers became more involved in distribution. Kaldor[3] and others claim that the heavier expenses of the new methods of promotion gave monopoly power to the manufacturer.

V. DETERMINANTS OF ADVERTISING EXPENDITURES

To say that business firms advertise because they find this to be profitable, although true, does not advance our understanding of the subject. We must look more closely at the mechanism of advertising. To this end let us consider how advertisers choose media for a given product, say, baby food. Potential customers are mothers of babies. Hence the advertiser wants media whose audience includes a sizeable number of females in this category. Television programs such as baseball games might be less suitable than weekly comedy programs after 8:00 P.M. In general the advertiser will attempt to allocate the funds in his advertising budget among the various media so as to obtain the maximum number of potential customers for his product. This may seem obvious, yet it goes far in explaining why some products are more advertised than others. Some products have so few potential customers that it does not pay to advertise them in any media, for example, glass eye balls. Such products are more efficiently promoted in other ways—by the use of salesmen or simply by relying on the buyers' ability to find the sellers for themselves, say, with the help of directories. This also explains why industrial products are less advertised than consumer products.

The same considerations explain the greater advertising of new than of established products. To illustrate, it is instructive to examine changes in advertising outlays on cigarettes during the past fifty years. At first cigarettes were a new product competing with cigars. During the twenties, advertising outlays were large and directed at women. By the thirties, penetration of both male and female markets had reached high and stable levels so that advertising outlays dropped to a point sufficient to maintain awareness among existing customers and to contact new potential customers as they came of age. After World War II there were new varieties—long cigarettes, filtered and mentholated ones, etc. To sell these new brands there were sharply increased advertising outlays. The ultimate reason for the appearance of the new brands was the connection between smoking and lung cancer and not the advertising in itself[7].

VI. BRAND LOYALTY

It is widely believed that advertising can reduce competition by the creation of brand loyalty for the advertised brands. This proposition is testable by comparing the brand-share stability of two classes of products, one which is more advertised and the other which is little advertised. The brand shares in the heavily advertised product class should be more stable over time than brand shares in the little-advertised product group. I tested this proposition by comparing the share stability of a group of toiletries and cosmetics, a heavily advertised product class, with a group of food items, a much less advertised product class [8]. Contrary to the hypothesis, brand-share stability is *lower* for the more advertised than for the less advertised group. The life-span of a brand in the cosmetic-toiletry category is shorter than for a product in the foods category. The explanation is clear. The high level of advertising results from the high frequency of introduction of new products in the cosmetic class. Far from creating brand *loyalty*, the high advertising outlays are the result of brand *disloyalty*. Consumers become dissatisfied with the existing brands of cosmetics, toiletries, and toothpaste and are constantly ready to test the promise of new varieties—promises hardly capable of fulfillment.

The conclusion is that some of the large advertising outlays are explained by the rapid rate of introduction of new products. It also appears that advertising by itself seems incapable of maintaining consumer acceptance of a product that is found to be unsatisfactory.

VII. ADVERTISING AND MONOPOLY

Closer study of the relation between advertising and competition is possible. One measure of competition in an industry, widely accepted by economists, is the concentration of sales among the four leading firms in the industry. The larger the share of the total going to the four leading firms, the less the competition. If advertising reduces competition, then there ought to be high levels of advertising in those industries in which the leading firms have a large share of total sales and low levels of advertising in industries where the leading firms have small shares. This seems to be true in some industries, for instance, soaps, cigarettes, and breakfast cereals, but it is false in other industries, drugs, and cosmetics. The best way to test the proposition is to examine the data for all consumer-product industries. Such an examination shows a negligible positive association between advertising intensity and concentration. In other words, the exceptions to the hypothesis nearly outweigh the conforming cases. Changes in concentration and advertising intensity ought to move in the same direction according to the hypothesis that advertising lessens competition. The data for the period 1947–57 show, if anything, the opposite relation—an inverse association between changes in advertising intensity and changes in concentration.

The weakness of the hypothesis claiming a positive association between advertising and monopoly is shown by another fact. Industries that make industrial goods hardly advertise and yet may be highly concentrated. Thus if all manufacturing industries were examined to determine the relation between advertising intensity and the concentration of sales among the leading firms, no systematic pattern would emerge. Advertising levels are better explained by the factors I have discussed above than by the state of competition in the industry. Characteristics of the customers of the product, their number, and the cost of contacting them by various media are much more important in explaining the level of advertising[8, 9].

Although a continuously high rate of profit year after year is a symptom of monopoly, occasional high profits are not, even if these may result from a successful advertising campaign. Some highly advertised consumer products strike the public fancy and yield a handsome return, and this can also happen to unadvertised goods for much the same reasons. Examples of the latter abound—best sellers, hula hoops, *Gone with the Wind*, and miniskirts. Neither Xerox nor IBM owes its profits to advertising.

VIII. ADVERTISING AND NATIONAL INCOME

The stability of advertising outlays as a percentage of national income results from the stability of the determinants of these expenditures. The turnover of consumers, the number of potential customers, their characteristics, and the rate of introduction of new products all determine the number of advertising messages that the sellers of goods and services wish to convey. In addition to these real factors, advertising outlays depend on the prices charged by the media. These prices depend on costs as determined by the nature of the audience relevant to the advertiser and by the forces affecting the average price level in the economy. The result is stability in the ratio of advertising outlays to national income. This stability has persisted for the past forty years despite the appearance of new media that might provide scope for increased advertising outlays. It should be borne in mind, however, that the new media substitutes for the old and that competition among the media, together with increased efficiency, checks the price of advertising services.

The cyclical behavior of advertising outlays has an equally prosaic explanation. When business declines unexpectedly, budgeted advertising is not reduced at first. Hence advertising outlays rise relative to income. When business unexpectedly improves, advertising outlays do not rise simultaneously, so that advertising outlays as a percentage of income fall.

In a static economy there would be less advertising. Information about goods and services, terms of sale, and the identity of buyers and sellers would not become obsolete. Catalogues and directories would never be changed. People would continue to use the same things in the same way. To the extent that advertising conveys pertinent information about such changes, it facilitates economic growth.

IX. CONSUMER PROTECTION

My analysis so far has dealt mostly with the more technical aspects of advertising. I have not said whether advertising is sufficiently informative, whether trivial product differences are overemphasized, whether advertising is truthful or deliberately misleading, whether there is too much advertising, whether the support of television out of advertising receipts debases the quality of television entertainment, and whether advertising stimulates too much useless change.

Central to many of these questions is the undeniable fact that as the economy grows richer it yields a larger array of complicated consumer goods. To purchase wisely requires a high degree of competence that only a specialist can acquire. This expertise cannot be obtained from a careful study of the content of advertising messages. The potential for abuse is present. Is it only the fear of government controls that checks the cupidity of the advertiser?

Surely not. To obtain the continued patronage of a satisfied clientele is often the goal of business enterprise, and not out of altruism. For experience has shown this to be the profitable course. Moreover, consumers can judge the quality of goods and services indirectly in many ways. They test the reliability of sellers through long experience. Department stores and mail-order retailers act in effect as expert buyers on behalf of their customers. These retailers have the knowledge to buy goods and get good value for their money. Competition forces them to sell these goods jointly with their expertise at reasonable prices. Nor is experience the sole mentor of consumers. Guaranties and warranties guard their interest. Finally, in cases of serious damage consumers can resort to the courts. Manufacturers of defective articles are liable for the damage they cause, and the risk of costly law suits increases their incentive to control the quality of their products. A wide reputation engendered by advertising in itself forces sellers to exercise closer watch on the quality of products.

The market also meets the demand for information about consumer goods in direct ways. A few magazines specialize in reporting to their readers about the attributes of numerous articles by brand. Nevertheless, some kinds of potentially useful information are strangely absent. Thus advertisers rarely compare their own products directly with competing wares. Most advertising is mere puffing, and very little is critical. Magazines and newspapers are also deficient because they do not provide their readers with news about consumer products. Perhaps because of pressures from advertisers there are few columns containing news about consumer items, although this might be expected to have considerable interest to many readers. The only consumer products criticized in newspapers and magazines are plays, books, movies, and television programs.

Though experience acquaints consumers with the good and bad qualities of products, it is sometimes a slow and costly teacher. Partly for this reason there has never been sole reliance on market forces. Weights and measures were among the earliest subjects of government control. The government inspects, controls, and licenses many goods and services ranging from meats to elevators, drugs, and physicians. The Federal Trade Commission scrutinizes advertising and prosecutes for false or misleading statements. At the same time, advertising of a product is considered to confer an implicit warranty that makes the manufacturer liable for faulty performance.

X. THE REITH REPORT AND THE BACKMAN STUDY

In concluding I wish to comment on two recent studies of advertising that have attracted much attention. The first, the Reith Report[6], was sponsored by the British Labor party and confines itself to British conditions. It avowedly resembles a Royal Commission Report in every way save for lacking the official imprimatur. Since it rests its analysis on the testimony of a number of interested parties who appeared before the "Commission," it brings forth no new material. Despite its critical approach to advertising, the report contains surprisingly mild recommendations. It favors the dissemination of more consumer information by an impartial board supported from public funds. This board is to publicize its findings about consumer wares through the use of advertising, I suppose on the theory of fighting fire with fire. The board, like our Federal Trade

Commission, is also to prosecute those who make false advertising claims. The Reith Report also appeals for more scholarly research on advertising and deplores the present lack thereof. No doubt its provincial concern with Great Britain accounts for its surprising ignorance of a number of recent American studies on the subject. The members of the "Commission" could reach no consensus on a tax on advertising, but they did recommend special safeguards on the advertising of medicines and cigarettes.

The second recent study on advertising was sponsored by the Association of National Advertisers and carries the signature of Jules Backman[1]. It surveys many advertising studies and contains no original contribution of its own. This study takes an uncritical position toward advertising. It is most valuable for its numerous references to the works of others.

XI. ADVERTISING AND TELEVISION

In closing I can hardly forbear comment on how the introduction of pay television can lead to improvement in the quality of television entertainment. The sponsorship of television by advertisers pressures networks to produce programs that will appeal to a mass audience at the expense of gratifying minority tastes. Under a system of pay television it would be possible to have programs appealing to smaller audiences who are willing to pay for them directly. Giving more scope to market forces in television would increase variety and quality, just as similar market forces in publishing permit high-quality magazines to survive with a relatively small circulation. Pay television can develop in many ways, and community antennas, CA-TV, give promise of leading to viable pay television, provided they are allowed to do so without hindrance from the Federal Communications Commission.

BIBLIOGRAPHY

1. Backman, Jules. *Advertising and Competition.* New York: New York University Press, 1967.
2. Harris, Ralph, and Seldon, Arthur. *Advertising and the Public.* London: Institute of Economic Affairs, 1962.
3. Kaldor, Nicholas. "The Economic Aspects of Advertising," *Review of Economic Studies,* XVIII (1950–51), 1–27.
4. Kaldor, Nicholas, and Silverman, Rodney. *A Statistical Analysis of Advertising Expenditure and of the Revenue of the Press.* New York: Cambridge University Press, 1948.

5. Palda, Kristian. *The Measurement of Cumulative Advertising Effects.* Englewood Cliffs, N.J.: Prentice-Hall, Inc., 1964.
6. "Report of a Commission of Engineering into Advertising" (Reith Report). London: Labour party, n.d. (mimeographed).
7. Telser, Lester G. "Advertising and Cigarettes," *Journal of Political Economy,* LXX, No. 5 (October, 1962), 471–99.
8. Telser, Lester G. "Advertising and Competition," *ibid.,* LXXII, No. 6 (December, 1964), 537–62.
9. Telser, Lester G. "The Supply and Demand for Advertising Messages," *American Economic Review,* Suppl. (1966), pp. 457–66.
10. U.S. Federal Trade Commission, *Distribution Methods and Costs.* Part V, *Advertising as a Factor in Distribution.* Washington: U.S. Government Printing Office, 1944.

5

Advertising and Changes in Concentration*

MATITYAHU MARCOS

I. INTRODUCTION

The effect of advertising on industry structure and firms' behavior is a topic which has stimulated much discussion, a limited number of hypotheses and still fewer empirically verified propositions. One well-known hypothesis, originally put forth by Kaldor, is that advertising will result in increasing industry concentration thereby affecting competition adversely [1, 5]. Tests of this proposition by Telser and Mann, Henning and Meehan, have yielded conflicting results. On the basis of his findings, Telser questioned the validity of the hypothesis while Mann, et al., found support for it in their study [6, 9].

It is the purpose of this paper to employ newer data and a more comprehensive test procedure in a reevaluation of this hypothesis.

II. THEORY

In order to evaluate properly the Kaldor–Bain hypothesis it is necessary to formulate a model of concentration changes and appraise the effect of advertising within it. The variables to be included in such a model will now be discussed.

A factor often mentioned in previous studies is the influence of industry growth on changes in concentration [7, 8]. Specifically, it has been suggested that concentration will decrease (or increase less rapidly) in rapidly growing industries. Arguing for this position, Shepherd pointed out that dominant firms in growth industries may find it difficult to expand as fast as the entire industry [8, p. 204]. Such inability may be due to a

*From *The Southern Economic Journal*, Vol. XXXVI, No. 2, October 1969, pp. 117–121. Reproduced by permission.

comparative disadvantage of large firms in adapting to changes which are characteristic of growing industries.

Another reason is offered by Nelson who points out that large firms may prefer to grow through product diversification rather than through an increase in their market share of a given product [7, p. 641]. With such a policy the firm could attain greater stability of growth and lessen the risk of conflict with the antitrust authorities.

Another factor is the current *level* of concentration. One may argue that the higher the concentration already achieved by the leading firms, the smaller is the likelihood of a given further rise. One reason for this is, of course, spurious; the closer is the share to 100 percent, the smaller is the *maximum possible* increase which is also the ceiling upon the magnitude of random increases in concentration. But more importantly, there are *economic* reasons for the negative effect of the concentration level. Consider, for example, attempts to expand market share by means of price reduction. Since the firm's own demand is more elastic (relative to the industry's demand elasticity) the smaller is its market share, the small firm will be able to realize a greater growth of sales for a given percentage reduction in its price.[1] In addition the prominence of the large firm reinforces its fear of undertaking a price reduction: attempts to increase its share are more likely to be noticed and lead to retaliation from competing large firms which are intent on maintaining their shares. In contrast, small firms are less conspicuous, as well as less menacing, and hence less likely to evoke retaliatory pressure.

The last factor to be considered, and the one of primary interest in this study, is the effect of advertising on concentration ratios. In arguing for his hypothesis, Kaldor suggested the presence of increasing returns on advertising which would favor the leading firms with their larger advertising outlays:

> "The reason for this is that the shift of the demand curve resulting from advertising cannot be assumed to be strictly proportionate to the amount spent on advertising—the 'pulling power' of the large expenditure must overshadow that of smaller one with the consequence that the larger firms are bound to gain at the expense of the smaller ones" [5].

---

[1] Let the market elasticity $(\partial q/\partial p)(p/Q)$ be expressed as E, the firm's own elasticity $(\partial q/\partial p)(p/q_i)$ as e_i, and its market share q_i/Q as s_i. Then, $e_i = (\partial q/\partial p)(p/Q_{s_i}) = E/s_i$. That is, if the supply of other firms is assumed to be unchanged the firm's (partial) elasticity is inversely related to its market share.

Kaldor does not go beyond this brief statement, nor has the possibility of increasing returns been examined at length by others.

Since advertising shifts the firm's demand curve outward it can be viewed as having an effect on price and/or quantity sold. If increasing returns relate to the effect of advertising on price (holding quantity sold constant), its impact on concentration is not hard to rationalize. Higher prices will lead to improved profitability which will, in turn, encourage and enable the achievement of a faster growth rate, thereby leading to the realization of Kaldor's prediction of increasing concentration.

If one assumes a uniform industry price, advantages to the larger firms due to the effects of advertising on price must be ruled out. Increasing returns may nevertheless be reflected in the effect of advertising on the volume of sales at a given price. Larger firms could then choose to expand their sales and market share at a lower advertising cost than small firms.

Another explanation for the predicted concentration rise in heavily advertising industries was offered by Bain. Without taking a position on the nature of returns to scale in advertising, Bain argues that the necessity to advertise (or cut prices) in these industries will raise the required amount of capital for successful operation thus constituting a barrier to entry of new firms. Such a condition can be expected to result in increasing concentration [2].

III. THE STATISTICAL TESTS OF THE MODEL

The data employed in our tests are found in a Federal Trade Commission publication *Industry Classification and Concentration* [4]. This source reports changes in concentration ratios for 213 four-digit manufacturing industries for 1947, 1954, 1958 and 1963. Eighty-one of these are classified as consumer industries and their degree of product differentiation is ranked as high, medium, or low on the basis of their advertising expenditures:

"The classification of consumer goods industries into product differentiation categories is closely associated with the level of advertising expenditures in the industry. Generally speaking, industries classified as undifferentiated made advertising expenditures of less than 1 percent of sales and those classified as highly differentiated made substantial expenditures for advertising, often in excess of 10 percent of sales and usually were heavy users of advertising media"[4].

The terms advertising and differentiation will therefore be used interchangeably in this paper.

Our statistical source is not subject to some of the problems faced by earlier authors; the data are reported for a large number of industries at the four-digit level for which concentration ratios are readily available. Its shortcoming is that advertising intensity is not treated as a continuous variable and instead a three-category classification is employed. However, since the underlying data sources had to be assembled from diverse sources it is also possible that specific dollar magnitudes of advertising would be subject to substantial measurement error.

Notation

CR_{it} = percentage of shipments, for industry i, year t, accounted for by the eight largest firms ($i = 1, 2, \ldots 78$; $t = 1947, 1954, 1958, 1963$).[2]

$d_{i_{t-1}}$ = change in eight-firm concentration ratio between 1963 and each of three previous years; ($d_{i_{t-1}} = CR_{i_{63}} - CR_{i_{t-1}}$; $t = 1963, 1958, 1954$).

$g_{i_{t-1}}$ = growth rate of industry; i.e., value of industry shipments in 1963 over shipments in each of previous three years.

MD = a dummy variable taking the value 1 for all industries classified as subject to medium differentiation in [4].

HD = a dummy variable taking the value 1 for all industries subject to a high degree of differentiation [4].

u = an error term with mean zero and constant variance.

The model and the results. Based on the reasoning developed in the previous section, we formulate the following model:

$$d_{i_{t-1}} = \alpha_0 + \alpha_1 g_{i_{t-1}} + \alpha_2 CR_{i_{t-1}} + \alpha_3 MD_i + \alpha_4 HD_i + u \qquad (1.00)$$

That is, changes in industry concentration ($d_{i_{t-1}}$) are a function of industry growth rate ($g_{i_{t-1}}$), base period concentration ratio ($CR_{i_{t-1}}$) and the advertising intensity class into which the industry falls (MD_i or HD_i).

The performance of the model can be evaluated on the basis of Table I.[3] The role of industry growth conforms to earlier findings by Nelson and

---

[2] In three consumer industries coverage definitions were changed and we therefore excluded them from the analysis. See note E in [4, p. 18].

[3] Although not strictly comparable with earlier formulations, the portion of variance explained by equations 1.01, 1.02 are quite satisfactory as results in similar studies go.

TABLE I. *Regression results: changes in eight-firm concentration ratios against several variables (Seventy-eight consumer industries)*

| Equation | Period | Independent variables | | | | Constant | R^2 (adjusted for degrees of freedom) |
		Industry growth (α_1)	Lagged concentration ratio (α_2)	Medium differentiation group (α_3)	High differentiation group (α_4)		
(1.01)	1947–63	−3.5482 3.6119	−0.1510 3.6266	8.1434 3.5157	17.5141 5.9698	10.8514	0.3425
(1.02)	1954–63	−3.8869 2.0740	−0.0989 2.9837	4.4633 2.4136	8.1187 3.3637	10.3925	0.1290
(1.03)	1958–63	−2.0343 0.7581	−0.0813 2.9332	1.2658 0.7954	3.6462 1.7592	8.2397	0.0626

Values below coefficients are *t*-ratios. The industries falling into each category are listed in a note to Table II.

Shepherd[7, 8]. The coefficient is negative in all cases, and statistically significant at the 0.01 level for the 1947–1963 period.[4]

The base concentration ratio behaves as hypothesized: for all three periods, $CR_{i_{t-1}}$ was negative and statistically significant at the 0.01 level.[5] We note that the (negative) impact of the lagged concentration level diminishes as the interval shortens. Such a pattern is not surprising; the longer the period, the more likely is the relative disadvantage of the more dominant firms to work itself through. As a further illustration of this point, we can express $d_{i_{t-1}}$ in equation (1.00) in its equivalent form $CR_{i_{63}} - CR_{i_{t-1}}$. Rearranging terms and ignoring all other variables whose coefficients will remain unaffected by this transposition, we obtain the following:

$$CR_{i_{63}} = (1 + \alpha_2)CR_{i_{t-1}} \qquad (1.10)$$

Using α_2 from equations (1.01), (1.02) and (1.03) we see that $1 + \alpha_2$ takes the values 0.8490, 0.9011 and 0.9187 respectively. That is, the shorter the time period, the more likely is the current concentration ratio to equal its lagged value (ignoring of course the effect of all other variables) and the less likely we are to detect the operation of factors which in the long-run militate against further expansion of firms with previously large market shares.

The performance of the advertising variables appears to confirm the Kaldor–Bain hypothesis. The coefficients representing the effect of advertising category (α_4-high differentiation, α_3-medium differentiation) are positive and display the expected relative magnitudes with α_4 larger than α_3 in all three periods; in addition, the coefficients are statistically significant for 1947–1963 and 1954–1963 (see note 5).

In interpreting the differentiation parameters it is to be remembered that α_4 and α_3 measure the effects of advertising intensity as a contrast to the effect of the omitted category (the low differentiation industries) which is embodied in the equation constant. Accordingly, equation (1.01) suggests that from 1947 to 1963 the eight leading firms in the medium differentiation group showed a rise in their market share of about eight percentage points *over* the change in concentration for the low differentiation group. During the same period, the increase attributable to high product differentiation was twice as large as that attributable to medium

[4]To determine this compare the "t" values reported in Table I with the following critical values based on a two-tailed test: for $v = 70, p\,(|t| \geq 1.994) = 0.05$, and $P\,(|t| \geq 2.648) = 0.01$.

[5]It must be noted, however, that α_2 is subject to downward bias; a regression of $CR_t - CR_{t-1}$ can be expected to result in a negative association if CR is subject to measurement errors even if the true values of CR_t and CR_{t-1} are uncorrelated.

TABLE II. *Eight-firm mean concentration ratios by year and industry grouping*

| | | Consumer industries | | | |
| | All (78 in-dustries) | High differen-tiation[1] (17 in-dustries) | Medium differen-tiation[2] (35 in-dustries) | Low differen-tiation[3] (26 in-dustries) | Producer industries (122 in-dustries)[4] |
Year					
1963	50.6	72.2	52.7	33.6	56.9
1958	47.4	68.4	50.0	30.3	56.3
1954	47.0	66.3	48.8	31.8	56.8
1947	46.4	60.9	48.4	34.2	57.1

Source: *Industry Classification and Concentration* [4].

[1]High differentiation industries: SIC 2043, 2072, 2073, 2082, 2084, 2085, 2086, 2087, 2111, 2121, 2771, 2834, 2844, 3421, 3633, 3717, 3861.

[2]Medium differentiation industries: SIC 2024, 2034, 2044, 2051, 2071, 2098, 2131, 2253, 2254, 2311, 2321, 2327, 2331, 2342, 2385, 2386, 2511, 2731, 3141, 3263, 3636, 3641, 3652, 3691, 3692, 3732, 3751, 3871, 3872, 3914, 3941, 3942, 3943, 3949, 3982.

[3]Low differentiation industries: SIC 2011, 2021, 2292, 2322, 2323, 2341, 2351, 2371, 2384, 2387, 2391, 2392, 2394, 2397, 2514, 2741, 3021, 3171, 3851, 3911, 3961, 3962, 3981, 3984, 3987, 3995.

[4]We excluded industries whose coverage definitions were changed. See note E in [4, p. 18].

differentiation, and larger by seventeen-and-a-half percentage points than the change for industries with lowest product differentiation.

Additional results of interest are presented in Table II. These show that concentration *levels* are also related to industry attributes. Bain's expectation that advertising intensity and industry concentration will be positively associated is found to be satisfied. In each period there is a perfect correlation between concentration levels and the advertising intensity rankings of the three industry classes. Furthermore, Table II clearly shows that *realized* changes in concentration differ sharply among the constituent subgroupings. Whereas the high-differentiation group showed a substantial and consistent increase in concentration during 1947–1963, the low differentiation group actually experienced a slight decrease. A similar, though less pronounced, divergence in trends is found when comparing concentration changes for (all) consumer and producer industries: the latter showing virtually no change against a moderate increase for the former. These findings demonstrate that concentration trends based on wide industry groupings may conceal important differences.

IV. CONCLUSIONS

Our main finding is that advertising can be expected to lead to substantial rise in industry concentration. This may raise concern about the long run impact of advertising on the nature and intensity of competitive behavior.

REFERENCES

1. Bain, Joe S., *Industrial Organization* (New York: John Wiley & Sons, 1959), p. 236.
2. Bain, Joe S., *Barriers to New Competition* (Cambridge: Harvard University Press), p. 142.
3. Comanor, William S. and Wilson, Thomas A., "Advertising Market Structure and Performance," *The Review of Economics and Statistics*, November 1967.
4. *Industry Classification and Concentration*, A Statistical Report of the Federal Trade Commission, Bureau of Economics, March 1967.
5. Kaldor, Nicholas, "The Economic Aspects of Advertising," *The Review of Economic Studies*, Vol. 18, No. 1, p. 13.
6. Mann, H. M., Henning, J. A., and Meehan, J. W., Jr., "Advertising and Concentration: An Empirical Investigation," *The Journal of Industrial Economics*, November 1967, pp. 34–39.
7. Nelson, Ralph L., "Market Growth, Company Diversification and Product Concentration," *Journal of the American Statistical Association*, December 1960, pp. 640–649.
8. Shepherd, William G., "Trends of Concentration in American Manufacturing Industries," *The Review of Economics and Statistics*, May 1964, pp. 200–12.
9. Telser, Lester G., "Advertising and Competition," *The Journal of Political Economy*, December 1964, pp. 542–544.
10. Weiss, Leonard W., "Factors in Changing Concentration," *The Review of Economics and Statistics*, February 1963, pp. 73–75.

6

"Antitrust and Efficiency: Product Extension Mergers": A Comment *

PETER ASCH

INTRODUCTION

In a recent paper [3] B. Joe Colwell argues:

1. that the Federal Trade Commission and the Supreme Court take efficiencies as a primary indicator of anti-competitive results in product-extension mergers; and
2. that this is a correct position under an anti-merger law (Section 7 of the Clayton Act) which is, after all, based "upon the most rudimentary concepts of a competitive economy, and ... is as much socio-political as it is economic" [3, 374]

Professor Colwell's conclusions are stated cogently. However, I should like to point out that his arguments depend in part upon: (a) a mistaken definition of efficiencies, and (b) a decision criterion for merger policy that appears irrational if it is extended to public economic policies generally.

EFFICIENCIES

Colwell discusses the Procter & Gamble decisions [4, 5] in order to show that the FTC and the Supreme Court will find a product-extension merger[1] illegal *because* it creates efficiencies. As he accurately indicates, however, the discussion of efficiencies in these decisions is couched in

---

*From *The Southern Economic Journal*, July 1970, pp. 100–101. Reproduced by permission.
[1]Product-extension mergers are defined as conglomerate-type acquisitions in which there exists some relationship between the products of the merging companies. They are, in other words, a kind of "non-pure" conglomerate.

terms of efficiencies *in advertising*. The Commission's ruling in fact seems to distinguish quite explicitly between pecuniary economies in advertising, which might result from quantity or volume discounts; and more genuine economies, which have to do with the fact that larger "units" of advertising permit reduced per-product cost and may be inherently more effective.[2] Both the Commission and the Court conclude that a large purchaser of advertising, such as Procter & Gamble, holds advantages which might reduce the vigor of competition among smaller established rivals and discourage the entry of new competitors.

In a strict sense, then, Colwell is correct. The Commission and the Court have held that a product-extension merger violates the law at least in part because of the efficiencies it creates. But there is a troublesome discrepancy here. Efficiency, within the context of the theory of the firm, refers to a relationship between productive inputs and output. When a firm becomes "more efficient"—whether by growth through merger, growth through internal expansion, or technological improvement—the implication is that the relationship between its inputs and output has changed in some specific way.

This is not, however, the implication of increased "efficiency" in advertising. Advertising may enable the firm to sell its output at higher unit prices or to sell more output at any given price. These effects might be said to comprise the "output" of advertising; but the "output" of advertising is not the same thing as the output of the firm. It is possible to speak of more or less efficient advertising, and it may be reasonable to suppose that larger firms are the more efficient advertisers [1]. But this simply is not equivalent to stating that such firms are more efficient in the usual technical sense.

It may of course be that the Federal Trade Commission and the Supreme Court *do* regard technical efficiencies in mergers as evidence of likely anti-competitive consequences. I would argue only that this proposition cannot be demonstrated with reference to advertising. A more compelling case might be based on the Court's hostility to vertical integration in the *Brown Shoe* decision [2], although there may be little direct implication for product-extension mergers here.

POLICY CRITERIA

Professor Colwell states that public merger policy *ought* to condemn as

---

[2]It is suggested, for example, that sponsorship of an entire television program is disproportionately effective in comparison with (less expensive) "spot" commercials.

anti-competitive those mergers which increase efficiency (I assume that he means technical efficiency rather than advertising efficiency). This proposition is well worth considering, regardless of whether it describes accurately the status of current policy.

The reason why efficiency-creating mergers ought to be stopped, according to Colwell, is that they are likely to increase the power of the merged firm. This is a plausible expectation, for more efficient firms are likely to gain at the expense of the less efficient. Increased efficiency thus can be interpreted as a sign that competition—defined in some rudimentary structural sense—may diminish.[3]

The notion that mergers ought to be prohibited because they increase efficiency, however, is unusual even if one accepts the assumption that more efficiency implies more centralized power. The expansion of production frontiers benefits society. This benefit may of course be outweighed by the costs of increased power concentrations, but it is the essence of rational policy-making that the costs and benefits be somehow *compared* [6].

Colwell's policy criterion implicitly precludes any such comparison. It is thus economically defensible only if one of the following assumptions is made:

1. that economic effects are *wholly irrelevant* to public merger policy; or
2. that economies of scale will be achieved as fully and as quickly without merger as with merger.

If the first assumption holds, then economic efficiency simply does not enter into policy calculations, perhaps because the policy is viewed as exclusively a social and political tool. Under the second assumption, the social benefit of merger is always zero, thus benefit–cost comparisons become superfluous.

Neither of these assumptions seems credible and Colwell does not suggest them. Yet unless one or both are correct, Colwell is in effect proposing that public policy act against any merger in which there is an identifiable cost. If such a criterion were applied generally, say to public projects, the results would be difficult to imagine. Indeed, there would be no public projects!

[3]The adequacy of such a definition of competition, however, is, at best, dubious.

A QUALIFICATION

It may be that I have misinterpreted Colwell's policy suggestion, and he has meant to condemn only those mergers which result in "efficiencies" of the advertising and pecuniary type. If this is the case, then I have no quarrel with his policy conclusion (the conclusion, however, becomes less interesting for it then ignores the troublesome issue of mergers that result in true economies). Whether or not I have misread Colwell, the discussion of "economies" and "efficiencies" in antitrust has become something of a semantic morass. The need to distinguish more clearly between technical economies and pecuniary kinds of gains is obvious.

REFERENCES

1. Asch, Peter and Marcus, Matityahu, "Increasing Returns on Advertising," *Antitrust Bulletin*, Spring 1970, 33–41.
2. *Brown Shoe Co. v. United States*, 370 U.S. 294 (1962).
3. Colwell, B. Joe, "Antitrust and Efficiency: Product Extension Mergers," *Southern Economic Journal*, April 1969, 369–75.
4. *In the Matter of Procter & Gamble*, Federal Trade Commission Docket No. 6901 (1962).
5. *Federal Trade Commission v. Procter & Gamble Co.*, 386 U.S. 568 (1967).
6. Williamson, Oliver E., "Economies as an Antitrust Defense," *American Economic Review*, March 1968, 18–36.

7

Conglomerates Revisited*

D. T. CARROLL

RECENTLY, conglomerates were much in the financial news. Their exploits and, particularly, their stock multiples attracted acclaim from some, consternation from others, and considerable curiosity from all. These reactions were accompanied by an outpouring of friendly and not so friendly comment, which attempted to explain the conglomerate phenomenon.

As the stock market began to sag and as the conglomerates began to demonstrate that they too could experience adversity, the comments began to dry up. The implications are that conglomerates were either a passing thing or no longer deserving of attention. It is my contention that neither implication is as yet justified by the facts.

In the case of the first, it is not possible to prove that conglomerates have or have not had their heyday. Only a market resurgence will demonstrate whether investors have lost or regained their confidence, and whether a new generation of conglomerates will be launched. Barring legislation aimed at conglomerates or a further enlargement of anti-trust interpretations (both unlikely) the prospects favor continued enthusiasm for conglomeration; the memories of successes in this area are too vivid and the failures too obscure to be a deterrent.

As for the assumption that conglomerates no longer warrant comment, I would argue that these difficult times may actually be a more appropriate time for conglomerate watching. Past commentaries, mine included, have probably been colored by the excitement of acquisitions and the accompanying confusion. In the relative quiet of acquisition inactivity, it ought to be possible to achieve a balanced view of the managerial skills of conglomerates. This view, if based on research, should be of considerable

*From *Business Horizons*, August 1970, pp. 42–44. Reproduced by permission.

value to both long-term investors and those contemplating the conglomerate adventure.

My own experience, while no substitute for research, suggests that certain conglomerates are actually making contributions to the art of management and that these contributions can significantly affect conglomerate well-being. There are three reasons for postulating these contributions. *First,* conglomerates, unlike their more stable counterparts, have rarely had the time or the resources to apply conventional management solutions to their problems. Instead, they have had to produce solutions of acceptable quality with new, or at least less traditional, methods. *Second,* conglomerates have been forced by their own ambitions to deal with an essentially unusual mix of businesses. This diversity has required reconsideration of the classic ways of decentralization and coordination. *Third,* conglomerates, with no real history to restrain or guide them, have had to give greater expression to the ideas and insight of their usually young management. Inevitably, the results have been innovative, if not always successful.

There is some evidence of the changes that conglomerates are bringing about. The list that follows is incomplete and inconclusive, but it indicates the genuine concern of many conglomerates with improved management technique.

METHODS OF PROFIT IMPROVEMENT

Much has been written about the ability of conglomerates to clean up losing or marginal businesses. Indeed, at least two of the more prominent ones seem to seek out only troubled businesses on which to practice their cost-cutting techniques. Unfortunately, the public hears only the anguish of employees who have been terminated, and presumes incorrectly that any such cost cutting is crude and largely involves reductions in payroll expense.

In the more successful conglomerates, the opposite is the case; profit improvement rather than cost reduction is the objective. Heading the list are improvements in purchasing. Conglomerates have been able to bring to bear such techniques as value analysis, competitive "sourcing," and make/buy analysis. Since many of their acquisitions have imprudently followed antiquated purchasing practices, conglomerates have had a field day in this area; six-figure savings are not uncommon, in even comparatively small divisions.

Another profit improvement area has been in salesman work loads.

Many conglomerate managements have been amazed at the substantial inequities existing between one salesman's work load and another's. Using some reasonably uncomplicated techniques of sales territory analysis, conglomerates have been able to distribute their selling capabilities more equitably and thereby gain increased sales productivity.

Another area concerns planning. A number of acquired companies simply had never planned in any meaningful sense, a fact that may have made them ripe for acquisition. The result of this nonplanning was invariably a series of uncoordinated programs, actions, and costs that were expensive and frequently redundant. As painful as the experience of introducing planning into a business has been, the rewards have been most impressive. It has revealed needed and unneeded products, facilities, cash, and personnel. An added dividend has been the more precise timing of these needs, so that otherwise idle dollars could be put to better use.

USE OF MANAGEMENT CONSULTANTS

Conglomerates have been quite perceptive in employing management consultants. First, they seem to have realized the importance of investing as much of top management's time and money as is necessary to make consulting principals intimately familiar with their objectives, practices, personalities, facilities, and products. This investment has made studies and recommendations more perceptive and compatible, but, more important, it has in effect established an inventory of versatile, knowledgeable resources that can be drawn upon at will.

A second characteristic of the conglomerate–consultant relationship has been a predetermining of the assignments to be handled "in-house" and those to be given to the consultant. Some have used consultants heavily in sizing up prospective acquisitions; others have not. Some have used consultants for profit improvement after acquisitions, while others have built a fairly elaborate internal staff for such work. Some have used consultants for finding key executives, and others promoted largely from within or used an internal personnel office. Some have augmented their own marketing staff with consultants only in instances where a third party's viewpoint was needed. Large-scale systems studies have usually been the consultant's responsibility.

Finally, some have used consultants for executive compensation studies to assure competitiveness and confidentiality; others have preferred to keep such matters entirely private. The pattern of use within a

single conglomerate has been reasonably predictable, but among conglomerates there has been little uniformity.

STYLE OF MANAGEMENT CONTROL

Much can be written about the innovations or, perhaps better, the
adaptations which conglomerates have made in the theses of decentralization contributed by Alfred P. Sloan, the organizer of General Motors.
Faced with decentralized and dissimilar businesses, the better conglomerate executives never deluded themselves into thinking that they could
subsist on a classic reporting system, even if well-conceived and automated for instantaneous response. Instead, they have supplemented the
usual budgetary processes with styles that have suited their personalities
and purposes.

One element of such style could be characterized as total absence or
total presence. A smoothly functioning business within a conglomerate
may not be aware of the conglomerate superstructure, while its troubled
counterpart is inundated with corporate talent to such a degree that actual
control may have passed from divisional to corporate personnel. In part,
this saturation technique has stemmed from the need to sustain an image
with investors, and in part from a realization that diverse problems
require highly skilled talent, which cannot be present in *all* divisions.

Another element of this style is full centralization of cash management.
Conglomerate management recognized the importance of this critical
coordination long before money became increasingly scarce. As a matter
of fact, they were motivated by the desire to activate idle funds and inject
planning into the cash cycle. Prime rate increases only served to confirm
this degree of prudence.

The final element of style is the conglomerate's continuous involvement
in the selection of incentives for management. Like traditional corporations, conglomerates have fairly constantly sought star performers, but,
unlike these corporations, conglomerates seem much more reconciled to
executive turnover. The conglomerate manager has not been too dis-
mayed with a resume which described a "job hopper." If the man has the
experience needed and can be expected to respond to financial incentives,
the conglomerate may employ him while making due allowance for the
probability that he will move on in a couple of years.

Given the rising rates of executive mobility, conglomerates may be
proven to be more foresighted than opportunistic. As unhappy as the
prospect may be, the job hopper is becoming more commonplace in our
economy.

PART V

Capital Budgeting and Profit

Introduction

Capital budgeting, which is sometimes referred to as capital expenditure, is concerned with the investment decisions made by the firm. This encompasses a wide variety of decisions such as investment in a new project, expansion, replacement, and retirement. It also deals with the decisions on different kinds of assets such as machines and equipment, research and development, and advertising. These decisions are usually considered to be concerned with assets from which benefits extend more than a year even though the analysis can be applied to a shorter period. Historically, capital budgeting received the major contribution from capital theory. However, the contribution of actuarial science, engineering economy, and more recently corporate finance and portfolio analysis, should not be underestimated.

The problem in capital budgeting is to evaluate the investment alternatives available to the firm and select the most profitable one. This requires the undertaking of four major steps:

1. Researching for investment opportunities (management problem).
2. Estimating the net capital outlay (engineering problem).

3. Predicting future yields for the project (forecasting problem).
4. Selecting a proper method of evaluation (a problem of multiple dimensions).

When managerial economics texts discuss capital budgeting they usually address themselves to the fourth step. Selecting the articles in this part followed the same approach. However, this should not be construed as underestimating the first three steps. On the contrary, the editors would like to emphasize that unless the first three steps are properly and accurately arrived at, any method of evaluation would be a waste of time and energy. Materials introduced in Part II of this book will be useful in arriving at the third step, and the first two will not be discussed because they should be handled in their appropriate areas.

Barring some short-cut formulas, most methods of evaluating investment projects require, beside the three steps mentioned above, the following:

1. Computing the cash flow (usually net accounting income after tax plus depreciation).
2. Measuring the cost of capital or the use of some discount rate to account for the time value of money.
3. Including some measure of risk.

The two most widely discussed methods in the literature are the rate of return and the present value. The first approach requires finding the rate of return and comparing it with the cost of capital. The rate of return is defined as being that rate which equates the present value of the future cash flows expected from the project with the present value of the capital outlays. The decision to invest is made if the rate of return is greater than the cost of capital. In the second approach the present value of the future cash flows from the project is found by discounting these cash flows with the cost of capital. If this value is greater than the present value of capital outlays the project is accepted.

These two methods are rooted in different economic schools. The basis for the present value method seems to be the demand for capital in the new classical school. The capitalized value concept is the present value of an infinite income stream for a durable asset discounted with the long-run interest rate. The Keynes marginal efficiency of capital is the same as the rate of return with the minor exception that the supply price of the asset is the relevant price—not its original cost. However, these economists ignored the finer points concerning the calculation and the implicit assumptions of these methods, probably because they did not consider them important enough. This could be the reason why a wide interest was not generated in capital budgeting techniques and their application to individual firm's investment decisions until a surprisingly late date. It was left to Joel Dean's book of 1951 to generate such interest.

SUMMARIES OF ARTICLES IN PART V AND COMMENTS

Article 1

The relatively recent development in capital budgeting created some confusion concerning the concepts being used to evaluate firms' performance. One of these concepts is the rate of return on investment. Ezra Solomon, in "Alternative rate of return concepts and their implications for utility regulation," addresses himself to such a problem. Even though this rate is a widely used concept in financial analysis it is measured in two completely distinct units—book rate and discounted cash flow units. The book rate b is defined as being the ratio of accounting net income to the book value of the net invested capital. The DCF rate r is defined as being the rate that equates the present value of the prospective cash flows with the investment outlay. Between these two rates there are three basic differences:

1. Income vs. cash flows.
2. Net book value vs. original cost of investment.
3. Current vs. current and future.

The two rates are used interchangeably even though, given the above differences, it is highly unlikely that their measures would lead to equal numerical values. This fact causes considerable confusion in financial analysis particularly in utility regulations.

In the major portion of the rest of his paper, Solomon illustrates the extent of the variation between b and r as follows: In an asset of $1000 that generates a yearly cash flow of $229.11 for 6 years with a salvage zero value, the DCF rate is 10% regardless of the accounting practice. Assuming that the firm invest in one asset every year in the steady state it will have six assets. Given a straight line depreciation and zero expensing policy, b would be 12.6% (zero taxes). Any increase in expensing policy would increase b until it reaches ∞ at 100% expensing. This wide variation occurs while r is still 10%. Since expensing policy is a form of depreciation, a change in depreciation policy would bring about the same change in b and again none in r. The above example is not a mere intellectual exercise. Companies do have different accounting practices and thus they are bound to show different book rates even though their performance is similar. In spite of these facts, different opinions tried to explain the variation in companies' book rates by such factors as risks, monopoly, and efficiency.

The difference between b and r is not affected by accounting practice only. Such variables as the duration of the project, the company's growth, and the pattern of cash flows have a significant effect too. The second example given in the article shows three kinds of assets with different durations, but each has an r of 10%. Only in the asset with one year maturity is b equal to r. With increasing maturity, b increases. On the asset with a 6 year duration b was computed before as being 12.6%. On the asset with a 30 year duration, b is computed as follows (still in the steady state and with zero taxes and straight line depreciation);

Net cash flow	$30 \times 106.08 = 3182.4$
Depreciation	$30 \times 1/30 \times 1000 = 1000$
Net book income	$= 2182.4$
Net book value	$1/2(30000) = 15000$
Book rate b	$2182.4/15000 = 14.5\%$

Since the steady state may be unrealistic, growth is brought into the picture. Again it is shown that while growth has no bearing on r its effect on b is significant. This is so because growth affects the relative weights assigned to assets with different ages while equal weights are assigned to each asset in the steady state. At a high rate of positive growth the weights given to new assets are dominant, while at a high rate of negative growth the weights of the old assets dominate. Since the new assets are low yielding b and the old ones are high yielding, the higher the rate of positive growth, the lower is b. In the example on the 6-year-old asset the book rate on the one year old is $(229.61 - 116.67) \div (1000 - 166.67) = 0.07$ while the rate on the 5-year-old is $(229.61 - 166.67) \div 166.67 = 0.38$.

So far b and r are dealt with as measures of performance. The same confusion arises if these rates are used as a basis for determining the required rate of returns or what is more accurately called the cost of capital. If the performance is measured by r, then the cost of capital k must be computed by DCF units. If the performance is measured by b, then the cost of capital β must be computed by net income and net book value units. However, a rate based on these units differs with accounting practice and cash flow configuration as has been mentioned above. Thus, when the investments used to compute β are subject to significantly different accounting practices from those investments being evaluated, a proper adjustment is needed. Please note that in this context the cost of capital would be the rate of return of the best alternative forgone when investing in the assets being evaluated.

To understand this article the student is advised to be acquainted with the following concepts:

Cash flow   Depreciation
Net book income   Expensing
Net book value   The cost of capital
Discounted cash flow units   Opportunity cost

Practicing the arithmetic of the following two concepts would be useful:

1. The rate of return r based on DCF units.
2. The rate of return b based on book rate units.

Article 2

While Solomon's article was concerned with the various measures used to evaluate the performance of different firms, Joel Dean's article, "An approach to internal profit measurement," deals with the problem that arises when attempting to measure the profit of each division (internal profit measurement). The question here is not whether one method of measurement is preferred to the other method. Rather it is whether internal profit measurement is useful at all. To answer this question two steps are needed. The first is to specify the appropriate objectives of internal profit measurement and the second is to consider whether this measurement enables management to achieve these objectives.

Is the objective of internal profit measurement to show correctly the division profit? The answer is no since the division does not control all the costs and revenues included when measuring the profit. Is the objective to provide a set of financial statements for outsiders to look at? The answer again should be no. The requirements of auditors and tax collectors do not necessarily fit the needs of management. For example, a tax collector requires that the records show only realized profit, while for top management purposes these records must show the unrealized profit also.

Dean argues that there are two main objectives for a system of internal financial measurement:

1. To assist the division managers in making optimal decisions.
2. To provide top management with a reliable estimate of the division performance.

Unfortunately internal profit measurement can satisfy neither of these objectives. To the manager, maximizing his division's profit is a complex task that is hard to fulfill since many variables that affect this profit are outside of his control. It would be more meaningful if he is asked to make optimal operational decisions such as making vs. buying, and product scheduling. Allocating the costs incurred by the central administration, such as the president's salary or lawyer's fees, would not in any way help division management in making optimal decisions.

For the same reason internal profit measurement is not useful in evaluating the division performance. The desire of the top management that the division cover all costs, direct and indirect, though legitimate, would not be made closer to realization by allocating the cost incurred by the central administration. In addition these costs render any historical review of the division results invalid since good and bad years would be leveled out by the inherent instability of most systems of allocations.

Breaking a large company into various divisions is done so that the company gains some advantages that small firms enjoy such as flexibility and competitive spirit. At the same time these divisions are not made completely independent, so they can still benefit from the efficiency of joint costs. The use of internal profit measurement implicitly implies that these divisions are separate companies.

The author recommends that a system of measurement should be separated from the complex task of evaluating divisions' performances. The installed system should help but not resolve top management decisions concerning divisions' performances. This is a task with which the top management's job should start.

Understanding well the following concepts would help the students appreciate the points raised in the article:

Profit   Indirect cost
Internal profit measurement   Profit maximization
Unrealized profit   Optimal decisions
Direct cost

Article 3

It has been mentioned in the introduction for Part V that while economic theory provided the basis for capital budgeting methods, economists in general did not emphasize the finer points regarding the calculation involved in and the implicit assumptions of these methods. The following two articles deal with these fine points. Solomon's article is concerned with the reinvestment assumption in different methods while Curran's article is concerned with the assumption about depreciation.

In "The arithmetic of capital-budgeting decisions" Ezra Solomon addresses himself to the problem of choosing the proper approach to evaluate investment alternatives. The two methods considered are the present value method and the rate of return method. As was stated before, in the first approach the rate of return is compared with the cost of capital and the decision to invest is made if the former is greater than the latter. In the second approach the decision to invest in a project is made if the present value of its future cash flows is greater than the present value of its capital expenditure. The rate of return method has been criticized on two major grounds:

1. It leads to decisions that are in conflict with the decisions that would be arrived at when using the present value method. (The assumption here is that the present value is the more accurate method.)
2. Sometimes the use of this method does not lead to a unique rate of return on a project.

The author argues that if the decision is whether the investment proposal should be accepted or not, either of the two methods could be used and the answer would always be the same. If the investment decision is to choose among two or more mutually exclusive projects, then the above two methods may lead to contradictory recommendations. However, the apparent contradiction between the rate of return and the present value methods is a product of improper assumption rather than of a real difference. Applied to projects with different durations, the rate of return approach assumes that the reinvestment rate is at least equal to the rate on the project of the longer life. The present value approach implies that the reinvestment rate is equal to the company's present cost of capital. If so the comparison should not be made between two methods but rather between two courses of action. If the reinvestment rate is assumed to be equal to the company's future cost of capital then both methods would always lead to the same results. The author illustrates the above by using a simple and very clear example.

The criticism that the rate of return on a project may not be unique seems to be more serious. Solomon argues that this happens only in complex projects where later cash flows may be negative. In this case the usual prescription for finding the rate of return cannot be applied. The author gives an excellent example demonstrating the absurdity of such an application. In this example the rate of return increases with the increase in capital expenditure even though the cash flow is assumed to be constant. However, the rate of return method would still be valid if a different prescription for arriving at it is used. This can be done by explicitly estimating the yields derived from the incremental cash flow.

The above article is frequently quoted because of its power in demonstrating the implicit assumptions of two widely used methods of capital budgeting computations.

The student is advised to get acquainted with the following concepts:

Cash flow and net cash inflow   Discounted cash flow
Cost of capital   Mutually exclusive projects
Capital outlays

In addition the student is advised to practice the computational aspects of the rate of return and present value methods.

Article 4

In "Depreciation in economic theory and capital budgeting" Ward S. Curran complements the preceding article since it is concerned with a second implicit assumption dealing with depreciation in economic theory and capital budgeting.

In new classical literature the capitalized value is defined as being the present value of an infinite income stream. This implies that depreciation must be sufficient to maintain the income stream through the reinvestment in another asset or restoring the productivity of the existing one. In the new classical technique depreciation is arrived at by finding the uniform payments that if discounted by long term interest rate would be equal to the original capital outlay. On the other hand, Keynes defines the marginal efficiency of capital (MEC) as being the rate that equates the present value of the series of annuities given by the returns expected from the capital asset with its supply price. In addition, Keynes assumes that the original cost should be the basis for depreciation. Thus, in the Keynesian analysis the implicit assumption is that depreciation is reinvested at a rate equal to the MEC. Depreciation would be calculated by finding the uniform payment that if invested for the life of the asset in a rate equal to its MEC would produce the original cost. There are two major differences in the assumptions of both analyses concerning depreciation:

1. In the Keynesian analysis the depreciation figure would be arrived at by equating the value of the payments representing depreciation at the end of the investment period with the capital outlay. In the new classical analysis the value of these payments at the beginning of the investment period is the one to be equated with the capital outlay.
2. In the Keynesian analysis the reinvested rate is the MEC while in the new classical thinking the discount rate is the interest rate.

In the following example we calculate the depreciation implied in the rate of return and the present value methods, assuming that the Keynes treatment of depreciation applies to the former and the new classical to the latter.* This example is a supplement to the one offered by the author.

From a project with an outlay of $3605 that produces yearly income of $1000 for 5 years and with zero salvage value we get the following values of depreciation implied in three different approaches:

1. The rate of return approach:

$$\$3605 = \frac{D[(1.12)^5 - 1]}{0.12} = 6.3528D, \ D = \$567.$$

2. The present value approach:

$$\$3605 = \frac{D[1 - (1.10)^{-5}]}{0.1} = 3.791D, \dagger \ D = \$951.$$

3. The accounting approach:

$$\$3605 = 5D,$$

$$D = \frac{3605}{5} = \$721.$$

Disregarding the new classical assumption concerning depreciation and assuming instead that depreciation is reinvested at a rate equal to the cost of capital, the depreciation figure in the present value approach would be:

4. $$3605 = \frac{D[(1.1)^5 - 1]}{0.1} = 590.5.$$

*Replacing the supply price of the asset with its original cost in the MEC produces the rate of return and applying the capitalized value to a limited income stream after using the cost of capital instead of the interest rate produces the present value.

†Please note that 0.12 is the rate of return derived from the following equation;

$$3605 = \frac{1000[1 - (1 + r)^{-5}]}{r}$$

and that 0.1 is the assumed cost of capital.

The editors believe that this is a more appropriate figure for depreciation than the one derived in 2 for two reasons:

    (a) It is consistent with the assumption in the present value approach that reinvestment is made at the cost of capital. (See Solomon's preceding article.)

    (b) It is consistent with the other two approaches in defining cash flow as being accounting net income plus depreciation. This is in contrast to the second approach which implies that cash flow equals economic profit plus depreciation.

As an example, if the present value of future cash flows is equal to the capital outlay then depreciation would be equal to the yearly cash flow and this means that net income is zero. But this is true only if the zero stands for economic profit (accounting net income–cost of capital).*

This article is useful because it relates the current capital budgeting techniques to different economic schools and brings out another hidden assumption in economic writings concerning depreciation.

To understand this article the students are recommended to familiarize themselves with the following concepts:

Depreciation	The net present value
Marginal efficiency of capital	Accounting net income
Capitalized value	Economic profit
The rate of return method	Cash flow
The present value method	The cost of capital

In addition the following formulas would be helpful.

1. The sum of a uniform series P:

$$S = \frac{P(1+r)^n - 1}{r}.$$

2. The present value of a uniform series P:

$$V = \frac{P[1-(1+r)^{-n}]}{r}.$$

*This is not the exact definition of economic profit. The term is used conveniently to be distinguished from accounting net income.

Article 5

Those who were trying to reach rational solutions to capital budgeting problems realized soon enough that the world of certainty assumed in economic analysis is not suitable for their purpose. Business firms operate in an uncertain world, and any rational approach to decision making must account for this fact. Various approaches have been suggested to discount for the risk involved in estimating the future cash flows used as the basis for most capital budgeting techniques. In his article "The consideration of risk and uncertainty in capital investment analyses" John R. Canada summarizes these approaches which vary from the simple increase in the discount rate or decrease in the estimated cash flows to the sophisticated use of decision theory and portfolio analysis. The summary is useful in focusing on the problems encountered when either risk or uncertainty is to be measured. For examples of their uses and for additional explanations of these techniques the student is referred to the articles in Part I of this book, particularly articles 2, 3, 4, 6, and 8.

In addition, the understanding of the following concepts would improve the student's awareness of the differences among the various approaches surveyed:

Risk	The Monte Carlo technique
Uncertainty	The expected value
Skewness	The variance
Probability distribution	Subjective probability
Taylor's expansion	

Article 6

Regardless of the method used to evaluate the firm's investment decisions, a measure of the cost of capital seems to be needed either to discount future yields with or to be compared with the rate of return on investment.

Modigliani and Miller's (M–M) conclusion that any financial structure (the debt–equity ratio) is necessarily optimal both startled and intrigued the financial world. The reason given for this conclusion is the ability of any stockholder to offset an undesirable debt–equity ratio by selling or buying some of the firm's stocks and bonds. If the firm's debt–equity ratio is lower than is desired, a stockholder can offset this by selling the firm's bonds and buying its stocks or buying its stocks on the margin if he does not own bonds. On the other hand, if the firm is highly leveraged, a stockholder can undo this leverage by buying its bonds and selling its stocks. This process is called the homemade leverage.

William J. Baumol and Burton G. Malkiel in "The firm's optimal debt–equity combination and the cost of capital" argue that the M–M conclusion would be true only if taxes and transaction costs are not included. In Fig. 1 of this article a company's opportunity curve CC' is shown to be a function of expected earnings per dollar and the safety level. The optimal point for a stockholder X is the point at which his indifference curve is tangent to the opportunity curve (point D). If transaction cost is included and the company chooses point E, X would not be able, by homemade leverage, to move along the transformation curve into D. The transaction costs would reduce his earnings and thus a new opportunity curve SS' will be available to him which now will be assumed to the left of C at all points except at (E). Homemade leverage enables the stockholder to move to point T which is at a higher indifference curve than E but at a lower indifference curve than D. Had the company chosen D instead of E, the stockholder would have been better off. In other words, the company's capital structure at D is not optimal for this or any other stockholder whose optimal point is to the left of E.

When the discussion regarding the effect of transaction costs on the individual stockholder's opportunity curve becomes more specific the curve looks more like SS' in Fig. 2. If the stockholder desires to be to the right of point E, then he can do so by buying stocks on the margin and, after exceeding the limits allowed, he may have to borrow from other sources. Since the interest paid by the individual investor is usually more than that paid by the company, the SS' to the right of E will be lower than CC'. On the other hand if this investor wishes to move to the left of E he purchases the company's bonds and stocks instead of its stocks alone. However, the commission on bonds is not more than that on stocks (slightly less) which means that to the left of E, SS' will be the same level as CC'. SS' extends to the left further than CC' because the investor can hold 100% bonds.

Adding taxes in addition to transaction costs increases the divergences of SS' from CC'. This relationship is shown in the graph to the far left of Fig. 2. This graph implies that an individual investor may actually benefit if he invests in a company that has a higher debt–equity ratio than he desires. This is so because of the tax advantage given to a highly levered company, an advantage that cannot be duplicated by risky portfolios of individuals. The advantage is allowing the company to deduct the interest paid on debt from its taxable income.* The above analysis leads to an interesting conclusion. If the company has a high leverage, investors can undo this leverage if they so desire without being hurt from the company's decision. These same investors cannot offset a low leverage point chosen by the company without being hurt. However, it should be understood that beyond a certain point an increase in the debt–equity ratio of the firm begins to threaten its solvency and its opportunity curve drops sharply. This point is more likely to be an optimal point for most investors, which means an optimal point for the firm.

The authors use the preceding illustrations to measure the cost of capital. Their analysis leads to the following conclusions:

1. The cost of capital of retained earnings, given that they are not needed by the shareholders, is cheaper than that of new stock issues because of the relatively heavy cost needed to float these issues. If income is needed the shareholders are forced to sell some stocks to compensate for the loss in dividends. Even then a policy of retention is likely to be preferred by most investors, since the tax rate on dividends is higher than on capital gains, and transaction costs on floating the new issues may be higher than on the sale of a few shares.

2. Disregarding transaction costs and taxes, the cost of capital of debt financing is equal to the cost of capital of equity. In general this cost is smaller than the earnings per share and greater than the interest rate paid on debt. This is so because equity financing usually increases the firm's safety level and debt financing reduces it. In other words the cost of capital differs from the nominal cost of both methods of financing.

At the end of this article the authors argue that the standard approach in finance which considers the cost of capital as a weighted average of the cost of alternative sources does not contradict the approach of economic analysis. In economic analysis the cost to be considered, given the availability of various resource alternatives, is the cost of the resources from the cheapest supply. In the finance approach the weights are assigned to the nominal costs of debt and equity to arrive at the real cost. Whether the weighted average may be considered a good approximation to the real cost of each source is a question of a different nature, and the answer to it needs further investigation. The use of either the cost of debt

---

*Notice that a risky capital structure results from a high debt–equity ratio while a risky portfolio for an individual results from a low bonds–stocks ratio.

or equity when capital structure is optimal is consistent with economic analysis, since the two costs are equal. The optimal solution arrived at is a corner solution; this is, floating new equity should be zero and the source of equity should be retained earning.

This article should be very useful in enabling students to understand the concept of the cost of capital and the assumptions under which the M–M thesis is valid. It also provides excellent illustrations concerning the effect on the M–M conclusion of removing some of these assumptions, and it clarifies an apparent but not a real contradiction between a standard finance approach to measuring the cost of capital and economic analysis.

Concepts to be acquainted with:

Safety level	Opportunity locus (curve) or transformation
Dividends	curve
Retained earnings	Homemade leverage
Earnings per share	Nominal cost of debt and equity
Equity	Real cost of debt and equity
Debt	Cost of capital
Indifference curve	Corner solution

In addition the instructor may wish to discuss with this article the following problems:

1. Why is the point of tangency between the opportunity curve and the individual indifference curve an optimal point?
2. The debt–equity ratio and its relationship with safety level.
3. The cost of capital when funds are assumed to be unlimited vs. the cost of capital when funds are limited (the first case is the one discussed in this article, the second is the opportunity cost concept).

Article 7

In the last article, Richard T. Hise and Robert H. Strawser in "Application of capital budgeting techniques to marketing operations" survey the application of capital budgeting techniques in such areas as advertising, marketing research, and sales management. The responses of the firms surveyed provide interesting information related to the different methods used and the various problems encountered.

1

Alternative Rate of Return Concepts and Their Implications for Utility Regulation*

THE rate of return on invested capital is a central concept in financial analysis. It is widely used as a basis for decisions, both in the unregulated sector and in utility regulation.

If the "rate of return on investment" were itself a single, unambiguous concept, the only difficulties we would encounter in using it for either purpose would be difficulties involving correct estimation of the measure. But the concept is not unambiguous: quite apart from trivial variants such as pre-tax vs. post-tax measures or a total capital vs. an equity capital basis for the concept,[1] there is a non-trivial problem which arises from the fact that "rate of return" is measured in terms of two altogether distinct units: book rate units, and discounted cash flow units.

Book rate units

These are more properly called book-ratio units. The "rate" being measured is defined as the ratio of income during a given period of time (as defined by the usual accounting measure of this term) to the net book-value of invested capital outstanding during the period (as defined by the balance sheet corresponding to the income statement from which the numerator is derived).[2] This version of the rate of return will be

---

*From *The Bell Journal of Economics and Management Science*, Vol. 1, No. 1, Spring 1970, pp. 65–81. Reproduced by permission.

[1]These are trivial in the sense that they are obvious and therefore lead to no confusion. To simplify the exposition, I shall ignore these two potential differences in definition by assuming throughout most of this paper, that income taxes and long-term borrowing do not exist.

[2]Another potential, but trivial, ambiguity arises from the fact that we can measure the accounting net book value figure on a beginning-of-period basis, an ending-of-period basis, or somewhere in between.

symbolized as *b*, and it represents the most commonly used basis for reporting and analyzing "rate of return on invested capital."[3]

DCF units

Unlike the book-ratio, this measures the return on capital in terms of the annual rate at which the "future" (actual or prospective) net funds flows (or cash flows as these are commonly called) from an investment have a discounted value equal to the value of the investment outlays required to bring about these funds flows. Hence the name DCF units, which refers to the "discounting cash flows" process required to calculate this version of rate of return on investment.

This basis for measuring rate of return is the most commonly used one for theoretical purposes. It will be symbolized by the letter *r*.[4]

CONCEPTUAL DIFFERENCES BETWEEN THE DCF RATE AND THE BOOK-RATIO

There are three major conceptual differences between the two measures, *b* and *r*.

(1) The book-ratio, *b*, defines its flow variable (income) as "cash flow" (meaning funds flow) minus depreciation and minus the expensed portion of current period investment. In contrast, the DCF rate, *r*, defines the flow variable as "cash flow" before these two adjustments.

(2) The book-ratio, *b*, defines its stock variable (investment) as the net book value of capital as this would appear on the balance sheet consonant with the definition of the income variable, i.e., the balance sheet number, which is linked by the inexorable rules of double-entry accounting to the income definition. In content, the DCF rate, *r*, defines the stock variable (investment) as the total initial outlay of funds required for generating the cash flows counted on the flow side of the equation.

(3) Finally, the book ratio, *b*, defines the rate of return in a given period of time, or over a period of time, as the arithmetic ratio of its flow variable

---

[3]For reporting, see *Fortune's* 500 Largest Industrials Directory: *Fortune's* 50 Largest Firms in Merchandising, Banking and Transportation: FTC-SEC Quarterly Financial Report on Rates of Return in Manufacturing; First National City Bank of New York's Annual Return on Capital series; FPC and other regulatory agencies' Annual Reports on "Return on Investment."

For analysis, see [3], [8], [11], and [18].

[4]For prospective investments it is equal to the expected marginal productivity of capital (or the marginal efficiency of capital in Keynesian analysis), or the "initial rate of return." For investments in long-term bonds it is called the "effective yield to maturity."

to its stock variable. In contrast, the DCF rate, *r*, defines the rate of return as that rate of compound discount (or interest) at which the time adjusted (present) value of the flow variable (cash or funds flows) is equal to the time adjusted (present) value of the stock variable (investment outlays).

Given these basic differences in definition between *b* and *r*, it is highly unlikely that their numerical values will be equal. Yet both carry the same label "percent per annum rate of return on investment," and the two are frequently used as if they were freely congruent and interchangeable measures of the same thing. Some examples are:

1. For a single company or industry the rate, *b*, is often treated as if it were an unbiased measure of *r*;
2. When several companies or industries are analyzed it is generally assumed that differences in *b* reflect corresponding differences in *r*;
3. Estimates of fair or reasonable rates are often calculated in DCF units, i.e., in terms of the *r* measure, and applied to net book value estimates without regard to the essential differences between DCF units and book rate units. Alternatively, a company may set its required rate of return for *ex-ante* capital budgeting purposes in terms of DCF cost of capital units and then measure *ex-post* performance in terms of book rate units.

These, and other forms of confusion between the two conceptually and numerically different yardsticks, can and do lead to considerable confusion in many forms of investment analysis, both in the unregulated sector and, more particularly, in utility regulation.

The rest of this paper is an attempt to explore the nature and magnitude of the differences between the *r* version and the *b* version of rate of return measurement and, on the basis of this analysis, to examine potential uses and misuses of the two concepts for interpretive and regulatory purposes.

COMPANY PROFITABILITY: *b* VS *r* IN THE STEADY STATE

In order to analyze the level of *b* relative to any given level of *r*, we take a hypothetical company or companies which acquire or can acquire only a single type of investment whose cash inflow characteristics are known. For illustrative purposes we can take the investment mentioned above: $1,000 of outlay generates level cash inflows of $229.61 a year for 6 years, after which the asset is scrapped at zero salvage value. The DCF rate of return on this investment is 10 percent, and hence any company which holds a portfolio consisting exclusively of such projects must be earning a DCF rate of 10 percent per annum.

What book rate b will such a company show? As we shall see, the answer to this depends on several factors. Two factors which have a powerful effect on the size of b relative to r deserve detailed consideration. These are:

1. Accounting practices used in defining book income and net book capital, and
2. The pace at which the company acquires new investments over time.

In order to understand the effect of each of these factors, we will deal with them one at a time. Assume, to begin with, that the company acquires new investments (or projects) by investing an equal amount of money each year. This will be referred to as the "steady-state" condition (it could equally well be called the zero-growth case). Our hypothetical company which invests an equal amount each year in the basic type of project outlined will reach a "steady state" after six years. Beyond this point it will always hold six "investments." When it acquires its seventh investment, the first one it acquired is scrapped, when it acquires the eighth the second is scrapped and so on.[5]

The Book Rate of Return *b*

The book rate of return for a company in the steady state, which holds only investments identical to the basic project outlined, will depend on the accounting procedures used—in particular, on the fraction of each original investment outlay which is expensed for book purposes, and the specific depreciation formula which is used in deriving income, period by period, over each project's economic lifetime.

The book rate can be calculated by (1) defining the general value of b in algebraic terms and (2) solving such an equation for any given set of values of the accounting variables. However for any situation other than full capitalization of investment outlays and straight-line depreciation and zero growth, the algebraic expressions for the book rate of return can become exceedingly messy and sometimes complicated. Happily a graphical approach, even though partly intuitive, makes it possible to bypass explicit algebraic solutions and still make the relevant points.

To begin with the simplest situation, assume that the company capitalizes all of its investment outlays and uses a straight-line depreciation

[5]Inflation is assumed to be zero in this portion of the analysis.

formula. The income statement of such a company after it reaches a steady state will show:

Net Cash Flow = 6 × $229.61 = $1,377.66
Depreciation = 6 × 1/6 × $1,000 = $1,000.00
Net Book Income = $377.66

Its balance sheet, in the steady state, would show a net book value equal to one-half of the original outlay for the six "investments" it holds in its portfolio. This is shown in Fig. 1. The original outlay is $1,000. This is written-off continuously as time passes, i.e., the net book value of each asset is diminished along the line AB. After $t = 6$ the company holds six vintages of investment ranging from one 0.5 year old to one 5.5 years old, and together they have an undepreciated net book value equal to the area under the line AB. We can see by inspection and our knowledge of Euclid that this is $1,000 × 6/2 or $3,000.

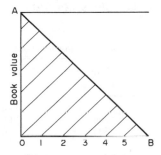

FIG. 1. Straight-line depreciation. $1000 original investment.

Thus the book rate of return for this company is $377.66 ÷ $3,000 or 12.6 percent.

We now also have a tool which permits us to vary our accounting procedures and to discover the consequent effect on b of doing so *without* engaging in tedious algebraic expressions. (Meanwhile we still retain our basic assumption that all companies are in a "steady state," i.e., that our company acquires its investments through *equal* annual outlays.)

VARIATION IN EXPENSING PROCEDURES

We can begin our analysis by assuming again that all companies acquire only the one basic investment we have outlined ($1000 which generates $229.61 a year for six years) and that all use straight-line depreciation.

However, now they are free to alter their expensing procedures, i.e., they may charge off any fraction of the $1000 as current expenses. (Recall that we are ignoring the tax-impact of expensing policies on net cash flows.)

As far as before-tax cash flows are concerned, there is no change if the company's accountant charges part of each year's $1000 outlay to current expenses rather than to book capital. Therefore accounting procedures do not affect the DCF yield r. It remains at 10 percent on each investment held, and hence at 10 percent for all of them collectively.

Do these accounting variations in the fraction of each year's $1000 outlay which is expensed affect the flow of company income? In the steady state (equal investment outlays each year) the answer is "No." This can be seen clearly in Table 1. Regardless of the amount expensed each year, the total annual charge of expensing plus depreciation adds up to $1000.

What Table 1 shows is that (in the steady state) the flow of reported income (after depreciation of non-expensed capital and the expensed portion of current investment) does not vary at all with the expensing policy adopted.

TABLE 1. *Straight-line depreciation*

Expensing policy	Annual cash flow	Annual amount expensed	Annual depreciation	Annual book income
0	$1377.66	$0	$1000	$377.66
20%	1377.66	200	800	377.66
50%	1377.66	500	500	377.66
100%	1377.66	1000	0	377.66

Although expensing policy has no effect on book income (ignoring taxes) it does have a profound effect on the net book value of capital. Returning to Fig. 1, we see that with a zero expensing policy the straight-line depreciation function (Line AB) produces a company net book value of $3000, i.e., the net book value figure is equal to the area under the depreciation curve (or line).

With a 100-percent expensing policy, the depreciation function will follow the right-angled line AOB. The area under this curve is zero. Such a company would have no net book capital. But, as we have seen in Table 1, its net income is $377.66. Its book rate of return b will therefore be infinity. The corresponding net book value and book rate of return for different expensing policies (straight-line depreciation) are shown in Table 2.

TABLE 2

Expensing policy	Annual book income	Company net book value	b (percent)
0	$377.66	$3000	12.6
20%	377.66	2400	15.4
50%	377.66	1500	25.2
90%	377.66	300	125.9
100%	377.66	0	∞

The effects of expensing policies on book rates of return are clearly powerful. What this means is that two companies which are in fact generating the same DCF rate r might in theory show book rates $b_a, b_b, b_c, \ldots b_z$ which range all the way from less than r percent at one extreme to ∞ percent at the other. The empirical question is: Do companies or divisions of companies, in fact, use different expensing ratios as far as investment outlays are concerned? The answer is that they do. Many companies capitalize all or almost all of their investment outlays. Others expense a high fraction. Companies with high research and development expenditures use a high expensing policy. Companies with high long-range advertising expenditures (i.e., expenditures which contribute little to current period cash flow but which contribute to future cash flow) do in effect use a high expensing policy. Producing departments of petroleum companies or primarily producing companies in the oil and gas industry also expense a high fraction of outlays in the form of exploratory, developmental, and intangible drilling costs.

Because our model, thus far, is confined to steady-state situations (equal or approximately equal investment outlays each year) it is premature to extrapolate our findings to the real world, but the results are suggestive. For example, the producing segment of the integrated oil industry, or oil and gas companies which are primarily producers rather than refiners and transporters, tend to have significantly higher book rates of return than the integrated companies. For example, Amerada earned an average book rate on equity capital of 21.6 percent during the period 1964–1968 as opposed to a corresponding rate of about 12.0 percent for the integrated petroleum industry as a whole. Likewise, pharmaceutical companies and cosmetic companies (which also follow a higher-than-typical expensing policy with respect to investment outlays) consistently show significantly higher rates than the rest of the manufacturing sector. For example, according to the Fortune Directory, the pharmaceutical industry has shown the highest return on invested capital year after year. For 1968 it was again in first place with a median book rate of return of 17.9 percent (compared to the *all*-industry median rate of 11.7 percent). The soaps and cosmetics industry was in second place with a median book rate of return of 16.9 percent.

The conventional explanation for these higher-than-normal rates of return for companies or industries is that they are either:

(1) riskier (this is the standard explanation for the producing sector of the oil and gas industry),
(2) more efficient, or
(3) have monopoly powers (this is frequently applied to the phar- maceutical sector).

While these three conventional explanations may be correct in varying degrees, they all assume that the observable book rates accurately reflect commensurate DCF rates. The fact that many high-book-rate companies or industries also follow high "expensing" policies suggests strongly that a fourth potential explanation is too important to ignore: namely that the observable book rates significantly overstate the underlying DCF rates actually being earned.

VARIATIONS IN DEPRECIATION METHODS

In addition to variations in accounting expensing policies, companies and industries use varying methods of depreciating the capitalized portion of their investment outlays. This is also a potential source of disturbance as far as the book rate of return is concerned. Since "depreciation" is a variant of "expensing" (which is instantaneous "depreciation") or vice- versa (depreciation is a form of "expensing" over time), it has similar effects on the DCF rate and the book rate of return.

OTHER FACTORS AFFECTING THE RELATION OF *b* TO *r*

Variations in accounting policies have a powerful effect on the size of rate of return measured in book rate units relative to the size of rate of return measured in DCF units. But they are not the only factors affecting the $(b \sim r)$ relationship. Three other influences are:

1. The economic duration of each investment outlay,
2. The time lag between outlays on the one hand and the commence- ment of net cash inflows on the other,
3. The time pattern of net cash inflows after they commence.

All three of these items can be summarized under a single caption—"The configuration of net cash outflows and inflows" from each investment.

Below is an example illustrating the effect of economic duration on the $(b \sim r)$ relationship.

Figure 2 shows three kinds of assets, all of which yield a DCF rate of 10 percent. Each of these shows outlays (below the horizontal line) and the size and duration of annual inflows (above the line). The first figure, 2a, is a depiction of the standard investment we have used for illustrative purposes thus far: $1000 buys $229.61 a year for 6 years. The DCF rate on this is 10 percent, but the book rate is 12.6 percent.

The second figure, 2b, is a short-duration investment in working capital. $1000 buys an inflow of $1100 in 1 year. The DCF rate (annual compounding basis) is 10 percent. So is the book rate. For this case $b = r$. And possibly this is how someone originated the idea that a rate could be measured accurately by taking the ratio of book income to book value of capital (or possibly it came from another favorite example in elementary commercial arithmetic—the case where $1000 produces a net inflow of $100 a year in perpetuity).

Finally the third figure, 2c, shows a long-duration investment, $1000 outlay producing a net cash inflow of $106.08 a year for 30 years. The DCF rate is still 10 percent. But the book rate for such a project, or for a "steady-state" company holding different vintages of such projects, would be 14.5 percent.

In short, in the steady state the longer the "duration" of each asset, the greater the discrepancy in the book rate unit measure relative to the DCF

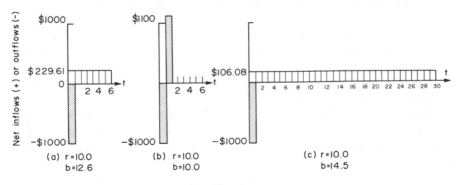

FIG. 2.

rate unit measure. Since, on working capital alone, the book rate is equal to the DCF rate, otherwise similar companies (with identical DCF rates) would show different book rates merely because each uses a different fraction of working capital relative to depreciable fixed capital.

THE EFFECT OF GROWTH

In this section we lift the steady-state assumption to deal with another major factor which influences the level of the book rate for any given set of the variables outlined above: This is the pace at which the company invests over time. To keep the analysis straightforward we assume that these outlays increase (or decrease) steadily at a given rate g.[6]

If all of the assets it acquires generate a common DCF rate of return equal to r percent, then clearly a company will be earning a DCF rate of r percent regardless of its growth rate g.

But unless the book rate b for such a company is equal to r in the steady state, variations in the pace of growth will cause changes in the observable book rate. The reason for this is simple and can be illustrated clearly in terms of our original "assumed" asset: namely the $1000 outlay which generates a level net cash flow of $229.61 for six years. Regardless of growth rate, a company holding only this form of asset holds six vintages of capital. In the steady state, the book rate earned on each vintage is a function of (a) the expensing and depreciation policy used and (b) the age of the vintage. With full capitalization and a straight-line depreciation policy, the net cash flow and net income attributable to each vintage is constant—at $229.61 *less* $166.66, $62.95.

But the midyear net book value of each vintage shrinks with age from [$1000 − 83.33] for the latest vintage to [$1000 − 3(83.33)] for the vintage acquired the preceding year, down to $83.33 for the oldest producing asset.

Hence the book rates of return, by vintage, vary: Very low for the mostly undepreciated asset to very high for the almost fully depreciated asset. The book rate for the company (earlier shown to be 12.6 percent) is simply a weighted average of the individual vintage book rates (with the net book values used as weights).

Introducing positive or negative growth into the analysis leaves the individual vintage book rates unaltered, but it changes the relative weights and, hence, the overall company rate (which is its weighted average).

[6]Growth here is defined as real growth; i.e., inflation is still assumed to be zero.

With positive growth, the "low yielding" newer vintages get a higher weight relative to the "high yielding" older vintages. Thus the company's overall book rate falls.

In contrast, when growth is negative (i.e., the company's new investment outlays shrink steadily over time), the opposite phenomenon occurs and the company's overall book rate rises.

The relationship of the book rate to the growth is shown in Fig. 3. Curve A shows the company's DCF rate, i.e., 10 percent, which is of course invariant to the growth rate (since each asset held is earning 10 percent). Curve B shows what the company's book rate would be at various assumed rates of growth (positive and negative). As growth rates become very large the company's overall rate will be dominated by the newest "low yielding" vintage, i.e., curve *B* approaches the yield for the newest vintage. At very fast rates of decay (negative growth) curve *B* approaches the yield for the oldest vintage.

Curve *C* on the same chart shows the same company, but under the assumption that it expenses 50 percent of each investment outlay when the outlay is made and uses a straight-line depreciation policy for the

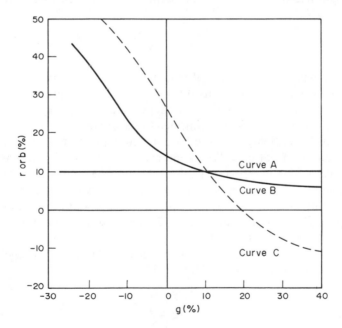

FIG. 3.

remaining 50 percent. The individual vintage book rates will now be even further apart. The newest vintage, which has charges of $500 of its acquisition price as an expense in its first year of life, will show a negative book rate of return, whereas the rate of return for the oldest vintage will now be more than twice as high as it was in the 100 percent capitalized situation. The effect of growth on curve C is therefore even more pronounced.

An interesting point on the growth axis is that at which the book rate b is exactly equal to the DCF rate r. This is the same for both curve B and curve C. And it will also hold for other curves $D, E \ldots Z$, which can be drawn for other combinations of the variables which affect the book rate of return. Why should this be so? A rigorous proof is beyond the scope of this paper, but one based on intuition runs as follows.

Taking very small intervals of time, we have by definition:

$$b_t = \frac{F_t - D_t}{B_t} \tag{1}$$

This says the book rate is equal to income (cash flow in period t less depreciation and expenses outlays in period t) divided by net book value. Also

$$g_t = \frac{I_t - D_t}{B_t} \tag{2}$$

This says that the growth rate of investment (which is also the growth rate of net book value) is equal to the net additions to net book value (new investment outlay in period t less depreciation and expense outlays in period t) divided by the existing net book value.

Now the condition $g = r$ (the growth rate equal to the DCF rate) exists only when all of net cash flow generated is reinvested. (An easy way to see this is to think in terms of a barrel of wine increasing in value with age. The annual DCF rate of return on holding this barrel of wine is also the rate at which the barrel increases in value each year—but only if one does not drink part of the contents!) In short $b = r$ only if all the net cash flow is reinvested, i.e. only if $I_t = F_t$.

But if $I_t = F_t$ we can see from equations (1) and (2) above that the conditions $g = b$ must hold. Hence: If

$$g = r$$

we have $g = b$

and thus $b = r$.

In other words, the book rate is an unbiased and accurate measure of the DCF rate for a company which is growing steadily at a rate equal to r (or b).[7]

So far we have dealt with rates of return as measures of performance of real assets and the two basically different units in which these rates can be, and are, counted. The same holds true for the other facet: Rate of return as a measure of the "required," "fair," or "target" standard, also known as the "cost of capital." This facet too can be, and is, measured in terms of the two units of account, one a DCF unit usually symbolized as k, and one a book rate unit, which I will here symbolize as β. Both are called "cost of capital," and both use the label "percent per annum required rate of return."

USES AND MISUSES OF DISPARATE "RATES"

The rules for the "correct" usage of these concepts and measures are fairly simple. If the actual or prospective performance of any investment is measured in DCF units, and if this rate is being assayed against some target or "reasonable rate standard," it is clear that the relevant standard must itself be calculated in DCF units. In short, r must be matched against k (the cost of capital) in order to produce rational decisions and judgments. Sometimes adjustments may be required, either to r or to k to allow for perceived differences in riskiness between the kind of investment being assayed and the kind of investments from which the k measure has been derived.

By the same token, if book rate units, b, are used to measure actual or prospective performance, the proper standard of comparison is against β. Here too risk adjustments are legitimate. In addition, adjustments may be necessary if the investment or collection of investments being assayed differ significantly with respect to the set of variables that affect the book rate of return from the collection of investments from whose performance the estimate of β has been derived.

The potential misuses of these tools of thought involve all the inconsistent comparisons which can be made among the four measures. What is surprising is that almost every conceivable form of misuse is being practiced today. Some examples are:

1. A regulatory authority measures the cost of capital in DCF units (k)

[7]The exact condition is that the company has been growing at this rate for at least n years, where n is the length of each underlying asset's productive life.

and then translates this number into "required revenues" by multi-plying it against a net book value estimate (or one based on net book value).

2. The same authority measures the cost of equity capital (k_e) in DCF units and the cost of debt in book rate units (embedded cost), and uses the weighted average of these two rates as the figure to be multiplied against a net book value rate base.

But regulation is not the only arena in which the disparate units are used as if they were interchangeable estimates of a common concept. Companies which have moved toward the measurement of investment worth in terms of a promised DCF rate still use book rates as a basis for setting the financial standard rate against which this promised DCF can be compared.

In some cases, DCF rates are used for *ex-ante* capital budgeting purposes, but an unadjusted book rate measure is used for later (*ex-post*) audit purposes, to check whether or not the investment lived up to its promise.

Finally, there is still a great deal of implicit acceptance that widely differing observed book rates are unbiased measures of actual profitability.

Understanding and avoiding these potential misuses of "rates of return" will not in itself provide correct answers. Important differential effects of price level changes on all measures, and the random effects of estimating errors, remain as significant barriers to be overcome, both for regulators and for private managers. Meanwhile, understanding that book rate measures and DCF rate measures are not different estimates of the *same* thing but rather estimates of *different* things should eliminate at least part of the confusion surrounding "rates of return on investment."

REFERENCES

1. Bierman, H. "Depreciable Assets—Timing of Expense Recognition," *The Accounting Review*, October 1961, pp. 613–18.
2. Carlson, R. *Measuring Period Profitability.* Unpublished doctoral dissertation, Stanford University, 1967.
3. Cottle, S. and Whitman, W. *Corporate Earning Power and Market Valuation.* Durham, N.C.: Duke University Press, 1959.
4. Gordon, M. J. "The Payoff Period and the Rate of Profit," *The Management of Corporate Capital,* edited by Ezra Solomon, New York: Macmillan-Free Press, 1959, pp. 48–55.
5. Gordon, M. J. and Shapiro, E. "Capital Equipment Analysis: The Required Rate of

Profit," *The Management of Corporate Capital*, edited by Ezra Solomon. New York: Macmillan-Free Press, 1959, pp. 141–47.

6. Harcourt, G. C. "The Accountant in a Golden Age," *Oxford Economic Papers*, New Series, Vol. 17, No. 1 (1965).

7. Johnson, O. "Two General Concepts of Depreciation," *Journal of Accounting Research*, Spring 1968, pp. 29–37.

8. Kuznets, S., ed. *Income and Wealth, Series II.* Cambridge: International Association for Research into Income and Wealth, Bowes-Bowes, 1952.

9. Lanzilloti, R. F. "Pricing Objectives in Large Companies," *American Economic Review*, Vol. 48 (1968), pp. 921–40.

10. Laya, J. C. *A Cash-Flow Model for Rate of Return.* Unpublished doctoral dissertation, Stanford University, 1965.

11. Minhas, B. S. *An International Comparison of Factor Costs and Factor Use.* Amsterdam: North-Holland Publishing Company, 1963.

12. Solomon, E., ed. *The Management of Corporate Capital.* New York: Macmillan, 1959.

13. Solomon, E. "Research on Return on Investment: The Relation of Book-Yield to True Yield," in American Accounting Association, *Research in Accounting Measurement*, 1965.

14. Solomon, E. "Systematic Errors in Book Rates of Return," Society of Petroleum Engineers, SPE 655 (1963).

15. Solomon, E. *The Theory of Financial Management.* New York: Columbia University Press, 1963.

16. Solomon, E. "The Variation Between True Yield and Book Rate of Return in the Oil and Gas Producing Industry," Testimony before Federal Power Commission, Area Rate Proceedings AR-61-1 (1961).

17. Solomon, E. and Laya, J. C. "Measurement of Company Profitability: Some Systematic Errors in the Accounting Rate of Return," in *Financial Research and its Implications for Management Decisions*, A. A. Robichek, ed. New York: John Wiley & Sons, 1966, pp. 152–183.

18. Stigler, G. J. *Capital and Rates of Return in Manufacturing Industry.* Princeton, N.J.: Princeton University Press, 1963.

19. Vatter, W. J. "Income Models, Book Yield and the Rate of Return," *The Accounting Review*, October 1966, pp. 681–98.

20. Wright, F. W. "Toward a General Theory of Depreciation," *Journal of Accounting Research*, Spring 1964, pp. 80–90.

2

*An Approach to Internal Profit Measurement**

JOEL DEAN

OBJECTIVES OF INTERNAL PROFIT MEASUREMENT

Let us start our investigation by setting down what seem to me to be the two main objectives of a system of internal financial measurement. These are, first, the guidance of the division or other internal managements whose results are being measured and, second, the assistance of top management and its staff in their tasks of appraising and guiding divisional performance. There is no need to argue which of these objectives is the more important in any particular case if we can agree that both are certainly important enough to be taken into account in setting up an internal measurement system. And, aside from such usually desirable characteristics as simplicity, these are the *only* objectives of a measurement system. We can, therefore, appraise any particular measurement system or some feature of such a system by answering little more than these two short questions:

1. Does it assist division management in making business decisions in ways that will maximize the company's profits?
2. Does it give top management a reliable summary of the financial record of each division's performance?

IRRELEVANT CRITERIA

By contrast here are two questions that need not be asked about an internal financial measurement system:

*From *Management Accounting* (formerly *N.A.A. Bulletin*), Section 1, Vol. 39, March 1958, pp. 5–12. Reproduced by permission.

366

1. Would the division results qualify as a conventional set of financial statements?
2. Does the internal performance measurement correctly show the division's net profits?

The first question need not be asked because we are not concerned here with how the reports might look to a tax collector or an uninformed outsider. One of the objects of the present form of conventional accounting statements, the kind that appears with the auditing firm's letter somewhere in the back of the annual report, is to protect stockholders against any arbitrary and possibly misleading manipulations of the books of account by management. They do this by guaranteeing that none of the traditional costs are overlooked, that objective methods of dealing with such hard-to-guess costs as annual depreciation are rigorously applied throughout, that no profits are shown until there has been a sale to a genuine outsider, etc.

The situation is very different where reports are made exclusively for insiders who may be presumed to be intelligent, informed and able to follow up or supplement these reports through personal investigation or staff work. Here we are free from the restraints of tradition, stockholder ignorance or the Securities and Exchange Commission. Management can, therefore, decide just what information it wants or does not want and how it is to be presented.

For example, unrealized profits can and often should be included in divisional profit measurements. The fact that no sale took place to outsiders and that the price of the internal transfer was determined by company executives rather than directly by market forces would disqualify the transaction for auditors' certification, but this is an irrelevant criterion for managerial use.

The treatment of inventory values and materials costs can well be quite different where managerial accounting is the object. Whether or not the company uses "lifo" in its stockholder and tax accounting, some system for costing materials on a replacement basis can often help division management and top management make better decisions. And, even if the company does use "lifo" for other purposes, managerial accounting objectives may require explicit recognition of inventory gains or losses where these are an important part of the responsibilities of division management.

As a final example, divisional financial measures can depart from the conventional kind in their treatment of depreciation charges and the net property accounts, which can be adjusted to reflect changing general price levels or windfall gains and losses in the market values of particular assets. In some cases, they might even be altered to record the division's investment in such things as research or a long-range advertising program, even though tax wisdom and the dictates of conservative stockholder accounting call for expensing these items on the regular books of account.

I am not saying that all of these things should always be done or that they are always easy to do, but I do say we should feel free to do them and that there are many cases where they *should* be done, both in order to give the right kind of guidance to division management and to permit top management to make the right kind of evaluation. Further, I am confident that they *can* be done well enough to be worth doing in such cases. Perhaps this is a heresy, but you will see that it is an old one if you will think back to the days before widespread securities ownership and the Federal income tax. In those days, owner-managers had their financial reports made up to suit themselves, and they often did such things as ignoring formal depreciation charges altogether, out of a belief that their own informed judgment was as reliable as any other guide to what the business was worth and how fast the fixed assets were losing economic value. Thus we need not be disturbed by the fact that internal profit measurements would not qualify for certification by independent auditors.

The second question we do *not* need to ask about an internal financial measurement system is: does the internal performance measurement correctly show divisional net profits? The word "profits" always seems to imply that the division financial measurement system should somehow apportion all the corporation's revenues and costs, especially the costs, to the divisional income statements. I suppose that the real reason for this is top management's worry that the divisional managers will not work hard enough unless they are exposed to the full, staggering burden of corporate overheads. It certainly seems reasonable that division managers should not be led to believe that the corporation's profits are any higher than they really are. I suggest, however, that the internal financial measurement system will usually work better if, instead of going to all the work of trying to calculate something like a traditional "net profit" for each division, we settle for a more simple and reliable measure. In fact, I doubt whether any routine divisional net profit computation along traditional full-cost lines can ever mean anything useful to either the divisions or top management.

DECISIONS OF DIVISION MANAGERS

Consider first the system's function in guiding the decisions of division management. Division management ought to have the clearest possible understanding in advance as to just how its performance is to be measured. If nobody tells them, they will guess, because executives have strong incentives to maximize whatever they think will be given the most weight in the corporate scoring system, whether this be divisional earnings, a clean desk or low golf score. It is inevitable and desirable that a corporate decision to rely heavily on financial performance measures will be reflected in the myriad of day-to-day decisions made by the division.

For the most part, these are business decisions between alternative ways of doing something. One example is make-or-buy; another might be the choice between a policy of occasional expensive overtime operation versus one of steady production. Steady production would incur the cost of either higher peak inventories or more frequent out-of-stock situations. For all these decisions, the financial criterion that the company wants the division manager to apply is that of maximizing company profits. But, so far as the division manager is concerned, he will make his decisions correctly if he maximizes something a good deal simpler, which we can call his operating result and define loosely as a dollar measure that takes no account of any costs beyond the division's current ability to control.

Examples of such uncontrollable costs might include the president's salary or office rent, the expenses of defending an antitrust suit, and perhaps even the annual depreciation charge on the division's own plants. The allocations and re-allocations of costs such as these take time and can generate many arguments that serve only to undermine confidence in the measurement system at all levels. These allocations serve absolutely no purpose in helping a division manager with the current economic or managerial decisions he has to make. He cannot change them by any constructive action he can take. Moreover, the mere fact that he may succeed in covering whatever portion of these costs may have been allocated to him, should not be a cause for self congratulations or any lessening of effort on his part. Clearly, the division does not benefit from a system of internal profit measurement that aims at showing conventional net profits at the division level.

APPRAISAL OF DIVISION'S PERFORMANCE

If we turn now to the system's functions of giving top management a basis for financial appraisal, I think we find an even stronger case for avoiding the usual net profit concepts. After all, the president knows what his own salary is and how it is determined. Of what help is it to him to see how somebody thinks it ought to be spread over the various divisions? So it is with such expenses as those of a major antitrust suit. The corporation certainly would like the earnings of its divisions to cover these, but that desirable state of affairs will not be made any more likely by allocating them to divisional profits and losses. Instead, allocations of such corporate costs only get in the way of evaluating divisional performance. They attribute costs to the divisions over which the divisions have no control and which will not be affected by any remedial action that top management can possibly direct at the divisions. In addition, the inherent instability of most systems for allocating such costs impairs the validity of any historical review of annual division results, since good and bad years can be leveled out or interchanged by the way the allocations fall. One of the lessons we can learn from the best outside security analysts is that a long historical perspective can be valuable in appraising the current status and prospects of a complex economic unit. Most good analysts prefer to work with simple and consistent data and to make their own special adjustments instead of accepting those they find in the published reports.

In setting up a system of profit center performance measurement, we are striving for the benefits of breaking the company up into a number of small firms. We wish to secure the advantages of a small firm, and to:

1. Associate responsibility and control.
2. Increase flexibility of profit center management.
3. Stress competitive instead of political skills.

At the same time, it would be well to remember that profit centers are not really small companies; if they were, there would be no point in holding several of them together under one corporate roof. This must mean that the important economic advantages of the profit center system will entail some joint costs incurred by the parent corporation in the interests of more than one division. It usually means that some restrictions will be imposed to prevent individual profit centers from behaving with complete independence in every case. Many of the financial effects of these joint costs and common policies cannot be allocated to the division in any sensible fashion. They need not be allocated for the profit centers to operate smoothly. In fact, if they are allocated, they are likely to distort the primary functions of the profit center.

This does not mean that these items are not real or are not important. What it does mean is that they can best be attributed to the central office and top management. They are not pertinent for the purpose of the profit center's decisions and their impact on evaluation of the center is too complex to try to summarize by mere allocation.

MEASUREMENT SEPARATE FROM EVALUATION

It would be both useful and satisfying to be in a position to distribute fully and finally to the divisions every last dollar of corporate revenue and expense, to set an economically correct depreciation charge for each division, to determine a managerially correct capital charge and risk allowance for each division, to do all this routinely by the use of nothing but desk calculators and junior clerks, and thus to derive automatically a series of divisional profit and loss figures that has real meaning for top management. It would be even better if the resulting figure could be made to point infallibly toward the source of any particularly good or bad performance that occurred. Since it is impossible to do all of the things at once, we must continue to rely on top management's judgment for many important evaluations and decisions. Since that is so, however, we can at least recognize that measurement is often properly separated from evaluation of such a complex thing as divisional financial performance, and that the evaluation is likely to be better if the measurements are made without trying to prejudge the result of a management review. A well-made measurement system can help management to see clearly the financial aspects of what the divisions are like, what they have done and what they are doing. It cannot resolve but can only contribute to the managerial decision as to whether a particular division is doing as well as it can or should do, why this is so, and what, if anything, should be done about it. Security analysts, whose work offers so many interesting parallels elsewhere in our task of measurement and evaluation, have little to offer on this point, because the analyst's job is over when he has decided how much a security is worth. This is the point where management's job really begins, because top management's responsibility is to identify and help to improve upon unsatisfactory performance, to learn from and reward performance that is of high quality, and to keep the company moving toward areas of high promise.

Perhaps I can summarize the important points I have been trying to make by saying that the fullest potentialities of the developing science (or art) of internal financial measurement can best be realized by being willing to take a fresh look at our reasons for measuring divisional results and then trying to lay out a measurement system with these unique purposes in mind, not merely by imitating some other currently used reporting systems that were originally devised at other times for other purposes. If I have judged these unique purposes correctly, it means that a good internal measurement system ought to aim at providing a well-ordered factual summary of current developments and their historical background, should make it as easy as possible for management and staff to arrive at their own evaluations of these facts and should recognize that a well-informed top management will derive little benefit from attempts to substitute a number of conventional and routine calculations for their own good judgment.

OTHER PROBLEMS OF INTERNAL PROFIT MEASUREMENT

I am acutely aware that I have done no more than outline one phase of this fascinating and fast-developing problem of internal financial measurement. I hope that the approach sketched here will help you to grapple with such other important problems as these:

1. *Divisional boundaries*—Which activities should be grouped together in divisions and which should be made into separate divisions or put in service centers? How well division boundaries are drawn and redrawn to keep pace with changing circumstances can make the difference between a system of profit center decentralization that works and one that creates even more problems of measurement and control.
2. *Pricing internal transfers of goods and services*—Should transfer prices be freely negotiated by the buying and selling divisions or should they be subject to central supervision and control? Pricing of transfers can make profits for any one division high or low and the method of pricing can have profound effect upon divisional results and incentives. What is needed is a system that yields meaningful divisional measures, which means that transfer pricing policies are central to a successful divisionalization program.
3. *Capital management decisions*—How do you get good capital investment decisions without compromising the position of the profit center manager? This problem is vital, because the manager is

usually thinking in terms of results for this year and next, whereas many investment decisions will affect results for the next five years, ten years or even more. One practical problem here is how top management can make sure that a division manager will not make unwise investments for the sake of dressing up his performance measure with short-run cost savings.

3

The Arithmetic of Capital-budgeting Decisions*

Ezra Solomon

IN ORDER to make correct capital-expenditure decisions, corporate management needs at least three sets of information. Estimates must be made of net capital outlays required and future cash earnings promised by each proposed project. This is a problem in engineering valuation and market forecasting. Estimates must also be made of the availability and cost of capital to the company. This is a problem in financial analysis. Finally, management needs a correct set of standards by which to select projects for execution so that long-run economic benefits to present owners will be maximized. This is a problem in logic and arithmetic. This paper is concerned exclusively with the last of these three problems.[1]

With respect to the question "Should this investment proposal be accepted or rejected?" the problem of arriving at a correct decision is uncomplicated. Either one of two approaches to measuring the investment worth of a proposal will provide a correct answer.[2] In the usual form in which these approaches are used as capital-rationing criteria, they are:

The rate-of-return approach.—This approach expresses each project's estimated value as a single over-all "rate of return per annum." This rate is equal to the rate of interest at which the present value of expected capital outlays is exactly equal to the present value of expected cash earnings on that project. The concept is identical with the "effective yield

*From *Journal of Business*, Vol. 29, No. 2, April 1956, pp. 124–129. Reproduced by permission.

[1]For a discussion of the first two problems see Joel Dean, *Capital Budgeting* (New York: Columbia University Press, 1951), and Ezra Solomon, "Measuring a Company's Cost of Capital," *Journal of Business*, XXVIII (October, 1955), 240–52.

[2]There are other criteria in use, e.g., determining capital budgets by size of department, by pay-out periods, or by the postponability of projects. It has already been shown that these are at best crude approximations to a correct solution (see Dean, *op. cit.*, chap. ii, and M. J. Gordon, "The Payoff Period and the Rate of Profit," *Journal of Business*, XXVIII [October, 1955], 253–60).

to maturity" on a bond that is purchased at some price other than its par value. It has also been called the "internal rate of profit"[3] or the "marginal efficiency of capital."[4]

If the rate of return on a project is greater than the company's cost of capital (also expressed as a percentage per annum rate), then the project should be accepted.

The present-value approach.—For each project, find the present value of the expected capital outlays, using the cost of capital as a discount rate. Likewise, find the present value of the expected cash earnings. If the present value of earnings is greater than the present value of outlays, the project should be accepted.

These two approaches give the same results for "accept or reject" decisions. This is so because the computed rate of return on a project will be higher than the cost of capital in all cases for which the present value of earnings, discounted at the cost of capital, is greater than the present value of outlays. Or, conversely, if a project promises a rate of return greater than the company's cost of capital, then the present value of its earnings, discounted at the cost of capital, will be greater than the present value of its outlays.

For problems which involve more than a simple "accept or reject" decision, the application of these two criteria, as they are generally defined, often yield contradictory or ambiguous results. The purpose of this paper is to explore the reasons for these contradictions or ambiguities and to reformulate this general approach to measuring investment worth so that it always provides a unique and correct basis for decision making.

MUTUALLY EXCLUSIVE PROPOSALS

It is often necessary for management to ask not only "Is this project worth undertaking?" but also "which of two projects is the better one?" This latter question is crucial whenever two or more projects or proposals are mutually exclusive. For example, the proposals may be alternative ways of doing the same thing. Both might be profitable in an absolute sense. But since only one of the two can be undertaken, the problem is to decide which alternative is the better one.

When the *relative* merit of alternative proposals is at issue, the

[3]See Kenneth L. Boulding, *Economic Analysis* (rev. ed.; New York: Harper & Bros., 1948), chaps. xxxv and xxxvi.

[4]See J. M. Keynes, *The General Theory of Employment, Interest, and Money* (New York: Macmillan Co., 1936), pp. 140 ff.

rate-of-return criterion, as defined earlier, and the present-value criterion, as defined, can yield contradictory results. With the increased interest in applying rational approaches to the solution of capital-investment decisions, this possible conflict between the two generally acceptable criteria has received renewed attention. Several recent papers have shown that when projects are ranked by the rate-of-return standard, the results may differ from a ranking of the same projects based on the present-value standard.[5] For analytical purposes, the simplest example of such a conflict will suffice: Assume that there are two investment opportunities available. Both are profitable in an absolute sense, but only one can be undertaken because the two are mutually exclusive.

Project X requires an outlay of \$100 now, at time t_0, and promises to return \$120 exactly 1 year hence at time t_1. Project Y also requires an outlay of \$100 now and promises to return \$174.90 exactly 4 years hence at time t_4. Assume also that the degree of certainty attaching to each project is identical and that the investor's present "cost of capital" is 10 per cent.

The "rate of return" on project X is 20 per cent, and on project Y it is 15 per cent. The present value of project X, discounted at the cost of capital, is \$109.09. For project Y, the present value, discounted at the cost of capital, is \$119.46. If the two projects are ranked by their rate of return, project X is the better one. If, on the other hand, they are ranked in terms of present value, project Y is the better one. Which should the investor choose?

In order to resolve the problem correctly, it is necessary to isolate the source of the conflict between the two approaches. The easiest way to do this is to compare the two investment proposals in terms of their relative value as of the terminal date (t_4) of the longer-lived project.[6]

According to the data given, proposal Y will provide the investor with \$174.90 at time t_4. All we know about proposal X is that it provides \$120.00 at time t_1. What happens to these funds between time t_1 and t_4 is obviously an important piece of necessary information. Neither the rate-of-return approach nor the present-value approach answers this question

[5]See James H. Lorie and Leonard J. Savage, "Three Problems in Rationing Capital," *Journal of Business*, XXVIII (October, 1955), 229–39; George Terborgh, "Some Comments on the Dean-Smith Article on the MAPI Formula," *Journal of Business*, XXIX (April, 1956), 138–40; and A. A. Alchian, "The Rate of Interest, Fisher's Rate of Return over Costs, and Keynes' Internal Rate of Return," *American Economic Review*, XLV (December, 1955), 938–42.

[6]The "terminal date" refers to the date at which cash earnings from the longer-lived of the two competing projects cease.

explicitly. But they both answer it *implicitly* and in different ways. This is the source of the conflicting results that they yield.

Those who use the rate-of-return approach, as it is usually defined, would choose project X over project Y. Hence they must assume that this choice will yield a larger terminal value than that promised by project Y, i.e., $174.90. This, in turn, implies that the $120 obtained from project X at time t_1 can be reinvested between time t_1 and t_4 at a rate lucrative enough to accumulate to more than $174.90 by time t_4. *In general*, the implicit assumption made by the rate-of-return approach is that the reinvestment rate is at least equal to the rate promised by the longer-lived of the two projects, in this case, 15 per cent.[7]

The present-value approach, as usually defined, assumes that the funds obtained from either project can be reinvested at a rate equal to the company's present cost of capital, i.e., 10 per cent. Using this assumption, the investor will end up at time t_4 with only $159.72 if he chooses project X. With project Y, he would have $174.90. Thus, according to this approach, project Y is the better choice.

The question of which assumption is likely to be the more justified one is important, but it is not relevant to the argument being made in this paper, namely, that the apparent conflict between the two approaches results only from differing assumptions that each makes about the future. If a common assumption is adopted, both approaches will always rank projects identically.

Let us assume, for example, that the investor can put money to use between time t_1 and time t_4 at an average return of 12 per cent. The following computations and results would ensue:

Terminal value.—For project Y this is $174.90. For project X we have $120 at time t_1, plus interest at 12 per cent per annum for 3 years. This would accumulate to $168.47.

Rate of return.—For project Y this averages 15 per cent up to the terminal date at time t_4. For project X the rate would be 20 per cent for 1 year and 12 per cent for 3 years—an over-all rate equal to 13.9 per cent.

Present value.—For project Y this would be $174.90, discounted from time t_4 back to time t_1 at 12 per cent[8] and back from time t_1 to t_0 at 10 per

---

[7]For example, if project Z, a third alternative, yielded 15 per cent in perpetuity and project X yielded 20 per cent, the rate-of-return approach would choose project X over project Z. Hence the approach must assume that funds received from project X can be reinvested at least at 15 per cent.

[8]This is the relevant rate because we are assuming that the investor can earn 12 per cent on his funds between time t_1 and time t_4.

cent. This gives $113.17. For project X the present value would be $120 discounted from time t_1 to time t_0 at 10 per cent, or $109.09.

All three criteria rank the two projects in the same order. With the particular assumption we used, project Y is the better one by any standard. Using some other assumption, the ranking might be reversed, but the alternative approaches would still yield identical results.

Our conclusion is that correct and consistent ranking of the investment worth of competing proposals can be obtained only if the following factors are taken into account:

1. The valid comparison is not simply between two projects but between two alternative courses of action. The ultimate criterion is the total wealth that the investor can expect from each alternative by the terminal date of the longer-lived project. In order to make a fair comparison, an explicit and common assumption must be made regarding the rate at which funds released by either project can be reinvested up to the terminal date.
2. If the rate of return is to be used as an index of relative profitability, then the relevant rate is the per annum yield promised by each alternative course of action from its inception to a common terminal date in the future (usually the terminal date of the longer-lived project).
3. If the present value is to be used as an index of relative profitability, the expected reinvestment rate or set of rates should be used as the discounting factor. These rates will be equal to the company's present cost of capital only by coincidence. When comparing two projects requiring different outlays, it is necessary to compare "present value per dollar of outlay" rather than the absolute present value of the projects.

THE PROBLEM OF "DUAL RATES OF RETURN"

In a recent paper Lorie and Savage[9] have drawn attention to a second problem involving the arithmetic of capital budgeting. In this paper the authors attempt to show that certain rare and complex investment situations exist which cannot be expressed in terms of a single, unique "rate of return." In such situations the application of the usual prescription for finding *the* rate of return yields two solutions, and thus "the rate-of-return criterion for judging the acceptability of investment proposals,

[9] *Op. cit.*

as it has been presented in published works, is ambiguous or anomalous."[10]

In order to understand the problem involved, it is helpful to recognize two basic types of investment situation, classified according to the pattern of estimated cash flows that are projected. In the usual type of situation, which we will call "pattern A," the stream of net cash inflows promised by a project ends either before or when it reaches that point in time beyond which the value of net *future flows* is negative. In other words, the project is assumed to terminate before the stage beyond which its continuation yields a net loss to the investor. The second situation, which we call "pattern B," is a much rarer one. Projects which fall into this category continue beyond the point defined previously, i.e., the terminal section contains a net cash outflow (a net loss). Such a pattern obviously exists only if there are contractual or other compelling reasons which make it impossible for the investor to avoid the terminal losses.

As far as pattern A projects are concerned, it is always possible to express the investment worth of the project as a single, meaningful "rate of return" and hence to make a clear-cut decision on the basis of such a criterion. For pattern B projects the application of the usually prescribed method of finding the appropriate "rate of return" can yield more than one answer.[11]

Let us take a specific example of a pattern B investment project. The proposal being considered is the installation of a larger oil pump that would get a fixed quantity of oil out of the ground more rapidly than the pump that is already in use. Let us assume that, by operating the existing pump, the investor can expect $10,000 a year hence and $10,000 two years hence. Let us assume that, by installing the larger pump at a net cost of $1,600 now, he can expect $20,000 a year hence and nothing the second year. The installation of the larger pump can be viewed as a project having the cash-flow characteristics shown in Table 1.

TABLE 1

Time period	Incremental cash flow due to investment
t_0	− $1,600
t_1	+ 10,000
t_2	

[10] *Ibid.*, p. 237.
[11] Lorie and Savage explain the general basis for dual rates (*ibid.*, p. 237).

The usual prescription for finding the rate of return of a project is to find that rate which makes the discounted value of net cash flows equal to the discounted value of capital outlays. Alternatively—and this amounts to the same thing—find that rate which makes the algebraic sum of the discounted cash outflows and inflows equal to zero. The application of this method to our example will yield two answers, namely, 25 and 400 per cent. In other words, using a 25 per cent rate, the discounted value of the cash flows is exactly equal to the outlay of $1,600. However, a rate of 400 per cent also equates cash flows with capital outlay. Which of the two "rates" is the correct measure of the investment worth of the project, 25 or 400 per cent?

The answer is that neither of these rates is a measure of investment worth, neither has relevance to the profitability of the project under consideration, and neither, therefore, is correct. The fault lies in the incorrect application of the "usual prescription" for finding the rate of return. A closer look at the implications of defining the rate of return in this context as that rate (or rates) which reduce the discounted cash flows to zero reveals the gross error that such a process entails. In order to find this error, let us vary the net outlay required to install the larger pump (keeping all other cash flows constant) and solve for the "rate of return," using the usual prescription. We get the following absurd results:

1. If the larger pump costs nothing, then the project is worth 0 per cent i.e., at 0 per cent, the discounted value of the net cash flows is equal to the value of the outlay.[12]
2. If the larger pump costs $827, the project, according to this method, suddenly becomes quite profitable and is rated at 10 per cent, i.e., at a rate of 10 per cent, the discounted value of the net cash flows is equal to $827.
3. The more the pump costs, the more "profitable" the project becomes! At a cost of $1,600 the rate of return is 25 per cent; at a cost of $2,500 it yields 100 per cent. The method would have us believe that the engineer who first thought of the idea of installing the larger pump could have a gold mine if only he could persuade the pump manufacturer to charge him enough for the installation.[13]

Needless to say, any definition of "profitability" that leads to these absurd results must itself be in error.

[12] Alternatively, one could say that the rate is infinitely large.
[13] This increase in the "rate," as the cost of the pump increases, reaches a maximum level, after which the relationship is reversed.

The correct solution for the investment worth of the project is simple and straightforward. But it requires an explicit answer to a relevant question: "What is it worth to the investor to receive $10,000 one year earlier than he would have otherwise received it?" This is actually all that the installation of the larger pump achieves. If the investor expects to be able to put the $10,000 to work at a yield of x per cent per annum, then getting the money a year earlier is worth $100x$. If x is 23 per cent, for example, getting $10,000 a year earlier is worth $2,300. In other words, if he spent $1,600 on the larger pump now (at time t_0), he would end up at time t_2 having $2,300 more than he otherwise would have had. This can be stated as an equivalent "rate of return," which in this case would be about 20 per cent ($1,600 at 20 per cent per annum would amount to $2,304 at the end of two years). Using this approach, a unique and meaningful rate of return can always be found for any set of cash inflows and outflows.

SUMMARY

The rate of return is a useful concept that enables us to express the profitability of an investment proposal as a single explicit value. This value automatically adjusts for differences in the time pattern of expected cash outflows and inflows. It is also independent of the absolute size of the project. Thus it provides a useful standard by which all types of projects—large and small, long-run and short-run—can be ranked against each other in relative terms and also against the company's cost of capital, in order to judge their absolute worth. The arithmetic involved in rate-of-return computations is generally straightforward. However, there are two situations in which such computations require a careful consideration of the logic that is involved.

1. When mutually exclusive proposals are being compared, it is necessary to compute the rate on each alternative course of action up to the terminal date of the longer-lived alternative. This requires an explicit estimate of the yield to be derived from the cash flows generated by each of the alternatives being considered.
2. When a rate is being computed for complex proposals that have negative terminal values, the usual mechanistic prescription for solving for rates does not apply. This situation also requires an explicit estimate of the yield to be derived from incremental cash flows generated by a project. Given this estimate, the equivalent dollar value of the incremental cash flows can be computed

explicitly. A comparison of this value with the outlays required for the project will give a correct and unambiguous measure of the project's rate of return.

If these concepts and methods are used in defining and computing rates of return, this criterion will always provide an unambiguous investment standard, the use of which will lead to a maximization of the investor's net present worth, in so far as the estimates used are accurate.

4

Depreciation in Economic Theory and Capital Budgeting*

WARD S. CURRAN

IN THIS paper I have two objectives: (1) to sketch in limited detail the treatment of depreciation in both the economic theory of the firm and in capital budgeting; and (2) to develop from the discussion of the alternatives presented the techniques which would appear to yield the most satisfactory solution to the capital budgeting problem.

I.

In the neoclassical world of certainty, the firm exists indefinitely for the purposes of capital theory. Individual assets depreciate but "given enough time some significant fraction of specialized assets can be transformed into other specialized assets without any sacrifice in income."[1] The amount of capital available will be invested in a succession of perishable capital goods or durable assets.[2] Thus if V represents capitalized value, I the net productivity or income from a durable asset, and r the long-run market rate of interest, then

$$V = \frac{I}{(1+r)} + \frac{I}{(1+r)^2} + \frac{I}{(1+r)^3} + \cdots + \frac{I}{(1+r)^n}.$$

As $n \to \infty$ for $r < 1$,

$$V = \frac{I}{r}.$$

*From The Quarterly Review of Economics and Statistics, Spring 1968, Vol. 8, No. 1, pp. 61–68. Reproduced by permission.
[1]Donald Dewey, Modern Capital Theory (New York: Columbia University Press, 1965), p. 28.
[2]J. B. Clark, The Distribution of Wealth (New York: Macmillan, 1899), Ch. 9, especially pp. 116–21.

Following this line of reasoning, a firm purchases not an asset but an income stream whose capitalized value depends upon its size and the long-run rate of interest. Assume that a perpetual income stream of $100 is capitalized at a long-run market rate of interest of 10 percent. This assumption does not preclude the firm from purchasing an asset with a finite income stream. It simply means that the depreciation must be sufficient to maintain that income through its reinvestment in another asset. Alternatively the funds could be reinvested so as to restore the productivity of the machine. In either instance there is a perpetual annual income of $100 a year from one or more assets. The capitalized value of this sum is $1,000.

Pursuing this argument still further, one can derive, assuming no indivisibilities, a firm's demand curve for capital. Because of diminishing returns as the total amount invested (that is, the total capitalized value) increases, the capitalized values of incremental individual income streams decline.[3] Hence the demand curve is downward sloping with respect to the volume of investment (Chart 1).

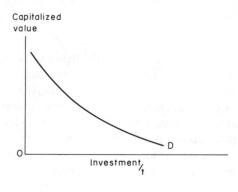

CHART 1.

The total volume of investment expressed as the summation of the capitalized values of individual projects approaches some finite sum and the capitalized value of each successive investment declines toward zero.[4] With appropriate modification, to be discussed in the next section,

[3]Even in the long run some relevant factor of production, perhaps entrepreneurial ability, must be fixed.

[4]Since the curve is a continuous function implying no indivisibilities, the income stream to be capitalized approaches zero.

one has in this model the basis for the "present value" technique of capital budgeting.

The foregoing discussion is not meant to imply that the concepts employed are agreed to by all economists. Keynes, for example, was particularly critical of what he called the "classical" school of thought on interest and capital.

In launching his attack, Keynes defined and made use of his now famous concept, the marginal efficiency of capital. In his words: "... I define the marginal efficiency of capital as being equal to that rate of discount which would make the present value of a series of annuities given by the returns expected from the capital-asset during its life just equal to its supply price".[5]

Whether Keynes was correct in assuming that this definition was consistent with the concepts employed by others, particularly Irving Fisher, need not detain us.[6] What is important for the purpose at hand is that instead of finding the present value of an income stream under conditions of certainty and without reference to the specific assets involved, one finds the rate of return which equates the prospective dollar return (that is, the prospective marginal product gross of depreciation) with the supply price of the specific asset to be purchased. The supply price is "the price which would just induce a manufacturer newly to produce an additional unit of such assets, i.e., what is sometimes called replacement cost."[7]

Thus if a machine has a replacement cost of $12,000 and a useful life of three years with no scrap value at the end of the period, and if the prospective annual marginal products or yields gross of depreciation are

[5]John M. Keynes, *The General Theory of Employment, Interest and Money* (New York: Harcourt Brace, 1936), p. 135.

[6]See A. A. Alchian, "The Rate of Interest, Fisher's Rate of Return over Costs and Keynes' Interest Rate of Return," *American Economic Review*, Vol. 45, No. 5 (December, 1955), pp. 938–42. Fisher's rate of return over cost, which Keynes thought to be identical with his concept of the marginal efficiency of capital, is the rate which sets the difference in present worth of two investment options equal to zero.

Keynes, however, was developing a marginal efficiency of capital schedule to determine the volume of investment which a firm would undertake. Unlike Fisher, Keynes incorporates uncertainty into his analysis. What he discounts is the "prospective yield" or prospective marginal product. The marginal efficiency of capital is therefore the expected rate of return. Each investment is undertaken under the assumption that accepting one investment does not alter the productivity of the others.

[7]Keynes, *op cit.*, p. 135.

$7,000, \$6,000, and \$5,000 respectively,

$$\$12,000 = \frac{\$7,000}{(1+r)} + \frac{\$6,000}{(1+r)^2} + \frac{\$5,000}{(1+r)^3}, \text{ with}$$

with $r =$ marginal efficiency of capital
                     = 25 percent.

Applying this technique to each individual asset, one can generate a marginal efficiency of capital schedule which, if one assumes no indivisibilities, approximates a smooth curve (Chart 2). Along the ordinate is the marginal efficiency of capital for each project, and along the abscissa is the supply price or replacement cost of the assets.[8]

In his definition of depreciation,[9] Keynes accepts original cost as the basis for calculation. As a consequence, the only fundamental difference between the yield method espoused in the literature of capital budgeting and the marginal efficiency of capital seems to be the substitution of original cost for replacement cost of the asset involved. If one interprets "the price which would just induce a manufacturer newly to produce an additional unit of such assets" literally, even this distinction vanishes. The original cost for a proposed investment is the current supply price.

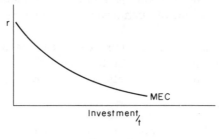

CHART 2.

[8]For Keynes, the negative slope of the marginal efficiency of capital curve stems not only from diminishing returns but also from the fact that the supply price of capital will rise because "pressure on facilities for producing that type of capital will cause its supply price to increase." The second of these factors is "usually more important in producing equilibrium in the short run, but the longer the period in view the more does the first factor take its place." *Ibid.*, p. 136.

[9]Depreciation is included as part of his definition of user cost or "the sacrifice of value involved in the production" of output sold. *Ibid.*, p. 50. See also pp. 52–73.

II.

It would be folly to suggest that professional interest in a rational approach to capital budgeting began in 1951 with the publication of Joel Dean's *Capital Budgeting*.[10] But it would be less than accurate to argue that the publication of this book and his subsequent writings[11] failed to stimulate widespread interest in the subject. However, those seeking a more rational approach to capital budgeting through application of economic analysis soon discovered the limitation of their own techniques. For example, profit maximization in a world of certainty underlies the economic theory of the firm, yet this assumption cannot be equated with the basic premise underlying the literature of capital budgeting, that is, maximization of the market value of ownership interests in a world of uncertainty. Attitudes toward risk must be incorporated into the analysis.

As to the problem at hand—the treatment of depreciation—even the "realistic" model which Keynes popularized is not without pitfalls. Keynes did recognize that uncertainty was a factor and it played a major role in his analysis of investment spending and the business cycle.[12] In fact, his major reason for developing the marginal efficiency of capital concept was not that he wished to explore the finer points of calculation but that he intended to use it as part of his general theory. Consequently, his attention focused mainly on the slope of the curve and on the reasons for fluctuations in it over time. The fact that the marginal efficiency of capital schedule contains assumptions as to the depreciation allowance and the rate at which depreciation is reinvested which differ from the accounting data that would be used in practice to determine the dollar yields either escaped him or was of no concern to him. Periodically, it seems these points are discovered or rediscovered. Ezra Solomon's 1956 article,[13] which is perhaps the most widely quoted, is a case in point. Even his concern is with the reinvestment assumption as it applied to the

[10]New York: Columbia University Press. See, for example, George A. Wing, "Capital Budgeting Circa 1915," *Journal of Finance*, Vol. 20, No. 3 (September, 1965), pp. 472–79.

[11]See, for example, Joel Dean, "Measuring the Productivity of Capital," *Harvard Business Review*, Vol. 32, No. 1 (January-February, 1954), pp. 120–30.

[12]He was, however, vague in suggesting a method of quantifying this allowance. Instead, he sought refuge in the observation that ". . . human decisions affecting the future . . . cannot depend on strict mathematical expectation, since the basis for making such calculations does not exist." *Op. cit.*, p. 163. Nevertheless, work in this area is proceeding along lines which build upon subjective-probabilistic foundations. It may yet result in a solution to the problem which Keynes felt was intractable. See William Fellner, *Probability and Profit* (Homewood: Irwin, 1965).

[13]Ezra Solomon, "The Arithmetic of Capital-Budgeting Decisions," *Journal of Business*, Vol. 29, No. 2 (April, 1956), pp. 124–30.

whole of the dollar yield, or, in capital budgeting parlance, to the net cash flow rather than the depreciation component. A more detailed analysis of this problem can be found in the works of Hunt[14] and Merrett and Sykes.[15]

A simple example can best illustrate the nature of the assumptions underlying the marginal efficiency of capital schedule. Suppose a firm is considering a capital project with an outlay of $2,361.60 resulting in an annual net cash flow of $1,000 a year for four years. The asset has no scrap value. The net cash flows are defined as the sum of the anticipated after-tax profits and noncash expense. In this case assume the latter is solely depreciation. For the present at least, assume also that the accounting technique for depreciating the asset is unknown. The rate of discount which equates the annual net cash flows to the original cost of the asset is as follows:

$$\$2,361.60 = \frac{\$1,000}{(1+r)} + \frac{\$1,000}{(1+r)^2} + \frac{\$1,000}{(1+r)^3} + \frac{\$1,000}{(1+r)^4};$$

$$r = 25 \text{ percent.}$$

This rate can be called the marginal efficiency of capital for this investment opportunity.

Implicit in the discounting process, however, are the figures for net income and depreciation. The annual dollar income is $590.40, or 25 percent of $2,361.90. The depreciation is $1,000 − $590.40, or $409.60. The results of reinvestment at 25 percent are shown in Table 1.

TABLE 1. *Reinvestment results*

End of year	Depreciation	Amount
1	$409.60 (1.25)^3	$ 800.00
2	409.60 (1.25)^2	640.00
3	409.60 (1.25)	512.00
4	409.60	409.60
		$2,361.60

If one applies the neoclassical technique to a finite income stream, he can read into it different figures for depreciation and net income. Here the rate of interest (or more appropriately, the cost of capital) is given.

[14]Hunt, *op. cit.*, pp. 9–37.
[15]A. J. Merrett and Allen Sykes, *The Finance and Analysis of Capital Projects* (New York: Wiley, 1963), pp. 33–43 and 163–71.

Assume that it is 10 percent. Then:

$$P = \frac{\$1,000}{(1-.10)} + \frac{\$1,000}{(1-.10)^2} + \frac{\$1,000}{(1-.10)^3} + \frac{\$1,000}{(1-.10)^4};$$

$$P = \$909.04 + \$826.45 + \$751.31 + \$683.01;$$

$$= \$3,169.86.$$

The present value of the cash flows is greater than the outlay. The net present value or addition to total profits that comes from adopting the project is $\$3,169.86 - \$2,361.60 = \$808.26$.

In this example, instead of dealing with a rate which equates the cash flows with the original outlay, that is, with a rate of return on the investment, one is asking another question: What is the annual depreciation allowance which will recoup the original outlay, recognizing that there is a cost of 10 percent per annum in employing these funds in this project? A depreciation allowance of $745.01 will satisfy this condition. When discounted at 10 percent it recoups the original investment of $2,361.60. Similarly an annual net income of $254.99 when discounted at 10 percent will equal the net present value of $808.26.[16]

Now drop the assumption that the accounting technique for depreciating the asset is unknown. Assume that the annual cash flow has been the sum of the straight line depreciation allowance of $590.40 ($2,361.60 ÷ 4) plus the after-tax accounting profit or net income of $409.60. Then the rate of return on the original outlay is 17.34 percent ($409.60 ÷ $2,361.60).[17] The reason that the depreciation figure in the former example becomes the profit figure in the latter stems from the differences in the reinvest-

---

[16]To calculate depreciation:

$$\$2,361.60 = x\left[\frac{1-(1.10)^4}{.10}\right];$$

$$\$2,361.60 = 3.16987x;$$

$$x = \$745.01.$$

To calculate profit:

$$\$1,000 - \$745.01 = \$254.99$$

$$\$254.99\left[\frac{1-(1.10)^{-4}}{.10}\right] =$$

$$\$254.99\,(3.16987) = \$808.28.$$

The discrepancy of $0.02 is due to rounding in the tables employed.

[17]One could, of course, use some form of accelerated depreciation which would change the profit figure and hence the return on the original outlay. Regardless of the depreciation technique, a zero reinvestment rate is still implicit in the "accounting approach."

ment assumptions. Implicit in the "accounting approach" is a reinvestment rate of zero. If a reinvestment assumption of less than 25 percent were introduced, as it was in the present value approach, then the annual net income would fall toward $409.60 and the size of the depreciation allowance would rise toward $590.40.

Thus we have three separate values for depreciation and three separate figures for net income. These are summarized in Table 2.

TABLE 2. *Values of depreciation and net income*

Technique	Net income	Depreciation
Marginal efficiency of capital	$590.40	$409.60
Accounting approach	409.60	590.40
Present value	254.99	745.01

Each has been derived under different assumptions. In the marginal efficiency of capital schedule, capital is recovered by reinvesting depreciation at 25 percent. In the accounting approach no reinvestment assumption is made, and under the present value technique the cost of capital is considered in arriving at the depreciation allowance. The net income figures in each instance follow accordingly. None of these figures necessarily results in a measure of net income that would be completely satisfactory to an economist.

Since the differences in figures result from the assumptions implied in the procedures employed, it appears that any "correct" approach to budgeting capital would include provisions for making these assumptions explicit.

III.

In this article I have attempted to compare the treatment of depreciation in economic theory, at least as the theory pertains to the firm, with the role accorded it in capital budgeting. It is apparent that the tools inherited from economics contained implicit assumptions which were of minor consequence in the literature of a market-oriented discipline but which cannot be ignored in a firm-oriented subject such as business finance.

5

The Consideration of Risk and Uncertainty in Capital Investment Analyses *

JOHN R. CANADA

This article will summarize a broad cross-section of approaches or procedures which can be used to consider the risk and uncertainty in capital investment analyses. These approaches can be categorized roughly into two main groups according to degree of sophistication involved. The two groupings are listed below. Some of the names of the approaches are long-established and some are arbitrarily used by this author.

A. Basic, Traditional Approaches
  1. Assumed certainty
  2. Conservative adjusting
  3. Risk discounting
  4. Sensitivity study
B. Advanced Approaches
  1. Probabilistic monetary
  2. Decision tree
  3. Expectation-variance
  4. Variable discounting
  5. Statistical decision theory
  6. Miscellaneous models and rules

BASIC, TRADITIONAL APPROACHES

Assumed Certainty

The most common approach presently used for making economic analysis is to "assume certainty", i.e., use only single estimates for each of the individual elements so as to arrive at a single value for the measure of merit. The estimates are usually intended to be expected values, so that the

*From *Management International Review*, Vol. 7, No. 6, 1967, pp. 47–55. Reproduced by permission.

resulting measure of merit is some kind of approximation of the expected outcome. The effect of risk or uncertainty in the estimates of the individual elements is taken into account only subjectively. This approach, sometimes coupled with one or more of the next three approaches, is the economy study procedure traditionally advocated in engineering textbooks (1, 11). This has flourished in practice because it requires less estimating information and is less difficult to perform than other quantitative means. However, it entails the weakness of failing to explicitly consider variation.

Conservative Adjusting

The conservative adjusting approach is an offshoot of the assumed certainty approach in which any or all element estimates are adjusted in a conservative direction to reflect the uncertainty of those estimates. For example, estimated periodic receipts may be adjusted downward, estimated periodic disbursements may be adjusted upward, and/or estimated project life may be shortened. John McArthur (21) has made efforts to gain quantitative accuracy in applying this approach when considering the variation of project life only. He developed tables which show what "adjusted economic life" is appropriate for various skewness and model characteristics of life distributions.

The conservative adjusting approach is weak, for it involves difficult and subjective estimates of how much adjustment should be made for varying degrees of risk or uncertainty. Further, in adjusting several elements at once, one may tend to be inconsistent and overly conservative in the final calculated analysis results.

Risk Discounting

The risk discounting approach is like the assumed certainty approach except that the standard for the minimum acceptable rate of return is varied according to the associated degree of risk. In general, the greater the degree of risk or uncertainty, the higher the minimum acceptable rate of return used. Elaborations can be found in Grant and Ireson (11, pp. 143–144) and in Bierman and Smidt (4, Chap. 9). This approach is weak because the specification of what interest rate is appropriate for what degree of risk is difficult and subjective and because it fails whenever a project has a very short life such that discounting has little effect on the calculated results. Also, the approach can give results which are opposite to what is intended when costs only are being considered, for a higher interest rate to reflect higher risk would result in a lower weighting of any future costs.

Sensitivity Study

The final basic, traditional approach, which is also commonly used to supplement the assumed certainty approach, is the performance of subsequent sensitivity analyses. A sensitivity study involves changing estimates of one or more elements to one or more possible alternate values of interest and subsequently determining the effect on the analysis outcome under the new condition(s). This procedure gives some indication of the effect if one or more of the original estimates were either too optimistic or too pessimistic. Often, sensitivity studies are pursued with the aim of determining just how much change in one or more elements of an analysis will just reverse a decision among alternatives.

It is difficult for one to draw precise conclusions about the possible effect of combinations of errors in estimates of element outcomes when performing sensitivity studies. Although this approach is often cited as a good means of exploring the effects of risk one must conclude that it has the limitations of lacking conciseness and comprehensiveness.

Now that we have briefly examined four closely-related approaches which are commonly used and advocated but which are quite limited in facilitating the explicit consideration of risk and uncertainty, let us turn to descriptions of more advanced, sophisticated approaches. Several of these advanced approaches seem to have good potential for increased future usefulness, so those approaches will be discussed in some detail.

ADVANCED APPROACHES

Probabilistic Monetary

The probabilistic monetary approach involves constructing a mathematical model or models of the prospective investment project or projects to reflect the variation of elements thought to be important in the analysis and from this determining desired parameters or characteristics of the probability distribution of the measure of merit. The results of a study using this approach could be in the form of: 1. expected outcomes or measures of merit (such as expected net present worth); or 2. expected outcomes together with some measures of the variabilities of those outcomes; or 3. shapes of probability distributions of the outcomes.

If a probabilistic monetary model involves simple variation functions for the individual elements considered then sometimes it can be mathematically manipulated so as to obtain directly the desired parameters of characteristics of the measure of merit. Use of the Taylor Series expansion is often convenient for obtaining analytical approximations. On the other hand, if the model involves variation functions such that the model cannot be handled feasibly by analytical mathematics, then a practical way to obtain approximations of the desired parameters or characteristics of the measure of merit is to use the Monte Carlo technique of simulation. The technique of Monte Carlo simulation involves repeated generation of random outcomes for elements or variables which vary according to their respective distributions, and putting these outcomes together so as to form estimates of the desired distribution information.* The Monte Carlo technique is quite powerful, and its practicability is greatly facilitated by the use of digital computers to perform all needed outcome generations and calculations. One advantage of the technique is that it can be used so that one can take into account non-independence of outcomes of the various elements or factors important to the analysis if the nature of the non-independence can be specified.

The information which can be obtained by use of the probabilistic monetary approach can be quite useful as opposed to the information obtained from one or more of the basic, traditional approaches. As an example, David Hertz (13) reported on a rather elaborate study in which there were 9 elements considered. In using the assumed certainty approach the calculated rate of return was 25.2%. Using the Monte Carlo technique to evaluate a probabilistic monetary model, the expected return was 14.6% and further valuable information on the variability of that return was made available.

Decision Tree

Another approach which provides for explicit consideration of the risk and uncertainty of the future is the use of decision tree or branching analyses. The name comes from the appearance of the diagram which results from tracing out the future alternatives and decision points which can result from an initial decision. Quantification of the outcomes and subjective probabilities for each alternative together with the accompany-

---

*(*Editor's comment*): Cummings' article in Part II illustrates how the Monte Carlo technique can be used to estimate a distribution which is based on a set of separate probability distributions.

ing analysis enables one to make an initial decision which includes consideration of the risk and effect of the future.

Two good articles on the use of decision trees were published by Magee in the *Harvard Business Review* (18) (19). Magee later expanded the article material into a short book (20) which features descriptions of the decision tree approach in several different investment analysis situations such as plant modernization programs, new product introduction, and research and development exploitation.

The idea of applying decision methodology to the analysis of sequential investment decisions over time seems to have good possibilities for future development. The main drawbacks of this approach are the common difficulties of performing the needed voluminous computations in cases where there are a large number of decision points and related outcomes.* However, it should be acknowledged that digital computer programs can be written to handle these computations.

Expectation-variance

This relatively new approach to the consideration of risk and uncertainty is also commonly referred to by the name "certainty equivalence". In general, the certainty equivalent of an investment, V, can be said to be a function of the expected value of the outcome or measure of merit of the investment, u, and the variation of that outcome, σ. While the nature of this function is open to question in most cases, there is general agreement that increases in an investment's expected outcome tend to increase the desirability of the investment, while increases in the variation tend to decrease the desirability of the investment. One simple model which reflects this is:

$$V = u - A\sigma, \tag{1}$$

where A is commonly referred to as a "coefficient of risk aversion." Morris (22, pp. 215–216) and Farrar (10, p. 26) have recognized the relation of the expectation-variance and expected utility approach by stating that the choice of the coefficient of risk aversion, A, represents a measure of the utility associated with the confidence with which an investment is made. Farrar further points out that as long as there is a diminishing marginal utility of money (which is a reasonable condition for a very wide range of

*(*Editor's comment*): Heuristic programming may be used to prune the decision tree.

investment situations) the coefficient of risk aversion is equal to the negative of $\frac{1}{2}$ of the second derivative of the utility vs. monetary outcome function evaluated at the mean monetary outcome. Incidentally, Farrar developed a specialized version of the expectation-variance approach in the form of a mathematical programming model which presents good possibilities for further development for general investment analyses.

Variable Discounting

Another approach is to use a time-varying rate of discounting such that the further one estimates into the future, the progressively higher will be the rate of discounting. This approach has been advocated by J. Morley English (8) (9) as a means of taking into account the increasing uncertainty coincident with more distant future by lowering the weighting of future outcomes relative to prior outcomes. As an example of such a time-varying interest rate, the interest rate at any time in the future, t, could be said to vary according to the function

$$r(t) = r_0 e^{at}, \tag{2}$$

where r_0 is the initial (risk-free) rate and a (which is greater than zero) is the coefficient which determines the rate of increase. As another example, an "operationally useful discount function" advocated by English in (8) is:

$$r(t) = \frac{1}{t} \log_e \frac{1}{1 - r_0 t} \tag{3}$$

The advantage of this approach is that it provides a way to reconcile the differences in risk caused by differences in timing. However, it should be noted that apparently the use of time-varying discount functions has not attracted much attention, for there is a dearth of further development and integration of them in the literature.

Statistical Decision Theory

An approach which has been used very little in investment analyses to date but which has possibilities for future development and application is the use of the concepts and techniques of statistical decision theory. Statistical decision theory can be viewed as a body of knowledge which integrates the processes of collecting the data, drawing the inferences from the data, and determining the decision. It often involves the use of Bayesian statistics to adjust "priori" subjective probabilities to more reliable "posteriori" probabilities based on the results of sample evidence. A more complete description is outside the scope of this paper, but the interested reader is referred to Chernoff and Moses (5), Schlaifer (25), and Weiss (28).

There are some drawbacks to statistical decision theory which limit its applicability in the analysis of the effect of risk and uncertainty in economic evaluations of capital investments. The most important is that analyses for investment decisions do not permit sampling in the usual sense because of the lack, in most cases, of a parent population from which to sample. Instead, they involve estimations which are based, at least in part, on past data. One goal of statistical decision theory is the determination of how much study cost is justified in order to gain certain reductions in uncertainty in the decision problem. Robert Schlaifer's (25) development of a rationale for calculating the expected opportunity loss or expected cost of uncertainty has provided an approach for achieving this goal. Weinwurm (27) presents an easy to-understand example of the application of this approach.

Miscellaneous Models and Rules

There are numerous specialized models which have been developed for application to particular investment situations involving risk and uncertainty. For example, Naslund and Whinston (23) developed a mathematical programming model for choosing a group of investment projects so as to maximize the monetary gains subject to probabilistic constraints on the maximum loss during each of the various time periods under consideration. As another example, Eisen and Leibowitz (7), showed how to handle probabilistic variation in determining when to replace randomly deteriorating equipment. As a final example, Gordon Kaufman (16) developed procedures for making sequential investment decisions under uncertainty for restrictive situations such that the investor's expectations about future investment opportunities are taken into account.

The existence of some arbitrary decision rules for choosing between alternatives when there is the element of complete uncertainty about certain probabilities should be mentioned. William T. Morris (22) gives a good description of these rules which are variously known as the maximin or minimax rule, the maximax or minimin rule, the Savage rule, the Laplace rule, and the Hurwicz rule. No attempt will be made to describe the rules here, but it should be mentioned that the choice of a rule such as one of these is often rather arbitrarily based on taste, intuition, and judgment of appropriateness for the particular situation. The greatest defense for the use of any of these rules or principles is that their use will promote explicitness or consistency in decision-making.

SUMMARY

This paper has summarized a broad cross-section of approaches or procedures which can be used to quantitatively consider the risk and uncertainty in capital investment analyses. These procedures are, for the most part, disjoint. Some have broad application, some are limited. Most of the procedures are still in need of development and/or testing in actual use. Like all formal analysis tools, use of any such approach should serve to supplement and not supplant executive judgment. Because of the importance of investment decisions to the welfare of the firm, it seems safe to prognosticate that the use of quantitative techniques and approaches such as the above will become increasingly important in the future. Hence, it behooves the analyst of investment projects to be aware of these developments, so as to be able to judge which can be applied or adapted usefully for his particular investment analysis needs.

REFERENCES

1. Baris, N. N., *Economic Analysis for Engineering and Managerial Decision Making*, McGraw-Hill, New York, 1962.
2. Bernhard, Richard H., *The Theory of Capital Investment Planning*, Ph.D. Dissertation, Cornell University, 1961.
3. Biermann, H., Fouraker, L. E., and Jaedicke, R. K., *Quantitative Analysis for Business Decisions*, Irwin, Illinois, 1961.
4. Bierman, Harold, Jr., and Smidt, Seymour, *The Capital Budgeting Decision*, Macmillan Co., New York, 1960.
5. Chernoff, Herman and Moses, Lincoln E., *Elementary Decision Theory*, John Wiley and Sons, New York, 1959.
6. Cramer, Robert H., and Smith, Bernard E., "Decision Models for the Selection of Research Projects", *Engineering Economist*, Vol. 9, No. 2, Winter, 1964.
7. Eisen, M., and Leibowitz, M., "Replacement of Randomly Deteriorating Equipment", *Management Science*, Vol. 9, No. 2, January, 1963, pp. 268–276.
8. English, J. Morley, "A Discount Function for Comparing Economic Alternatives", *Journal of Industrial Engineering*, Vol. XVI, No. 2, March–April, 1965.
9. English, J. Morley, "New Approaches to Economic Comparison for Engineering Projects", *Journal of Industrial Engineering*, Vol. XII, No. 6, November–December, 1961, pp. 375–378.
10. Farrar, Donald Eugene, *The Investment Decision Under Uncertainty* (reprint of Ph.D. Dissertation, Harvard University, 1961), Prentice-Hall, New Jersey, 1962.
11. Grant, Eugene, and Ireson, W. Grant, *Principles of Engineering Economy*, Ronald Press, 4. Edition, 1960.

12. Hirschleifer, Jack, "The Bayesian Approach to Statistical Decision: An Exposition", *The Journal of Business*, Vol. XXIV, No. 4, October, 1961.
13. Hertz, David B., "Risk Analysis in Capital Investment", *Harvard Business Review*, Vol. 42, No. 1, January–February, 1964.
14. Hillier, Frederick S., "The Derivation of Probabilistic Information for the Evaluation of Risky Investments", *Management Science*, Vol. 9, No. 3, April, 1963.
15. Hillier, Frederick S., "The Evaluation of Risky Interrelated Investments", Technical Report No. 73, Department of Statistics, Stanford University, July 24, 1964.
16. Kaufman, Gordon M., "Sequential Investment Analysis Under Uncertainty", *Journal of Business*, Vol. 36, No. 1, January, 1963, pp. 39–64.
17. Kells, Lyman N., *Calculus*, Prentice-Hall, New York, 1947.
18. Magee, John F., "Decision Trees for Decision Making", *Harvard Business Review*, Vol. 42, No. 4, July–August, 1964.
19. Magee, John F., "How to Use Decision Trees in Capital Investment", *Harvard Business Review*, Vol. 42, No. 5, September–October, 1964.
20. Magee, John F., *The Decision Tree*, Arthur D. Little, Inc., 1964.
21. McArthur, John H., "The Estimated Economic Life of an Investment Under Uncertainty", *Engineering Economist*, Vol. 5, No. 4, Spring, 1960, pp. 16–40.
22. Morris, William T., *Engineering Economy*, Irwin, Illinois, 1960.
23. Naslund, Bertil, and Whinston, Andrew, "A Model of Multi-Period Investment Under Uncertainty", *Management Science*, Vol. 8, No. 2, January, 1962, pp. 184–200.
24. Roberts, Harry V., "The New Business Statistics", *Journal of Business*, Vol. 33, January, 1960.
25. Schlaifer, Robert, *Probability and Statistics for Business Decisions*, McGraw-Hill, New York, 1959.
26. Wald, Abraham, *Statistical Decision Functions*, John Wiley and Sons, New York, 1950.
27. Weinwurm, Ernest H., "Measuring Uncertainty in Managerial Decision Making", *Management International*, Vol. 3, No. 3/4, 1963.
28. Weiss, Lionel, *Statistical Decision Theory*, McGraw-Hill, New York, 1961.

6

The Firm's Optimal Debt – Equity Combination and the Cost of Capital *

WILLIAM J. BAUMOL and BURTON G. MALKIEL

I. THE PROBLEM

This paper undertakes to provide a model that at least offers an approach to an optimality analysis of the firm's capital structure. In this construct transactions costs and risk will turn out to play important roles just as they do in the theory of money, where, without them, it is difficult to see why anyone would want to hold any money at all. In addition, corporation and personal income taxes will be integrated explicitly into the analysis. It will be seen that the Modigliani–Miller[1] result, which states that any financing decision is necessarily optimal, is an artifact (albeit a highly instructive one) of their frictionless world, in which we should never be surprised to encounter behavior about as peculiar as the permanent flight of a ball that is thrown in a frictionless physical universe. It should be made clear, however, that this paper is not intended in any way to be critical of Modigliani and Miller (henceforward M and M). On the contrary, it will rely very heavily on their pathbreaking work.

In addition to its attempt to provide a formal optimality analysis this paper undertakes several other tasks. It describes exactly what is involved in the M and M "homemade leverage" process, which the individual investor utilizes to provide for himself whatever degree of risk he wishes to undertake when investing in a company. We show exactly what the investor must buy or sell to achieve any specified degree of

*From *The Quarterly Journal of Economics*, Vol. LXXXI, No. 4, November 1967, pp. 547–578. Reproduced by permission.

[1]Franco Modigliani and Merton H. Miller, "The Cost of Capital, Corporation Finance, and the Theory of Investment," *American Economic Review*, XLVIII (June 1958), 261–97.

leverage and the extent to which specific institutional obstacles impede this process. We describe also how the formal analysis of corporation finance fits in with the standard value theory of economic analysis and, in the process, reconcile some apparent inconsistencies between the two, particularly in the definition and measurement of the "cost of capital."

II. A FEW FORMAL RELATIONSHIPS

In order to get on with the substance of the analysis we will assume throughout that the goal of the firm is maximization of the wealth of its stockholders. We begin by providing a few simple and fairly well-known relationships that will prove useful in the discussion that follows. By definition, earnings per dollar of equity are given by

$$i = (X - rD)/S \tag{1}$$

where i = earnings (after interest payments) per dollar of equity
X = total company earnings before deduction of interest payments
S = total equity at current market value
D = total debt at current market value and
r = the effective rate of interest payments on company debt (D).

Given the prospective earnings of the firm and the riskiness of its operations, then, according to M and M the market values D and S, its debt and equity, will satisfy the relationship

$$S + D = V \text{ (constant)}. \tag{2}$$

The surprising feature of this proposition is its implication that the market value of the firm, $S + D$, is totally independent of the firm's capital structure—the ratio between its debt and equity. No matter whether the company's indebtedness is heavy or light, given the expected value and the other moments of its anticipated earnings stream, $S + D$ will remain equal to V. The reason this is so in their analysis is that if a company's leverage, its debt/equity ratio, D/S, is not at the level desired by some particular stockholder, he can utilize a process which M and M call "homemade leverage" to rearrange his own holdings in a way that achieves for him exactly the financial returns that would flow from his preferred value of D/S. Suppose for simplicity that the individual holds some stocks and some bonds in our company and that he wishes the company would increase its leverage (increase its expected return per share even though this increases his risk). He can achieve the same effect by selling some of his bonds and using the money to purchase more of the company's stocks, thus increasing his expected overall rate of return as well as its variance. Even after he has sold all of his bonds he can increase the leverage of his personal portfolio further by borrowing money (in effect selling his personal bond) and using it to purchase still more stock. In this way he can offset completely any leverage decision by the company management. As a result, to each and every stockholder, any financial structure for the company will be just as good as any other and so equation (2) must hold regardless of the ratio between D and S.

III. A DIAGRAMMATIC APPROACH TO COST OF CAPITAL

To examine the effects of transactions costs it becomes convenient to utilize a graphic procedure including an indifference curve representation of investor attitudes on risk and expected earnings.

In Fig. I let CC' represent the opportunity locus or transformation curve giving the combinations of expected earnings on equity and safety levels corresponding to different leverage ratios. On the horizontal axis we measure expected earnings per dollar of equity and on the vertical axis we have some sort of index of "safety"—a magnitude that varies inversely with some measure of risk, however selected.[2]

Now from the point of view of the stockholder the optimal financial arrangement is given by the point of tangency, D, between one of his indifference curves[3] I_1, and the opportunity locus CC'. Suppose instead that management decides on the leverage ratio corresponding to some

---

[2]The equation for the opportunity locus is $y = f(\bar{\imath})$, where y represents safety level and $\bar{\imath}$ represents expected earnings. The definition of safety level is not obvious and a number of alternatives are possible. Among the more intuitively attractive are a measure which takes the safety level to be some fixed number of standard deviations below expected earnings:

$$y_1 = \bar{\imath} - k\sigma.$$

Alternatively, we may assume that there is some plausible range of earnings such that earnings outside this range are so improbable that they can be neglected. Let $i_{min} = X_{min} - \tau D$ be the lower bound of this range. Then a second possible definition of safety level is

$$y_2 = X_{min} - \tau D.$$

It will be noted that the opportunity loci lie entirely below and to the right of a 45 degree line through the origin because y, the safety level, will always be lower than the expected earnings, the value of the abscissa, except if there is no risk, in which case they will both be equal.

[3]For the moment we ignore the complications introduced by differences in the indifference maps of the various stockholders. We will see later that their consequences are not so serious as they appear to be at this point.

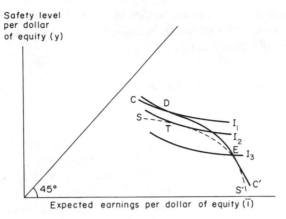

FIG. I.

other point, say *E*. In that case, if the investor can do nothing about it, he will simply end up on a lower indifference curve I_3.

But, if homemade leverage is free, the investor can do something about it. On his own initiative he can move to any point on *CC'* and so he can simply proceed to his optimal point *D*. The choice between financing by debt and equity therefore makes no difference to him and all capital has the same cost as far as he or any other stockholder is concerned.

However, if homemade leverage incurs transactions costs, as it does in reality, he cannot move from *E* to any point on *CC'*. Instead he may have open to him only the stockholder opportunity locus *SS'* which is somewhat less advantageous to him than *CC'*. It will coincide with *CC'* at the company decision point, *E*, because no transactions costs are incurred in homemaking of leverage at this point, and will perhaps curve more sharply toward the axes. With any given degree of homemade leverage, his net earnings may be less than if the company itself had chosen that leverage ratio, since the stockholder's expected stream of net earnings will be reduced by a stream of payments equal in present value to his transactions-cost outlay. We will see later that in practice the relative shapes of *SS'* and *CC'* are not exactly as they are shown here, but for our present discussion that does not matter. What is important here is that the investor will end up at a second-best point of tangency, point *T* on *SS'*. This will get him onto an indifference curve I_2, better than that through the company decision point *E* but not so good as that at the optimum point *D*.

We see then that, once transactions costs enter, the financial structure of the company is not irrelevant to the stockholder, and from his point of view there is an optimal point, *D*, because any other point must land him on a lower indifference curve.

IV. TRANSACTIONS COSTS AND TAXES IN PRACTICE

We will now try to specify the transactions expenses and other costs involved in homemade leverage in real capital markets.[4] We will first discuss matters in general terms and after examining specific illustrations in which the numbers are chosen to be representative of those encountered in practice, we will show how the geometry of the analysis can be used to determine the optimal financial structure.

First consider the case where the company's leverage is lower than that desired by the investor (he wishes to move toward the right in Fig. I). To increase his earnings and his risk, the investor must simultaneously purchase stocks and borrow money. Normally he will do this by buying stocks on margin. His brokerage costs will be greater than would otherwise have been the case simply because he must purchase a larger volume of securities than he would if the firm had provided the degree of leverage he desired. In addition, our investor must pay the interest on his loan, the real interest rate being significantly higher than that which is normally paid by the corporation. Once the individual has taken full advantage of the margin permitted him by law he can borrow from other sources, but, since he cannot legally use his stocks as security for the loan, his borrowing rate is now likely to rise substantially. All of this means that if the stockholder wishes to move toward the right of the company's decision point (point *E* in Fig. I), as he must do if he wishes to increase the leverage in his holdings (higher expected earnings but a lower safety level), he will find a difference between his opportunity locus *SS'* and the company locus *CC'*, and the distance between them will normally

---

[4]In a long-run comparative statics analysis it is not legitimate to include the readjustment costs of current stockholders who are induced to change their portfolios when the company varies the composition of its funds. In our analysis we must consider different company leverage ratios as alternative long-run choices, and the transactions cost incurred in the homemade leverage process must be that of the investor who is switching his holdings from cash to securities, given whatever leverage ratio happens to have been selected by the firm. It should also be noted that we are not the first to introduce taxes and transactions costs into a discussion of financial decision-making. For example, John Lintner has previously examined the effects of transactions costs and taxes on optimal financial policy in a somewhat different context. See his "Dividends, Earnings, Leverage, Stock Prices and the Supply of Capital to Corporations," *Review of Economics and Statistics*, XLIV (Aug. 1962), 243–69.

increase considerably the further one gets from *E*. For some (e.g., institutional) investors whose borrowing for this purpose is limited by law or tradition, the individual opportunity loci *SS'* may simply fall vertically, at least after a point, i.e., there will for them be an absolute limit to the extent to which they can increase the leverage of their holdings via the homemade leverage process.

Consider next what happens if the investor feels the company's stock is overlevered, i.e., he wishes to move to the left of the company decision point *E*. Now he will find (again neglecting tax considerations for the moment) that *homemade leverage imposes on him virtually no added transactions costs*. The investor simply purchases a combination of stocks and bonds rather than stocks alone, and, since this does not affect the total volume of his security purchases, he can do it with little change in brokerage cost. Indeed, the transactions charges for dealing in bonds are often slightly smaller than those applicable to common stocks. Moreover, the cost of this process is not changed by the extent to which he uses it because when he lends, the relevant rate of interest will not vary with the magnitude of his bond purchases—unlike the case where he borrows to increase leverage, when the rate of interest is likely to go up with the volume of his borrowing. Thus, to the left of the company decision point, *E*, the company locus *CC'* and the individual locus *SS'* will correspond for a stretch. The investor who buys a combination of

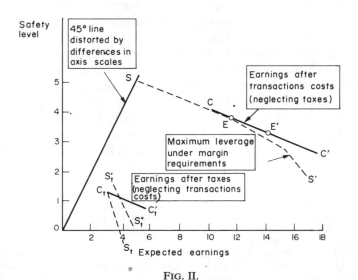

FIG. II.

stocks and bonds can receive precisely his pro rata share of the interest payments and earnings made by the corporation, and the brokerage cost in purchasing a bond is not materially different from that on a stock.

Thus the individual opportunity locus takes the general form shown by SS' in Fig. II. We note also that the individual locus extends leftward for a considerable stretch SC beyond the end of the company locus. This additional segment of the individual locus involves what might be considered homemade negative leverage—a proportion of bonds in the individual portfolio so great that its safety is greater than that which would be provided by an unlevered equity stream, i.e., by company stocks in the case where the company's debt was zero (point C). The left-hand end, point S, of the individual's opportunity locus corresponds to a portfolio consisting exclusively of bonds.

Next we consider the role of taxes and the fact that interest payments, unlike dividends, are not subject to the corporate income tax. The first effect of corporate income taxes is to reduce proportionately both the expected earnings and the safety level of the shareholder.[5] More important, the difference in tax treatment of debt and equity will tend to increase substantially the divergence between the company opportunity locus CC' and the stockholder opportunity locus SS', because the stockholder is not able through the homemade leverage process to duplicate the tax advantages available to the corporation. This is so because the corporation, by shifting from equity to debt, can actually increase the total amount of interest plus dividend payments that can be distributed to its security holders. It is as if the company provided by itself each dollar of dividend payments made, but received a matching grant from the government of one dollar for each dollar of interest distributed. In fact, this tax arrangement can cause the two opportunity loci to intersect as they do in the lower left-hand corner of Fig. II (curves $C_tC'_t$ and $S'_tS''_t$). The individual who wants little leverage may actually gain by investing in a highly levered company that obtains the maximal tax advantage, and then purchasing bonds in sufficient quantity to undo the leverage to whatever extent he desires.[6]

---

[5]This is so because the safety level itself is a potential level of corporate income—one that is relatively low and so it is also reduced in proportion to the tax rate. Of course, if the safety level corresponded to corporate earnings less than $25,000 per year, or if it involved a loss, a lower tax rate (or even a rebate) would apply to the safety level and the conclusion in the text would have to be modified.

[6]The tax advantage of capital gains can produce an offsetting divergence between the individual and the company opportunity locus. The individual who unlevers his holdings, in effect, accepts a contract to receive part of his payments in the form of interest on which he

One other related observation completes our a priori discussion of the influences affecting the shape of the opportunity loci. If the firm is subject to a rising marginal cost of borrowing, the CC' curve may begin to fall more steeply at its lower end (it will curve downward toward the right)[7] and the degree of divergence between the two loci may be reduced (since the individual stockholder who wishes to increase leverage for himself may be able to escape some of the rising interest costs that the company must pay). Moreover, the introduction of a risk concept more general than the "safety level," that has been used here for illustrative purposes only, would provide additional reasons to expect that the company opportunity locus would be nonlinear. For example, consider the inclusion of the risk of insolvency. Even if insolvency did not lead to the ultimate ruin of the stockholders through the liquidation of the assets of the company at forced-sale prices, it entails, at least, a costly reorganization and disruptive effects on company operations that would impair the expected earnings stream. It is reasonable to suppose that, after a maximal "safe level" of debt has been reached, perceived risk increases sharply with any increase in leverage.

V. A FEW COMMENTS ON THE OPPORTUNITY LOCI

It should be made clear to the reader that the curves in Fig. II have not been drawn in an arbitrary manner. Rather, they have been based on rather careful calculations intended to constitute realistic numerical examples. Thus, the curves CC' and SS' which take into account transactions costs but not taxes, are based on the following assumptions whose empirical basis is described in the Appendix: That there is a 1 per cent commission on the purchase of stocks and a $\frac{3}{4}$ per cent commission on the purchase of bonds, and that an individual can borrow on margin at

---

must pay his marginal personal income tax rate, and none of which will be plowed back to receive favorable tax treatment at the lower capital gains rate. On the other hand, the individual who buys stocks on margin can receive part of his income in favorably taxed capital gains and can deduct the interest he pays on his personal debt at ordinary marginal income tax rates. For individuals to whom this can make a very significant difference, then, the relation between individual and company opportunity loci may be a bit closer to that shown in Fig. I. However, it should be recognized that some very large security holders are nonprofit institutions—foundations, universities, etc. Capital gains clearly offer them no tax advantage.

[7] If the cost of borrowing rises far enough, the lower end of the CC' curve may even begin to bend backwards—further borrowing will not only increase risk—it will also reduce the expected earnings per dollar of equity. This will occur if r exceeds $\bar{X}/(S + D)$.

a rate of $5\frac{1}{2}$ per cent while the corporation's borrowing rate is 5 per cent. Similarly, the lower curves in the figure are based on a 50 per cent corporate tax rate and on the premise that the stock purchaser is in the 50 per cent marginal tax bracket so that his capital gains are taxed at 25 per cent.

The striking conclusion demonstrated by the graph is that, even in the absence of transactions costs, homemade leverage is not an effective substitute for company leverage. Despite the fact that we have allowed for a tax advantage to the individual who buys common shares (some of the return is taxed at preferential capital gains rates), the individual cannot homemake the same menu of returns and safety levels that firms can produce by alternative leverage ratios. In the lower portion of Fig. II, we can see clearly the asymmetric effects that result when an individual rolls his own leverage and unmakes company leverage. If the company chooses a levered capital structure, the individual who desires no leverage is actually better off than he would be buying unlevered common shares directly—the relevant portion of the individual opportunity locus $S_1'S_1''$ actually lies well above the company locus. Only when the individual makes more leverage than the company has chosen, is he in a worse position than he would be if he bought common shares in a company that had itself made use of the desired amount of debt in its capital structure.[8]

It can also be shown that the shape of the curves shown in Fig. II is not a fortuitous matter of the numbers chosen in our calculation.* These curves will all have the general characteristics displayed in the diagrams (see Fig. III).

VI. CHARACTERISTICS OF AN OPTIMAL FINANCIAL STRUCTURE

We can now discuss the implications of our analysis for the nature of the firm's optimal financial decision. It will be recalled that if we ignore taxes, the company and individual opportunity loci will be as shown in the upper part of Fig. III. This suggests that it will be advantageous to

---

[8]This suggests that in practice (in contrast with a pure M and M world) the dividend payout ratio is not irrelevant to the stockholder. For example, if the degree of leverage that currently characterizes the firm is below the optimal level, then stockholders would be better off if dividends were increased and, instead, more debt were used to finance the company's investment plans.

Editor's note: For a further discussion on the shape of these curves see Appendices A and B of the unedited version of this article.

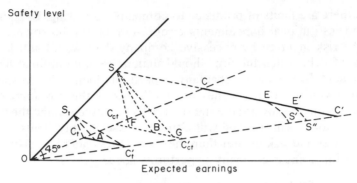

FIG. III.

stockholders for the company to move as far to the right on CC' (to borrow as much) as is consistent with prudence and legal and institutional limitations.[9] For, consider the zero tax case, for simplicity, and suppose E is the company's decision point whereas some investor would prefer E'. Homemade leverage will not permit him to reach this point because his opportunity locus $SCES'$ lies well below it. Suppose next that positions are reversed: that the stockholder wants to get to E but the company decision point is E'. Any individual opportunity locus must go through the company's decision point since the stockholder always has the option of holding a portfolio consisting exclusively of company stocks. Hence, with the company decision point moved to E' the individual opportunity locus must shift to $SCE'S''$, which it will be observed, enables the stockholder to arrange to get back to E if he wishes. As we have seen (lower curves in Fig. III) tax considerations may well make these relationships even stronger. A highly levered company may as a result offer both higher earnings and greater safety even to the investor who desires little or no leverage in his personal portfolio.

It follows that, for such a company, failure to finance enough of its investment by borrowing may indeed cause a reduction in its market value. Particularly institutional investors, whose holdings of risky high-return securities is severely circumscribed by law, may bid up the shares of more highly levered companies relative to those of our firm so that, for the two companies, the ratio between earnings and $S + D$ will no longer be equal.

---

[9]A similar conclusion is reached by Solomon. See Ezra Solomon, *The Theory of Financial Management* (New York: Columbia University Press, 1963), p. 103.

Yet, there are limits of prudence to company borrowing. Even if there were no institutional impediments circumscribing the borrowing of the firm, the risk incurred by excessive company debt would still limit the amount of debt which the firm should undertake in an optimal financial arrangement. In Fig. IV the company opportunity locus, CC', is shown to curl downward as it approaches point C'. For as the firm increases its borrowings (moves toward the right) its risk of insolvency and the interest rate on its loans will rise and will ultimately rise sharply. Thus, earnings will be lower and risk greater than they would be under the assumptions that call for a linear company opportunity locus.

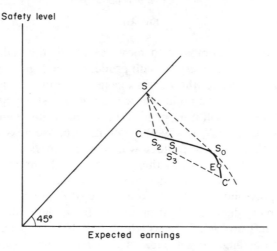

FIG. IV.

Now consider the linear segments such as SS_0, SS_1, and SS_2 of the various individual opportunity loci corresponding to the different decision points (S_0, S_1, S_2, etc.), the segments lying to the left of these decision points. These are the line segments connecting the various points on CC' with a fixed point[10] S on the 45 degree line where S lies above and to the left of CC'. Hence it is to be expected that one of these, SS_0, will be a segment of a line tangent to CC'. Point S_0, the point of tangency, will for a

---

[10]Strictly speaking, S will not be fixed for company decision points lying sufficiently far to the right. When company debt grows sufficiently great, the rate of return on debt can no longer be considered riskless. Hence a given number of bonds might now offer a lower expected return and certainly a lower minimal return. Thus, for example, the individual opportunity locus through point C' might look like S_3C' which lies entirely below the company locus. However, this observation does not appear to affect the conclusions of the text.

considerable portion of its stockholders normally represent the company's optimal financial structure. For SS_0 will then be the highest opportunity locus available to any individual investor who does not have so strong a desire to speculate that he wishes to be at a point to the right of S_0. Thus, only from point S_0 can any such stockholder reach his highest attainable indifference curve. This conclusion then has the remarkable property that it may be *independent of the shape and position of most stockholders' indifference curves.* This is so because any other company decision offers poorer opportunities (higher risks and lower earnings) to *all* stockholders who do not wish to bear extremely great risks.

In fact, it is possible that in a wide variety of cases point S_0 will be optimal for all potential stockholders—including those who prefer even greater leverage. For as Fig. II indicates, in practice, transactions costs at first only cause a very gradual displacement from linearity of the *individual* opportunity locus. On the other hand, once the firm exceeds conventional standards of prudent leverage, the *company* opportunity locus may curve sharply downward because normal debt sources will be unwilling to provide additional debt to the firm. In that case the individual locus (SS_0 and its rightward extension in Fig. IV) would not lie below the company curve CC' at any point.[11]

VII. THE REAL MARGINAL COST OF DEBT AND EQUITY

The preceding materials have immediate implications about the cost of various sources of capital from the point of view of our stockholder.

To get at the *cost* of an increment in company funds we must avoid any confusion that would result if one were to introduce into the discussion the revenues that will be produced by the investment financed with these moneys. In Fig. V we therefore show what would happen to the company opportunity locus C_1C_1' if it were to raise some additional funds and simply keep them idle. That is, the figure takes into account only the costs of these additional funds and abstracts from any yield they may subsequently produce.

Suppose first that the firm were initially at its all equity point C_1 (with a high safety level and relatively low expected earnings) and that it increased its capital by the raising of new equity. Since we are deliberately ignoring any revenues that could be obtained with the aid of these

---

[11]Still, it is conceivable, even in such a case, that a "nonoptimal" locus will for some interval lie above the "optimal" locus (SS_0 extended) at the extreme right of the diagram, and in such a case, SS_0 extended might not be preferred by all investors.

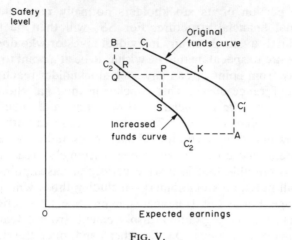

FIG. V.

funds, the added equity must cause a reduction in the expected earnings per dollar of equity (along BC_1) because earnings must now be spread over a larger amount of equity. Some change in the safety level (C_2B) is also likely to result, so that we will be brought to some new point such as C_2. Similarly, were we to start out from a highly levered position, C'_1, and just issue new bonds, this would reduce the safety level and reduce earnings per share (after the increased interest payments) and so it would land us at a point such as C'_2. There would then be some curve $C_2C'_2$ that connects these extreme points and represents the locus opportunities corresponding to different debt-to-equity ratios in the additional funds.

The difference between retained earnings and a new stock issue as means for increasing equity can readily be described in terms of our diagram. Consider, for example, the case of a company whose shareholders have no need to consume the income from their holdings. The flotation of securities usually involves very heavy transactions costs which would be escaped by retention.[12] Since these transactions costs can be translated into an equivalent stream of payments, they are tantamount to a long-term reduction in earnings. Hence the CC' curve corresponding

---

[12]The increase in equity will certainly reduce both i and σ by (9) and (10) (Appendix B) so that it may or may not change safety level, $i - k\sigma$. On the other hand, if we define the safety level as $(X_{min} - rD)/S$ (see fn. 2, p. 402), the increase in S holding D constant must certainly reduce the safety level.

to a new issue of stock will, other things being equal, lie below and to the left of the curve involving retained earnings. This means that in such a case new equity is simply an uneconomic way to raise funds unless increased earnings retention is just not possible.

Of course, the situation is changed if the shareholders want to consume the income from their holdings. In this case, a policy of retention forces the shareholder continuously to sell off part of his holdings and so it is the stockholder, rather than the corporation, who incurs the transactions costs. Even in this case, however, it is likely that retention will still frequently be the optimal method for raising new equity capital. Tax rates on capital gains are lower than those on dividend income. Moreover, the transactions costs involved in the sale of new equity issues are usually substantially larger than the brokerage costs involved in the sale of shares by small stockholders.[13]

We can also describe somewhat more explicitly the difference between the effects of new debt and that of added equity on the welfare of the shareholder. In Fig. V suppose the firm's initial financial position had corresponded to point K. If it were now to increase its debt, this would reduce expected earnings by some amount KP, and it would also reduce the safety level by an amount PS, thus moving us to a point S on the lower opportunity locus C_2C_2'. The *nominal* incremental cost of the added debt is simply KP, the amount of interest required by the funds in question, which causes a corresponding reduction in expected equity earnings. But we see that the *real* marginal cost of the debt is greater than KP since the indifference curve through the debt point, S, will lie below the indifference curve through the nominal-debt-cost point, P.

Similarly, if from K the company were to move to C_2C_2' with the help of new equity, expected earnings per dollar of equity would be decreased by some larger amount, KQ, than it would with the issue of debt. But because the leverage ratio would thereby be reduced, the variance of earnings per share would fall and there might even be an increase in safety level, QR, so that the real marginal cost of equity would then be lower than its nominal amount, QK.

---

[13]In addition many of these shareholders are in high marginal tax brackets and therefore receive after-tax dividend returns far smaller than the actual number of dollars paid. This provides an additional reason for them to prefer having new equity capital raised through retained earnings. Retention allows them to realize their returns through favorably taxed capital gains.

VIII. A MEASURE OF THE COST OF CAPITAL

We may now develop an explicit measure of cost of capital and see the effect of homemade leverage upon its magnitude. In Fig. VI we add three stockholder indifference curves to our previous diagram. The first, I_1, is tangent to the old opportunity locus at initial point K, which for simplicity is assumed to have been optimal. The second indifference curve is that tangent to the new lower opportunity locus, with optimal point E. Finally, the third indifference curve is that through point S, the increased debt point.

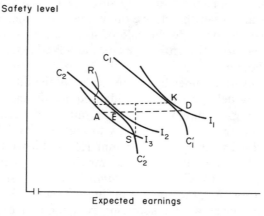

FIG. VI.

Let us define as an index of the marginal cost of capital the increase in expected earnings per dollar of equity necessary to get the stockholder back to his initial level of satisfaction after the change in financing. Again, for the moment, assume taxes and transactions costs to be zero. Let us (in analogy with the Fisher–Hirshleifer construct[14]) consider the investor to undergo a two-step adjustment process. First the added debt moves him from K to S. Then he may use homemade leverage to move himself along C_2C_2' to his optimal point E. If he does so, it is clear that from point E an annual cash payment equivalent to an increase in expected earnings ED will move him back to his initial level of utility. This, then, is the incremental cost of debt capital to him. However, had homemade leverage or even a partial adjustment been ruled out for any

[14]See Jack Hirshleifer, "On the Theory of Optimal Investment Decision," *Journal of Political Economy*, LXVI (Aug. 1958).

reason, so that he would have been forced to remain at point *S*, then he would have been on a lower indifference curve and the real incremental cost of capital (the compensating variation in earnings) would have been the larger amount, *AD*.[15]

It is easy to see that had we drawn another indifference curve through point *R* (the new equity point), then we could have produced a precisely analogous representation of the marginal cost of equity both with and without homemade leverage. With no transactions costs and taxes it is clear that the stockholder can get to optimal point *E* just as easily from *R* as he can from *S*. Thus with homemade leverage his cost of equity would also be *ED*, and we have the M and M result: with homemade leverage costless, the real marginal costs of debt and equity are always equal.

Figure VII now shows the effects of taxes and transactions costs. If the new financial decision point is *P* on C_2C_2' and *P* is not the optimal point,

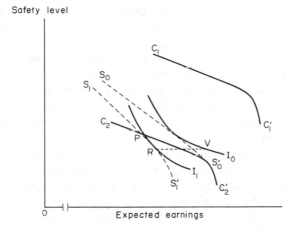

FIG. VII.

S_0', the stockholder opportunity locus will be S_1S_1', which lies below C_2C_2' to the right of point *P*. Again, taking the investor to undergo a two-step process, having been moved to point *P*, the best adjustment available to him involves a further move along S_1S_1' to the point of tangency, *R*, with his indifference curve I_1. This is a second-best adjustment which leaves

[15]Clearly this measure suffers from the same ambiguities as the measures of consumers' surplus. The compensating variation, the horizontal distance between two indifference curves, varies with the height at which this distance is measured. See J. R. Hicks, *Value and Capital* (New York: Oxford University Press, 1939), Chap. 2, Appendix.

him better off than he was at P, but does not get him to his optimal indifference level, I_0, the level he could attain if the company were to make an optimal financial choice (point S_0') from which opportunity locus S_0S_0' becomes available to the stockholder. Thus there is an added real cost to the acquisition of capital by a nonoptimal method as compared with the zero-tax, zero-transaction-cost case, a cost which may be represented by distance RV. Note that, since the magnitude of RV varies with the location of point P, the marginal real costs of debt and equity need no longer be equal.[16]

IX. CAPITAL AS A WEIGHTED AVERAGE

Our analysis can perhaps help to clear up a point which, as it now stands in the literature, appears to constitute a cleavage between the logic of financial theory and ordinary economic analysis. In standard economic theory, when a *homogeneous* resource can be obtained from any of several different sources, the real cost of that resource is always taken to be the price charged by its cheapest supplier. For there is no motivation for the purchaser of that item even to consider any other source since it would be irrational for him to buy any of this item from anyone else.

But in the theory of corporation finance there is a standard proposition which would appear to conflict with that result. It states that the cost of capital is a weighted *average* of the costs of capital from the alternative sources available.

However, the two propositions refer to different matters and there is therefore no real conflict. The point is that these costs are only *nominal* costs and constitute neither the real cost of debt nor that of equity. This is most obvious in the case of the interest rate on debt, which as we have seen, understates the true cost of debt because it makes no allowance for the leverage risk incurred by additional borrowing. Similarly, the corresponding rate of return which is used to measure the cost of equity fails to take into account the risk reduction that results from the decreased leverage ratio when there is a *ceteris paribus* increase in the amount of

---

[16]If we were to plot a graph representing RV plus an appropriate constant K, as a function of the leverage ratio, D/S, we would have a curve showing how the *total* cost of capital varies with the debt/equity ratio. For if K were chosen to be the cost of capital at the optimal debt/equity ratio (however defined), $K + RV$ would represent that cost at nonoptimal points because RV is by definition the excess of the cost of capital at any arbitrarily chosen point P over the cost at the optimal point.

equity. Whether in the presence of taxes and transactions costs this calculation still provides a valid approximation to the true cost of capital is a matter that requires further investigation.

So much for the nominal costs of debt and equity. It remains for us to see that their real costs accord with the standard economic proposition that one borrows only from the cheapest sources. As M and M show,[17] when both sources are utilized neither has a lower real marginal cost, just as standard economic analysis requires. But we have seen that, because of taxes and transactions costs, new equity is more expensive than added debt or retained earnings and it will not pay to issue additional shares. Our optimal solution will then be a corner solution in which the amount of funds derived from the issue of new stocks is zero, and the marginal cost of new shares will not affect the real marginal cost of capital to the firm.

X. CONCLUSION

The main purpose of this article has been to show that there is no basic conflict between the conclusions that emerge from the new theory of corporation finance and much of what one observes in company behavior, and that these two in turn are consistent with the precepts of received economic theory. It has been shown that in practice there *is* an optimal capital structure for the firm, and that its existence really follows from the logic of the M and M analysis supplemented only by a few simple institutional observations.[18] In general, the tax advantages of bond financing and the near zero transactions costs incurred in *un*doing leverage make it desirable for the firm to employ as much debt as is consistent with considerations of financial prudence. It turns out that,

---

[17]See Modigliani and Miller, *op. cit.*, Sec. IIA.

[18]There is, however, one unfortunate consequence of the softening of some of the more paradoxical M and M conclusions. It means that it may be even more difficult than has been thought to test empirically the relative merits of the M and M analysis as against the more traditional views on the consequences of different degrees of leverage for the value of a company's securities. For it follows from our discussion that even in an M and M world, but one in which transactions costs are present, a curve representing the value of $S + D$ as a function of the leverage ratio D/S is likely to have a maximum point rather than being a horizontal line as it would be in a pure M and M model. Thus the predictions of the M and M analysis and of the traditional approach are not easily distinguished in statistical terms. Empirical testing would require some sort of a priori specification of the degree of curvature in the $S + D$ functions predicted by the alternative models, and since we really know very little about the shapes of the curved portions of the opportunity loci this may well be a very formidable task.

despite differences in preferences, the financial decision toward which this result points will, in fact, be preferable for wide classes of stockholders. The prescriptions for optimal financial policy that emerge seem to be consistent with general company practice, where capital structure is considered a matter that requires highly careful decision making and where management seems characteristically to turn to the issue of new stocks only as a last resort when all other reasonable sources of funds have been utilized.

7

Application of Capital Budgeting Techniques to Marketing Operations *

RICHARD T. HISE and ROBERT H. STRAWSER

CAPITAL budgeting techniques are not usually viewed as being applicable to marketing decisions. This may be because of the feeling that marketing outlays are not quite the same as those for plant and equipment. These expenditures are made for assets that involve substantial outlays and require a time period in excess of one year to generate a return.[1] It should be noted, however, that marketing resources are no different. They may be considered assets, they involve sizeable outlays, and they may extend to time periods in excess of one year. The application of capital budgeting techniques to marketing operations would thus appear to be justified. This has been suggested in the literature, with the areas of sales management, channels of distribution, new product development, marketing research, and advertising often identified as the most promising.

SALES MANAGEMENT

The sales manager's effectiveness should be based on the return on investment generated in his territory, with the value of the inventories and accounts receivable employed serving as the investment base and the contribution margin (sales minus cost of goods sold and direct expenses) representing the net profit. The appropriate formula would be:

$$\frac{\text{Net Profit}}{\text{Sales}} \times \frac{\text{Sales}}{\text{Investment}} = \text{Return on Investment}$$

Although it is obvious that the sales figures would cancel out, leaving

*From *MSU Business Topics*, Vol. 18, No. 3, Summer 1970, pp. 69–76. Reproduced by permission.
[1]Robert W. Johnson, *Financial Management* (Boston: Allyn and Bacon, 1966), pp. 161–63.

net profit divided by investment, for purposes of control it may be better to perceive the concept as consisting of these two separate segments. For example, an increase in sales with the profit percentage and investment base the same would yield a greater return on investment because the turnover of assets would be increased.[2]

CHANNELS OF DISTRIBUTION

Two basic factors are critical in the selection of channels of distribution; these involve marketing and financial considerations. Generally speaking, the more direct the channel, the more *control* (a marketing consideration) that may be exerted by the firm. However, in order to increase its control, the firm will be required to commit additional financial resources. This is because as the firm eliminates middlemen it will be forced to assume those marketing functions that were formerly handled by the middlemen.

In selecting channels of distribution, a capital budgeting approach · might be employed. Eugene Lambert, Jr. says: "The application of the techniques of capital budgeting to the selection of a marketing channel involves a comparison of the estimated rate of return on funds required for each choice with the firm's cost of capital. If the anticipated earnings on the resources used to expand the marketing functions performed by the firm exceed its cost of capital, the change will be profitable."[3]

Firms will not automatically employ all channel combinations that yield rates of return in excess of their cost of capital. Logically, they should choose those alternatives that would yield the highest rates of return. In making this selection the marketer must consider the return on investment from the alternative uses of the funds freed when it uses longer trade channels. Such released funds could be used, for example, to expand the firm's manufacturing operations "if it is determined that total profit can be increased by using more capital in manufacturing, the channel should be shortened until the anticipated rate of return on capital employed in marketing is equal to the estimated rate of return on capital employed in expanding manufacturing operations."[4]

[2]Michael Schiff, "The Use of ROI Sales Management," *Journal of Marketing*, July 1963, pp. 70–73.
[3]Eugene Lambert, Jr., "Financial Considerations in Choosing a Marketing Channel," *MSU Business Topics*, Winter 1966, p. 22.
[4]*Ibid.*, pp. 22–23.

MARKETING RESEARCH

Twedt presents a means of measuring the return on investment from marketing research using the marketing research budget as the investment base. If, for example, we assume this to be $1,000,000, the value of the information obtained by the marketing research should then be calculated. Let us suppose this was $500,000; the percentage of times that the best alternative would have been chosen without the help of marketing research should be estimated. If we assume this to be 30 percent, a return of $350,000 is attributed to marketing research (100 percent minus 30 percent times $500,000), and a return on investment of 35 percent results ($350,000 divided by $1,000,000).[5] James H. Myers and A. Coskun Samli, when considering the problem of establishing controls over expenditures for marketing research, suggest a present value approach for both individual projects and the firm's total marketing research program.[6]

ADVERTISING

Joel Dean has long been an advocate of including advertising in the firm's capital budget. Advertising is an investment rather than an expense, according to Dean. The best way to measure the productivity of advertising is by the profit it generates. In order to most effectively appraise this profitability, discounted cash flow analysis is necessary. Thus, the expected discounted cash flow rate of return must exceed the firm's cost of capital in order for an advertising project to be undertaken.[7] It appears that there is ample justification for the application of capital budgeting techniques to marketing operations; the examples we have cited from the literature illustrate how this might be done and also indicate that some firms are indeed doing so.

A question that remains to be answered, however, is how widely capital budgeting techniques are utilized in making marketing decisions in practice. This is a pertinent question since the few earlier studies have dealt only with the area of new product development. Accordingly, in this article we will describe the results of a survey of the nation's 500 largest manufacturing firms involving a wide range of marketing functions.

---

[5]Twedt, "What is the 'Return'?," pp. 62–63.
[6]James H. Myers and A. Coskun Samli, "Management Control of Marketing Research," *Journal of Marketing Research*, August 1969, p. 269.
[7]Joel Dean, "Does Advertising Belong in the Capital Budget?," *Journal of Marketing*, October 1966, p. 21.

THE SURVEY

A mail questionnaire was sent to the 500 largest manufacturing firms in the United States, *Fortune's* 500. The questionnaire had four major objectives: (1) to determine the incidence of usage of capital budgeting techniques by these firms in making marketing decisions; (2) to ascertain which specific capital budgeting techniques are being utilized, particularly as they relate to the decision areas of sales management, channels of distribution, new product development, marketing research and advertising; (3) to examine in detail some of the technical aspects of capital budgeting as practiced by these firms, especially risk, useful life, and rates-of-return; and (4) to secure an indication as to how effective respondents feel these techniques are and what problems they believe exist with their usage.

The number of responses received totaled 261, a response rate of slightly more than 52 percent. Forty of the respondents indicated that they did not utilize capital budgeting methods at all in making marketing decisions for which the time period involved exceeded one year. Of the 221 that did, thirty-one declined to complete the balance of the questionnaire. Thus, the sample for the results that follow is 190 of the nation's 500 largest manufacturing firms.

Respondents were asked to indicate the percentage of all marketing decisions with a time dimension of greater than one year for which capital budgeting techniques were employed. The mean average percentage for all firms was 73.5 percent. When this finding was analyzed in terms of specific functional areas, it was found that capital budgeting techniques were used in 90.0 percent of the decisions involving channels of distribution. For new product development it was 80.9 percent, while for sales management, advertising, and marketing research, respectively, the percentages were 64.0 percent, 49.6 percent, and 49.5 percent.

Four basic capital budgeting methodologies were examined in some detail: payback, average rate-of-return, present value, and discounted rate-of-return. Each approach was very carefully explained and examples were provided so that respondents would have available a uniform definition of each technique. Accordingly, they were asked to indicate which of these were most frequently used by them by assigning a ranking of one to the method most often employed, a two to the next most frequently used, and so on. Three methods had virtually the same scores when mean averages were calculated. These were the payback, discounted rate-of-return, and present value approaches with mean scores of

2.05, 2.07, and 2.08. The average rate-of-return method was a distinct fourth, with a mean score of 2.56. When analyzing the responses according to the percentage of firms that ranked each method *first* in frequency of usage, it was found that the payback and discounted rate-of-return methods were used most often; each was ranked first by about one-third of the respondents. Table 1 indicates the degree to which the four capital budgeting techniques are used in making decisions within the various functional areas of marketing.

TABLE 1. *Percentage of marketing decisions in various functional areas for which specific types of capital budgeting methods are utilized*

Capital budgeting method	Functional area				
	Channels of distribution	Sales management	Advertising	Marketing research	New product development
Payback	18.2	20.7	39.1	32.4	29.1
Average rate-of-return	20.5	24.1	13.0	14.7	15.2
Present value	25.0	20.7	13.1	23.5	24.1
Discounted rate-of-return	36.3	34.5	34.8	29.4	31.6
Totals	100.0	100.0	100.0	100.0	100.0

The discounted rate-of-return approach proved to be most frequently utilized for three functional areas: channels of distribution, sales management, and new product development. For these functions, about one-third of the firms indicated that this methodology was employed. For advertising and marketing research, the payback method was allocated the first place position, followed by the discounted rate-of-return approach. The present value technique was used most often in the channels of distribution sector where one-fourth of the decisions made involved this approach, while the average rate-of-return approach was used most frequently in the area of sales management, with a 24.1 percent figure reported.

Almost 42 percent of the respondent firms indicated that they always consider risk when employing capital budgeting techniques in marketing decision making; 45.5 percent that they usually consider risk, whereas 12.7 percent indicated that risk is seldom accounted for. None of the 190 firms stated that they never recognize the risk factor.

Table 2 indicates the manner in which firms account for the factor of risk. Almost one-fourth (24.7 percent) of the respondents cited the practice of increasing the rate-of-return desired as the method whereby they recognized risk, while 21.7 percent revealed that risk was accounted for by the assignment of probabilities. Surprisingly, about one-fifth (19.6 percent) of the firms indicated that they had no specific procedure for considering risk. Other methods reported as being used were approximations (that is, decreasing the estimated sales, increasing operating costs, decreasing the useful life, and increasing the estimated original outlay).

TABLE 2. *Methods utilized to account for the factor of risk*

Method	Percentage of firms indicating use of the specific method
By increasing the rate-of-return desired	24.7
By assigning probabilities	21.7
Not explicitly figured, merely accounted for	19.6
By decreasing estimated sales associated with the investment	11.2
By increasing operating costs associated with the investment	9.3
By decreasing the useful life of the investment	8.3
By increasing estimated original investment outlay	5.2
Total	100.0

The estimated useful life of an asset is a significant consideration in the more traditional applications of capital budgeting methods. Accordingly, respondents were asked to indicate the useful lives of their various marketing "assets." The mean average useful life for channels of distribution was reported to be 15.2 years. This was considerably longer than those indicated for sales management (8.3 years), marketing research (7.9 years), new product development (7.8 years), and advertising (7.2 years).

In order to use the payback approach to capital budgeting, it is necessary to delineate a payback period. In this regard, respondents were requested to indicate the payback periods they associate with specific functional areas of marketing. The mean average payback period for channels of distribution was 7.6 years, followed by new product development (3.8 years), marketing research (3.3 years), sales management (2.6 years), and advertising (2.3 years).

SOME PROBLEMS ENCOUNTERED

Almost 43 percent of the firms studied indicated that their application of capital budgeting techniques in marketing decision making had proven to be "very effective." A higher percentage of respondents (46.9 percent) revealed that these methods had been "somewhat effective." Only 2.0 percent of the firms believed them to be ineffective, while 8.2 percent of the respondents stated that they were unable to assess the effectiveness of the capital budgeting techniques used.

Table 3 identifies the most significant difficulty encountered by firms in applying capital budgeting methods to their marketing operations. Singled out most frequently was the problem of estimating sales cited by almost one-third (32.7 percent) of the respondents. Accounting for the factor of risk was indicated by 27.3 percent as the most significant problem. Slightly less than one-fifth (19.9 percent) of all firms believed that the major difficulty encountered was that of implementing capital budgeting techniques.

TABLE 3. *Problems encountered when using capital budgeting techniques*

Problem	Percentage of all firms indicating this problem as the single most important difficulty
Estimating sales	32.7
Accounting for the factor of risk	27.3
Getting the techniques accepted and implemented	19.9
Estimating operating costs	7.3
Determining useful life of investment	5.5
Determining acceptable rate-of-return	5.5
Estimating original investment outlay	1.8
Determining firm's cost-of-capital	0.0
Total	100.0

Since many marketing decisions involve choices from among a number of alternatives, there is a definite need for a well-defined process to ensure that the best alternative is selected. Capital budgeting methods provide assistance in implementing such a process, and with the realization that marketing assets are essentially similar to the more traditional notion of assets, there have been recommendations that these methods are indeed applicable to the marketing operations of firms. In particular, the areas of sales management, advertising, marketing research, new product development, and channels of distribution appear to be especially appropriate areas for applying capital budgeting methodologies.

The current research found that a significant number of large manufacturing firms employ capital budgeting in making about three-fourths of their long term decisions. However, the fact that capital budgeting methods are employed for less than half of these decisions in advertising and marketing research would seem to indicate that there is a less than universal application of these techniques across all functional areas of marketing.

FACTOR OF RISK

Many firms frequently utilize the less sophisticated capital budgeting tools, particularly the payback approach. Although the payback and average rate-of-return methods have the advantage of simplicity, it would seem desirable that the major emphasis should be on those approaches that recognize the time value of money, with the pay-back and average rate-of-return methods serving in an adjunctive position. Although all firms consider risk, only slightly more than 40 percent do so all the time. Similarly, about one-fifth of those who consider the factor of risk indicated no specific methodology for doing so. Because of the uncertainty that beclouds many marketing decisions, it would seem that there should be a greater cognizance of risk.

CONCLUSION

Current research indicates that marketing departments of the largest manufacturing firms are consistently applying capital budgeting technique to a preponderance of their long-range decisions and that, in general, they seem to be fairly well satisfied with the results obtained.